SPITFIRE LEADER

SPITFIRE LEADER

ROBERT BUNGEY DFC, TRAGIC BATTLE OF BRITAIN HERO

DENNIS NEWTON & RICHARD BUNGEY

AMBERLEY

To the memory of Sybil and Robert Wilton Bungey, and so many others like them, who have sacrificed and fought the good fight for the good cause, their loved ones and their country.

Half title page: Wing Commander Bob Bungey DFC RAF. When the *Melbourne Express* arrived in Adelaide on 6 May 1943, Bob Bungey disembarked to find the press waiting for him. He was photographed but declined to be interviewed. (Richard Bungey)

Title page: The picture of a Spitfire Mk I that Bob brought home for his family. It was duly framed and given pride of place on the wall. It still has pride of place at the time of writing. (Richard Bungey)

First published 2019

Amberley Publishing
The Hill, Stroud
Gloucestershire, GL5 4EP

www.amberley-books.com

Copyright © Dennis Newton & Richard Bungey, 2019

The right of Dennis Newton & Richard Bungey to be identified as the Authors of this work has been asserted in accordance with the Copyrights, Designs and Patents Act 1988.

British Library Cataloguing in Publication Data.
A catalogue record for this book is available from the British Library.

ISBN 978 1 4456 8435 2 (hardback)
ISBN 978 1 4456 8436 9 (ebook)

Origination by Amberley Publishing.
Printed in the UK.

Contents

Acknowledgements from Richard Bungey

Special thanks must go to my wonderful, understanding wife, Allison, who has been a tower of strength with the encouragement she has given me in my quest to tell my father's story. She has put up with a lot and at times I must have been a right pain in the neck, but in the wash up I want to say from the bottom of my heart thank you, my love. Without your support I would not have been able to complete my mission.

Special thanks are due to my grandparents, Ernest and Ada Bungey; my aunt, Pauline Hannaford (née Bungey); and my uncle David Ernest Bungey, who was always a kind considerate and generous man. God bless you David and thanks a million for the life that I've been able to live due to your guidance.

Thank you to the RAF and RAAF people who knew my father and who aided me in my quest, including ex-452 Squadron pilots Raife Cowan and his wife Joan, Ian Milne and his wife, Fred McCann, Bill Jefferies, and Bill Thorpe; former 452/457 Squadron ground staff Bill Maudlen and Jack McKenna, Feardar 'Dickie' Finucane and Ray Finucane (brother of the extraordinary Brendon 'Paddy' Finucane), and the first commanding officer of 452 Squadron, Roy Dutton.

So many others have helped so much: Mary Clisby, sister of Leslie Clisby, and her mother Faye; Jane Waddy; Jon Waddy; Jack Marx; Fiona McWhirter; Ray Fairminer; Nan Wawn; the widow of ex-452 pilot 'Bardy' Wawn; Carolyn Grace, the pilot and owner of the two-seater Spitfire; Milton Howard and Jim Rogers from the Aviation Museum at Port Adelaide; and Bill Denny, South Australian State President of the RSL.

And what can I say about the amazing *60 Minutes* team from Channel Nine Network Australia. They were Nick Greenaway (producer); Liam Bartlett (interviewer); Greg Barbara (cameraman); Andy Shaklis (sound); Steve (dogsbody) our ubiquitous driver; Kirsty Thomson (executive producer); and Vanessa for the organisation of accommodation, tickets, etc. When we went to the UK to film segments for the story on my father, I found all the crew great and so very helpful. Nick, we thank especially. Ali and I appreciated what you did for us very much.

Richard Bungey

Acknowledgements from Dennis Newton

This book began for me with a telephone call. It was from Richard Bungey who asked in his own direct way if I would like to write a book about his father, Robert Wilton Bungey. I jumped at the chance.

While researching for my first book, *A Few of 'The Few': Australians and the Battle of Britain*, I had been amazed at how many times Bob Bungey's name kept cropping up in various publications. There he was flying bombers in France; there he was flying fighters in the Battle of Britain; there he was again intercepting intruders in the winter of 1940/1; and there he was yet again in 1941/2 leading the first, and most successful, Australian Spitfire squadron of the Second World War. But then it all stopped abruptly with a brief footnote appearing in the official RAAF history of the Second World War stating that he died in June 1943. Intriguing. How and why did he change from bombers to fighters? How did he contribute to making 452 Squadron so successful? What happened during the year between him leaving the squadron and returning to Australia in 1943? There were so many questions and I remained intrigued for years. Suddenly I now had the opportunity to investigate further.

I sincerely thank Richard who inspired and provided the impetus for this work and allowed access to his own research and his father's memorabilia. Thank you, too, to both Allison and Richard for their great welcomes and outstanding hospitality. (They also have the best private display of Christmas lights in Adelaide!)

I thank Stewart Wilson and the staff at Wilson Media who have allowed me to write the 'Skywarriors' segment in *Aero Australia* magazine for over ten years. The research which was necessary in order to write the column has been of inestimable value finding extra data for this book and so too has the feedback generously volunteered from readers.

In addition, a work such as this could not reach its fruition without the help and co-operation of many people and organisations, many of whom Richard has already mentioned. The also include Gordon Olive, Tom Scott, Winston Ramsey, Don Clark, the Australian War Memorial, Australian Archives, the National Library of Australia, RAAF Historical Section, RAAF Museum Point Cook, *Wings* – the official magazine of the RAAF Association NSW,

8

QLD and WA, NSW Library. In England: the Ministry of Defence, the National Archives, Commonwealth War Graves Commission, Imperial War Museum, Battle of Britain Museum, RAF Museum, Andrew Rogers, Wallingford Town Clerk, and of course the staff of Amberley Publishing, particularly Cathy Stagg and Shaun Barrington. Many thanks, and if any have been overlooked, I apologise for the unintended omission.

Special acknowledgment has to be made of the efforts of my son, Scott, who went out of his way to help throughout, as well as carry out much-needed and challenging last-minute research.

Last, and by no means least, I give special recognition and thanks to my wife, Helen, for her support and patience through some difficult times. Without her the book could not have been finished.

Dennis Newton

Abbreviations

AASF	Advanced Air Striking Force
AC	Aircraftman
AFC	Air Force Cross, Australian Flying Corps
AHQ	Air Headquarters
AI	Aircraft Interception (airborne radar equipment)
AIF	Australian Imperial Force
A/Cmdr	Air Commodore
AM	Air Marshal
AOC	Air Officer Commanding
AOC-in-C	Air Officer Commanding-in-Chief
ARP	Air Raid Precautions
ASR	Air-Sea Rescue
AVM	Air Vice-Marshal
BAFF	British Air Forces in France
BEF	British Expeditionary Force
Brig	Brigadier
BV	Blohme and Voss
Capt	Captain
Cdr	Commander
C-in-C	Commander-in-Chief
CIB	Criminal Investigation Branch
CO	Commanding Officer
Co-op	Co-operation
Col	Colonel
Cpl	Corporal
DFC	Distinguished Flying Cross
DFM	Distinguished Flying Medal
DH	de Havilland
Do	Dornier
DSO	Distinguished Service Order

E/A	Enemy Aircraft
EATS	Empire Air Training Scheme
EFTS	Elementary Flying Training School
FAA	Fleet Air Arm
F/Lt	Flight Lieutenant
F/O	Flying Officer
F/Sgt	Flight Sergeant
FW	Focke-Wulf
GAF	German Air Force
Gen.	General
GOC	General Officer Commanding
Gp/Capt	Group Captain
He.	Heinkel
HMS	His Majesty's Ship
HQ	Headquarters
IFF	Identification Friend-or-Foe airborne radar identification device
IRA	Irish Republican Army
JG	*Jagdgeschwader*
Ju	Junkers
LAC	Leading Aircraftman
Lt	Lieutenant
Lt/Col	Lieutenant-Colonel
Lt/Gen.	Lieutenant-General
Maj.	Major
Maj./Gen.	Major-General
Me	Messerschmitt. *See* Note 1, Chapter 4.
NCO	Non-commissioned Officer
NZ	New Zealand
O.	Observer
Ops	Operations
ORB	Operations Record Book
OTU	Operational Training Unit
P/O	Pilot Officer
POW	Prisoner of War
PTSD	Post-traumatic Stress Disorder
RAAF	Royal Australian Air Force
RAF	Royal Air Force
RAN	Royal Australian Navy
RCAF	Royal Canadian Air Force
RDF	Radio Direction Finding (Radar)
RFC	Royal Flying Corps
RN	Royal Navy
RNZAF	Royal New Zealand Air Force

RSL	Returned Services League (of Australia)
R/T	Radio Transmitter
RUC	Royal Ulster Constabulary
SAAF	South African Air Force
SASO	Senior Air Staff Officer
Sgt	Sergeant
Sqn	Squadron
USAAF	United States Army Air Force
USN	United States Navy
VC	Victoria Cross
WAG	Wireless Air Gunner
W/Cdr	Wing Commander
W/Ldr	Wing Leader
W/O	Warrant Officer
W/T	Wireless Telegraphy

Foreword

Wing Commander R. W. Bungey DFC had a distinguished career as an RAAF Officer in the RAF after graduating from RAAF No.1 Flying Training School, Point Cook, in June 1937.

It was a career destined for the upper echelons of the service had it not been cut short by his tragic and untimely death on a lonely South Australian beach at Brighton on Thursday, 10 June 1943.

Bob Bungey served in France from late November 1937 to August 1940 in Bomber Command, No.226 Squadron, flying Fairey Battles on bombing reconnaissance and strafing operations against the German forces in the early stage of the enemy occupation of France.

Bob was one of the few survivors of this campaign, and after his return to England participated in the Battle of Britain with another RAF squadron, namely 145, which was operating Hawker Hurricane fighters. By this stage of the war Bob had gained valuable experience in single-seater fighter tactics. He was subsequently promoted to squadron leader and on 9 June 1941 he was posted to command No.452 Squadron, the first Australian Spitfire unit formed in Britain. It was initially based at Kirton-in-Lindsey in April 1941.

During his time with 452, Bob was an outstanding squadron commander, whose qualities as a leader and fighter pilot won the respect of every member of the squadron.

It was during Bob Bungey's time as CO of 452 that the squadron recorded the highest number of enemy aircraft destroyed for three consecutive months out of all RAF operational squadrons in Fighter Command.

He was posted from the squadron on 25 January 1942 to take command of an RAF Wing at Shoreham – on which occasion the squadron bade farewell to a courageous, skilful and dedicated leader.

When Richard invited me to contribute a foreword for this book about his father, under whom I served during his time as CO of 452, I was delighted to do so, and I commend Richard for writing this book as it is a story that needs to be told.

Raife Cowan
Ex-452 pilot[1]

Note: This foreword was written originally for Richard Bungey's initial work about his father, *The Story of Wing Commander R. W. Bungey DFC RAAF.* (Richard Bungey's Private Papers, *c.* 2000).

Prologue

The fighting over southern England had been bitter all summer but with winter approaching it had slowed down considerably. The Nazi bombers were only coming at night now. Hurricanes and Spitfires had knocked them out of the sky during the day. October had been 'Messerschmitt Month' – German fighters and fighter bombers coming over in great force making it very dangerous for the Royal Air Force defenders, but safer for the people below. Even that was tapering off – at least it had seemed so until now...

Stuka dive-bombers were reported to be after shipping near Portsmouth. Eleven Hurricanes from 145 Squadron were scrambled at 1.50 p.m. and ordered to patrol near the Isle of Wight. F/Lt Bob Bungey was leading 'B' Flight. Then they were instructed to return to base and patrol at 20,000 feet (6,000 m), but suddenly enemy fighters appeared all around them. Three formations of fast and deadly Messerschmitt 109s were shadowing them; one group ahead, one astern and the third flying on a parallel course to the south.

It was a trap!

There were about fifty of them!

Fifty against eleven!

The Hurricanes could not attack any gaggle without putting themselves at the mercy of the others. All they could do was stay alert and keep gaining more height as they waited for the 109s to make the first move.

And they did.

Breaking formation in pairs, they began attacking the Hurricanes of 'B' Flight at the rear.

They came in fast...

1

The Royal Australian Air Force

Bob Bungey was working as an insurance clerk with the Atlas Insurance Company in Weymouth Street, Adelaide, when he noticed the newspaper advertisements early in 1936. They invited young men to apply for cadetships in the Royal Australian Air Force.

These cadetships entailed a year of study and flying training at Point Cook, after which one could expect to graduate as an officer pilot in the RAAF. There might also be an opportunity to transfer across to the Royal Air Force in England. To fly and travel was definitely far more exciting than insurance! But what was the likelihood of him being accepted? Hundreds, possibly thousands, across Australia would probably be applying.

* * *

On Thursday, 31 March 1921, *Commonwealth of Australia Gazette* No.28 proclaimed that a new force 'to be called the Australian Air Force, be constituted as part of the Australian Military Forces as from the thirty-first day of March, One thousand nine hundred and twenty-one'. Personnel strength on its formation consisted of twenty-one officers and 130 enlisted men. The new service also had 151 aircraft. This total included 128 – less one lost in 1920 – war surplus aircraft with supporting equipment presented by the British government in appreciation of Australia's part in the Great War of 1914–18.

The roots of this 'new force' went further back. Mankind's first controlled, powered flight in a heavier-than-air machine had taken place only eighteen years earlier, on 17 December 1903 in North Carolina, USA. On that fateful Thursday at Kill Devil Hills, Kitty Hawk, the Wright brothers, Orville and Wilber, successfully launched and flew their *Wright Flyer* four times. The total airtime they achieved was 1 minute 38 seconds. From these faltering small steps, a worldwide revolution began at an accelerating pace.

In Australia less than seven years later, brothers John and Reg Duigan designed and built their own aircraft and flew it at Mia Mia, Victoria, in July 1910. The following year, Minister for Defence, Senator G. F. Pearce, convinced his government colleagues of the need for a military aviation corps. The Australian Flying Corps (AFC) was established in 1912. By doing this, Australia became the only dominion to act on a decision taken during the Imperial Conference of 1911 in London that the armed forces of the British Empire should exploit the air as a means of warfare. Applications were sought for 'two competent mechanists and aviators' to be given the responsibility of forming it.

The men selected were Henry Petre and Eric Harrison. Both were in England. Petre was an English barrister, who had designed, built and flown the Petre monoplane with his brother, and was currently a pilot with the Deperdussin Company at Brooklands. Eric Harrison was an Australian from Castlemaine, Victoria, working for the Bristol Aeroplane Company.

Petre arrived in Melbourne in January 1913 and was commissioned as a lieutenant in the Australian Army. He selected Point Cook, Victoria, as the site for a flying school and 734 acres were purchased for £6,040 2s 3d. Harrison, who was also commissioned into the army, arrived from England with two mechanics, H. J. Chester and A. E. Shorland, on 25 April 1913. Five aircraft (value with spares: £14,031 16s) were also shipped to Australia.

When flying training started at the new Central Flying School (CFS) over a year later, Petre and Harrison were the instructors and the first four trainees were Lt R. Williams (later Air Marshal Sir Richard Williams), Capt T. W. White (later Sir Thomas White, Australian High Commissioner in London), Lt G. P. Merz and Lt D. T. W. Manwell. Lt Merz was the first student to fly (on 18 August 1914) and Lt Williams was the first to win his 'wings' (on 12 November). Williams actually had to purchase his own wings for his uniform at a cost of 3s 6d (35 cents). This school and these men were the nucleus of the AFC, forerunner of the newly proclaimed Australian Air Force of 1921.

Before 1914, few people believed that the aeroplane had any military use except for reconnaissance. Experiments in firing guns from aeroplanes, and dropping bombs and torpedoes from them, were not taken very seriously at first by senior officers of the world's armies and navies. As a result, at the beginning of the First World War when Britain's Royal Flying Corps (RFC) crossed the English Channel to support the British Expeditionary Force in France, its pilots flew unarmed aircraft.

Military leaders on both sides did not take long to appreciate the value of aerial reconnaissance. It could report and photograph every movement of the opposing armies on the ground behind their own lines and could guide artillery bombardments. The same leaders began to press for methods of stopping the reconnaissance activities of their enemies. Eventually, aircraft designers devised ways of mounting and firing a machine gun from an aircraft without shooting off its own propeller in the process. Reconnaissance aircraft began to suffer heavy casualties at the hands of the new scout planes. Friendly scouts began to accompany the reconnaissance machines to protect them from attack. So began air-to-air combat.

During the 1914–18 war, Britain and Australia were the only Commonwealth countries to have their own flying corps. Aside from a small contingent that did not see action when it went with a force to take over

German possessions in New Guinea, the first AFC unit sent overseas was the famous Mesopotamian Half Flight. George Merz, who went with this unit, was the first Australian aviator to be killed in action.

Meanwhile, Australia responded to Britain's request to send skilled airmen for war service. Some were partially trained in Australia and then sent to England to complete their training before joining one of the AFC's four operational units there, No.1 in the Middle East or Nos.2, 3 and 4 Squadrons in France. Four more AFC squadrons were set up for training in England. Other Australians, who were already overseas, mostly in the AIF, joined the AFC or RFC, or Britain's Royal Naval Air Service (RNAS) direct. The exploits of these men built up an enviable reputation of skill, courage and audacity.

The first Australian flier to win the Victoria Cross was Lt Frank McNamara of No.1 Squadron AFC. Although wounded and under fire, he courageously landed in enemy territory on 20 March 1917 and rescued a downed pilot, Capt D. W. Rutherford. No.1 Squadron's highest scoring ace, and most highly decorated member, was Capt Ross Smith who also piloted the giant Handley Page 0/400 bomber, the only one of its type in the Middle East at the time.

Flying with the RNAS, which amalgamated with the RFC to form the Royal Air Force (RAF) on 1 April 1918, Capt Robert Little, credited with forty-seven victories, was the highest scoring Australian pilot of the war, closely followed by Major Roderic Stanley 'Stan' Dallas, who was usually credited with thirty-nine. The AFC's leading air ace was Capt Harry Cobby, who flew Sopwith Camels in No.4 Squadron and accounted for twenty-nine enemy aircraft, including five observation balloons.

After the Great War – supposedly the war to end all wars – the AFC was replaced by the Australian Air Corps (AAC) and its squadrons were disbanded. The AAC manned Point Cook airfield more or less as a caretaker and the government constituted a new Air Board on 9 November 1920. Its recommendation that the 'Australian Air Force' be formed was sent to the Air Council on 15 February 1921. Lt/Col Richard Williams, the first Australian to win his 'wings' in 1914, was the First Air Member of the AAC Air Board, and as Wing Commander Williams, he became the First Air Member, Director of Intelligence and Organisation, of the Air Board for the Australian Air Force. Britain's King George V approved using the prefix 'Royal' in June and, effective from 31 August 1921, the Royal Australian Air Force (RAAF) came into being.

Like the aviation industry in general, for the new service the period between the two world wars was difficult, particularly at first. It was one of survival, gradual development, fighting for funding and trying to acquire up-to-date equipment. Expansion was far from rapid, particularly during the years of the worldwide Great Depression in the early 1930s.

***

Robert Wilton Bungey was born at Hutt Street Private Hospital, Adelaide, on 4 October 1914, the first child of Ernest Bungey and his wife Ada (née Rough). He was initially educated at Glenelg Primary School and then

Adelaide Boys' High School before starting his working life as an insurance clerk. Academically, he judged that he was in good shape to apply to join the RAAF.

Bob's younger brother, David, was with the Commonwealth Bank and his sister, Pauline, was still at school. David Ernest Bungey had been born on 9 February 1919, Ada and Ernest's second child. At that time, the family was living in Gladstone Street, Fullarton, where they stayed briefly before moving to 3 Tarlton Street, Somerton Park, when young David was four years old. Their new home was about 350 yards (320 m) from the beach and both boys became strong swimmers. David had already learnt to swim before he went to school at the age of five.

Like Bob, David attended Adelaide Boys' High School where he excelled at sport and eventually became a prefect. He represented the school at swimming, tennis and cricket, and was especially good at football. He captained the school's football team, winning the Gosse Medal for Best and Fairest in the Adelaide Students' Association. Though he left school in 1933 to work in the bank, he continued with sport, going on to represent South Australia in amateur football in 1933 and 1935. In 1936 he was lining up to play Australian rules for Glenelg.

Ada and Ernest's third child, Pauline Rosalind Bungey, came into the world on 22 July 1921. Pauline began her school life at Woodlands Church of England Girls' Grammar School where she attended to Grade 4. From there she went to Black Forest Primary School and then to Adelaide Girls' High School where she would successfully complete 4th Year.

Physically, Bob Bungey was in good shape as well. The air force was only interested in people who were physically very fit and the family's physician, Dr Kenneth Steele, had written a glowing recommendation. Bob and David both enjoyed sport and trained with enthusiasm, often together. A favourite pastime was swimming and they could frequently be found in the beautifully clear, normally calm water of Holdfast Bay in the Gulf of St Vincent.

Brighton was the next beach suburb just south of the Bungey home at Somerton Park. Its landmark was Brighton Jetty, a long pier stretching out from the beach. Almost equidistant to the north of Somerton Park was historic Glenelg, the place where Governor Hindmarsh had arrived a hundred years earlier aboard HMS *Buffalo*. There the governor had read his famous proclamation declaring South Australia would be settled by free people. Glenelg, of course, had (and still has) its own famous long jetty, just a tram ride from Adelaide's CBD.

The long pier at Brighton Beach was usually a safe place to swim, but just ten years before it had been the site of the state's first recorded fatal shark attack. Kitty Whyte had taught children to swim at Brighton in the 1920s and she had been awarded a Grand Diploma from the Royal Life Saving Association in 1919 for saving a swimmer, Miss Sybil Davies, from drowning. While on holiday visiting her parents at Brighton on 18 March 1926, she took her usual class of children and afterwards returned for a swim herself. She dived off the springboard but suddenly screamed and threw up her arms.

Witnesses saw her dragged under the surface by a 12-foot black shark. She was brought ashore by onlookers but she had been badly mutilated. She collapsed and died before reaching hospital. Afterwards, she was buried in the family plot at St Jude's Cemetery. Kitty had been very popular in the area and a fountain was erected in her honour. This is now on the Brighton Jetty. Sharks, when they came, appeared during summer. That was the case three years later on 22 January 1936 when thirteen-year-old Ray Bennett was taken while swimming at West Beach on the other side of Glenelg. Passer-by Len Bedford heard the boy scream. Then he saw a large white shark leap from the water and the swimmer disappeared. The attack was fatal. Despite such incidents, the long, continuous stretch of beaches has remained ever popular with swimmers.

Living so close to the sea, Bob and David Bungey could reach the water by walking a short distance westward from their home along Phillip Street, then over the road to walk straight ahead across the yellow stretch of sand. If they turned right they could walk along to Glenelg. If they turned left they could walk to Brighton. Alternatively, they could cut across the sand dunes either way through low bush and coastal shrubs.

It is easy to imagine the pleasure and mounting excitement of the two young men as they neared their destination, and perhaps made a last minute dash to the water. Would the sand be hot underfoot? How cold would the water be? Would there be girls there? Did you bring an old tennis ball to play with the dog? Oh, what relief on a long hot summer's day! They could be very hot in Adelaide. Races along the sand and in the water. Usually they swam north to Glenelg Bathing Box. Afterwards, as they made their way back across the dunes to home, they would be relaxed and happy – at peace with the world. These were good times – happy times for the whole family.

Meanwhile, for an Australia emerging from the effects of the Great Depression, the mid-1930s were beginning to show greater promise, particularly in the skies. Aviation was the future and its prospects captured the imagination. Records were being set almost daily. Two years earlier, on 23 October 1934, an estimated 40,000 people had gathered at Flemington Racecourse in Melbourne to watch the finish of the MacRobertson International Air Race from England to Australia. The event was staged to celebrate the establishment of Melbourne and the state of Victoria. C. W. A. Scott and T. Campbell Black in the de Havilland DH 88 Comet, G-ACSS *Grosvenor House*, arrived overhead, and then flew off to land at Laverton. They received the £10,000 first prize and, of course, the MacRobertson Trophy.

F/Lt O. Cathcart-Jones and Ken Waller in a second Comet, G-ACSR, commenced their return flight to England from Laverton four days later and arrived at Lympne, England, on 2 November creating an out-and-back record of 13 days 6 hours and 38 minutes. Even while this was happening, Sir Charles Kingsford Smith and Capt P. G. Taylor had taken off from Brisbane in the *Lady Southern Cross* on 21 October to make the first west to east crossing of the South Pacific. They arrived at Oakland, California, on 4 November. Such exciting events inspired young men, especially one who had just turned twenty years of age and was sitting at a desk in an insurance office. Opportunities in aviation seemed to be appearing almost every day.

Closer to home, in 1935 a new company, Adelaide Airways Ltd, began running air services from Adelaide to Port Lincoln, the Yorke Peninsula and Kangaroo Island. A service to Broken Hill in NSW was inaugurated on 26 November and connected with Western and Southern Provincial Airlines to Sydney. In February 1936 the company announced the purchase of two de Havilland Rapides for services to Melbourne and Broken Hill flying three trips per week instead of two, and there was talk of acquiring the Perth – Adelaide service from West Australian Airways.

The RAAF was building up again too. Minister for Defence, Mr R. A. Parkhill, announced in April that there had been significant progress in the expansion and re-equipment programme following the setting up of No.2 Aircraft Depot at Richmond NSW in January 1936 with the provision of necessary facilities for aircraft. As from 30 April, recruiting additional personnel made it possible to create more units. These included a Station HQ and a fighter-bomber squadron at Laverton, a Station HQ and Army Co-operation Squadron at Richmond and upgrading of the Fleet Co-operation Flight to squadron strength to become No.5 Squadron.

Another three-year defence programme was being considered but there were delays due to the failure of English companies to deliver £1.7m worth of orders. They defaulted because of their primary commitment to the Royal Air Force's own expansion programme, which was gaining momentum in England – particularly in the light of the unsettling events in Germany under the Nazis. The Commonwealth government had been considering the manufacture of the latest British-designed fighter either in a government factory or by arrangement with private aviation companies suitably subsidised by the government. Now, it might have to look elsewhere, perhaps to the USA?

Such happenings did not go unnoticed by young men like Bob Bungey. He was keenly interested in aircraft, his room at home in Tarlton Street was decorated with photographs and sketches of aeroplanes such as the legendary Sopwith Camel and the like from the Great War – the war to end all wars. Through books and magazines he knew of such aces as Mick Mannock, the dreaded Red Baron and Billy Bishop, and the Australians Robert Little, Stan 'Dice-with-Death' Dallas and Harry Cobby. He was in good shape as well.

The RAAF thought so too. Bob was accepted. He had to report for training to No.1 Flying Training School Point Cook, Victoria, on 15 July 1936.

Flying Course 'A' No.20 was a large course. They came from all over the country, forty of them, and several were from South Australia. There was Kevin Walsh who lived in Maturin Road, Glenelg, not far from the Bungeys; Wally Skinner was another Adelaide boy. So was one of the cadet NCOs, Leslie Clisby, who was originally from McLaren Vale. Like Bob Bungey, he came from a Methodist family background and he was enthusiastic about sport. The Clisbys had moved to Walkerville, a suburb of Adelaide, in 1919. Leslie Clisby had actually joined the RAAF the year before. His main interest then had been in anything mechanical. A favourite pastime of his was to buy an old motorcycle, dismantle it and then reassemble it. Next, he would kick over the engine to check for any defect. If there was, he would take the bike apart all over again, repeating the whole process until it was right. This interest led him to the air force. He joined as an aircraftsman in engineering and found himself at Laverton. His first commanding officer was none other than Frank McNamara, the AFC's famous Victoria Cross winner from the Great War. Meanwhile, Leslie realised he wanted more than to just pull aeroplanes apart so he applied for a flying course. He had already logged around 50 hours flying time when he applied, with McNamara's blessing, for the officer cadet course at Point Cook.

Many of the new arrivals were from New South Wales. Allan 'Mull' Mulligan had been born in Bingara but he was living in Sydney when he joined up. Ellis 'Rossy' Ross, who came from Tamworth, was already forming a close friendship with Mulligan. Fate would lead them to the same squadron in England, and they would fail to return from the very same special mission.

Jack Kennedy was a big, tall, strong fellow from Waverley near Bronte Beach in Sydney's Eastern Suburbs. He was very quiet, and people soon realised he was really a 'gentle giant'. Charles Fry was the fourth child in a family of five boys and three girls. They lived in Toronto on Lake Macquarie where you either swam or sailed – or both. Although it was the time of the Great Depression and employment was scarce, Charles found work as a jackeroo in southern Queensland and he drove trucks for his father's business in Newcastle. That was before he presented himself to Victoria Barracks in Sydney at the end of October 1935 to be interviewed for the air force.

Oliver John Trevor Lewis – Johnny Lewis – was from Artarmon in northern Sydney, and Allan Farrington, although born in Young, was living on the same side of the harbour at Manly when they applied. An electrical fitter by trade, Allan was also enthusiastic about sport and took part in riding, rugby football and diving. He represented NSW in diving competitions from 1932 to 1936 and competed at international level in NSW summer events in 1935. From 1933 he served in the Australian Signals Corps rising to corporal and his Adjutant wrote an excellent reference to attach to his application for an RAAF cadetship. Between 1927 and 1933, Allan had attended Sydney Technical High School, where he first met Bill Edwards from Leichhardt in western Sydney. The two became good friends. Bill was another of the July 1936 cadets.

They came from the other states too. Stuart Walch was from a well-known Tasmanian family. His father was the managing director of J. Walch & Sons, a successful publishing house in Hobart. Despite leaving the Hutchin's School in 1935 and going into the business, Stuart realised his heart was not really in the book publishing industry and after several months he announced his intention to join the RAAF.

The same thing had occurred in another eminent Tasmanian family just six months earlier. Bob Cosgrove had told his father, an eminent figure in the state's Labour Party government, that he was joining the RAAF too. He was currently in the senior course that had started at Point Cook in January, and was sharing a room with Pat Hughes, a boisterous fellow from Haberfield in NSW. Next door to them were Peter McDonough whose family had moved from Ulverstone, Tasmania, to Victoria, and Gordon Olive, a talkative, lightly built young man from Queensland. Despite being in different courses, everybody mixed together – especially on the sports field.

Back in Bob Bungey's group, Norman Messervy was another Queenslander. His family knew Gordon Olive's family in Brisbane. Greg Graham of Gunbower, Victoria, had actually been born in Foster in the same state. Everyone called him 'Shorty'.

During the intense twelve-month officer cadet course the RAAF endeavoured to cover some twenty-two subjects. Many of these applied to the problems of flying such as navigation, the theory of engines, the theory of flight, and airmanship – the art of 'conducting oneself around an aerodrome and an aeroplane in an intelligent and safe fashion'. Then there were subjects relating purely to the service such as general administration, air force organisation and a comparable knowledge of the army and navy, and of civil aviation. Air Force Law had to be clearly understood.

Tactics and strategy were only words when the cadets started their course, but they had to be studied most carefully and were to be the found in the content of numerous 'lengthy and profound', but dull, books. Meteorology was another obscure and inexact science, as was the case with photography and photographic interpretation. Morse Code had to be learnt by buzzer and using lights and each cadet had be able to read semaphore, the procedure of sending messages by flags.

In a more practical vein, the knowledge of armaments was essential. Guns of various calibres and bombs of numerous types had to be understood, their construction explained and remembered, and the theory of ballistics studied. The application of these to the aeroplane and the theory and practice of their use were important. Other requirements were that the anatomy of machine guns, bombs and cameras, had to be known to the extent that cadets could dismantle and reassemble them 'without enough parts left over to go into the second-hand business'.

There were also the practical sides of engineering and rigging that had to be mastered. This involved dismantling and reassembling aero engines and repairing damaged aeroplanes parts.

It was a formidable array of subjects, as was the six-day routine each week. The cadets' day began at 0600 hours (6.00 a.m.) with the blast of a bugle. From then on, the pace was hectic – beds made, rooms tidied, shower, shave and breakfast. Out on the parade ground at 0700 in immaculate order with boots, buttons and all leather polished followed by forty-five minutes of 'tramping up and down the parade ground learning the finer points of ceremonial drill'. Then it was back to the barracks to divest themselves of rifles, belts and paraphernalia, and grab books, pencils and notepaper ready for the mile-and-a-half march around the perimeter of the aerodrome to 'the Flights'.

'The Flights' was an area of old sheds, hangars and lecture rooms where they worked for the rest of the morning. At 1200 hours, they marched the mile and a half back to the mess for lunch. Forty minutes later they were on their way back to 'the Flights' on foot for the afternoon sessions.

For the most part, the days were divided into two basically different sessions of theory and practice. If the morning was all theory, the afternoon was practice; that is, learning to send and understand Morse Code, practical work on engines or air frames or on guns or bombs and the like, and hopefully soon, flying. On alternate weeks the days were reversed with practical work in the morning, followed by theory in the afternoons.

At 1600 hours, the cadets were marched back to the barracks for a 10-minute tea break before sport which was from 1630 to 1800. The choices were cricket, tennis, football or hockey and everybody mixed in. There was no let-up here either. If the instructors found anybody shirking, they were sent for a run around the perimeter of the aerodrome, or out to a line of trees roughly a mile and a half away. The victim had to be back within a given time, or he had to do it again each evening until he could.

From 1800 to 1830 hours, cadets were permitted to clean up their personal gear, clean boots and so on, and prepare for dinner or supper at 1900. This was a formal meal and then everyone had to be back in their rooms studying at 2000 hours. At 2145 hours, a whistle was blown, allowing 15 minutes to tidy up and get to bed. Lightsout was at 2200 hours sharp and by 2201 nearly everyone was asleep from pure exhaustion, particularly at the beginning of the course.

The severe system of training and discipline left many new cadets in constant fear of being dropped from the course, an attitude which tended to make some fail. To overcome this fear, the attitude had to be one of 'do your best and to hell with the consequences'. For all this the rate of pay, was £3 10s per week, with uniforms supplied. Most of the cadets adjusted to the long hours of work fairly quickly.

It was not all work and no play. Despite the pace, there was still time for some 'mucking about'. Dereck French, who joined as a new cadet in January 1937, recalled some of the initiation rites that were inflicted on his group behind the scenes:

> The custom was that the members of the senior course introduced those of the junior term into the system, which involved a rather vicious form of bastardry – initiation ceremonies and penalties for minor offences. At our initiation we were made to strip and run naked across the drome to the hangars along the foreshore, there we were painted with colourful aeroplane dope – only on parts of us which could not be seen when we were in uniform. In this condition we were forced to walk the plank into the sea. One or two of us could not swim and nearly drowned – then we had to take part in a race, pushing peanuts along the concrete tarmac with our noses.
>
> All rather stupid and childish, yet it was condoned by the senior staff as it was supposed to make us group together and bend to discipline...

For the first three weeks new cadets were not allowed away from the aerodrome. From then on, one Sunday each month was allowed as time off to go to the city or visit friends or relations. This day of freedom was anticipated with great relish, and about the worst disciplinary restraint in the book of penalties for misbehaviour was to be confined to barracks for that particular Sunday.

After weeks of intense preliminary training, the cadets at last saw the inside of an aircraft. One of the practical subjects actually was flying! For just about everyone, this made up for everything. Flying training began using de Havilland Gypsy Moths. The DH60 Moth series had been a direct result of the worldwide surge of enthusiasm for flying in the 1920s and it had revolutionised popular aviation. First flown in the UK on 22 February 1925, the Moth proved highly suitable for school and private use in flying clubs all over Britain. Many civil examples were exported, and military tandem two-seat trainer models were delivered to various air forces, including those of Britain, Australia, Canada, Irish Free State, Sweden, Finland and Japan.

The later de Havilland DH60G Gipsy Moth was the outcome of nearly four years and more than 4 million miles of experience with the earlier versions. The main changes included the installation of a 100–120 hp (74.5–89.4 kW) Gipsy I, II or III engine, split-axle landing gear and cleaner lines. It remained in UK production until 1934, by which time it was in worldwide use and was built under licence in Australia, France and the USA.

In Australia, it was in a Gipsy Moth that Francis Chichester flew across the Tasman Sea in 1932. Gipsy Moths were used in the first public crop-dusting demonstrations, such as at the 1934 Laverton Air Pageant. At the very same show, W/Cdr George Jones DFC, who later became the RAAF's Chief of Air Staff, did what may have been a world first – piloting the first Moth glider. This was a special machine with its propeller removed and a quick-release cable attached to the crankshaft. It was towed aloft behind another aircraft and then cast off at 2,000 feet (600 m). Jones looped the Moth twice and then glided to a perfect landing directly in front of the VIP grandstand.

Gipsy Moths were one of many trainers still on RAAF strength at No.1 Flying Training School at Laverton in 1939. They were the air force's main elementary trainers in the important pre-Second World War period. Slow, stable and safe enough for beginners, the cadets flew dual with instructors for about 10–12 hours before attempting to go solo. Initial flying training included aircraft handling on the ground as well as in the air, tuition in the techniques of take off and landing, and some local flying.

'Bob Bungey took to flying like a child to a secret place,' Jack Marx noted poetically in his book, *Australian Tragic*:

> Suspended in the sky, looking down upon the once tall buildings and impassable rivers, their tributaries now silver little lightning bolts impressed into the earth, he felt as one having leapt from the frame in which all life remained, the streets and houses, the people going to and fro about their tiny business, all captives of some vast equation only he had solved. All the things that ever mattered were now literally beneath him, falling away from his panorama with the tilting of the wings, all humankinds existence made to wait for his return. It was the greatest thing in life, and risking life was worth it.

The training course at Point Cook consisted of two six-month terms. New courses started every January and July, so there was always a senior and a junior course running. This meant that Point Cook was crowded – too crowded for some. Despite all the pressure, the first six months for Bob Bungey and the others went by very quickly and two glorious weeks of leave loomed ahead as Christmas approached. It also meant graduation for those in the senior course – and for them a choice that had to be made.

Twenty-five from the course could go to the United Kingdom under a deal that existed for the RAAF to provide trained pilots for the Royal Air Force. If they wished, graduating cadets could nominate themselves for five-year short service commissions in the RAF, with their year at Point Cook counting as the first year.

This scheme had its beginnings back at the Imperial Conference in London in 1923. It was seen as desirable to develop the air forces of the Empire along common lines, as far as practicable. British representatives proposed a system of reserve training for RAAF officers at courses in England through a system of short service commissions in the RAF. These commissions would be made available to a proportion of the pilots trained annually at Point Cook. There were advantages for all concerned. By adopting this method, it was reasoned that a reserve of trained aircrew would be built up, which could be drawn on to reinforce RAF squadrons in an emergency, and Australia would benefit when the men returned home after four years of practical operational training at British expense. As an incentive for agreeing to this uniform scheme, Britain's Air Ministry would credit £1,500 per head to a special fund in London from which Australia could draw to pay for other goods and services to be provided to the RAAF. Australia's fledgling air force was only two years old and so it stood to benefit enormously.

With the Australian Defence Minister's approval of the scheme, the first cadets were selected from the Point Cook course that completed training at the end of October 1926. Seven graduates, not ten as originally stipulated, nominated to go and they sailed for England the following month to begin their RAF service.

Although the original agreement involved each RAAF transferee receiving a five-year short service commission, less one year because of their Point Cook training, the RAF soon showed interest in retaining some of the men for a longer period, perhaps even permanently. The Commonwealth was agreeable, subject to a satisfactory financial adjustment.

In November 1928, F/O Lee Murray, an officer who had been sent in the first group, was considered for a permanent RAF commission but shortly afterwards he transferred for compassionate reasons to the RAAF Reserve and was no longer available. Nevertheless, the administrative groundwork had been laid.

In October 1930, the Commonwealth was asked if it wished to limit the number of officers to be accepted for permanent transfer. With the effects of the Depression resulting in retrenchments in the services at that time, Australia did not place any restriction on numbers. When Britain announced measures to build up her air strength in 1935, the Air Ministry suggested extending the short service commission scheme from five to six years. Again, the Air Board raised no objection.

The RAF was eager to have as many Point Cook-trained pilots as possible. The Chief of Air Staff, Air Chief Marshal Sir Edward Ellington, said the RAF would like to increase its intake of Australian pilots to twenty–twenty-five per year, and that it was looking for as many as fifty pilots in 1936.

Most of the senior course that year chose to go, twenty-five in all, filling all places. For them it meant a complete severance from the RAAF for four or five years at least, but it was a great opportunity to see the world. Most thought that they would return to Australia and pick up the threads once again. This would benefit the service, and mean greater opportunities for themselves because of their overseas experience. Bob Cosgrove and his roommate, Pat Hughes, were among those who chose to go. So too was Gordon Olive, but Peter McDonough decided to stay.

During the second six-month term, which started after Bob and the others returned from leave in January 1937, flying training switched to Westland Wapitis, single-engined two-seater biplanes that were larger and heavier than the Gipsy Moths.

The Westland Wapiti was a general-purpose biplane, which incorporated in its design several component parts in common with the de Havilland DH9A of First World War vintage. The prototype flew for the first time in the UK in March 1927. An initial order for twenty-five production Mk I Wapitis included an aircraft specially modified with a more luxurious rear cockpit for the Prince of Wales to fly in. Mk I models were powered by 420-hp (313-kW) Bristol Jupiter VI engines, but subsequent Mk IIs and Mk IIAs had 460-hp (343-kW) Jupiter VI and 525-hp (391.2-kW) Jupiter VIIIF or similar engines respectively. Small numbers of lengthened Wapiti Vs and unarmed Mk.VI trainers brought total production for the RAF to 501. The type was also adopted by Australia, Canada, China, India, and South Africa, where it was built under licence.

The RAAF received nine Mk I Wapitis and twenty-nine Mk IIAs beginning in 1928. The first nine were subsequently upgraded to Mk IIA standard. Another six ex-RAF Mk IIAs were taken on charge in 1936. The type had a maximum speed of 140 mph (225 km/h), a range of 360 miles (579 km) and for armament it housed one forward-firing Vickers machine gun and one rear-mounted Lewis gun, plus it could carry up to 500 lb (227 kg) of bombs. By now, however, both the Gipsy Moth and the Wapiti were obsolescent, the RAAF's equipment being years behind that of the RAF.

The Wapiti's Bristol Jupiter radial engine drove an 11½-foot-diameter propeller through a 2:1 reduction gear, which allowed the prop to tick over unbelievably slowly when the engine was idling. There was a legend about this that was related to all the cadets.

The incident happened at Point Cook a couple of years earlier. A pilot taxied his Wapiti onto the tarmac by the hangars and signalled to his rigger that one of his oleo legs needed attention. He left the engine ticking over slowly as it was only a quick adjustment that was needed and he was going to fly again. The rigger grabbed his tools and came in along the leading edge of the wing. He did what was necessary to the oleo leg, picked up his tools and, without thinking, proceeded to walk out forwards, straight towards the spinning propeller. Amazingly, he walked right through its spinning arc without being hit. A few steps in front of the aircraft he stopped, turned round, realised what he had done, and fainted. Others who were watching the incident had already turned away or covered their eyes in horror at what they expected to see. They were astounded to find the collapsed man quite untouched. It was blind luck that he had not been killed or maimed, and a haunting object lesson in safety that nobody forgot.

Flying was now a matter of applying the theory of flight and the lessons of flying learnt during first term to the practice of warfare. To begin with, there was considerable close formation flying that was soon mastered. This was necessary in order to take a number of planes through thick, dense cloud and be in a position ready to fight without the necessity of trying to rendezvous over a featureless mass of cloud.

Next there was instrument flying. To do this a canvas hood was pulled over the pupil's cockpit so that he could not see out and had to rely on his machine's primitive instruments.

Another practice was high altitude flying. For this, the Wapiti took off fully loaded, as if for a wartime operation, and climbed up to 20,000 feet (6,000 m). The last few thousand feet were gained very slowly and painfully. At that altitude the temperature was around 15°C below the temperature at sea level. Because in Victoria during winter the weather was seldom above 15°C, the corresponding air temperature at 20,000 feet (6,000 m) could be down to 0°C. The Wapiti's crew would be up there sitting in unheated, open cockpits with a 100 mph (160 km/h) wind whistling around them as they flew sluggishly about. They could freeze very quickly and 2-hour trips were not unusual. By the time they landed, they were at the very least cold and miserable.

Far more popular was dive-bombing practice and air to ground gunnery. Both were startling to begin with. At first, the target was approached very slowly at about 2,000 feet (600 m). Then the pilot dropped the nose down into a 45° to 50° dive, which left the pupil's stomach behind at 2,000 feet. This always felt as if it was a vertical dive and the Wapiti gathered speed very rapidly. The wires in the rigging between the mainplanes 'howled and vibrated' impressively under the extraordinary stresses.

The idea was obviously to release the bomb or fire the guns at the lower part of the straight dive, and then pull out in time so as not to plunge down into the target. The lower you went before releasing or firing, the better were the chances of hitting the target. These two exercises soon showed up the differences in temperament of the various cadets. Those who were more nervous tended to pull out high, and the reckless ones went down low. A few could be unpredictable – too high one time, and much too low the next – and they were potentially dangerous. Fortunately, not many were in this category.

The RAAF had eight Bristol Bulldogs and they were based at Laverton, 5 miles to the north. This type was the standard RAF interceptor fighter from the late 1920s until it was progressively replaced in the mid-1930s by the Hawker Fury and Gloster Gauntlet. It was an unequal-wingspan biplane with a sturdy structure mostly of light alloy with fabric covering. From its first flight on 17 May 1927, handling was found to be excellent. To rectify some minor faults that showed up in the first prototype, Bristol quickly produced a Mk II prototype with a longer fuselage and other changes, and this was accepted for RAF service.

Altogether, ninety-two Bulldog IIs were built, and of these seventeen went to Latvia, twelve to Estonia, three to Sweden, two to the US Navy, two to Siam, one to Chile and eight to Australia in 1930. Bulldogs remained in RAF service until 1937 and they were with the RAAF until 1940.

The Australian Bulldogs performed at various aerobatic displays to great applause, and for the Point Cook cadets they provided the first exhilarating experiences of air-to-air combat. The manoeuvres were exactly those of the dogfights of the First World War. It was fun for the instructors too.

Mostly the Bulldogs would attack an 'unsuspecting' Wapiti from above and behind, and if possible from out of the sun. If the instructor was alert, he would whip the Wapiti around and dive under the angle of their dive forcing them into an outside loop if they tried to keep their sights on him. Then he would haul up and straight into a steep climbing turn, which he could maintain inside the Bulldogs' turning circle, forcing the fighters to break off. The Wapiti pilot then had the chance of fastening onto their tails.

Once the cadets understood the rules, it was fascinating to follow the whirling tactics as they indulged in these pitched mock battles. It was fortunate no bullets were fired! Half-an-hour of this was breathtaking and exciting but after the rush of adrenalin wore off, it could result in a very tiring session.

The last six months went quickly, and suddenly it was almost over. The graduating cadets were scheduled to be awarded their wings on 29 June and like those in the previous class, they were faced with the same choice. Before them was a great opportunity to see England, the 'Mother Country', and experience the world outside Australia for five years – and at the same time be paid for it! On top of that, there would be opportunities to fly the latest in British-designed aircraft. Who could tell where such valuable flying experiences might lead? Like those before them, twenty-five cadets opted for short service commissions in the RAF. Bob Bungey was one of them.

Significantly, although by choosing to go overseas they were leaving the RAAF behind, none were required to hand back their issued RAAF uniforms and regalia. They considered they were still 'air force', and again like those before them, did not doubt that they could return to home and transfer back again into the RAAF.

The nervous young men of almost a year ago were now feeling 'pretty good'. They all had a sense of achievement and significant success, confident that they had shown skill at the pilot's trade. Altogether, Bob had amassed 125 hours of flying in his RAAF Log Book. This total included 25 hours 15 minutes of solo in the Gypsy Moth, 37 hours 25 minutes solo in the Wapiti, and 15 hours instruction in cloud and under-hood flying.

On 17 July 1937, the 20,000 ton Orient Line Steamship *Orama*, left Sydney Harbour bound for England via the Suez Canal. She was a regular ship on the Australia–England route. Listed among those on board were fifteen Queenslanders and New South Welshmen of the RAAF party setting out with the aim of joining the RAF. They were:

Dilworth, J. F.
Edwards, W. H.
Farrington, A. L.
Fry, C. H.
Gibbes, A. R.
Hubbard, A. L. G.
Hunter, D. H.
Kennedy, J. C.
Leighton, J. W. E.
Lewis, O. J. F.
McGhie, A. F.
McKinlay, J. F.
Messervy, N. H. E.
Mulligan, A. R.
Ross, E. H.

The ship sailed southwards to Melbourne where the Victorians and Tasmanians joined the group on the 20th:

Ambrose, B. S.
Blom, W. M.
Graham, G. F.
Sadler, J. F. B.
Walch, S. C.

Next, it was westward to Port Adelaide where the four South Australians came aboard on 22 July:

Bungey, R. W.
Clisby, L. R.
Skinner, W. B.
Walsh, K. H.

There was just one more to go and he joined the *Orama* at Fremantle in Western Australia on the 26th.

Reed, R. J.

That made twenty-five on their way to England. Air Chief Marshal Sir Edward Ellington had what he asked for. He said the RAF wanted fifty pilots in 1936, and they came, twenty-five each, from that year's January and July classes.

Departing from Fremantle and voyaging out into the vast Indian Ocean, the young men on the *Orama* watched with mixed emotions as Australia's coastline disappeared beyond the horizon.

2

226 Squadron RAF

Bob Bungey's first flight in an RAF aircraft took place on 2 September 1937 at No.8 Flying Training School (FTS) at Montrose on the north-east coast of Scotland, an area jutting out eastward into the cold North Sea. He was the passenger in Hawker Hart K5006 piloted by F/Lt Reid. It was 55 minutes of 'General Flying Practice', after which Bob took Hart K5894 up alone while Reid watched from the ground. Similar familiarisation flights were repeated next day. After this, F/Lt Reid's name disappeared from Bob's brand new RAF Pilot's Flying Log Book.

From this point onwards, Bob was teamed up with Allan Farrington, the diving champion from Manly. Immediately after the Australians had arrived in England they'd had to report to the RAF Depot at Uxbridge in Middlesex. This was on 26 August 1937, but within a week they had been dispersed to advanced flying courses at various bases throughout the United Kingdom. Bob and Allan were posted to the course at Montrose.

Over the next three months, the pair flew together in Harts and Hawker Audaxes in a series of familiarisation cross-country flights and flying exercises, alternating their roles of pilot, passenger or observer or navigator or bomb-aimer, as required.

The Hart two-seat light bomber, which first flew in June 1928, introduced an unrivalled dynasty of interwar military aircraft for the Hawker Company. It was an early product of Sydney Camm, a promising draughtsman/designer who had joined the firm three years earlier. He and engineer Fred Sigrist devised a system of bolted duralumin tubes that became the constructional characteristic of Hawker aircraft.

The Hart was an elegant design that boasted a matchless performance for its time. With the RAF needing a replacement for its lower-performance Westland Wapiti aircraft (the same type that Bob and the other Australians had trained on earlier at Point Cook), the Hart was chosen as the service's new light day bomber. Nearly 1,000 were built and there were large export orders. It proved to be one of the most adaptable aeroplanes in RAF history, and spawned further development as the Demon, Audax, Hardy, Hind, Hector, and Hart Trainer, which Bob and Allan had started flying in their new surroundings.

Hawker's Audax involved comparatively minor changes to the basic Hart design, such as installing a message pick-up hook, to satisfy an army co-operation requirement.

As for their surroundings, Bob and Allan found that picturesque Montrose was located in the county of Angus between Aberdeen and Dundee, some 38 miles (61 km) north of Dundee between the mouths of the North and South Esk Rivers. It was the northernmost coastal town in the county and the airfield was situated a mile further north. The town itself evolved and developed at a natural harbour where there had been a flourishing trade in skins, hides and cured salmon during medieval times. A 220-foot (67-m) steeple, designed by James Gillespie Graham and built between 1832 and 1834, dominated the skyline. It was an easily identifiable landmark from the air, as were features on the red cliffs and long beaches of the rugged Scottish coastline. On a clear day, to the west, the Grampian Mountains could be seen rising from a cold, green, damp rural landscape that was so different from the much drier, hotter Adelaide Hills and plains back home.

Bob and Allan stood out. They stood out because they were easy to see. All the former Point Cook cadets had permission, for now, to wear their distinctive, much darker RAAF uniforms and these immediately set them apart from the others who wore RAF light blue. There were, however, at least two other Australians on the base. Their names were Anderson and Moreland but they had joined the RAF direct and so were wearing RAF blue. Between the late 1930s and 1940, young men from various Commonwealth countries took their chances and travelled to England in the hope of gaining one of the widely advertised short service commissions in the RAF. This resulted in the RAF having a growing influx of New Zealanders, Canadians, South Africans and others as well as the Aussies. When their RAAF uniforms were worn out the Australians were expected to change over to RAF light blue.

Bob's mate from Adelaide, Leslie Clisby, was not far away, training at Leuchars in Fifeshire, 4 miles (6.5 km) north-west of St Andrews with its famous golf course. He had been posted to No. 1 FTS of which he wrote:

> No.1 Flying Training School is for training of seconded Naval and Army Officers, the other Air Force men learn the first part of flying at a civil school and then come here for service type A/C flying – a course which lasts three months. They push them off here just as soon as they can go up and land safely. Our flying is streets ahead of theirs – they think we are crack pilots. From here they go into the Fleet Air Arm on Fleet Carrier ships doing deck landings. I wouldn't really mind, I like ship life. We Australians (6 of the original 25 from Aust.) are the first Air Force Officers to do any flying training here.

Leslie loved Scotland, and wished that he could describe its beauty adequately in his letters to his family. He bought a car and made many trips around the countryside. On 23 November he wrote home: 'Drove down to Montrose to see Bob Bungey and three other Australians. They are leaving for their new postings next week. We will be scattered all over England.'

The advanced flying course at Montrose ended four days later on the 27th. Bob Bungey and Allan Farrington were both assessed as 'above average', but at the same time, for reasons unknown, Allan received fail marks in armament and navigation and also as a pilot. This was in spite of the fact he had already qualified for his Flying Badge, his 'wings', in the RAAF on 29 June back in Australia. Somehow compromise was reached. The RAF authorised him to wear his wings with effect from the original date regardless of the so-called fail marks.

The same day the course ended, Allan and Bob were notified of their postings. They were to go separate ways. Allan was posted to 211 Squadron at Grantham in Lincolnshire. Bob was going to 226 Squadron at Harwell in Berkshire, about 11 miles (18 km) north of Newbury. Both were Bomber Command units but in just six months' time Allan Farrington and his squadron would transfer to the Middle East.

Leslie Clisby, meanwhile, received a posting to fly fighters with No.1 Squadron, 'the crack squadron of the RAF' he wrote in a letter home from Tangmere in Sussex.

No.226 Squadron RAF had formed as a light bomber squadron at Upper Heyford on 15 March 1937. This was actually its second birth. It had been originally formed on 1 April 1918 at Pizzone in Italy as a unit of No.6 Wing of the former Royal Naval Air Service (RNAS) based at Taranto. This was also the date in the First World War when the RNAS and the Royal Flying Corps (RFC) were amalgamated to create Britain's new Royal Air Force.

Equipped initially with de Havilland DH4s and later with DH9s, reconnaissance and bombing missions were flown over the Adriatic to raid Austrian bases in Albania and Montenegro. Anti-submarine patrols were also carried out. In October 1918, the squadron moved to the Aegean to make attacks on Turkish targets. These continued until the end of the war, after which it returned to southern Italy later in November. It was disbanded on 18 December 1918.

The new 226 Squadron was at first equipped with Hawker Audaxes but in October 1937 it began swapping these for Fairey Battle light bombers. Bob Bungey's first flight in a Battle took place on 2 January 1938. He was a passenger for a 35-minute 'air test' in aircraft K7588. His pilot was P/O Pitfield, another Australian. Alan Pitfield had been at Point Cook a year before Bob as a member of the July 1935 course.

Bob took the controls of a Battle (K7586) for the first time five days later on the 7th, and this marked another series of firsts for him. This was his first time as the pilot of one of the new 'modern' monoplanes. Prior to this, all of his flying had been done in biplanes with open cockpits and fixed undercarriages. This new, almost all-metal machine was more powerful, though it still only had one engine, had retractable landing wheels and its cockpit was under a long greenhouse-type glazed canopy that could be fully enclosed. There was far more to understand and apply. There were the new flaps and a variable pitch propeller, and learning to cater for a crew of three. The Battle itself had already undergone a considerable number of changes too.

When it first flew on 10 March 1936, the prototype, K4303, represented a vast improvement over the earlier Hawker Hind, Hart and Gordon light bombers. It emerged as an aesthetically pleasing, low-wing cantilever monoplane with its crew of two accommodated under a lengthy glazed canopy. Powered was supplied by a Rolls-Royce Merlin 'F' engine driving a Fairey-Reed three-blade, fixed-pitch metal propeller fitted with a streamlined spinner. The spinner merged beautifully into the contours of the cowling with its flush exhaust ports, and no problems occurred during the initial flight tests. The Merlin engine appeared to provide sufficient power while its compact frontal area resulted in a clean, streamlined profile and a good performance by 1936 standards.

The retractable undercarriage folded rearwards into wing positions that left part of the wheels exposed. This was supposed to be handy in the event of a wheels-up landing. A fixed castor tail wheel was fitted under the rear fuselage.

Public attention was first drawn to Fairey's new bomber, which had been given the name 'Battle' on 2 April, at the annual RAF Display at Hendon on 27 June 1936. The prototype appeared in the 'New Types Park' with an overall silver finish and a large black number '4' on the fuselage ahead of the roundel. Originally envisaged as having separate cockpits, one for the pilot and one for the gunner, these had been modified to reduce the effects of drag and noise by having the long greenhouse canopy enclosing both.

Flight testing of the prototype was delayed owing to problems with early development of the Merlin engine, but by July K4043 eventually arrived for handling and performance trials at the Aeroplane and Armament Experimental Establishment (A&AEE) at Martlesham Heath in Suffolk. These showed that the Battle outclassed all of the RAF's contemporary day bombers. It had a maximum speed of 257 mph (414 km/h) at 15,000 feet (4,575 m). Its cruising speed was 200 mph (322 km/h) carrying a 1,000-lb (454 kg) bomb load at 14,000 feet (4,260 m) over a range of 980 miles (1,570 km). Even so, the Battle's performance was considered disappointing for a potential front-line aircraft.

The Air Ministry then made matters worse by deciding a third crew member should be carried. It decreed that a separate bomb-aimer would be needed so that the rear gunner could concentrate entirely on defence during combat. This crew member was to sit between the pilot and rear gunner, and carry out his duty bomb-aiming from a prone position on the fuselage floor. His extra weight had an adverse effect on performance. The first production machine, Battle K7558, flew in April 1937 and when tested with a full load including the third crew member, it could only manage 241 mph (388 km/h) maximum speed at 13,000 feet (3,960 m).

Fuel was contained in a 45-imp. gal. (205 litre) fuselage tank and two 106-imp. gal. (482-litre) wing tanks. Bombs were housed in four cells incorporated in the wing roots, a normal load consisting of four 250-lb (113.5-kg) bombs carried on hydraulic crutches which, in a dive-bombing attack, swung the bombs clear of the Battle's fuselage and propeller arc. External underwing racks could carry an additional 500-lb (227-kg) bomb load.

Offensive armament consisted of a fixed, forward-firing 0.303-inch (7.7-mm) Browning machine gun in the starboard wing root and for defence it had one 0.303-inch (7.7-mm) Vickers 'K' gun in the rear cockpit. The rear of the long glazed canopy that contoured smoothly into the rear fuselage decking was hinged to allow the gunner maximum movement when operating his Vickers gun – that was the theory anyway.

Production Fairey Battles featured improved internal equipment, the introduction of external 'kidney' exhaust manifolds on the engine cowlings and a de Havilland variable-pitch propeller instead of the original Fairey-Reed fixed-pitch type. The new de Havilland propeller made removal of the original streamlined spinner necessary because the larger spinner needed to cover the pitch-changing mechanism would have required alterations to the profile of the engine cowling.

The first RAF unit to receive Battles was No.63 Squadron based at Upwood, Huntingdon, and its first Battle, K7559 (the second production aircraft), arrived on 20 May. This was one of several early-production Battles with dual controls to aid conversion of crews to the new monoplane. By the end of the year, the squadron had fifteen on charge. From 2 July 1937 until 21 March 1938, No.63 Squadron carried out various trials, and became known as the Battle Development Unit. It was also the first Battle squadron to reach operational status. Others that received Battles during 1937 were No.105 Squadron at Harwell, No.226 Squadron also at Harwell, No.52 Squadron at Upwood and No.88 Squadron at Boscombe Down in Wiltshire, in that order.

Experience showed that the aircraft was strongly built and heavy – heavy enough to ignore the bumpy air when being flown at a low level. The wing section near the wing roots was thick enough to conceal a 1,000-lb (454-kg) bomb while it seemed to lumber along and wallow behind its spinner-less, variable-pitch propeller. Its designated top speed was, in reality, beyond its reach.

Bob found the pilot's cockpit comfortable enough, but it was totally unlike anything else he had flown. It felt confined with the hood closed but it was quite roomy. Forward visibility over the engine cowling, unobstructed by an upper wing, was good, but the vision to the rear was poor.

The rear gunner's position was a long way back and uncomfortable. Although the tilting hood screened his back from the slipstream, the backdraught it created curled in and slapped him full in the face. The single rear gun itself had a poor arc of fire, and the large rudder and tailplane effectively blocked much of the arc anyway.

To perform his task, the bomb aimer needed to move from his seat to lie face down in the prone position in the bomb-aiming gap and peer through a Perspex panel (usually oil stained) in the floor to aim his bombs. The unpleasant hot, oily stench from the engine made any lengthy stay in that hole an absolute impossibility.

During 1938, twelve more Bomber Command squadrons converted to, or were formed with, Fairey Battles. This was all due to the increasing urgency of the RAF's expansion programme in light of the worsening political situation in Europe.

* * *

After the Great War of 1914–18, German national pride smarted over the harshness of the 1919 Treaty of Versailles. Military aviation had been banned in Germany and civil aircraft construction was also prohibited until 1922, when it was permitted again under certain conditions. The Germans were quick to adapt. By the mid-1920s there was a highly efficient aircraft industry that included Dornier at Friedrichshafen, Focke-Wulf at Bremen, Heinkel at Warnemünde, Junkers at Dessau, and Messerschmitt at Augsburg. While the victorious Allies were still flying obsolete wood and fabric biplanes, German designers were already developing advanced all-metal monoplanes with cantilevered wings, variable-pitch propellers, and retractable undercarriages.

As far as the outside world was concerned, air-minded young German men could only gain flying experience by joining local gliding clubs, but all was not as it seemed. In reality, German civil aviation was highly centralised and largely controlled by the military class. In contravention of the Versailles Treaty, *Lufthansa*, Germany's civil air transportation company, restructured and secretly created a small elite air force within the framework of its organisation. Military crews could train to become proficient in night and all-weather flying at four *Lufthansa* flying schools. At the same time, the airline established flying routes throughout Western Europe and quickly became the most technically advanced air service in the world.

Following the rise to power of Adolf Hitler, the German Air Arm was developed in secret under *Reichskommissar* for Aviation, Herman Göring. To build up the new service, trainee pilots were sent clandestinely to the Soviet Union and Italy for training on military aircraft. In March 1935, Hitler repudiated the conditions of the Versailles Treaty, restored conscription and announced that Germany's army would be raised to a peacetime strength of more than half a million men. At the same time, the pretence was dropped and the existence of the new *Luftwaffe* was unveiled to an astonished world.

Noticeable signs of German rearmament, and the collapse of the League of Nations Disarmament Conference in July 1934, had already triggered a move to expand the RAF. At that time, in an organisation known as the Air Defence of Great Britain, subdivided into 'Western Area' and the 'Central Area', the bomber force based in the UK was made up of twenty-eight squadrons. Most of these were light bomber squadrons and, apart from those at Bircham Newton in Norfolk, they were all based in the counties of Wiltshire, Hampshire, Berkshire and Oxfordshire. This disposition revolved around the assumption that air attacks on Britain could only be made from France.

The whole air force itself was made up of short-range biplanes able to fly just modest speeds and capable of carrying only moderate bomb loads. Several new types such as the Fairey Battle, Bristol Blenheim, Armstrong Whitworth Whitley, Handley Page Hampden and Vickers Wellington were under development, but they were still on the drawing boards and nowhere near being put into production.

RAF expansion was programmed in a series of successive schemes noted alphabetically, each the result of rethinking future requirements in the light of changing circumstances. None were ever fully implemented. The first plan, Scheme 'A', announced in July 1934, was aimed at boosting first-line numbers in order to impress Hitler. As far as the bomber force was concerned, the idea was to enlarge it over a five-year period ending on 31 March 1939, to reach forty-one squadrons, twenty-two of which were to be of light bombers.

The arrival of the Fairey Battle on the scene in March 1936 meant that this would be the type chosen. It was a relatively cheap option, which had the advantage of enabling a greater number of pilots and aircrew to be recruited and trained to an operational level, but as far as aircraft were concerned, it gave up quality for quantity. Fairey Battles did not have the range to fly from England to attack targets in Germany, but they were the only choice if rapid expansion was to proceed to create an apparent deterrent. For them to be of any practical use, they would have to be based somewhere on the Continent closer to their potential targets.

By February 1936 Scheme 'F' was being announced and, among other things, it called for an extensive increase in the RAF's striking power by replacing light bombers with medium bombers plus the creation of much larger reserves. All of this needed to be achieved within three years but there were huge practical problems. The aircraft industry was in a state of flux. It was already adapting itself to the radical change from biplanes to monoplanes and from fabric-covered to stressed metal-covered construction. It simply could not cope with the enormous complex workload that Scheme 'F' demanded. In order to produce these new, highly sophisticated modern aircraft, factories needed to be restructured. Stocks of basic materials had to be changed, and the traditional small-scale production methods replaced by the jigs, dies, tools and new assembly line techniques of mass production. Not only that, workers had to be retrained for their new tasks.

A far-sighted system known as the Shadow Factory Scheme was instituted in April 1936 to rectify the situation. Initially, this was introduced as a means of utilising the resources of Britain's motor vehicle industry to provide extra production capacity. It involved building new state-owned aero engine, airframe component and assembly factories that were equipped and run by such leading motor companies as Austin, Daimler, Rootes and Standard. They would turn out products designed by a 'parent' organisation within the aircraft industry. This scheme was quickly underway, and was complemented early in 1938 by an additional shadow scheme that provided for the erection of more state-owned factories managed by approved firms in the aircraft industry to further increase production.

Enlargement of the RAF necessitated a major reorganisation too. On 18 June 1936, the Air Council abolished the Air Defence of Great Britain and created two separate entities, Bomber Command and Fighter Command, each with its own Air Officer Commanding-in-Chief directly responsible to the Air Council. At the same time, Coastal Command and Training Command were formed by restructuring the former Coastal Area organisation.

Bomber Command initially comprised four groups, Nos.1, 2, 3 and 6, the latter being an auxiliary group. To accommodate the expanding bomber force, a chain of new bases was built in eastern England. In 1937 the first concrete runways were laid but by the outbreak of war two years later, the majority of bomber airfields were still all-grass.

The training of incoming crews was complicated by the fact that the new all-metal monoplanes were vastly more complex than their lumbering biplane predecessors. They introduced as standard such items as constant-speed propellers, automatic pilots, retractable undercarriages and power-operated gun turrets. With the new bigger bombers, such as the Hampden, Whitley and Wellington requiring more crew members, navigation became the duty of a specialist, and many more gunners were needed too.

In Fairey Battle crews, the pilot was also expected to navigate. To gain proficiency in this, Bob Bungey attended the School of Air Navigation in south-east England from the end of November 1938 to the end of January 1939. It was situated at Manston in Kent, about 12 miles (19 km) east of Canterbury. During his two months training on Avro Ansons, he accumulated 45 hours 5 minutes as a navigator. This consisted of 34 hours 55 minutes of daylight flying and 10 hours 10 minutes at night. It was a skill that would serve him well.

From early in 1938 Britain's prime minister, Neville Chamberlain, had been seeking a general appeasement throughout Europe, which would assure peace. To do this he and his partners in the League of Nations had to make concession after concession to the wishes of the expanding Third Reich. In return, Chancellor Hitler would give assurances that the re-emerging Germany had no further territorial claims, but this was false. The German Army marched into Austria in March 1938; in September it threatened Czechoslovakia. Chamberlain flew three times to Germany to negotiate with Hitler, and at Munich he took part in negotiating the agreement that weakly ceded Czechoslovakia's Sudetenland to Germany for more hollow assurances.

The immediate crisis was over but Chamberlain's assertions of 'peace for our time' as he held up a paper signed by the German government totally ignored what had been going on in Spain since 1936. Germany, Italy and the USSR were locked into a bloody struggle, the Spanish Civil War – a dress rehearsal for what was to come. In any case, to have opposed Germany in September 1938 would have been suicidal. What had become painfully clear was the fact that Britain's armed forces, particularly the RAF, were not ready.

Facing the *Luftwaffe's* strike force of an estimated 1,200 modern bombers, RAF Fighter Command would have only been able to muster ninety-three of its new eight-gun monoplane fighters, including all reserves. The remainder of its 666 aircraft were outdated biplanes. No Spitfires were yet in the line; and the Hurricanes, being without heating for their guns, were useless above 15,000 feet (4,500 m), even in summer.

After Prime Minister Chamberlain held up his scrap of Munich Agreement paper, the world breathed a sigh of relief, but the realities of the international situation – an almost inevitable drift to war – became more widely realised. The Munich Agreement did at least have one positive effect, that of gaining a breathing space, giving Britain and France more precious time to rearm and plan.

British Intelligence and a combined-services planning section compiled a list of potential targets that would be vital to any German war effort. As a result, the Air Council drew up sixteen detailed directives known as 'Western Air Plans', which were approved on 1 October 1937. The main assumption of the planners was that Germany would immediately commence operations in Western Europe either with intense bombing raids on Britain, or with a land offensive through France and Belgium. The assumption was flawed.

Bomber Command's main war plans – Western Air Plans Nos.1, 4 and 5 – were designed to counter whichever of these moves the Germans made. If they started bombing, the RAF would attack the *Luftwaffe's* airfields and supply depots. If the German Army attacked France, its supply lines to the battle front would be targeted. A third major plan was for strategic raids to be made on Germany's war industry, particularly on oil refineries and storage depots in the Ruhr, Rhineland and Saar. There were other plans for other possibilities and for various minor operations – but no plans were in place for the prospect of the Germans attacking in the opposite direction – towards Poland.

As time passed it became apparent that the *Führer* aimed next to occupy the free city of Danzig, which lay across the Polish Corridor. Hitler's disregard for all his assurances at Munich led the British government to offer guarantees of support to Poland in the event of attack. As far as Bomber Command was concerned, it was difficult to see how the Poles could be helped. Poland was too far away. Its nearest point was 700 miles (1,125 km) away from the RAF's bomber airfields. The only possibility would be to establish a force in France close to the German border, which would create the impression of a threatening second front.

Plans were made for the army to send a British Expeditionary Force (BEF) to France. This force was to have an Air Component under the operational direction of the C-in-C, Viscount Gort, and there would be an Advanced Air Striking Force (AASF) for short-range offensive operations across the German frontier.

By August 1939, short-range light/medium bombers (Battles and Blenheims) designated under the war plans to go to France with the BEF were based in the Oxfordshire/Berkshire area; whilst the long-range striking force of Bomber Command were situated at bases nearest Germany, in the counties of East Anglia, Lincolnshire and Yorkshire. Bomber Command's strength at this date was fifty-five squadrons and it was organised as follows:

- Headquarters Bomber Command was at Richings Park, Langley, Buckinghamshire, but a new location was being prepared at High Wycombe. The C-in-C was ACM Sir Edgar Ludlow-Hewitt.
- No.1 Group was commanded by AVM A. C. Wright; HQ at Abingdon, Berkshire; with Nos.12, 15, 40, 88, 103, 105, 142, 150, 218 and 226 Squadrons, all equipped with Fairey Battles.
- No.2 Group; HQ at Wyton; commanded by AVM AM C. T. Maclean; with Nos.21, 82, 101, 107, 110, 114 and 139 Squadrons, all equipped with Bristol Blenheims.
- No.3 Group; HQ at Mildenhall; under AVM J. E. A. Baldwin; with Nos.9, 37, 38, 99, 115 and 149, 214 and 215 Squadrons, all equipped with Vickers Wellingtons.
- No.4 Group. HQ at Linton-on-Ouse; commanded by Australian-born AVM A. Coningham; with Nos.10, 51, 58, 77, 78 and 102 Squadrons, all equipped with Armstrong-Whitworth Whitleys.
- No.5 Group; HQ at St Vincent's House, Grantham; under AVM W. B. Callaway who was due to be replaced by AVM A. T. Harris

from 11 September; with Nos.44, 49, 50, 61, 83, 106, 144 and 185 Squadrons, all equipped with Handley Page Hampdens.

- No.6 Training Group with Nos.7, 18, 35, 52, 57, 63, 75, 76, 90, 97, 98, 104, 108, 148, 166, and 207 Squadrons; and the New Zealand Flight with a mixture of aircraft including Ansons, Battles, Blenheims and Wellingtons.

The Whitleys of 4 Group could carry the heaviest bomb loads and had the greatest range, but they were slower than the others and therefore more vulnerable to fighter attack. For this reason, the Whitley squadrons were trained exclusively for night operations. It was intended that the main bombing operations for Battles, Blenheims, Hampdens and Wellingtons would be carried out in daylight using tight, self-defending formations. The Battles and Blenheims were restricted by their limited range but the other three types could reach most of Germany, except for the extreme east.

The RAF's move to France was planned to occur in three stages. Phase One would take place three days after the orders were issued for mobilisation. The First Echelon was the AASF consisting of ten squadrons of Fairey Battles paired into five wings, which would fly across to France to bases in the Rheims area. With this move, No.1 Group would all but cease to exist in England. Although it would form the bulk of the AASF, it was proposed it would remain part of Bomber Command and under its control from Command HQ in England – a clumsy arrangement.

Ten to eighteen days after mobilisation, Phase Two would follow. The Second Echelon of the AASF was to be Blenheim bomber squadrons from 2 Group and its first units would fly across the English Channel to bases and satellite airfields prepared for them. During this period too, the Air Component forces of two squadrons of reconnaissance aircraft would move out to their bases.

Phase Three would take place between nineteen to twenty-six days after mobilisation. This would be the second flight of the Second Echelon crossing the Channel. Altogether, the plan envisaged that within twenty-six days of mobilisation, twenty bomber squadrons of the AASF and the Air Component's two reconnaissance bomber squadrons, six army co-operation squadrons and four fighter squadrons would be transferred to France – a significant achievement if it could be done.

On 4 April 1939, a meeting took place between Britain's Secretary of State for Air and the French Air Minister, primarily to discuss the state of French aircraft production. France's representatives explained that the *Aimée de l'Air* had no modern aircraft at all. At that time it consisted of 1,200 out-of-date aircraft, with a further 5,000 machines that were obsolete but could be used for other military purposes. The best French fighters were only capable of about 240 mph (385 km/hr) and their bombers were so slow they could only be used at night or with cloud cover. To help, it was agreed that the UK should consider supplying Merlin X engines with propellers to France, and examine the possibility of standardising specifications for their air forces.

The next step was to set up advance airfields in the Rheims area, and in May a stockpile of British bombs and munitions was sent to those airfields allocated for AASF use. The transaction was to be in the guise of a sale to the French Air Force.

In the meantime, training intensified for the Fairey Battle squadrons of No.1 Group, which were scheduled to be the first RAF aircraft to transfer to France. From Harwell during May, 226 Squadron moved temporarily to Warmwell in Dorset for a bombing practice camp. Bob Bungey logged no less than twenty-four flights for the month, most of them bombing practice from high-or low-level, or dive-bombing, but some of it was preparation for the Empire Air Day display. There was also air-to-ground firing practice for the rear gunners and mock attacks on the aerodrome from different directions. All this happened to coincide with Bob's yearly flying assessment and his bombing results were graded as 'Above Average'.

He had a break from bombing practice on the 11th. Bob flew F/O Cameron from Warmwell to Old Sarum in Wiltshire where they collected forty parachutes. Douglas Cameron was another Australian in the squadron, an 'old boy' from Croydon in Victoria. He had trained at Point Cook in 1930, embarked for the UK in January the following year, and stayed. Later that day, Bob dropped two passengers back at Harwell and returned again to Warmwell.

Bob only had three flights in June, probably due to leave being granted after his intense but successful bombing camp. The flights were significant. On the 6th, the 4-hour flight was written in his Log Book as a tactical exercise from Harwell to Andover, Andover to Dover, Dover to Andover and back again to Harwell. On the 13th, it was a high-altitude flight up to 22,700 feet (6,900 m) using oxygen while carrying a full bomb load. Two weeks later on the 26th, he carried out a high-altitude cross-country return flight to Liverpool at 15,000 feet (4,600 m), again using oxygen. Perhaps the second break in his flying time was due to additional leave to celebrate his promotion to the rank of flying officer.

It was summer now and while on leave, there was time for some vigorous exercise, swimming training again, but where was a good place to go? Despite the season, the sea around England always seemed much colder than off Brighton, Somerton Park or historic Glenelg back home. There was more convenient swimming closer to hand along the River Thames at Wallingford, which was not far from Harwell and in the same county. The open-air swimming pool there was a good option.

Wallingford was (and still is) an old country market town in the upper Thames Valley, located on the western side of the river at the foot of the forest covered Chiltern Hills and picturesque Berkshire Downs. Across the river was the village of Crowmarsh Gifford, which was linked with Wallingford by a 900-foot-long medieval stone bridge built over the river and the adjacent floodplain. The southern end of the town bordered Winterbrook in the parish of Cholsey.

If he thought Glenelg was 'historic', to the young South Australian so far from home Wallingford was something else again! It had many links with ancient and medieval history – and pre-history. Flint tools from the Stone Age were found nearby but Wallingford itself was originally established by the Saxons, who built a defensive wall around the town for protection against the Danes. It was reputedly the best-preserved example of a Saxon town in England. The long bridge spanning the Thames was where William the Conqueror crossed in 1066, and in 1155 King Henry II held a 'Great Council' in Wallingford and gave the town a royal charter. As well as its magnificent medieval bridge, Wallingford had the remains of a great castle, a Town Hall dating back to 1670 and many fine Georgian buildings. It was one of the oldest towns in England and situated in an Area of Outstanding Natural Beauty.

The Wallingford and Watlington Railway (W&WR) had opened between Cholsey and Wallingford in 1866. It took a large share of the freight previously being carried on the Thames but the income from the traffic was not enough to allow the W&WR to build the extension it had planned to Watlington. The company sold the line to the Great Western Railway (GWR) in 1872, and it became known as the 'Wallingford Bunk'.

The open-air swimming pool in Wallingford Park alongside the River Thames was where Bob first met an extremely attractive local girl by the name of Sybil Ellen Johnson. She was nineteen and the eldest daughter of Wallingford's GWR stationmaster, Mr Arthur Sydney Johnson, and his wife Lucy (née Lott).

The members of the family were proud of their lineage. Sybil's grandfather had for many years been the stationmaster at Windsor and apparently Queen Victoria had remarked that she would not travel from the station unless 'nice Mr Johnson was there'. Her great-grandfather, Charles James Johnson, had been an NCO (troop sergeant major) in the 13th Light Dragoons, 1831–1859. He was one of four brothers in the cavalry, as was their father. Another relative, Thomas George Johnson had served with distinction during the Crimean War and had been present at Balaclava, where his horse had been severely wounded.

With her 'dark eyes and lustrous upswept hair', Sybil was described by an admirer as 'the most beautiful person I have ever known' and Bob was certainly more than just very impressed. They would see each other again – and again. This was the start of a budding romance.

Back from leave, in July the tempo of the squadron's flying picked up again and Bob's Log Book shows it included a tactical exercise on the 9th, flying 720 miles (1,160 km) above cloud for a practice raid on Bristol; on the 13th another tactical exercise, flying 700 miles (1,125 km) above the clouds for raids on Northampton and Skegness; and on the 31st there was a display and flypast at Tangmere in Sussex.

Meanwhile, Bob's flight commander, Alan Pitfield, received a posting to No.12 Squadron, which was stationed at Bicester in Oxfordshire. This too was a Fairey Battle squadron.

At another meeting between British and French representatives on 25 July, arrangements were made for 216 Rolls-Royce Merlin III engines to be supplied to France by February 1940 and 175 Merlin X engines by June 1940. The Merlin Xs were to be delivered as parts, so French technicians would gain valuable experience assembling them. As well as this, 303 de Havilland-Hamilton propellers would be delivered at the rate of thirty per month. The meeting was conducted amid the realisation that time was starting to run out.

August was busier for the Battle squadrons and the work was even more war related. On the 6th, during another tactical exercise, Bob flew as the sub-flight leader for the first time.

The 17th in particular was full of activity. For the first flight Bob had a ZZ training exercise scheduled at Abingdon. ZZ was a method of making a blind landing approach. The pilot was required to land solely by obeying verbal orders over the R/T from ground control. It was meant to build the pilot's confidence in his instruments and instructions from the ground until he trusted them completely. Then that evening, after a night test flight lasting twenty minutes, Bob flew a nocturnal cross-country exercise to Mildenhall in Suffolk and back.

Bob's two short flights on the 27th had an ominous purpose. On the first, he carried two unnamed civilian passengers – camouflage experts. Harwell aerodrome was being camouflaged in case of bombing attacks and the work needed to be inspected from the air. The second flight was with the civilian who was in charge, again to check what could be seen from above. Two days later, with the same man aboard, he had permission to carry out mock low-level attacks on the aerodrome which he obviously enjoyed immensely as he described them in his Log Book as a 'glorious beat up'. On the 30th, it was back to Warmwell again to for air-to-air firing practice for the rear gunner.

In August too some RAF bomber squadrons were allowed to fly over France for familiarisation and experience, and as part of joint midsummer manoeuvres. These were probably intended to boost confidence in the co-operation between the two allied powers and perhaps to create awe in any German observers. During the manoeuvres, the French Air Force mounted a raid with escorted bombers. British fighter pilots that were 'scrambled' to intercept were confronted by what seemed like hundreds of aeroplanes, but they were far from being impressed. The French aircraft were mostly old biplanes and they were woefully slow.

One of the pilots in Leslie Clisby's Hurricane squadron remarked, 'How gay they looked in their red, white and light blue markings! But how pathetically out of date...' Leslie himself wrote in a letter home to his family: 'We are all ready if anything comes of an unexpected crisis – we are on from 5 in the morning until 9 at night, dressed in protective clothing, gas masks, eye shields etc. Running in and out of dugouts and chasing French and English bombers. It is as realistic as possible – and will give us a good idea of what it could be like!'

Gordon Olive, who had been in the senior course when Bob started at Point Cook, was now flying a Spitfire in 65 Squadron and he wrote, 'The exercise may have heartened the French, but it did not provide us with much hope. If that was all the French could do, God help us!'

Expectations of war were rising daily and they were being taken more and more seriously. During the evening of 23 August, all RAF units received orders to mobilise inconspicuously to war establishment.

Next day, green envelopes bearing the word 'MOBILISATION' in large letters (so much for being inconspicuous!) began to arrive at the homes of members of the Royal Auxiliary Air Force (RAuxAF), the main body of the

Reserve, and 3,000 of the Volunteer Reserve (VR). At the Royal Air Force Club in Piccadilly, a flood of telegrams threatened to engulf the entrance. Secret mobilisation of the AASF and Air Component was ordered. Leave was cancelled, kits were packed and equipment was made ready for transfer.

It was accepted by now that the AASF would proceed to airfields in France whether Britain decided to declare war or not.

In Germany on the last day of August, Adolf Hitler issued the order to march against Poland the next morning. His forces were already poised and in position. The sky was still dark on that morning of 1 September 1939 as German aircrews climbed into the cockpits of their waiting fighters and bombers. Blue flames spurted from the exhausts of the engines as the planes warmed up. At the first signs of dawn they took off, spearheaded by deadly *Stuka* dive-bombers.

Simultaneously, without a formal declaration of war, 1,250,000 German troops organised in sixty divisions, nine of them armoured, invaded Poland from the north, west, and south. It had started.

That very same day, the AASF Headquarters in Rheims opened for business.

3

The Phoney War

When the embittered, disillusioned tones of Britain's prime minister announced on Sunday morning, 3 September 1939, that Britain was at war with Germany, the RAF thought it was ready... but was it?

By the previous evening, Saturday the 2nd, Operation *Fall Weiss*, the German offensive in Poland had brought the invaders speedy, crushing advantages in the fighting in just two days, thanks to superior German equipment and tactics. The Germans were gaining rapid, but expensive, victories in fierce frontier battles. In the air, the story was the same as the *Luftwaffe* applied its new principles of *blitzkrieg* and created chaos in the Polish rear. Polish courage and defences were being overwhelmed as Britain and France tried to decide what to do.

An emergency meeting of the British government debated well into that Saturday evening to formulate its response. The final result was an official note that the British ambassador in Berlin handed to the German government. It stated that unless Britain heard by eleven o'clock the following morning that Germany was prepared to immediately withdraw its troops from Poland, a state of war would exist between Britain and Germany.

Sunday dawned clear and balmy and RAF squadrons everywhere in England were called to 'Standby'.

In London, high-ranking officers and civil servants gathered in a room in Richmond Terrace, Whitehall. On a table ready to be consulted was a copy of the Government War Book. In it had been set out the actions to be taken on the outbreak of hostilities by the Royal Navy, the Army and the Royal Air Force and by all Departments of State. The men did not refer to the book for they all knew the directions it contained. Many of them had helped to revise it since the blustering day six months ago, 15 March 1939, when German armoured divisions had entered Prague. All precautionary measures had been taken. Reservists of the three services had joined their posts or were hastening to join them. The flying squadrons of the RAuxAF had been put on a war footing; members of the Observer Corps were manning their posts; and the ARP Services were ready. Those assembled in that room did not talk much. They were waiting for the message from Berlin. Few, if any, doubted what it would say.

The deadline came and went.

A message arrived at Whitehall. It was from the ambassador in Berlin. Hitler had not replied to the government's ultimatum. As the men present discussed this, the Cabinet Secretary entered and declared, 'Gentlemen, we are at war with Germany. The Prime Minister directs that the "War Telegram" be despatched immediately.'

It was a few minutes after eleven. In the streets outside men and women watched as barrage balloons began climbing into the sky around the city.

From the Cabinet Room at No.10 Downing Street at 11.15 a.m., Prime Minister Neville Chamberlain made his announcement. People gathered around their radios listened intently as the last few bars of orchestral music were followed by the BBC announcer introducing the prime minister. In simple language and a flat voice he said: 'I have to tell you now that no such undertaking has been received, and that consequently this country is at war with Germany.'

Operations orders for Britain's forces had been worked out well beforehand. While Chamberlain was still at the microphone, the War Telegram went out to all units appointed to receive it – but RAF units were already on the Continent even before his declaration of war. The Government War Book had seen to that. Existing plans to send the BEF to France had already been put into effect the previous day.

The procedure for the sending the AASF to France had moved smoothly. As soon as the possibility of war with Germany became acute, ground parties from those squadrons marked for overseas service had transferred across and started preparing for the arrival of their planes. At the same time back in England, stores were massed and equipment gathered together. Some was put on one side to be taken over by air, while bulkier items were sent to the docks for immediate shipment.

The AASF's Battle squadrons had begun leaving for France on the morning of Saturday, the 2nd. First to depart was 15 Squadron based at Abingdon. At 10 a.m., its sixteen Battles took off for Bétheniville, situated 15 miles (24 km) east of Rheims. Next to go were sixteen Battles of 40 Squadron at noon, also from Abingdon, although some of this squadron's ground crews had left earlier by civil aircraft at 9.40 a.m. All but one Battle landed at Bétheniville. The missing aircraft had developed engine trouble over the English Channel and ditched 15 miles (24 km) north of Dieppe. It sank in two minutes. The pilot suffered slight concussion but both of the others in the crew were uninjured and they were all rescued by a cross-Channel steamer.

After lunch, fifteen Battles from 226 Squadron, led by its CO, W/Cdr Sydney 'Poppy' Pope DFC AFC, left Harwell and flew to Rheims. Pope had been a First World War fighter pilot so France was familiar to him. Bob Bungey's Log Book shows that the flight took 2 hours 20 minutes. His aircraft was Fairey Battle K7709 and the members of his crew were Sgt D. E. Bingham and LAC L. Smith. They would be his two 'regulars'.

Also leaving early in the afternoon were Nos.12 and 105 Squadrons from Bicester and Harwell. No.12 Squadron's sixteen Battles and one Miles Magister landed at Berry-au-Bac, near Rheims, at 4.45 p.m. No.105 Squadron's sixteen Battles headed for Rheims too but one aircraft had to force-land in a field near Poix when a broken engine con rod broke through the sump, stopping his engine. The crew were unhurt but the Battle had to be written off.

Nos.103, 218, 150 and 142 Squadrons flew out as the afternoon progressed. No.103 landed at its base at Challerange in the Ardennes at 5.30 p.m. Meanwhile, its ground party was on its way by train to Southampton to board ship. No.150 Squadron from Benson followed 103 into Challerange 45 minutes later. No.218 left Boscombe Down at 3.00 p.m. and landed at Auberieve, and 142 Squadron from Bicester landed their sixteen Battles at Berry-au-Bac without incident. All these squadrons had sent out advance ground parties by civil or RAF transport aircraft, but their main parties travelled across by various sea passages.

One unit that did not fly out that Saturday was 88 Squadron, which did not move to France until 12 September, when its sixteen Battles flew to Mourmelon-le-Grand, south-east of Rheims.

At the same time as the Fairey Battles were moving off, Italy declared its neutrality for the second time in two days and called for a peace conference. When they reached their destinations, the Battle squadrons were quickly refuelled and loaded with bombs. Pre-arranged, the Government War Book had seen to that too; bombs for the AASF had already been stockpiled in the Rheims area under the guise of a sale to the French Air Force.

The countryside in this, the Champagne district of France, was deemed ideal for air bases. There were some hills round Épernay and Rheims, and further east towards Verdun, but on the whole the land was level and made up of large unfenced fields, mostly beet fields. There were also many large pastures and these, as a Franco-British Survey Committee had decided some time before the war, would make ideal airfields.

Of all the Fairey Battle squadrons, Bob Bungey's 226 Squadron had what was said to be the 'cushiest billet'. (105 Squadron moved out from Rheims to Villeneuve-les-Vertus on the 12th.) It was established near the town itself on the large Rheims/Champagne aerodrome, which had been both a huge peacetime station for the French Air Force, and a civil airline terminus. The French still had several bomber squadrons at Rheims, mainly old night-flying Farmans, with a scattering of Potez 63s and Bloch 131s. These were concentrated over on one side of the enormous airfield, and the Battles were given the other side, with plenty of hangar accommodation for repair shops for the salvage section, and for the establishment of a wing headquarters, under Group Captain Field. This HQ was later moved to near Châlons.

Other squadrons were not so lucky. They found themselves put down miles from the attractions of the city of Rheims on satellite fields which were still just that – fields. They had to arrange for their own billets at the closest villages; organise the setting up of stores, fuel and ammunition dumps, vehicle parks, defences, camouflage, and all the other ground systems that air force units need.

The Anglo-French plan had been to have one squadron on each airfield, but the satellite landing grounds for the AASF Phase Two 2nd Echelon – the Blenheim bomber squadrons from 2 Group – were not ready. The plan to move in the 2nd Echelon was postponed and finally abandoned completely on 21 September when it was suggested that the Blenheim units might be better left in England for use against any German attack that might come through Belgium. This meant that the five main airfields which had been reserved for the 2nd Echelon were available for the Battle squadrons to spread out into, in accordance with the one squadron per airfield distribution idea. Accordingly, five of the Battle squadrons relocated but Bob's 226 Squadron remained at the Rheims/Champagne aerodrome.

During this period too, the Air Component forces of two squadrons of reconnaissance aircraft began to move out to their bases in France, as also did its selected Hurricane squadrons.

Meanwhile, French and British ground forces were marshalled along Germany's western border behind the great concrete, steel-turreted fortresses of the Maginot Line. This system stretched from the Swiss border northward to Montmédy. From there to the North Sea, a system of independent but outmoded fortresses extended along the Belgian border. They were the independent relics of pre-First World War defences. Across the German border was the similar, parallel, Siegfried Line, the west wall of the German defences. It was threatening but dormant – for the moment. Unknown to the Allies, Germany's mobile support troop strength had been reduced to a minimum owing to deployments to the Polish front.

Belgium and Holland meanwhile preserved strict neutrality in an effort to appease Germany. The horrors of the Great War – supposedly the war to end all wars – were still fresh in the minds of their people. Unfortunately, they clung to the hope they would be left alone and not engulfed by another castaclysm. Their policies prevented any united military co-operation with French and British planners as the almost 400,000-strong BEF was being transported across the English Channel and moved up to concentrate in the general area of Arras-Lille in the Allied line.

The first fifteen RAF Hurricanes arrived from England on 8 September and landed at Octeville, a new airfield near Le Havre. They belonged to No.1 Squadron. Leading the squadron was the CO, S/Ldr Patrick 'Bull' Halahan, a stocky Irishman. The Hurricanes had taken off from Tangmere and after a brief 'beat-up' of the airfield joined up into flights in sections astern, then went into aircraft-line-astern. Then it was down to Beachy Head for a last look at the cliffs of England before crossing the English Channel to France. Halahan's section included Bob's South Australian mate, Leslie Clisby, and Mark 'Hilly' Brown from Manitoba, Canada.

It was a bright and cloudless day and below there was an almost complete absence of shipping. The water was breathlessly calm and the sun made the heat most uncomfortable in the cockpits of the fighters. After 30 minutes Dieppe appeared through the heat haze and they followed the coast down to Le Havre. Prior to landing, the squadron closed up, broke into flights, then sections and gave an appropriate salute with an exhibition of formation flying over the town.

That evening was spent exploring the nightlife of Le Havre – the *Guillaume Tell*, the *Normandie*, the *Grosse Tonne* and *La Lune* (*La Lune* was a brothel, but its main attraction for the RAF boys was its drinking amenities). The town was full of Americans trying to escape the war zone.

They were full of admiration for the RAF's flying skill, and 'full of grog' too. After a memorable time (for those who could remember next morning) it was back to where they were billeted – in a commandeered convent!

By now, most of the Fairey Battle units were settled in at their new bases, and next day they carried out their first operational flights. No.105 Squadron put up three Battles on a reconnaissance mission to within 15 miles (24 km) of the France – Germany border. Likewise, 226 Squadron sent two separate formations of three to reconnoitre the frontier area around Thionville. The first trio was off at 1420 hours and back again by 1550. Ten minutes later the second section took off at 1600, and in it was Bob Bungey and his crew flying Battle K7709, their usual aircraft. Their recce was carried out at 3,000 feet (900 m). A single anti-aircraft shot was fired from the French battery at Thionville, possibly to warn them of German aircraft in the vicinity, but none were seen. The three Battles landed at 1730 hours without further incident.

Each day the Battle squadrons patrolled a little closer to the German frontier. Bob's next recce was on the 15th in the same section of three aircraft. Low cloud below 1,200 feet (365 m) meant that the mission could not be completed properly.

The Battles were patrolling to within 10 miles (16 km) of the border by the 17th and a section of three aircraft from 12 Squadron, one of them flown by Alan Pitfield, who had previously been Bob's flight commander in 226, finished the day by flying a reconnaissance only 5 miles (8 km) behind the frontier.

Although the bulk of the *Luftwaffe* had been deployed to the Polish front, about 1,300 aircraft, a formidable force including 600 single-engined fighters, were still stationed to protect Germany's western borders. On 20 September, the first *Luftwaffe* vs RAF engagement took place over the Western Front when three Messerschmitt Me109Ds of *JG 152* shot down two Fairey Battles out of a formation of three from 88 Squadron. At first, the three Battles came under French AA fire south-east of Bitche until the British aircraft fired off the colours of the day. Then the Messerschmitts pounced on them over Aachen. The Battles closed up for defence but one went down in flames almost immediately with no survivors.

The second stricken Battle crash-landed; its pilot suffered such severe burns that he had to be evacuated to a hospital in England. His rear gunner had been killed outright, struck in the head by a German bullet, and his third crew member was severely wounded. This man's leg was amputated in an effort to save his life, but he later died.

The remaining Battle lost height in a series of diving turns and escaped. The gunner claimed to have destroyed one of the Messerschmitts making it the first German aircraft shot down by an Allied airman in the Second World War.

As a direct result of this tragic action, it was decided to operate in greater numbers for better mutual defence. Two days later, on the 22nd, 226 Squadron went out in force with six Battles to fly a photographic reconnaissance of enemy territory between Briedenbach and Höheinöd from 20,000 feet (6,000 m). Bob Bungey, Sgt Bingham and the newly promoted Corporal Smith were, as usual, flying Battle K7709.

The promotion to corporal made Smith one of the 'chosen few'. In the AASF Battle squadrons, the air gunners, who also operated the wireless, were virtually all of aircraftmen rank – either AC1, AC2 or leading aircraftmen (LAC) and very occasionally, corporals. Prior to December 1939, they wore the 'winged bullet' emblem on the upper right arm of their tunic. This was replaced at the end of 1939 by the introduction of the 'AG' cloth brevet sewn above the left breast pocket. Although the rank of sergeant for air gunners was also approved, subject to qualification, there were virtually no sergeant air gunners in the AASF or even No.2 Group back in England.

Eight-tenths cloud cover from 4,000 to 8,000 feet (1,200–2,400 m) prevented Bob's squadron photographing the required area, so line overlap photos were taken from Selchenbach to Saahlautern instead. No activity was seen on the ground inside German territory but visibility was poor due to haze. F/O Thomas, flying in Battle K9182 as No.2 to S/Ldr Lockett who was leading the flight, broke away from the formation at Hombourg because of engine trouble and had to force land at Saint-Dizier. He did so successfully and returned to base at Rheims later.

In another clash on the 27th, a Battle from 103 Squadron force-landed with a wounded gunner on board but one Me109 was claimed shot down.

On the last day of the month, four out of five Battles from 150 Squadron were shot down when they were bounced (taken by surprise) by eight Me109s of 2/JG 53. After a long chase, the fifth Battle, which was badly damaged, managed to reach its base at Écury and land, but as it rolled to a stop the aircraft swung violently due to a burst tyre and fire broke out. The crew abandoned the doomed machine with 'extreme haste' and just managed to escape to safety by the narrowest of margins. Two Messerschmitts were claimed destroyed.

These first clashes provided sobering demonstrations of the Fairey Battle's lack of ability to survive in hostile air – and the AASF was made up of ten squadrons of them!

Earlier, on the 25th, Leslie Clisby's squadron had been ordered to move to Norrent-Fontes, near St Omer in the Pas-de-Calais. Bull Halahan led the Hurricanes to their new airfield on the 29th, and the pilots received a rude awakening. Their accommodation was under canvas, and rain that lasted for the next fortnight made their surroundings most unpleasant, to say the very least.

The squadron had hardly finished digging in at Norrent-Fontes when another change of plan came through, to move to a new airfield at Vassincourt. This news caused little disappointment. The move had been prompted by the Fairey Battle losses. It was becoming evident that if bombing operations had to be carried out in daylight using tight, self-defending formations as Bomber Command stipulated, losses could become extremely heavy, hence two fighter squadrons, Nos.1 and 73, were allocated to the AASF.

No.1 Squadron's Hurricanes stayed at Norrent-Fontes for another week. On 4 October Bull Halahan flew east with Leslie Clisby and Hilly Brown, to inspect the new airfield. On the way back from Vassincourt they called in to interview the mauled Battle crews at Écury.

From Écury it was just a short hop for Leslie Clisby to reach Rheims where Bob Bungey was stationed – and on top of that it was Bob's twenty-fifth birthday! This may well have been an additional motivation for making the trip that day. The two South Australians were firm friends, a bond that had only strengthened since they had arrived in England together two years ago. They held quite a reunion. Journalists, who were all thirsting for good news stories for their readers, made much of their celebration, and reported that Leslie Clisby had flown 300 miles (770 km) across France just for the occasion.

Among the journalists at Rheims were Charles Gardiner from the BBC and Noel Monks, an Australian who was the London *Daily Mail's* war correspondent with the RAF in France. In Bull Halahan's eyes, most reporters were 'very tiresome and incredibly ignorant of their subject matter'. He was very against individual publicity for his pilots in case it put the squadron's teamwork at risk. His pilots fully supported his stance and they were all relieved when reporters were banned from entering their officers' mess.

However, it did have to be admitted that some correspondents were doing a 'first class' job within the security limits imposed upon them. Noel Monks was a standout who became friends with many pilots in both Nos.1 and 73 Squadrons. Because he had once been on an Olympic team, Monks worried about such things as 'being in condition', so he did not drink or smoke, and when he finished a hard day's work he liked to go to bed early. Despite this, his hotel room at the *Lion d'Or* (the largest hotel in town) in Rheims became a regular meeting place for anyone who had some leave. It was one of the few places too where they could enjoy the luxury of a hot bath.

On one occasion Monks discovered that the RAF's beer was being overpriced to avoid upsetting local traders. He wrote an article about this, which was published in the *Daily Mail* and caused such an outcry back in England that the situation was remedied overnight. Of him it was said: 'Although severely restricted by the censor, his enthusiastic reporting did a great deal for the image of the RAF in France. In those dark uncertain days his stories provided a lot of cheer across the breakfast tables of England.'

Both Noel Monks and Charles Gardiner would have books published about the air fighting in France shortly after the campaign was over. The first Australian edition of Noel Monks' *Fighter Squadrons* came out in December 1940 and although it concentrated mainly on the exploits of Nos.1 and 73 Squadrons, it also contained some useful information on bomber operations too. Charles Gardiner's book, *A.A.S.F.*, came out late in 1940 as well. Both were subjected to the censorship restrictions of the day.

Meanwhile, cruel Fate would not allow Bob Bungey and Leslie Clisby to celebrate another birthday together.

* * *

Bomber Command's commander-in-chief, Air Chief Marshal Sir Edgar Ludlow-Hewitt, could not help but be worried. Bomber Command was the primary instrument of Britain's air power but on the outbreak of war his was a force almost without reserves and without an adequate training organisation to back it up. He had a total of fifty-three squadrons at his disposal, but in accordance with the agreed pre-war plans the entire strength of his No.1 Group, ten squadrons of Fairey Battles, had transferred to France where they would be attached to AASF Headquarters. Of the remaining forty-three squadrons, fourteen soon had to be assigned to a training role under the authority of No.6 Group, while six others were set aside to become Group Pool Training Squadrons. His operational capability was therefore reduced to six squadrons each of Wellingtons, Hampdens and Blenheims, plus five squadrons of Whitleys – a total of only twenty-three operational squadrons! This small force of light-and medium-range bombers, some of which were already approaching obsolescence, did not compare favourably with the estimated 1,500 modern bombers that equipped the *Luftwaffe*.

There were other restrictions. On the eve of war, US President Franklin D. Roosevelt had cabled the leaders of the major powers – Neville Chamberlain of Britain, Edouard Daladier of France, and Germany's Adolf Hitler – seeking an assurance from each that restraint would be exercised in the use of their bombers on targets where civilians would be placed at risk. Britain and France immediately signalled their agreement to the American president's proposals but because of the fighting going on Poland, Germany delayed. With this in mind, how would the powerful Third Reich react if France and Britain took the initiative on Germany's western frontier? Would the *Luftwaffe* retaliate by bombing French and British cities – and perhaps those of Belgium and Holland too? Little wonder that the Allies hesitated and puzzled over what to do next.

Having pledged to restrict its bombing operations, the RAF rearranged its priorities. To the Wellington squadrons of 3 Group and the Hampden squadrons of 5 Group fell the task of attacking the German Navy at sea. Leaflet raids were the province of 4 Group because its Whitley crews had been trained from the beginning for night flying – they would drop paper on Germany, not bombs; and reconnaissance duties fell to the Blenheims of 2 Group.

The roles of the two major elements of the RAF ordered to France were redefined too. The AASF's ten Fairey Battle light bomber squadrons had been meant for short-range offensive operations, but all they could really do was fly back and forth along the border, look threatening and try to take some photographs. The main tasks of its two Hurricane squadrons (Nos.1 and 73) were to protect the bombers and their bases, and general air defence of the British-occupied sector of north-eastern France. The Air Component's job with its Blenheim bombers and Lysander army co-operation aircraft was to support and protect the British Army. Among its units were another two Hurricane squadrons (Nos.85 and 87).

In mid-September Adolf Hitler considered the Polish question all but settled and he finally signalled that he would follow President Roosevelt's humanitarian request and avoid bombing civilians. What was actually happening in Poland was conveniently overlooked. On 13 September, a force of 183 *Luftwaffe* bombers began air raids on Warsaw – the first of many. In conformity with the Nazi-Soviet Pact signed in August 1939, Soviet troops swept over Poland's eastern border on 17 September. By 25 September, Warsaw was surrounded. To avoid being bogged down in costly street fighting, the Germans initiated Operation *Seaside*. Backed by thirty Ju52/3m transports dropping incendiaries, 240 *Stuka* dive-bombers were employed in around-the-clock bombing of the capital. The attacks lasted the whole day, by which time Warsaw was a mass of flames and explosions. Facing starvation and typhoid, the city offered to surrender next day. The Allies were helpless to intervene. The *Führer's* word was as unreliable as usual.

In reality, after the successful *blitzkrieg* which defeated Poland, Hitler wanted to immediately start a campaign in the west, but German Army groups and the larger part of the German Air Force needed to re-equip and rebuild before the next confrontation. The *Führer* summoned his generals to a conference, where he warned that Germany must strike first and hardest because time was on the enemy's side. The positional warfare of 1914–1918 had to be avoided at all costs; instead, the armoured divisions must force the crucial breakthrough, 'to maintain the flow of the army's advance, to prevent fronts from becoming stable by massed drives through identified weakly held positions'. Luxembourg, Belgium and Holland constituted '...the only possible area of attack'. He added: 'The start cannot take place too early. It is to take place if at all possible this autumn.'

German staff officers immediately set to work drawing up detailed plans for the offensive but some high-ranking officers genuinely thought that if Germany continued the war, the Fatherland would be defeated. The commander-in-chief of the German Army, General Walter von Brauchitsch, and chief of staff, General Franz Halder, presented a report to Hitler outlining the army's deficiencies.

On the Allied side, the British chiefs of staff were under no illusions. With occupied Poland now a buffer zone and the Russo-German agreement in place, Germany's flank and rear were protected so the west was obviously next on Hitler's list. The question was when would the German offensive come? How much valuable time did the Allies have left? In the meantime, with the onset of winter's rain and snow, there was a continual struggle against the elements. The airfields of northern France were poorly drained and they were being transformed into quagmires.

As November began, German preparations for invasion continued. On the 2nd, Hitler left for two days' inspection of the Western Front. As he visited the German positions he found his commanders were pessimistic about the prospect of success. He told his generals before returning to Berlin, 'My decision is unchangeable. I shall attack France and England at the favourable and earliest moment.' The date for the offensive was set for 12 November.

On Sunday, 5 November, as German units moved to their jump-off positions opposite Holland, Belgium and Luxembourg according to plan, General von Brauchitsch drove to the Chancellery to urge Hitler to abandon his plans for the offensive. He claimed the weather was unsuitable. Hitler replied that the enemy had to suffer exactly the same conditions. The general protested, claiming that the morale of the German troops was low. At this, Hitler raged until von Brauchitsch's resistance was broken. The *Führer* had already drafted proclamations justifying his invasion to make to the Dutch and Belgian governments – his pretext would be French violations of the Belgian border.

Meanwhile, weather conditions over the Western Front deteriorated dramatically. Low cloud restricted aircraft movement; mud churned up by tanks bogged vehicles and slowed men on the march; ditches were flooded with stormwater; and atmospheric static crackled wireless communications. The weather forecasters predicted worse to come. On the 7th, the assault had to be postponed for three days.

On the following day, Wednesday, 8 November, there was an unsuccessful assassination attempt on the *Führer* at the *Bürgerbräukeller* in Munich. The German invasion was postponed again and reset for 19 November. This postponement was followed thirteen more times at various intervals, mostly for reasons of poor weather.

The weather continued to decline. Belgium's roads became waterlogged and for the most part, impassable for heavy traffic. A major operation so late in the season was becoming less and less likely. If the German Army did not launch the offensive soon, Hitler judged, the opportunity for doing so with any hope of success was slipping away. The next chance would not be until spring.

Time was the key. Time was what the Allies desperately needed – to produce weapons, ships and aircraft; to build defences; train and to boost manpower; to be ready. The bad weather affected operations for both sides during much of December. It was obvious to the Allies by now that the Germans were in no hurry to invade France and would probably wait for the spring next year.

Some American war correspondents who were becoming disenchanted with the lack of real action to report, and frustrated with security restrictions, were calling it a 'Phoney War'.

From the beginning of December until Christmas, many dignitaries visited the British forces in France. On Friday, 8 December, after spending a day or two with the BEF, His Majesty, King George VI, visited Rheims accompanied by the Duke of Gloucester to inspect the AASF. Overhead, there was a continuous air umbrella of Fairey Battles and Hawker Hurricanes. The event was described by Charles Gardiner in *A.A.S.F.*:

> He spent the night in his train in the siding and arrived at Rheims Station about nine o'clock in the morning.
>
> It was a bitterly cold day and was snowing and I felt very sorry for the pilots of the Battles and Hurricanes which provided a constant escort for His Majesty. I wasn't surprised to find out later that one flight leader, Flight Lieutenant Kerridge of 226, had got frozen up and had had some trouble in keeping out of the hillsides.
>
> The correspondents had split up to cover the King's tour and each of us reported just one part of it, agreeing to form a pool of our information afterwards. This was to prevent a large convoy of cars as the authorities were quite rightly taking no risks.

Bob Bungey was one of six pilots from 226 Squadron selected to escort the king during his visit. In his Log Book Bob noted matter-of-factly on the 6th, 'Escort duties (The King) Rehearsal' and then on the 8th, 'Escorting The King'. On the day itself, he carried out the duty for 2 hours 45 minutes in Battle K9182 and with him as usual were Sgt Bingham and Cpl Smith. For Bob and his crew, the assignment of guarding the visiting monarch was a highlight and an honour.

Charles Gardiner continued:

The two places which I had to cover during the King's tour were a stores park and the aerodrome at Villeneuve. At the stores park His Majesty saw the famous dug-out 'Grosvenor House', which had been given a lot of publicity. He also had a good laugh at a very elaborate dog kennel which the men had made for a stray dachshund, which had come into the camp. This kennel was in the shape of a house and was complete with everything a dog could wish for ... even a miniature lamp-post.

At Villeneuve, His Majesty spoke to the crews of some Whitleys which were going pamphlet raiding that night, and there, as at every other station, the officers of the squadron were presented to him. He drove round to see the camouflage, and the rows of Fairey Battles, and then returned to Headquarters. The return drive was through Épernay, where British nurses lined the famous champagne street. Actually HQ had taken extra precautions in Épernay, which was always thought to be a big spy centre. A number of people had been arrested before the King's visit, and, if there were any suspects left, they caused no trouble. The drive passed off without incident. Some months later, during the *blitzkrieg*, it was freely rumoured that another large number of spies had been rounded up and shot at Épernay. Among them was supposed to have been a stationmaster.

Back at the Château Polignac the King was shown albums of pictures of the Siegfried Line which had been taken by our Battles during the first weeks of the war. He was very interested in them and was delighted when Air Vice-Marshal Playfair presented him with one of the albums.

Immediately after lunch His Majesty went off by train to Metz to see the Maginot Line, and all the correspondents rushed off with their stories of the visit to Rheims. We needn't have rushed, however, because for security reasons they were all held up until after the King had got safely back to London.

There were other visiting dignitaries. One was Prime Minister Neville Chamberlain on Sunday, 17 December. His was a much less formal affair. In the course of his French liaison duties, the Duke of Windsor was a reasonably frequent visitor. Other VIPs who were shown around the AASF included Winston Churchill, Sir John Simon, Mr Anthony Eden, who was then Dominions Secretary, and Mr James Fairbairn, Australia's Minister for Air.

Included in Mr Fairbairn's party were his secretary and Gp/Capt Frank McNamara VC of the RAAF. They stayed for lunch with No.1 Squadron at Vassincourt and were particularly interested to meet the squadron's resident South Australian, Leslie Clisby. For his part, Leslie was delighted to meet up again with the legendary VC winner who had been his first CO at Laverton in Victoria in 1935. Their relationship was no longer that of a lowly aircraftsman to his commanding officer and Leslie found that McNamara was a cheerful, unassuming and courteous companion who showed a genuine interested in his progress. Mr Fairbairn declared that when the first RAAF fighter squadron was formed in England, Leslie would be posted to it as a flight commander.

In early December too, the AASF began the first rotation of its squadrons back to England for re-equipment. This was in line with the policy of Scheme 'F' that called for the replacement of light bombers with medium bombers. Nos.15 and 40 Squadrons were sent home to swap their Fairey Battles for Bristol Blenheims, and they were replaced in France by Nos.114 and 139 Squadrons, which already had the twin-engined type.

Elsewhere that month, the Wellingtons of Bomber Command suffered badly at the hands of German fighters during daylight operations hunting for German shipping in the Heligoland Bight. In the first serious clash on the 14th, seven out of twelve Wellingtons survived the onslaught and retreated for home with their bombs still on board. Unfortunately, one of these was seriously damaged and jettisoned its bombs into the sea before recrossing the English Coast. The crippled aircraft crashed shortly afterwards killing three members of the crew, including the pilot, and most of the others were injured.

On 18 December, twenty-four Wellingtons set out to attack German shipping near Wilhelmshaven. Two-thirds of the way to the target, one aircraft aborted, followed by his wingman. The remaining twenty-two bombers continued and fell prey to the defending Me109Ds, Me109Es and Me110s. It was a massacre. In a running battle lasting 30 minutes, beginning north of Wilhelmshaven and continuing all the way along the Frisians to Ameland, the German fighters claimed no less than thirty-eight victories for the loss of two Me109Es and one Me109D with two of the pilots killed. The *Luftwaffe* subsequently disallowed eleven or twelve of these claims, but the claimed destruction of twenty-six or twenty-seven British bombers for such small losses represented a major victory for the German fighter defences. Yet this was still a larger number of aircraft than had been in the entire British formation.

Bomber Command's actual losses had been very heavy, but not as bad as those believed by the *Luftwaffe*. During the running combats eleven Wellingtons had fallen and two aircraft were left to limp home, shot full of holes with petrol streaming from their damaged fuel tanks. Gradually, both sank ever lower and lower until one of them went into the sea off the coast of Norfolk. The second crippled Wellington entered the water about 30 minutes later. This time four of the five-man crew were rescued. The body of the front gunner, who had been killed during the fighter attacks, went down with the aircraft. Five other Wellingtons were so badly damaged that they crashed or crash-landed on the English coast. Of the other five surviving aircraft that landed at their bases, two had suffered damage. Only three escaped more or less intact. Bomber Command's death toll amounted to ninety.

Earlier, at the end of September, an entire flight of Handley Page Hampdens had failed to return from a similar strike in the same general area. Bomber Command's daylight bombing experts preferred to think that during their low level attacks the bombers had been caught by the explosions of their own bombs. Later, when a German radio broadcast claimed that the Hampdens had met 'a hornet's nest' of fighters, an RAF enquiry concluded simply that the raids had been badly planned.

Experienced pilots and valuable crews had been lost in a most dramatic fashion. Air Chief Marshal Sir Edgar Ludlow-Hewitt did have good reason to worry. Such casualties could not be sustained. If they continued, Bomber Command would be brought to its knees very quickly. The same sort of losses might happen in France.

During December 1939 and January of the new year in France, winter strengthened its icy grasp. Autumn rains were followed by extraordinary falls of snow and widespread ice. Water transport was prevented because the rivers were frozen. Roads were impassable because of slush and mud. Soldiers huddled miserably under waterproof capes in their positions as they waited for an enemy that did not come. In the air, operations were almost non-existent.

The winter was so severe that RAF ground crews went about all the time wrapped in woollen scarves, coats and cloaks, and wearing balaclavas. The problem was to start the engines of the aircraft in the bitter cold. At one stage, teams of men went around each machine during the night, starting the engine every 2 hours to warm the oil and to keep some warmth in the metal so they would start in the morning, if they had to. Because of the extreme cold, the oil became so glutinous that it was hard to turn the engine over – even with the mechanical advantage of the long propeller blades, which were used initially to free the engine. The best way was to drain the engine oil into 5-gallon (23-litre) drums and heat them over a petrol-fed fire. By the time they worked their way back to the first aircraft again, the oil had recongealed.

The AASF squadrons operated when they could. The original intention in bringing the AASF to France had been to position the RAF's short-range bomber force within effective striking distance of German industry. This idea had to be set aside because of the vulnerability of the Battles when they were confronted by German fighters.

Several countermeasures were suggested to minimise casualties. The most obvious solution was provision of a fighter escort but there was simply not enough of them to go around. There were only two squadrons of Hurricanes allocated to the AASF at this stage and co-operation with the *Aimée de l'Air's* Moraine 406 and Curtiss P-36 units so far was lacking in co-ordination.

The Battle squadrons were well aware of the need for better defensive armament and in October, an observer in 150 Squadron improvised a third gun for one of their aircraft. His idea generated a great deal of interest. It was a Vickers 'K' gun fitted on a moveable mounting in the bombing aperture, which gave an admirable field of fire, fore and aft, under the fuselage. When it was trained aft, the gun was turned upside down and this necessitated the fitted of an extra set of sights.

Among the VIPs who inspected this field modification when it was brought to Rheims were ACM Sir Edgar Ludlow-Hewitt, C-in-C of Bomber Command, and AVM Philip Playfair. They both liked the mounting and Playfair instructed that the aircraft with the gun mounting be flown to Fairey Aviation's works in England for a demonstration.

Fairey Aviation responded quickly and gun mountings fixed to fire back and down from the observer's bombing hatch began reaching the squadrons before the end of the month. The crews that had to use the system were not all that impressed. The Vickers 'K' was mounted on a swivel with a mirror attached. The navigator had to crawl down on his stomach, open the trap, push the gun through, turn it upside-down and, by using the mirror, aim and fire. While it might prove useful for shooting up ground targets, its practical use as an effective defence weapon was open to question and doubted by the Battle crews.

Another measure suggested to reduce casualties was to operate at night like the Whitey crews of No.4 Group, who were the only ones specifically trained for night work. The Whiteys were over Germany on the very first night of the war – but they were not allowed to drop bombs for fear of hitting civilians. Thanks to President Roosevelt's cable, they could only drop printed pamphlets as part of the government's propaganda campaign. Code-named 'Nickel', the leaflets were loaded in bundles tied with string. The string was cut before they were released from either the flare chute or ventral gun turret of the aircraft. Down they went that night on Bremen, Hamburg and the Ruhr.

AVM Arthur Harris took charge of Bomber Command's No.5 Group (Hampden) shortly after the war started and he would eventually become marshal of the RAF, Sir Arthur Harris, the C-in-C of Bomber Command itself. He had no illusions about the value of the 'Nickel' flights: 'My personal view is that the only thing achieved was largely to supply the Continent's requirements of toilet paper for the five long years of war.'

There was one thing these 'Nickel' flights did do. It gave the RAF bomber crews valuable experience of operational long-distance flying at night. For achieving the best results they needed clear moonlit nights and precise navigation. The main hazard these crews faced early in the war on these long nocturnal excursions was not the enemy's flak or nightfighters but changeable weather. Casualties were light.

Sometimes the Whitleys staged through Rheims or other French airfields to extend their range of operations to the eastern parts of Germany or occupied Poland. Even so, a close watch had to be kept on the fuel gauges. A very rare incident occurred in mid-March.

The crew of a Whitley from No.51 Squadron at Driffield returning from a 'very tricky' flight over Poland found their fuel situation becoming critical. They had been up for 11 hours flying by dead-reckoning and battling with a headwind on the return journey to Villeneuve. Deciding that they were certain to be over French territory, the pilot chose a field he could see though it was still dark, landed and switched off. At the other end of the field they could see a group of peasants running towards them so the pilot and one of the crew went out to meet them about 200 yards from the plane. The pilot asked in French where they were. Imagine the shock when he was told Germany and one peasant obligingly pointed in the direction of the frontier 25 kilometres away! The Britishers immediately turned, bolted for the plane, started engines and took off before the others realised what was happening. A few shots were fired as the Whitley lifted off. There was just enough fuel to cross the frontier and land again, this time thankfully in French territory.

It made a good story for Charles Gardiner, who had also reported:

Incidentally, the Swiss manager at the *Lion d'Or* had become the most unpopular man in Rheims. He was always refusing to serve food to pilots who had just come in after long night-flights, and he made exorbitant charges for baths and other comforts. When argued with he became abusive, and there were several scenes. Once he was chased across his own foyer by two infuriated Whitley pilots who had been trying to get a ham sandwich at the unearthly hour of 11 p.m. On another occasion the hall porter had to defend him from an attack by a Battle pilot to whom he had been unjustifiably rude.

The biggest laugh we got out of the snow season was when some of the boys from 226 wedged this manager in his own revolving door, and pelted him with snowballs. They were all carefully hidden in the black-out, so he never knew who did it. We did, and bought drinks for everyone involved.

Gardiner never did reveal who the miscreants from 226 Squadron actually were but, of course, Bob Bungey would never be involved in such an exploit – or would he?

Up to January 1940, Bob had only logged 18 hours 45 minutes of night flying since joining the RAF, but that was about to change. On 10 January, he did half-an-hour of local night flying, his first night flight since the previous August. It was a sign of things to come.

On the night of 25/26 January, two Battles from 142 Squadron carried out local and cross-country flights on a six-leg course in the area of Laon-River Aisne, north and west of Berry-au-Bac. The night was pitch black with windstorms. The French beacon system proved inadequate because the signals being flashed were not always definite and they were invariably too long. An aircraft flying at low altitude was often past the beacon before it could be identified. For example, it took 20 seconds to flash the letter 'Q' and the problem was compounded by the bad weather. At a conference in Rheims in February attended by representatives from each AASF squadron, this was the main item on the agenda. The discussions brought about changes that allowed the crews to find, without difficulty, the 'lanes' to and from the frontiers and they became accurate and invaluable guides. Other lights indicated landmarks.

The RAF in France was reorganising too. The AASF and Air Component were placed under the overall command of Air Marshal Arthur 'Ugly' Barratt as the Air Officer commanding-in-chief of the British Air Forces in France

(BAFF). So too were the No.1 and No.2 Air Missions, which had arrived later, but most importantly, the BAFF was now an independent force. It disconnected the operational control of the AASF from Bomber Command back in England.

As they were within the RAF as a whole, Australian pilots were scattered throughout the BAFF too. Frequently they would pass through Rheims and Bob Bungey would meet up with them, swap stories and catch up on news about some of their friends. One of these pilots was Tasmanian Wally Blom who had been at Point Cook and come to England on the *Orama* with Bob. He had joined 150 Squadron at Écury-sur-Coole towards the end of September when he brought a replacement aircraft from England. Because of the casualties suffered by the squadron a week later, there was a re-allocation of duties and Wally took over as Squadron Armament Officer. Now, on 15 February, he was off to England to attend a course on the spraying of poison gas. Meanwhile, Wally's mate from Hobart, Stuart Walch, was flying Hurricanes back in England, Allan Farrington and Charles 'Digger' Fry were somewhere in the Middle East, and Jack Kennedy was with another former Point Cook cadet, Gordon Olive, in a Spitfire squadron.

The bad news was that Johnny Sadler had been shot down and killed in a Hampden at the end of September. It had happened while out hunting for German shipping in the Heligoland Bight. Suddenly, the 'Phoney War' seemed very real. It was startling to realise that one of them out of Bob's group of twenty-five from Point Cook, was no more. Who might be next?

Flying was severely restricted again in February with the weather worsening instead of improving. Bob only flew a total of 5 hours mostly in short low-level bombing practice trips or towing a drogue for air-firing practice in the last few days of the month. It was around this time that he was out of action for a while because of German measles and 'another minor ailment'. He did have time to catch up with correspondence to his family back home and he sent a No.226 Squadron silk scarf to his sister Pauline as a souvenir from 'somewhere in France'. The scarf had a dark blue background with four white Turkish crescent moons and light blue ripples. Explaining these, he said that the squadron was originally formed in the First World War to carry out anti-submarine patrols in the Dardanelles, hence the Turkish crescents set in the dark blue of the Eastern sky, with the light blue ripples representing the sea.

Progressing into March, Bob started flying more often as a section leader, and as an acting flight leader, as well as having more night flying tests, blind flying and 'head lamp landing' practice. He flew various aircraft depending upon servicing and availability but most often Battles P2255 and P2265. One of these may have been the machine on which he had kangaroos painted on the side. At this stage, numerous Battles were adorned with emblems such as the *Madam Harpy* or the *Jolly Roger*, but later, closer to the outbreak of the 'shooting war', this practice was officially frowned upon by authorities for 'security reasons'. Bob also made use of a toy koala, which he would hang from the back of the cockpit and transfer from one machine to another.

In April, with the weather improving, snow and ice slowly disappeared leaving the countryside lush and green but it also meant a heightened threat of invasion. It happened on 9 April, but in Scandinavia, not France – not yet.

That day at dawn, German forces attacked Denmark and Norway. The move into Denmark was by land and almost uncontested. Within hours, the country was occupied. The attack on Norway was carried out by sea and air landings, which were opposed by the Norwegians. Britain and France immediately declared their support for the two countries.

The Royal Navy, Bomber Command and Coastal Command were ordered to slow down the German advance in southern Norway while an Anglo-French expeditionary force could be assembled for landing at Narvik in the north. The bomber squadrons were ill-fitted for their new task. With round trips of up to 1,000 miles (1,600 km) entirely over the sea, the distances to be covered put them at a severe disadvantage and they would be without fighter escort. Only targets in Southern Norway, where the Germans would soon have full control, could be reached, and of course *Luftwaffe* fighters would be waiting. Meanwhile, the restrictions against bombing land targets in Germany remained in place. Ports in Northern Germany, well within the range of Bomber Command, would be left untouched throughout the entire Norwegian campaign.

As news of the fighting in Scandinavia reached France, most Battle squadrons were practicing cross country night flights so their pilots and crews would become familiar with their surroundings after dark and could improve their navigation skills. There was a spate of accidents as the Battle crews retrained to operate at night. According to his Log Book, Bob cancelled his cross country night flight on 7 April and landed back at Rheims 45 minutes after taking off to report that he had seen a crash. This may have been a Battle from 142 Squadron, which crashed and burst into flames 5 miles (8 km) south of Neufahatel. This accident has been reported elsewhere as happening on the 8th; however, it is not clear if this meant early in the morning or late at night. Several Battle squadrons lost their records for the month of April during the retreat in May so full details of their operations during this period are incomplete and many dates remain open to question. Very likely it occurred in the dark hours of 7/8 April, in which case Bob's Log Book and the other documentation would both be correct.

War correspondent Charles Gardiner became aware of the AASF's night flying activity at an early stage. He wrote:

No.226 Squadron had been busy night flying, taking advantage of a full moon. This piqued my curiosity, and I tried to find out why. It took some time, but, after pledges of great secrecy, I gathered they were training with a view to dropping mines in the Rhine at the next moon.

I don't know whether that was the true 'gen', or whether they were shooting a line, but the plan seemed feasible to me, so I half-believed it. On the other hand, it seemed more likely that they were getting in night-flying hours in order to drop leaflets and take some of the work off Home Command. If it was for mine-sowing, I hoped their navigation would be all right – because, if they missed the Rhine and dropped a mine on the bank, it might have started the air war off – bombing and all that!

The sowing, they said, would be done in shallow dives below the Rhine-hill level – tricky work, but on a good night it should have come off…

Of course, Gardiner's second guess was the right one. The first man from 226 Squadron to be ordered to fly a leaflet raid was F/Lt Brian Kerridge, and Gardiner was offered the privilege of going to the Rheims/Champagne aerodrome in the middle of March to see him off.

> Unfortunately, on my way... I got lost, and then ran out of petrol. By the time we had walked to the aerodrome in pouring rain, activities for the night were over. Actually, Kerridge had taken off, but had had to return with his radio not working, so we didn't miss very much.

During the second half of April, most of the Battle squadrons flew Nickel leaflet raids, after which they carried out reconnaissance sweeps. The French beacon and lighthouse system now proved very useful up to the frontier and the lights of Luxembourg, plus the glow of the blast furnaces at Thionville near the frontier, provided additional aids to navigation. The weather was bright moonlight and cloudless, with ground mist particularly heavy along the Moselle valley.

Bob Bungey and his crew had their first turn to drop pamphlets on the night of 20/21 April. It was recorded in 226 Squadron's Operations Record Book:

> At 0130 hours on Sunday 21/4/40 I took off in Battle P 2255, climbed to 8,000 feet and set course for Merzig via beacons on Route No.1 to frontier. At Thionville we were challenged by the French with a searchlight which held us for approximately 8 seconds – apparently they recognised us as friendly. The border towns in Luxembourg were well lit and were of assistance in navigation. Thionville and Metz were also easily distinguished. Set course from Merzig to Nickels point via Traben-Trarbach, 10 miles North East of Merzig we were challenged by a Green rocket which we ignored. We encountered a Battery of searchlights at KLJY which failed to catch us; they were always behind us – they searched the sky for 2 minutes then switched off. We continued on our course at 8.000 feet and dropped our Nickels at NFJV3807 from 8,000 feet between 0300 and 0305. Between our Nickels Point and Bonn we encountered numerous single searchlights which all failed to catch us. We arrived over Bonn and found it very difficult to locate the Rhine as it was covered with mist. As we continued our Recce of the Rhine it became clearer, (height at this time was 6.000 feet) but it was not clear enough to see whether there was any traffic. We set course from Coblenz for Merzig climbed to 8,000 feet. We encountered numerous single searchlights and one Battery at Zell NFJV0211. There was no flak fire.
> The towns in Luxembourg were again a good aid to navigation.
> Set course for Base via Route No.1 and landed 0430 hours.
> Weather perfect. No cloud and full moon.
> Rivers stood out clearly.
> Mist was seen in numerous valleys in Germany[1].

Aside from various night flights, engine tests and return trips to the satellite airfields throughout the month, Bob only flew one more time in

April – a 1-hour cross-country wireless test on the 25th. He did not record another entry in his Log Book for more than two weeks, until 13 May.

The arrival of the warmer weather meant the Nazis were likely to launch an invasion soon. They had gone into Denmark and Norway already. That might keep them busy for a while but it was only a matter of time. Now was probably the last chance for Bob to be granted long enough leave to get back to Wallingford. Leslie Clisby had returned from leave in England a couple of weeks ago and he was back with No.1 Squadron again at Vassincourt.

With his conservative upbringing and formal family life, and his accountant's organised mind, Bob's nature was to be methodical and thorough. He had to see Sybil again. They had met nearly a year ago now and it was time – time to ask her to marry him. But besides the looming threat of invasion, there could be other difficulties ahead.

The RAF's guiding principle regarding junior officer pilots being married was to discourage them. Any officer that married before the age of twenty-five, or before attaining the rank of squadron leader, would not be eligible for the usual married officer's allowance. Being without any additional private income could mean that they would suffer financial hardship for a while, but it would be worth it. Bob had turned twenty-five last October – with delight he recalled Leslie Clisby turning up at Rheims – but Sybil was not yet twenty-one. She would need the permission of her parents. Nevertheless, come what may, it was time – time to ask.

Bob and a Canadian mate left the squadron on leave at the same time. By the time they returned, things had changed for the worst.

The 'Phoney War' had turned ugly – and very deadly.

4

Six Days in May

By midnight on 9/10 May 1940, Germany had assembled some two and a half million men along her western borders with France, Belgium and the Netherlands. There were a hundred and four infantry divisions, nine motorised divisions and ten armoured divisions organised into three army groups: In the north from the North Sea to Aachen was Army Group B commanded by General Fedor von Bock comprising two armies; in the centre was the main force, Army Group A under General Gerd von Rundstedt, which consisted of four armies and a strong armoured (Panzer) group or army, in a relatively narrow zone between Aachen and Sarrebourg – most of the German Army's 2,574 tanks were concentrated in this command; and Army Group C commanded by General Wilhelm J. F. von Leeb, which consisted of two armies facing the French defences in eastern Lorraine and along the Rhine River.

Overall command was exercised by the *Führer*, Adolf Hitler, as commander-in-chief, with General Wilhelm Keitel as his chief of staff. Directly commanding the army was General Walther von Brauchitsch, who had been in command of the invasion of Poland.

The German plans, code-named *Fall Gelb*, were thoroughly prepared. Army Group B, supported by an overwhelming aerial bombardment, plus glider and parachute troops, was to swiftly overrun the Netherlands. Simultaneously, Army Group A would move more slowly into Belgium to decoy the Allied left-flank armies into rushing to the assistance of the Low Countries. The Germans anticipated (correctly) that the Allied plan was to meet the expected invasion by pivoting the Allied First Army Group about the northern tip of the Maginot Line to the River Dyle, the so-called Dyle Line of Belgium. With the Allies committed to this action, Army Group A would then suddenly thrust through the Ardennes Forest and make an armoured drive into France. The aim was to split the Allied armies, cutting off those who had advanced into Belgium. Army Group A would then continue westward to Calais and roll the northern portion of the Anglo-French forces against Army Group B in the Low Countries. Taking prompt advantage of the gap, attacks southward by Army

Group A would then push the severed French armies to the south, back on the Maginot Line, where Army Group C was ready and waiting.

Supporting the troops on the ground were two *Luftwaffe* air fleets, Air Fleet 2 and Air Fleet 4, with a combined force of 1,444 bombers and more than 1,000 fighters, mostly single-engined Me109Es and Me109Ds. The German aircraft were newer and far more modern than those of the Allies.

The *Luftwaffe's* bomber strength was predominantly made up of a trio of twin-engine aircraft types: the Dornier Do17; Heinkel He111; and Junkers Ju88.

The Dornier Do17 'Flying Pencil' was originally designed as a fast passenger and mail transport for *Lufthansa's* European express services. The first of three prototypes had its maiden flight in autumn 1934 but its slim fuselage was not suitable for a passenger carrier. They were 'moth-balled' but resuscitated in 1935 as a fast bomber project. A new series of prototypes was manufactured with a twin-fin arrangement replacing the original single tailfin. By 1937, Do17E and F-series bombers and reconnaissance bombers were entering air force service.

Export sales to Yugoslavia followed the Dornier's impressive demonstration at a Military Aircraft Competition held at Zurich in 1937. A specially prepared machine performed at a speed of 248 mph, which was superior to that of any of the foreign fighters at the meet. Do17Es and Do17Fs served with Germany's *Condor Legion* during the Spanish Civil War and the major production version, the Do17Z, appeared in 1939. In appearance, this featured a new deepened nose section incorporated a rear-facing ventral position for a prone gunner. When war broke out in September 1939, Do17s played a major role in the bombing of Warsaw, and now four *Geschwader* were ready to operate in the battles ahead.

Likewise supposedly designed in 1935 as a fast mail and passenger aircraft for *Lufthansa*, the Heinkel He111 prototype already had provision for three gun positions and a 2,200-lb (1,000-kg) bomb load. Its early configuration featured a conventional 'stepped' cockpit and nose section but the P-series that began to leave the assembly lines in 1938 had a new, straight-tapered wing and a completely redesigned, extensively glazed nose section that gave its distinguishing appearance. The He111B, D, E and F variants served with units in Germany and with the *Condor Legion* in Spain where, like the Do17s committed to combat there, they fared extremely well owing to their speed and defensive armament against the 'assorted' collection of fighters flown by the Republicans.

For defence the He111P also featured a new streamlined ventral gondola that replaced the unsatisfactory drag-producing retractable 'dustbin' gun position of the earlier models. Defensive armament consisted of three 7.9-mm MG15 machine guns in nose, dorsal and ventral positions. Power was supplied by two 1,100-hp Daimler-Benz DB601A-1 12 cylinder liquid-cooled engines. He111s operated over Poland and were ready in significant numbers for battles over France and the Low Countries.

Third in the triumvirate and less numerous were the Junkers Ju88, which first flew in December 1936. It was designed in response to a requirement by the *Luftwaffe* for a fast bomber. The V4 prototype saw the introduction of the characteristic ventral gondola and the blunt, glazed nose section built up of optically flat panels. This type would prove to be the most remarkably versatile of all German aircraft. It served with success throughout the war in many variants – as a dive-bomber, level bomber, torpedo bomber, mine layer, day fighter, night fighter, reconnaissance aircraft and close-support aircraft. Production began in 1938 and about sixty Ju88A-1s had been delivered by the end of 1939.

Two 1,200-hp Junkers Jumo 211B-1 twelve-cylinder liquid-cooled engines could provide a maximum speed of 286 mph (460 km/hr) at 16,000 feet (4,900 m). Defensive armament consisted of three 7.9-mm MG15 machine guns in front and rear cockpit mountings and the ventral gondola. It had to be treated with respect by all Allied fighter pilots.

After the overwhelming of Poland in just a month, the angular and ugly Junkers Ju87 *Stuka* dive-bomber with its spatted fixed undercarriage already had the reputation of being the terror weapon of lightning warfare, or *blitzkrieg*. It operated ahead of the panzer columns acting as long-range artillery by successfully pinpointing and destroying such worthwhile targets as bridges, road junctions, and troop concentrations. The term 'Stuka' was an abbreviation of the word *Sturzkampfflugzeug* meaning 'dive-bomber' but it was applied almost exclusively to the Junkers' machine. Screaming down in dramatic, almost vertical, dives it caused almost as much psychological damage to soldiers and civilians alike as it did in damaging physical objects.

The Junkers inverted gull-wing design originated in 1935 and it won a dive-bomber competition in 1936. The first Ju87As were delivered to the *Luftwaffe* the following spring. The Ju87B-2 was the main early production variant and both versions served in Spain, several *Stuka* B-1s arriving in time to take part in the last weeks of the civil war. The B-series was larger, more powerful with a 1,200-hp Jumo 211 engine and better armed than the 'A' version, going into production in 1938. By the outbreak of hostilities in September 1939 some 335 Ju87As and Ju87B were in service. Now the *Luftwaffe* had more than 700 of them, with around 420 of these in front-line units facing the West.

Ironically, Germany's deadly Messerschmitt Me109 fighter had originally been powered by a British engine, a Rolls-Royce Kestrel V.[1] The design was a marriage of the smallest practicable airframe with the most powerful engine available. It incorporated several features of the successful Me108 *Taifun* four-seater tourer, including leading-edge slats and slotted flaps. Development in the pre-war years saw the aircraft appear in more powerful and heavier armed versions and the Me109B and C models proved to be lethal weapons in the hands of the *Condor Legion* in Spain. When Germany invaded Poland on 1 September 1939, the Me109E-1 powered by a fuel injected 1,100-hp Daimler-Benz DB601A 12 cylinder liquid-cooled engine was the *Luftwaffe's* standard fighter, with 850 equipping twelve *Gruppen*.

The Messerschmitt Me110 *Zerstörer*, or 'destroyer', was the *Luftwaffe's* new long-range fighter, introduced too late to be deployed in Spain. The first true operational version was the Me110C-1 powered by two 1,100-hp Daimler-Benz DB601A engines and armed with four 7–9-mm MG17 machine guns and two 20 mm MG FF cannon plus one rear-firing 7.9-mm MG15 machine gun in the cockpit. The type saw limited service in the ground-attack role in Poland in September 1939 and small numbers were used during the invasion of Norway in April 1940. Such was the reputation of these fast new fighters that Air Marshal Sir Arthur 'Ugly' Barratt, who commanded the BAFF, sent out a memo saying that he would treat the first AASF pilot to bring one down to a dinner in Paris. The honour of the first Me110 kill eventually went to a section of Hurricanes from No.1 Squadron in April and true to his word, Barratt lived up to his offer. It had to be dinner for three because the squadron's CO, Bull Halahan, insisted that the 110 had been brought down by teamwork. And so, an air marshal, a flight-lieutenant, a flying-officer and a sergeant-pilot sat down to 'a slap-up dinner together' at Maxim's. Three hundred and fifty Me110s were now poised ready for the invasion of France and the Low Countries.

Along Germany's western frontier were Allied forces that, although more numerous in total, lacked cohesion. Remembering the horrors of the Great War of 1914–18, Belgium, the Netherlands and Luxembourg wanted to remain independent and neutral in the naive hope that the major powers would respect their borders. United we stand; divided we fall. There was no co-operation with the strategies of France and Britain – no unity of purpose.

To the south, facing the German armies behind the French border were more than two million men, mainly French, who were assembled in three army groups. The First Army Group occupied the area from the English Channel to Montmédy, and consisted of five armies, including the British Expeditionary Force (BEF). The Second Army Group of three armies was behind the Maginot Line from Montmédy to Épinal. The Third Army, comprising just one army, occupied the defences of the Maginot Line. The overall field commander was General A. J. Georges, who in turn was under the Allied commander-in-chief, General Maurice G. Gamelin. Altogether the Allies had 3,609 tanks, but these were scattered among three armoured divisions and several separate tank battalions attached to other units. In support was the French *Aimée de l'Air* of some 1,400 combat aircraft, most of which were obsolescent or obsolete, and about 300 RAF aircraft of the BAFF. Generally, the equipment of the Allies was far less modern than that of the Germans.

The storm broke in the early hours of 10 May. Following predawn bombardments of all major Dutch and Belgian airfields, German Army Groups A and B crossed the Belgian and Dutch frontiers. As planned, the main initial effort was on the right in the Netherlands by Army Group B. Drops of parachute troops in the vicinity of Rotterdam, The Hague, Moerdijk, and Dordrecht quickly paralysed the interior of the Netherlands. Glider and parachute units landed on the top of powerful Fort Eben-Emael, northern anchor of the main Belgian defence line, and neutralised it at the same time as other German troops crossed the Albert

Canal. The violence and success of the initial German attacks, combined with the bombing of the interior of both countries, threw the general populace into confusion and panic.

To the French Army GHQ, the main German attack appeared to be in the direction of Maastricht, Tongres and Gembloux, but some pessimistic reports of German Army movements in the Ardennes had been received since the early hours of the morning. Amid the confusion, scant attention was paid to this fresh intelligence.

Meanwhile, the AASF's Fairey Battle Squadrons were placed on 'Four Hours Readiness' notice at 4.00 a.m., and then changed to 50% of aircraft at 'Two Hours Readiness' at 5.00 a.m. Half-an-hour later this was changed again to '30 Minute Readiness' notice. The aircraft were loaded with four 250-lb (113-kg) bombs with 11-second delay fuses. Air Marshal Barratt waited impatiently for the Allied C-in-C, General Maurice Gamelin, to issue orders to attack the German spearheads.

As dawn came, so too did the *Luftwaffe* making widespread attacks on French airfields as well as on those in Belgium and Holland. At 4.35 a.m., 142 Squadron's airfield at Berry-au-Bac was bombed and machine-gunned by six Heinkel 111 bombers. Two Battles were damaged and the surface of the field was broken in several places. Scattered about there were several unexploded bombs. No.103 Squadron at Bétheniville was bombed as the sky lightened, but suffered no damage.

An hour later, Mourmelon, the home of 88 Squadron was bombed. Again two Battles were damaged, one severely, two soldiers were wounded and the oil dump was damaged slightly.

The base at Rheims/Champagne, 226 Squadron's home, came in for attention when German bombers dropped sixteen high-explosive bombs and about seventy incendiaries over the aerodrome but did no damage to British aircraft. No RAF personnel were injured but according to reporter Charles Gardiner, one hangar was blown up and two French soldiers were killed.

At 0800 hours, in response to Barratt's request for permission to attack, French Army GHQ informed him that operations at this stage were limited to fighter defence and reconnaissance sorties. In the Ardennes, Panzer units of Army Group A moved forward as French troops and the BEF moved across the frontier into Belgium to take up positions along the Dyle. French reservists were left to hold the Ardennes frontier.

At BAFF Headquarters, Barratt persisted with requests to be allowed to attack. It was not until late in the morning that enough information was available to have an idea of what was happening. Reconnaissance aircraft, those that managed to return, reported enemy armoured columns and troop formations stretching miles back into Germany. The direction of the enemy's advance into Belgium now seemed clear and there were obvious vulnerable targets, but still Gamelin refused Barratt's appeals. At noon, with his patience exhausted and still without permission, Barratt authorised AVM Playfair to deploy his Fairey Battle squadrons at last.

There could be no mass attack; targets seemed to be all over the place. As they became definitely known, the AASF's squadrons sent their aircraft off in flights, sections and half sections. They ran into withering ground fire and enemy fighters in overwhelming numbers.

Ideally, the procedure was for paired Battles to make a low level approach in tight formation and break at the last minute to deliver individual attacks with their four bombs from about 50 feet (15 m) at 30 second intervals. Then they were to reform after the attack for the return flight. That was the theory anyway.

By the end of the day, a total of twenty-one Battles had been lost, including those destroyed or damaged beyond repair in the early bombing raids. Of thirty-two Battles despatched in the afternoon, thirteen failed to return, one force-landed, and practically all that did return suffered varying degrees of damage. Other RAF aircraft lost included four Air Component reconnaissance Blenheims, four Blenheims from Bomber Command's No.2 Group, five AASF and Air Component Hurricanes, and five fighter Blenheims from 600 Squadron.

Because Bob Bungey was on leave, his usual crew, Sgt Bingham and Cpl Smith, flew with another pilot, Sgt Hubert Barren, in Battle P2180. It was the last mission of the day and 226 Squadron sent out four aircraft led by F/Lt Brian Kerridge shortly after 5.00 p.m. Bert Barron was Kerridge's wingman. The other Australian in the squadron, F/O Doug Cameron, led the second pair.

At 6.20 p.m., a German column of thirty to forty vehicles was found south-west of Luxembourg. The Battles broke formation and made their individual low-level dive-bombing attacks into an intense barrage of ground fire. Barron saw Kerridge's Battle crash in flames after dropping its bombs then he too was hit and wounded in the left leg, the bullet passing right through. As they pulled away from the attack, Barron saw the other two Battles caught in the middle of the ground fire. Doug Cameron's aircraft faltered and crashed. (The Australian survived the crash but died of his wounds two days later. His two crew members were captured.) The last Battle flown by Sgt Gerald McLoughlin swept low over the road with its gunner, Aircraftman Jack Russell, blazing away at anything on the ground until it was at last in the clear.

Despite his wounded leg, Bert Barron managed to fly back to 226 Squadron's base at Rheims/Champagne, bringing Sgt Bingham and Cpl Smith safely home. For this exploit, he was awarded the DFM later in the month.

Meanwhile, news of the early German successes aroused immense alarm in Paris and back in London. Prime Minister Neville Chamberlain's government was already faltering because of increasing, widespread lack of popular support, which was compounded by the frustrating British failures in Norway. This was the last straw. Chamberlain resigned leaving the way clear for Winston Churchill to take office at the head of a coalition government. Hopefully, it would be ready to meet the challenge.

The call went out for servicemen, such as Bob Bungey, who were on leave to return to their units immediately. They had to make their way back as quickly as possible by whatever means they could find.

Next day, Saturday, 11 May, the air-raid sirens at Rheims raised the alarm at 5.30 a.m. Shortly afterwards, the anti-aircraft guns opened fire at a formation of what appeared to be nine Junkers Ju88s directly overhead, flying calmly along at about 10,000 feet (3,000 m) in the beautiful clear morning sky. They were not the main danger. A few minutes later a number of Dornier Do17s came from nowhere to begin circling the town at 500 feet (150 m) or less. They commenced bombing and strafing.

Reporter Charles Gardiner raced to the window of his room at his hotel:

Down came the bombs – terrific thuds and lighter crack-cracks – while I wished I had made for the safety of an abri, instead of relying on the thin structure of the hotel. I looked out of the window and saw a Dornier circling at 500 feet or less – obviously about to make a second run on the target – which, from the direction of the noise, I presumed was the Headquarters building – Chateau Polignac.

I went out to watch – and as the crump of the bombs reached my ears, I also heard a second Dornier flying at nought feet down the main street and letting off with its pop-gun…

Then a lone Hurricane belatedly made an appearance and chased the Dorniers off – later, I was told, getting one of them down near Plivot. What happened to the Junkers I don't know, but presumably they were heading for some other target.

After the raid I found out that the Dorniers had dropped two-thousand-pounders at the chateau – and had missed both times – which is bad bombing, especially from their low height, and without interruption.

All the bombs did was to move masses of earth from a field (luckily it was soft earth and not hard *pave)*, and break some of the chateau windows. One crater was enormous.

For Rheims, it was the beginning of a day full of alarms after alarms.

By now the blueprint of the German assaults seemed clearer. In the north the situation in the Netherlands was growing more critical with the passing of every hour, while in Belgium and France two main thrusts were developing. One was aimed through Maastricht towards Brussels; the other, further south, was pushing through the supposedly impassable Ardennes according to reports by French reconnaissance aircraft. The French High Command believed because of its preconceived ideas that the most serious threat was posed by the move into Belgium. The Germans, thanks to its glider-borne troops who had captured the bridges immediately west of Maastricht intact, were already across the Albert Canal, and there were grave doubts whether or not the Belgians could hold on long enough to cover the Allied advance to the Dyle. It was on this threat, therefore, that attention was mainly focused.

Throughout the morning, RAF Component reconnaissance Blenheims tried to establish the strength of the enemy drive through Maastricht. German fighters were over the area in force. By midday out of eight aircraft that had been despatched, three failed to return and two limped back damaged.

The AASF launched just one operation in the morning against the more southerly Ardennes thrust. Eight Battles of Nos.88 and 218 Squadrons were ordered to make a low-level attack on a column that was inside German territory moving towards the border of Luxembourg. Seven of the Battles failed to return and the eighth landed at Vassincourt, previously the base of No.1 Squadron's Hurricanes (they had moved back to Berry-au-Bac the day before).

AASF bomber losses during the 11th added to Arthur Barratt's grave concern. At least seven Battles were recorded as lost and an eighth had to be written off. Added to these were eighteen AASF Blenheims lost, this figure including the aircraft of 114 Squadron that had been destroyed on the ground. Combined with the losses of the previous day, it was a rate of attrition that the RAF could ill afford.

Anxiety at BAFF HQ about the future of operations by his Battle squadrons caused Barratt to telephone the Chief of the Air Staff at the Air Ministry. He explained that he had not made further attacks during the day because of the obvious necessity to conserve his forces. Worse was to come.

By the 12th, the greater part of the Allied First Army Group, including the BEF, had reached their chosen line of defence, the so-called Dyle Line. The German advances via the captured bridges just east of Maastricht still appeared to pose the most serious threat so, in accordance with the instructions from the French High Command, Barratt now concentrated the RAF effort against this area.

In Maastricht there were two road bridges crossing the wide, slow-running River Meuse (or River Maas as it is known there) in the township itself, while outside the town two roads led over bridges crossing the Albert Canal. The Belgians had successfully destroyed the bridges in the town and at Kanne, but the concrete bridge on the Maastricht-Vroenhoven – Tongres road and the steel bridge on the Maastricht-Veldwezelt-Hasselt road were in German hands. These were the main targets. Another bridge to the north-east over the Albert Canal at Briegden had not been attacked by German paratroops, nor had it been blown up. The troops detailed to do the job had been killed when falling bombs destroyed their barracks. At Maastricht and the other breakthrough points, the Germans had quickly brought up and deployed 20-mm and 37-mm anti-aircraft guns, ready for counter-attacks by the Allied air forces.

At dawn, nine Blenheims of 139 Squadron were sent to attack an enemy column on the road from Maastricht to Tongres. They ran headlong into the hordes of German fighters. Only two Blenheims returned. This disaster, combined with the loss of 114 Squadron's aircraft destroyed on the ground the previous day, all but eliminated the AASF's Blenheims as an effective fighting force. The brunt of the fight now fell squarely onto the shoulders of the AASF's remaining Fairey Battles.

On the ground the Belgians had been trying in vain to deal with losing the intact bridges over the Albert Canal. The advancing *Wehrmacht* was moving the bulk of two *Panzer* divisions across the river. Counter-attacks made no headway and artillery fire proved ineffective. Bombing attacks from the air so far had only inflicted light damage on one bridge for the cost of excessive casualties. The Belgians then lodged a plea for help to the Allies. French aircraft fared no better, suffering the same unaffordable casualties for the same negative results.

Aware that the ever-increasing strength of the German defences made any new attempt against the bridges almost suicidal, Barratt took an extraordinary step. He instructed AVM Philip Playfair to despatch six Battles, but they were to be manned by volunteer crews only. Patrols could be flown over the area by Hurricanes from both the AASF and Air Component but there would not be a close escort. The lot fell to No.12 Squadron, known as the 'Dirty Dozen' and other less printable epithets.

It was indeed a 'dirty' job but when the crews learned that they had been chosen for the task they all volunteered. The briefing officer then asked the six pilots next on the duty roster to go. They did. Three were detailed to attack the concrete bridge at Vroenhoven, and the others the metal bridge farther north at Veldwezelt. The bridges themselves were of similar dimensions, about 370 feet long by 30 feet wide (110 m by 9 m), but 250-lb (113-kg) bombs were unlikely to have an effect on the concrete structure. They had to try.

The leaders of the two sections were F/O Norman Thomas and F/O Don 'Judy' Garland. Garland determined to carry out a low-level attack, while Thomas decided on dive-bombing. The task was badly timed because the morning sun would give the flak gunners a good view of the Battles as they approached from the south-west and it would hide the German fighters attacking from the east.

Fighter escort over the target would be provided by eight Hurricanes from No.1 Squadron led by the CO S/Ldr John 'Bull' Halahan, with his usual wingmen Leslie Clisby from Adelaide and Mark 'Hilly' Brown from Manitoba, Canada. The remaining five aircraft would be flown by F/O John 'Killy' Kilmartin, F/O Laurie Lorimer, P/O Peter Boot, P/O Richard Lewis and Sgt Frank Soper.

At Amifontaine when it was time for the Battles to take off, one crew found that their radio was u/s. The men quickly switched to another machine but found it had a hydraulic problem that prevented the bomb rack working. They had to abort the mission. The other five Battles were all away by 0822 hours.

Bull Halahan arrived over the metal bridge at Veldwezelt a minute before Garland's Battles were due. There were German fighters in small groups everywhere. As some Me109s were beginning to take an unhealthy interest in the Hurricanes, he made a wide sweep of the target area hoping to divert their attention away so that the Battles would not be noticed. At the same time he saw Garland's section heading for the bridge in a grimly determined low approach through a growing volume of flak. The Battles were hacked out of the sky, one by one. He saw Garland's aircraft in trouble but still flying on regardless until it either blew to pieces over the bridge or crashed and exploded on the bridge.

Another Battle flown by P/O Ian McIntosh, who was from Glen Innes NSW, arrived over the target still flying but brutally damaged and on fire. McIntosh dropped the bombs just before crashing. The Australian was pulled from the burning wreckage by his crew but then they were all quickly captured. 'You British are mad,' declared their captors, 'We capture the bridge early Friday morning. You give us all Friday and Saturday to get out flak guns up in circles all round the bridge, and then on Sunday, when all is ready, you come along with three aircraft and try and blow the thing up!'

No.12 Squadron lost five machines out of five that day, with four crews killed or captured. For their valour, Garland and his observer, Sgt Thomas Gray were each posthumously awarded the Victoria Cross but the third member of the crew, the wireless operator/air gunner LAC Lawrence Reynolds, inexplicably received no award.

In the wild dogfight overhead, Bull Halahan, Leslie Clisby and Frank Soper all claimed one Me109 shot down and Richard Lewis, in his first big action, hit two others in rapid succession and claimed them destroyed. The Hurricanes were split up and individual fighting ensued. Lewis bailed out when his aircraft was hit and caught fire. Two Me109s turned towards him as his parachute opened and Hilly Brown, fearing they might shoot at him as he floated down, dived at them and fired. He reported that the two Messerschmitts collided and spun down locked together.

Halahan's Merlin engine was hit by a cannon shell and as it died, he started to glide towards the Belgian lines. Along the way he encountered two Arado army co-op aircraft. He claimed them both shot down from head-on before crash landing safely in Allied-held territory.

Peter Boot claimed a Me109 soon after Halahan's Hurricane departed and then Clisby brought down another, his second. Kilmartin claimed a gull-winged German fighter shot down, which he identified as a Heinkel He112.[2] By now, Hilly Brown and Frank Soper had broken free of the fight but both of their aircraft had been damaged. Clisby, meanwhile, claimed his third Me109 destroyed just before Laurie Lorimer scored his first.

The only Hurricane Kilmartin could see after this was Leslie Clisby's plane below. It was coming in from behind a line of what he thought were Arado army co-op aircraft flying along sedately at low level. He heard Clisby 'whooping with delight over the R/T as he closed in behind and shot down the last three in the line'.

Kilmartin and Clisby then joined up and flew back to Berry-au-Bac together. Only Hilly Brown arrived home before them. The others had run out of fuel and landed elsewhere. It had been an astonishing battle for the South Australian who could claim six kills.[3]

While the Battles were attacking the bridges over the Albert Canal immediately west of Maastricht, Blenheims from Bomber Command's No.2 Group based in England were concentrating on the bridges in the town itself. Although these had supposedly been demolished by the Dutch, the Germans were already repairing them. The aircraft caused little damage but out of the twenty-four Blenheims on the raid, ten failed to return. An attack on the road exits at Hasselt and Tongres that evening was more successful.

German pressure through the Ardennes was increasing and before the end of the day, the AASF lost six out of fifteen Battles in attacks in this region near Bouillon. The Battles could not continue to suffer such devastating losses. Disregarding aircraft damaged, the loss rate stood as high as 40% during the sorties flown on 10 May, 100% on 11 May and 62% on 12 May. On the 10th there had been 135 serviceable bombers in the AASF. By day's end on the 12th, this number had shrunk to seventy-two.

That evening Barratt received a warning message from the RAF's Chief of the Air Staff, 'I am concerned at the heavy losses incurred by the medium bombers... we cannot continue indefinitely at this rate of intensity... If we expend all our efforts in the early stages of the battle we shall not be able to operate effectively when the really critical phase comes...' In actual fact, the 'phase' was becoming more 'critical' with every passing hour.

Such was the situation when Bob Bungey managed to return to Rheims/ Champagne. France was a dangerous place to return to with the *Luftwaffe* already so dominant in the air. 'I returned from leave fit and brown,' Bob remarked later, 'just in time to take a very active part in the invasion of Belgium and Holland.'

Continuing good weather conditions next morning favoured the German onslaught. They were through the supposedly impassable Ardennes and pushing further and further into France. A French force falling back to a line of defence north-east of Antwerp was in danger of being cut off. It was engaged in a race with an advance German motorised column. The Germans had to be stopped despite the fact Arthur Barratt needed to conserve his bombers. The job was allocated to No.226 Battle Squadron at Rheims/Champagne.

A study of maps of the area made it obvious that the Germans might be able to use either of two roads to overtake and get behind the French. The best places to stop, or at least delay, the German tank column for a couple of hours were at two road junctions, one at Boeimeer, just south-west of Breda, and the other at Rijsbergen. Both were marked down as targets. It needed to be done quickly, hopefully before any Me109s or 110s could interfere. Most likely the *Stukas*, probably with escorting fighters, would be up hunting for the retreating French force too.

Take off was at 1020 hours. Seven Battles were despatched, splitting into two groups. Bob Bungey, Sgt Bingham and Cpl Smith flew Battle L5438 in the formation that targeted Rijsbergen. The mission led to 226 Squadron being mentioned specially by the French High Command and receiving telegrams of congratulation from Air Chief Marshal Sir Cyril Newall in England as well as from Arthur Barratt. All the men who took part in the action described the job as being 'easy', but the French said that the Battles saved a very difficult situation, and enabled their troops to consolidate. One Battle had to force-land near Brussels.

Next day, BBC reporter Charles Gardiner interviewed two of the Battle pilots to prepare for one of his regular broadcasts to England. Bob was one of them. Gardiner later wrote:

... the scripts of the two Battle pilots I mentioned ... were all prepared, and though they were not broadcast, there may still be some interest in what the men were going to say. So here are the scripts:

'FLYING OFFICER BUNGAY [*sic*]: The part of the road which we had to block was north-west of Antwerp. We took off, and flew into Holland – and we arrived over Antwerp at about 800 feet. We picked out our road on the map, and then came down along it, losing height all the time until we were only about a hundred feet up. Our orders were to bomb any German troops we saw, and above all to block that road. Well, we flew along, but I couldn't see a sign of any Germans – although a machine gun did start up at us not far from our target. Several bullets from this gun went through my mainplane – and one of the other machines was slightly hit – but nothing serious.

Then, just as we arrived over the little village which was our target, we saw a group of about twenty Dorniers – which were heading back towards Germany. We kept on – and they didn't seem to notice us – which was a good thing – because a few seconds later we saw another lot of Dormers on the other side of our formation – so at the time we would have been sandwiched between two fires. However, nothing happened – and we made our run on the target. The village seemed to be deserted, and there weren't any civilians about – so we dropped our bombs. The idea was to collapse houses on each side of the road – so that they fell across the road itself. I dropped four bombs on my house, and the other two machines let theirs go as well. We did this from very low level – and immediately we'd dropped our loads, we turned back towards Antwerp – and we made our getaway safely, after catching a glimpse of a lot of wreckage which showed us that we'd found the mark.

GARDNER: Meanwhile the other flight of four of our Battles were making for their target – a junction in the same road – but a bit farther north. They were led by a flight lieutenant – and one of the other three pilots was the Canadian pilot officer who is here tonight.

FLYING OFFICER DAVID CROOKS (now DFC): After we'd got to Antwerp we came down really low – hopping over the tops of the trees that lined the road. We were so low that my rear gunner pulled in his gun in case he caught it in any branches – while the sergeant pilot in the next machine to mine actually hit a high-tension cable, without doing any damage to himself. We still don't know how he managed it, but he did, and we went flying on.

We, too, had been told to keep a look-out for enemy troops – but we saw nothing on the roads – though I caught one glimpse of a German running like anything for a machine gun in a wood. I heard noises from time to time which sounded like machine-gun fire – but nothing hit my plane, although I believe a bullet did come up through the floor of the leader's machine – and just missed his legs.

We dodged about a bit to avoid any possible attack from the ground – and then we arrived at the village which marked our road junction.

At the south end of the place we could see groups of civilians standing about – and the last thing we had to do was to injure or kill any of them. So the leader took us up and down the street once or twice to give the people plenty of time to get out of the way – and then he chose, as the place for the bombs, a site at the other end of the village – just to make doubly sure of not hitting anyone.

We made our run right low down – and we went for a three- or four-storied house on one side of the road – and what looked like an empty factory which stood right opposite it.

All four of us dropped our bombs one after the other – and then turned and made a low-level getaway. As we turned we could see both targets going up with big clouds of bricks and rubble and stuff shooting right into the air. We couldn't stop to take a full look at the damage, but it seemed obvious to us that no German troops would get past that lot for some time to come – so then we just flew home.

All seven of us got back safely – though one of us had to force land behind our own lines. He's all right though – and so's his machine.'

During the broadcasting of that last despatch, an air raid started outside, and I was able to take the microphone to the window and let listeners hear the crash of falling bombs...'

The Battle crews had been lucky, very lucky. This was the AASF's only bombing mission flown on the 13th. Arthur Barratt could not afford to risk any more of his precious bombers. The French too only sent out one bombing raid.

At Berry-au-Bac, No.1 Squadron's inspirational CO, Bull Halahan, had been grounded by the C-in-C after his narrow escape over Maastricht the day before. He was too valuable an executive officer to take further risks, he was told, but now Leslie Clisby was missing. Normally the Australian flew as his Number Two and they had become inseparable friends. They would have been together if not for the grounding order. Instead of being up there with 'the boys', all Halahan could do was await their return and check in each Hurricane as it arrived. Time dragged by and Clisby's aircraft, Hurricane N2326, was still not back.

The Hurricanes had encountered a group of Heinkel He111s escorted by Me110s south-east of Vouziers and afterwards he had failed to show up with the rest of his flight – he would be out of fuel by now. Halahan was concerned because people were saying that Clisby, who had earned the nickname of 'Leo the Lion', was becoming a little too reckless.

A few hours later, just as Halahan was giving up hope, a refugee cart drew up outside the mess. On board was Leslie Clisby who was 'in the best of spirits, having shared a large bottle of red wine with the peasant and his family,' the owners of the cart. His dark blue uniform was unkempt and his eyes were bloodshot. He jumped down and apologised for being late.

In his report he stated, 'I attacked Messerschmitt escort first and saw it crash in flames, then a He111 which gave out white smoke from both engines. But then I had to break off on account of an attack by a French Potez 63. On returning home, I sighted a He111 below and made an attack which used up my ammunition. Followed E/A until I saw it crash with wheels up. I then landed alongside and secured five prisoners – the entire crew – and handed them over to the French at Bourcq.' His Hurricane had suffered damage and had to be left behind where he had landed approximately 18 miles (29 km) south-east of Vouziers.

As the story was told and retold it was embellished with more colourful details, one account even claiming he brought one of the fleeing Germans to the ground with a rugby tackle. The squadron's diarist probably started it all when he humorously added that 'Clisby landed beside one of the machines and chased the startled crew all over the countryside, waving his revolver. He wanted their autographs!'

Charles Gardiner related: 'No one knew what had happened to him, until there came a story that he'd shot down three more Heinkels, and had landed alongside the third in an attempt to capture the crew. He was said to have been last seen chasing the Germans through a field with his revolver in his hand... he captured the Germans – and they've now been handed over to the French.'

The Australian reporter, Noel Monks, described how 'Three Germans climbed out of the Heinkel and made for a clump of bushes about a mile away. Drawing his service revolver, Clisby leapt from his damaged Hurricane and started in pursuit of the Nazis. They began to run when they saw him, so he sprinted after them, as fast as the rough nature of the field allowed. Gaining on them, he loosed a few shots over their heads. They stopped dead, and had their hands held high when, cursing and out of breath, Leo the Lion came up to them. He marched them away to the nearest village and handed them over to the French...'

It made good copy for the war correspondents, and was a good tale for telling over a few beers in one of the lighter moments that were becoming few and far between.

The war was going badly. As the *Luftwaffe* systematically bombed Allied communication, the Germans spearheaded by General Heinz Guderian's 1st and 10th Armoured Divisions occupied Sedan. Further north the German 7th Armoured Division reached the Meuse, level with Dinant. Crossings of the river were made on either side of Sedan and bridgeheads were established in Marfé Wood, at Houx north of Dinant and at Monthermé.

In Belgium, the French 1st Army and Lord Gort's BEF reached the bank of the Dyle and was deployed between Louvain and Wavre. The French were between Wavre and Namur. Liege fell to the Germans.

Further north, the Dutch army was on the point of collapse. The Netherland's High Command ordered a general retreat to defensive positions in an area called the 'Dutch fortress' which took in Amsterdam, Rotterdam and Utrecht. Meanwhile, Queen Wilhelmina and her government were evacuated to London on a British destroyer. There were potentially dire circumstances everywhere.

In Britain, Prime Minister Winston Churchill declared to the House of Commons: 'I have nothing to offer but blood, toil, tears and sweat.'

The serious news was reported to Arthur Barratt late in the evening. Before midnight he advised Philip Playfair that the AASF would be required to operate at what was left of its full strength the following day to support a major French counter-attack, but that was not all. Barratt also said he should also prepare plans for a withdrawal.

Early in the morning on Tuesday 14 May, ten Battles from Nos.103 and 150 Squadrons located German pontoon bridges at Nouvion and Douzy near Sedan and attacked them without loss. No enemy fighters were encountered. Buoyed by this good fortune, Barratt decided to arrange an attack on the bridgehead near Dinant, but before he could do so the French High Command called for a supreme effort at Sedan. It was an emergency. *Stuka* dive-bombers had already thwarted the proposed counter-attack before it even started. The ground forces that had been assembling had scattered so the situation was desperate.

Arrangements were made for the entire force of Allied bombers in France to be hurled against the Sedan bridgehead in a series of waves – a maximum effort. The really critical 'phase' had come. It began for the most part just after midday. The few French aircraft available – Bréguet 693s, Amiot 143s and LeO 451s totalling only twenty-six machines – went into action first, attacking bridges and columns of troops, but the Me109s that had been absent in the morning were now covering the spearhead. Losses were so severe that the remaining missions the French had planned for the day had to be cancelled.

Then it was the turn of the AASF. Between 1500 and 1600 hours the entire force of Battles and Blenheims available tackled the same objectives. The three-volume official history of the *Royal Air Force 1939–1945* by Denis Richards recorded:

No.12 Squadron lost four aircraft out of five; No.105 Squadron, six out of eleven; No.150 Squadron, four out of four; No.139 Squadron, four out of six; No.218 Squadron, ten out of eleven. In all, from the seventy-one bombers which took off, forty did not return. No higher rate of loss in an operation of comparable size has ever been experienced by the Royal Air Force.

What happened to 226 Squadron was not stated but other sources say that out of six Battles that took off, just three returned. 'A' Flight was on duty. It was the turn of Bob Bungey and 'B' Flight to just watch as S/Ldr Charles Lockett led the six Battles off at 3.25 p.m. They split into pairs to attack separate bridges.

Lockett's target was the bridge at Douzy but he and his wingman met withering ground fire as they attacked. Lockett's aircraft, Battle P2267, was hit and crashed. One of the occupants was seen climbing out and the squadron leader was later listed as a POW. His wingman's Battle was hit too, the port aileron and part of the tailplane being shot away, and the bombing gear was smashed. He had to abort.

The second section bombed the bridge at Mouzon and at least one bomb hit the bridge. Both Battles were damaged by intense tracer fire and one of the gunners was wounded in the right ankle but they managed to return.

The last two targeted the Mouzon Bridge too but neither returned home. Both crews, all six men, were later confirmed as killed.

Charles Gardiner was at Rheims/Champagne that afternoon.

I saw Squadron Leader 'Lucy' Lockett before lunch – but when I came down to the aerodrome again from the mess – he was missing. He'd gone out on a raid – and hadn't come back. Poor Hurst was almost beside himself. He had orders to send all his machines out to bomb this German bulge – and he hadn't a single Battle to send. Bungay [*sic*] and Crooks were both waiting to go – but there wasn't an aeroplane. ... There are lots of bomb craters on the field – but machines can still take off. Reports from other aerodromes show similar stories there – Battles going out and not coming back.

With Lockett missing, leadership of 226 fell onto the shoulders of F/Lt Hurst. Gardiner wrote: 'I'll never forget Hurst walking about an empty Rheims/ Champagne on the first day of that Sedan break through, saying 'Bomb the b------s, bomb the b------s, but for Christ's sake what with?'

Gardiner would also write: 'The work of the Battle squadrons, and of the Blenheims, is beyond praise in my inadequacy of words. The courage of those boys – outnumbered – attacked by hordes of fighters – defended by only two tatty little guns – and in slow aeroplanes – they have been going at those German lines of supply the whole time. We don't get any details of casualties now – but I imagine that many more of our friends have gone...'

The BBC reporter had a narrow escape himself at Rheims earlier in the day when two He111s swept low over the town and strafed the main street. Gardiner found himself trapped in the back of a car. 'I tried to get out, but the door was jammed. I yelled "Let me out of here" — and Noel Monks came running up and undid the damned thing. I just dashed inside a shop — and when I got my breath, I saw a Hurricane going at the Heinkels. The Heinkel, in its panic, nearly turned into its companion, and in the resultant flap it was shot down. I saw it stall and turn over, and then it went out of sight behind the houses. Others who could see better say that it caught fire. I must say that I viewed this with great pleasure. Not long ago I would have been disturbed at the unpleasant end of those Germans, but now I'm as jingoistic and bloodthirsty as anyone...'

In the evening, twenty-eight Blenheim IVs from No.2 Group, Bomber Command, continued the assault from the air around Sedan. They encountered fewer Me109s than the Battles, and had their own stronger fighter protection. Their losses were less severe – two from 21 Squadron (plus there was another heavily damaged and considered beyond repair) and five from 110 Squadron – but they were bad enough at 25% of the sorties flown.

Meanwhile, the French troops had regrouped and for a few hours the French High Command thought that the German breakthrough had been checked. It was a false hope. The situation was on a knife's edge.

Throughout the night AASF personnel stood by on their aerodromes to guard against possible landings by any enemy parachutists, troop carrying aircraft or gliders that might be attempted. The Germans had already used such tactics successfully in Norway, Holland and Belgium, but not yet in France. Transport vehicles were dispersed and the aircraft were staggered in positions with their rear guns manned. Rifle and machine-gun parties were distributed around the perimeters.

The large Rheims/Champagne airport was an easily recognisable landmark and a prime target. The decision was taken to shift several of the aircraft that were still flyable out of harm's way. Some of these were damaged machines under repair, others were being serviced ready for operations next day. Bob Bungey and his crew transferred Battle K9330 to a less obvious satellite airfield just 15 minutes away.

Those who had the chance to tried to catch up on some rest and sleep. Leslie Clisby snatched some time out by calling on Noel Monks in his hotel room at the *Lion d'Or* in Rheims. Monks wrote about the visit later in his book *Fighter Squadrons*:

> … young Clisby looked in on me for a bath. He was dog-tired, having been on five patrols since dawn, and while he stretched out in the hot water, sighing aloud with the luxury of it, I brushed up his old royal-blue Australian uniform.
>
> Poor old Clisby clung grimly to that uniform. He had permission to wear it for as long as it held together, then, he was told, he would have to get an RAF uniform. A young bomber pal of mine, Flying-Officer Bob Bungey, of Adelaide, was in the same plight. It was pathetic to see the way those two lads nursed their uniforms. In the shambles that followed the *blitzkrieg* I am afraid at least a year's peace-time wear was crowded into a week. Sleeping in a suit, for weeks on end, does not improve it.
>
> I remarked to Clisby, as he lay in his bath, that the old uniform would not hold out much longer, and asked why he did not get a new one, rub some dust and grease on it, and make believe it was his old one.
>
> He said, wearily, 'Brother, those old rags will see me through. But hell! Wouldn't I like to see dear old Aussie once more! Just one walk down old Collins Street in Melbourne, or a mug of beer at the South Australian in Adelaide.'
>
> I was with him, there, with all my heart.

When Clisby returned to his base, Bull Halahan was there waiting for him. They talked for some time. The Australian, who was described as 'a tough, uncompromising man, [was] not given to boast or exaggeration.

During the course of their discussion that night they established that Clisby had probably destroyed nineteen aircraft, fourteen of them during the past three days.'

It was another beautiful clear morning on 15 May. Berry-au-Bac had several light and fast hit-and-run raids early, but the Hurricanes were well dispersed and camouflaged in the wood and were not damaged. 'B' Flight, which was on duty, was relieved at 0800 hours by 'A' Flight. 'A' Flight remained at readiness until 1130 when the six Hurricanes were scrambled to meet a heavy raid approaching Vouziers. One of the pilots, Paul Richey, estimated there were well over 150 German aircraft, about forty Do17s escorted by Me110s.

After accounting for two 110s, one destroyed and one probable, Richey's Hurricane was hit in the glycol tank and he had to bail out. Another Hurricane had to force-land but the remainder managed to break free and were able to claim that no less than four more Messerschmitts shot down. Richey hitched a ride and returned to Berry-au-Bac.

Soon after tea, the six pilots of 'B' Flight, including Leslie Clisby, were sitting at readiness when about thirty Me110s flew overhead. There had been no order to scramble but one of the fitters begged and challenged the flight commander to go up after them. With that, they scrambled in pursuit. There was little chance of catching up but over Laon the Me110s turned and swung back into the attack. The Hurricane pilots were suddenly faced with huge, overwhelming odds.

One by one the Hurricanes returned to Berry-au-Bac – three of them. Bull Halahan could only wait helplessly for news of the others. One pilot had bailed out and landed in open country. He was safe but almost blinded by hot fluid from his punctured his glycol tank. There was no sign of Leslie Clisby and Laurie Lorimer.

As they waited, Paul Richey, who chronicled these events in his book *Fighter Pilot*, remarked: 'It won't surprise me if Leslie's bought it ... He's been rushing about the sky like a madman for the last five days. He's much too keen to rush into these bloody Huns.'

The words were prophetic. Neither Leslie Clisby nor Laurie Lorimer returned. This hit Bull Halahan and Noel Monks hard. The Australian war correspondent wrote: 'only two officers of the entire original squadron were lost. It was a crushing blow to the Bull that one of these two should be his dearest friend, Flying-Officer Leslie ("Leo the Lion") Clisby DFC, brilliant twenty-five-year-old Australian, who was last seen going down in flames near Rheims on May 15.'[4]

Across at Rheims/Champagne, Bob Bungey would have had no inkling yet that Bull Halahan had entered 'Flying Officer L. Clisby missing, believed killed' in No.1 Squadron's official log; nor that he had added Leslie's name to a list of pilots recommended for the Distinguished Flying Cross.

He may have been aware that in the north the Dutch army had already surrendered – after just five days of fighting. He may have thought that the breaches at Sedan had been closed and the German attack halted. He would have been wrong. He would not have known yet that by late in the evening German tanks would be only 12 miles (19 km) from Laon, and he could not have known that the French Army was about to collapse.

He was, however, painfully aware of the disastrous slaughter suffered by the bomber squadrons. He knew that all of the Battle and Blenheim crews had lost friends and companions over the last five days. Most of the men had been together for months, sometimes years. Some senior pilots had been with their squadrons since 1937. They had all flown, trained, played and lived together. As in most peacetime formations, they had been like family groups sharing all the pleasure and excitement, as well as the serious side, of air force life.

So many senior officers and NCOs had been killed or were missing. It had happened so quickly! Here, there was an empty chair; there, a vacant bed; personal belongings were left where they had been when the owner had hurried to his aircraft – poignant reminders that the owner was gone. They had flown to France at the beginning of the war for a 'great adventure'. Instead they had been forced to endure a long, harsh winter – and now, suddenly, so many of them were dead or missing.

Then Arthur Barratt issued orders that the Fairey Battle squadrons were no longer to be used on daylight operations – unless it was absolutely necessary. This at least was some welcome relief.

During the late afternoon, a Battle from 150 Squadron landed at the depot at Rheims. It had two pilots on board. Climbing down from the front cockpit Bob saw a familiar figure – it was Walter 'Wally' Blom, one of the Tasmanians who had been in his Point Cook class. Wally explained he was there with a replacement pilot to pick up a new Battle and fly it back. He had joined 150 at Écury-sur-Coole last October and was now the squadron's armament officer. He also had a harrowing tale to tell.

On the first day of the German attacks, he'd had a very narrow escape. He was leading another Battle in a search for a German motorised column reported to be advancing along the Neufchâteau/Bertrik road in Luxembourg when it happened. After crossing the frontier his plane was hit by ground fire. Petrol from the main fuel tank spurted into the cockpit drenching him and seriously blurring his vision. He and his crew were affected by the strong fumes too but they all decided to continue. Unable to locate their target, they found a second German column and attacked that instead, but ran into concentrated machine-gun fire. The other Battle was shot down. Wally's plane was hit repeatedly but he was able to place his bombs right in the middle of the Germans. Then, almost beyond control, he managed to fly the 90 miles (145 km) back and land safely on punctured tyres. His Battle was so badly shot-up that it was condemned as beyond repair.

Wally had been recommended for a DFC. And now 150 Squadron was making ready to move back to Pouan. Bob informed him that Doug Cameron had gone down while dive-bombing a German column south-west of Luxembourg that very same afternoon. Two Battles out of four had been lost.

There was some delay before the new aircraft was ready, making it close to dusk before Wally Blom and his companion finally took off to return home. The new pilot was alone in his new machine and Wally told him to keep hard on his wingtip so he would not get lost in the darkening sky. The new man had no chance of finding the aerodrome any other way. They both did, in fact, make it back safely.

Nevertheless, overall it was a sobering picture. The RAF's Fairey Battles could not seriously be called first rate bombers. In daylight they were flying deathtraps, abysmal aeroplanes in which to go to war. Used this way, the future for Battle crews was very limited.

But at least by flying night ops, there might be a better chance of survival.

5

Maydays

Between 11 and 15 May there were thirty-two air raids on the Rheims area. Some damage was caused to the AASF HQ Motor Transport section, Rheims railway station and to units at Rheims/Champagne aerodrome. Late in the evening on Wednesday the 15th, No.226 Squadron was instructed to prepare to leave. It seemed that Rheims could soon be overrun. All the Fairey Battle squadrons had to be ready to relocate, regroup and rebuild.

The order to depart came on Thursday morning. Everything possible was packed into trucks to join an evacuation to airfields in the Troyes area. Before moving off, 226 Squadron's stores, two spare engines and seven aircraft (including Battles L5418, K9383, P2180 and P2255) were destroyed. Then the last two flyable aircraft left for Faux-Villecerf, south of Épernay. The other Battle squadrons were in the throes of doing the same thing. At the same time 'the civil population fled with the AASF, and only the Mayor and the ARP men stayed behind,' recorded Charles Gardiner.

During Friday they were still in the process of their various moves. Some were delayed by refugees and diversions from the main roads to side roads. There seemed to be endless streams of refugees coming from the north, many pulling handcarts with elderly people aboard, sitting on small piles of their personal possessions. They were homeless, hungry and absolutely exhausted. When the RAF trucks became jammed in their midst the airmen were frustrated by the fact they could do nothing to help apart from offering small comforts by handing out a few bars of chocolate to the children and cigarettes to the adults.

Exactly a week had passed since the invasion began. Few people could have predicted how fast the Germans overwhelmed all before them and established a bridgehead across the River Meuse. The evacuation of the AASF squadrons to fields around Troyes placed both the River Marne and the River Aisne between the AASF and the German advance. At this stage of their attack, the Germans made no attempt to cross the Aisne and, in fact, they would soon use it to protect their left flank in a race to split the Allies by driving through to the Channel coast.

At midday on the 17th, AASF HQ noted that right then, the total strength of the seven Fairey Battle squadrons came to only forty machines, but few of these were ready for operations. At Faux-Villecerf, 226 Squadron had only three Battles. Bob Bungey used one of these, Battle L5468, to ferry two pilots, P/O David Crooks and Sgt Gerald McLoughlin, from Faux-Villecerf to Amiens, where he left them to pick up a couple of replacement aircraft.

The previous afternoon Britain's new prime minister, Winston Churchill, had flown to Paris with General Sir John Dill, Vice Chief of the Imperial General Staff, and Major-General Hastings Ismay to find out if the pessimistic reports coming out of France were true. In a meeting with France's Prime Minister Paul Reynaud, War Minister Edouard Daladier and General Maurice Gamelin he was told that the Germans had broken through north and south of Sedan on a 50-or 60-mile (80-to 96-km) front and were now advancing, unopposed, towards Amiens and Arras. They could then either charge for Paris, or dash for the coast.

After Gamelin finished his briefing there was a pregnant silence. Finally, a stunned Winston Churchill asked: 'Where is the Strategic Reserve?' 'There is none,' Gamelin answered.

The terrible extent of France's plight hit home. In the courtyard outside the room where Churchill was talking with the gloomy French leaders, secret papers were already being burnt 'by the wheelbarrow load' to prevent them falling into German hands. There could no longer be any doubts about the seriousness of the situation.

Churchill telephoned London, and at 11 p.m. the British Parliament met again for another late session. Cabinet was informed that the prime minister was urging that six more squadrons of fighters should be sent to France in addition to the four that had already been promised. And he wanted a larger portion of the RAF's heavy bomber strength to be employed over the coming nights in attacks on the German Army crossing the Meuse.

His wishes were less than welcome. Secretary of State for Air, Sir Archibald Sinclair, warned that if six more fighter squadrons were sent to France there would only be twenty-nine remaining in all of the United Kingdom. The number was critical. According to Churchill, the head of Fighter Command had already stressed to him that Britain could only be defended by an absolute minimum of twenty-five squadrons.[1]

Chief of Air Staff, Sir Cyril Newall, added more alarming details, 'There remains in the United Kingdom, now, only six complete Hurricane squadrons.' He pointed out as well that the French had neither the airfields nor the facilities to accommodate six extra squadrons. If support for the French was to be forthcoming, it would need to be given by fighters operating from bases on Britain's south coast.

An emergency compromise solution was suggested. Three of the six remaining Hurricane squadrons could be sent to Kent from where they could work in France from dawn until noon. After that they could be relieved by the other three squadrons which would fly an afternoon shift. This measure was approved as were instructions to be issued for the bombers to operate as the prime minister proposed.

In Paris, Churchill was notified of the decisions just after 11.30 p.m. In person, he at once informed Paul Reynaud and Edouard Daladier. After this, the prime minister slept at the British Embassy, from around 2 a.m., where he was only slightly disturbed by 'cannon fire in petty aeroplane raids'. A few short hours later, he prepared to fly back to London in time for the 10 a.m. Cabinet meeting.

That night was the beginning of the end for the BEF. As their withdrawal started, the troops blew up bridges behind them to prevent the Germans from overtaking. Little did the men know they had eighteen days of shock and bombardment ahead of them.

As Churchill was preparing to depart for London, RAF bombers were suffering another catastrophe. Because Arthur Barratt could not call on his Fairey Battle squadrons while they were in a state of transition, he had to ask Bomber Command in the UK to have No.2 Group mount a dawn raid on German armoured vehicles reported near Gembloux. The mission was given to 82 Squadron at Watton in Norfolk. Twelve Blenheims took off at 4.45 a.m. and by just after six o'clock, they were beginning to run into AA fire. One Blenheim was quickly shot down and before the others could reform for mutual defence, a large formation of Me109s pounced on them. Ten more Blenheims were downed – only one heavily damaged machine survived long enough to return to Watton.

For the rest of the day, Blenheims of the Air Component had to take up the fight in desperate attempts to stem the flow of the German offensive. Normally used for photographic reconnaissance in support of the BEF, now they carried bombs and searched independently or in pairs for armoured columns and enemy troops.

When the onslaught began, the Air Component was made up of four Blenheim squadrons for long-range reconnaissance as far as the Rhine, five squadrons of Westland Lysanders for army co-op and tactical reconnaissance, and four squadrons of fighters. Two of these were equipped with Hawker Hurricanes and the other two, Nos.607 and 615 RAuxAF, were in the process of converting from Gladiator biplanes to Hurricanes.

Unlike those of the AASF, the Air Component units were relatively untried. During the whole period of the 'Phoney War', with neutral Belgium between them and the German frontier, there had been no active role for the Lysanders at all. They began the battle untested. The Hurricane pilots had comparatively little practical combat experience aside from intercepting a few reconnaissance aircraft. Meanwhile, the Blenheims had flown eighty-two sorties since coming to France, but forty-four of these were regarded as 'definitely unsuccessful'.

By Sunday, 19 May, the German strategic plan was clear. Allied troops had not been bombed during their advance into Belgium because the Germans wanted to manoeuvre them into forward positions in order to break through via the Ardennes and split them apart. It was working in dramatic fashion – and they were not rushing to Paris! The Germans were pushing hard into Flanders with the obvious intention of completely dividing the Allied forces with a thrust towards the coast, along the River Somme. This would leave a large part of the BEF cut off and in retreat towards the coast between Boulogne, Calais and Dunkirk.

The Dutch were already out of the war. It would probably only be a matter of time before Belgium was crushed too. The Germans had simply gone around the static defences of the Maginot Line. Only a huge, last-minute counter-attack by the French, supported by the BEF, might stop the onrushing panzers; however, France's army groups were divided and scattered, their effective strength halved and they were constantly being harassed by the seemingly ever-present *Stuka* dive-bombers.

The British were being pushed back to the ports where they had landed. So far, the BEF was withdrawing in good order to the line of the canal running through Brussels but communications with the French were breaking down. The most serious threat was on the right flank where German armoured vehicles had penetrated the line but were, so far, being held.

A special reconnaissance reporting back to BAFF HQ around 9 a.m. showed that German mechanised columns, with infantry, were moving north towards the Neufchatel-Montcornet road, and that the territory immediately north of the Rethel-Blanzy stretch of the Aisne River was crowded with enemy troops. Air Marshal Barratt requested support from No.2 Group yet again because of this new threat, but he was refused. With some severe losses over France and Belgium, as well as up north with daylight anti-shipping strikes off Norway, Bomber Command's resources were being stretched to the limit. No.2 Group needed time to replace and repair aircraft, as well as bring in new crews.

By now most of the AASF's Battle squadrons had relocated and begun building up again for operations, but they were still far below proper strength. Arthur Barratt had no choice but to call on them for daylight missions, their first since the grievous losses suffered on Tuesday the 14th. It would have to be a maximum effort, but how many aircraft would be ready for it? At Faux-Villecerf, 226 Squadron could only muster two and 142 Squadron, which shared the airfield, three. Combined with the other five squadrons the numbers are said to have stretched to just over thirty, but then crews had to be chosen to fly them.[2]

The system for deciding who would fly was relatively simple. So many experienced crews had been lost over the past ten days that not that many remained who had actually flown Fairey Battles at night before. Those who had, were almost automatically reserved for the forthcoming night operations. For those who had not, the chances were that they would be rostered for day trips. Inexperienced replacement crews were therefore very likely to find themselves in action quicker than was healthy for them.

Having evacuated from Berry-au-Bac, No.142 had arrived at Faux-Villecerf the same day as Bob Bungey's squadron. It too had been involved in the early heavy fighting and suffered similar heavy casualties, including some among the Australians who were in the unit. When it had come to France last September, S/Ldr John Hobler from Rockhampton, Queensland, had been the squadron leader flying, responsible for all of the unit's flying activities, while F/Lt Ken Rogers, another Queenslander from Toowoomba, and F/Lt William 'Wiggy' Wight from Melbourne were the two flight commanders. Hobler had been at Point Cook in 1932; Rogers and Wight had been there in 1936 in the class six months ahead of Bob, who knew them from those days.

Back on 14 May, of the eight Battles from 142 Squadron which attacked bridges between Sedan and Mouzon, four had failed to return. Ken Rogers and his crew were among those killed in action. John Hobler did not come back either but his crew, Sgt R. Kitto and Cpl D. Barbrooke, did. Their Battle (P2246) had been shot up by Me109s but Hobler managed to successfully crash-land the crippled plane. He suffered serious facial burns while doing so, but neither Kitto nor Barbrooke were injured. They set fire to their aircraft, evaded the Germans and made it back to safety. Hobler was now on his way to hospital and England. No.142's other flight commander, Wiggy Wight, had to take over the role of squadron leader flying.

Richard Kitto teamed up with another Australian, or more accurately a British-Australian, F/Lt John Hewson. John's Irish father had immigrated to Australia; his mother was Australian born. His brother and sister were born in Australia, but in 1913 the family sailed to England for a holiday and this was where John was born in 1914. The family stayed in England during the years of the First World War. After the war, there was a family split and John's father returned to his property in western Queensland. John, his mother and sister remained in England and this was where he was raised. John learned to fly at Brooklands and he joined the RAF on a short service commission in 1936. His intention was to move to western Queensland afterwards but this idea had to be put on hold because of the outbreak of the war.

P/O Howard Taylor who was from Perth, Western Australia, was a later arrival in 142 Squadron. He had been at Point Cook twelve months after Bob. His group of seven former cadets had arrived in the UK in mid-1938. They were the last to reach England under the auspices of the RAF/RAAF Short Service Commission Scheme, which had started in 1926/7.

It was Taylor who led 142 Squadron's three Battles on 19 May. None of them returned. Two were shot down but the third force-landed 10 miles south of Épernay. The pilot, Sgt Ebert, who was formerly a member of 226 Squadron having switched to 142 Squadron in October 1939, returned safely later with his gunner, LAC R. Utteridge, but his observer, Sgt Tom Jones, had been wounded and later died. Months would pass before it was learned that Howard Taylor and his crew were all POWs.

So much depended on luck, particularly the good fortune of being in the right place at the right time. Two out of six Battles from 12 Squadron were shot down by Me109s and one Battle from 150 Squadron's half-dozen fell to heavy flak.

The two crews from 226 Squadron were blessed with the good luck when they attacked the crossroads on the Ecly to Seraincourt road. Concentrations were seen at Hauteville and vehicles were at the east end of the Château Porcein road junction, west of Conde. Flying along the roads, rather than across them, they made shallow dive attacks from around 7,000 feet (2,100 m), releasing their bombs between 4,000 and 2,000 feet (1,200–600 m). Their bombs fell on the western side of the crossroads, and the convoy at Hauteville was left in flames as they flew off.

They spotted and reported yet another column of tanks close to Hauteville, and thick smoke seemed to be hovering over Conde Village as well. Despite intense small arms firing from the ground, both Battles returned safely to Faux-Villecerf.

The tank force that these crews reported was obviously a juicy target, but Arthur Barratt could do nothing about it. He had no more aircraft available until well into the afternoon and by that time the tanks could have dispersed anywhere. No.2 Group was back in action next day, the 20th, each time successfully escorted by Hurricanes.

Meanwhile, French attempts to plug the gap created by the German Panzer spearhead using divisions from the French general reserve and her armies south of the German drive failed miserably. The only successful French attacks of the campaign were made into the German south flank by Brigadier General Charles de Gaulle's 4th Armoured Division from Laon between 17 and 19 May but, after limited gains, these were turned back by vigorous counter-attacks and the dreaded *Stukas*. General Gamelin was relieved of command on the 19th and General Maxime Weygand, who had been called from his post in the eastern Mediterranean, took over Supreme Allied Command.

Just ten days after the Germans began their drive to the west, the British were now forced to consider evacuating the BEF from mainland Europe. Authority was issued for withdrawing the squadrons of the Air Component. Some units were ordered to re-establish in the area north-west of Paris. The next step for the Air Component was to move its Lysander army co-op squadrons, with the exception of a few aircraft, across the Channel to the south of England.

Driven by the vigorous leadership of General Heinz Guderian, the German Panzers completely split the Allied forces. He moved his armour faster than all the others, rejecting a call to briefly halt and regroup. He believed in fully exploiting the advantage of his impetus. By the evening of the 20th, he had taken Amiens and Abbeville within that day and reached the coast line west of Abbeville at Noyelles. Earlier, General Erwin Rommel's 7th Panzer Division occupied the heights round Arras. The German tanks had opened a breach in the Allied line some 20 miles (32 km) wide from east to west. North of this gap was the French 1st Army, nine divisions of the BEF and the Belgian army; to the south of Guderian's spearhead were four French armies in disarray – from west to east, the 10th, 7th, 6th and 2nd.

By reaching the sea, the Germans had virtually surrounded forty-five Allied divisions in Flanders and the north-east tip of France with the German 4th, 6th, and 18th Armies pressing in on them from the east. Guderian now wheeled his armour in three prongs northward from the coast towards Arras.

Arthur Barratt's too-vulnerable-for-daylight-missions Fairey Battle squadrons began their nocturnal raids on the night of 20/21 May. Nos.12, 88, 103, 142 and 226 Squadrons were selected to take part. Five Battles from 12 Squadron bombed Montcornet and Mézières between 11.17 and 11.55 p.m., and the target for five aircraft from 103 Squadron was Fumay in Germany itself.

At Faux-Villecerf, 226 Squadron put up seven aircraft. Bob Bungey and his crew took off at 2 a.m. in Battle P2335, less than half-an-hour behind Sgt Annan and his crew in aircraft K9176. Bob's target was at Montcornet, just 15 minutes' flying time away.

Four Battle crews of 142 Squadron were assigned to fly as well but for them things went horribly wrong. At first, F/Lt Wiggy Wight and his crew had to abort, not taking off because the wireless was u/s.

As the next aircraft prepared to taxi out, a parachute flare being carried on the inboard racks of the port wing exploded. With the port mainplane on fire, the crew – P/O Sutton, Sgt Hall, LAC Duckers – jumped out and ran clear. They had good reason as the aircraft was carrying four 250-lb (113-kg) GP bombs! By the time a fire tender arrived on the scene, the Battle was blazing fiercely. When the fire crew attempted to spray the fire they were ordered to take cover. Soon afterwards the port petrol tank exploded, but not the bombs. Thinking they were probably safe, the squad moved in again but at that point the bombs detonated. Five men were killed outright: four of the fire crew, and one of the squadron's instrument repairers who was watching nearby. The driver of the fire tender was seriously injured too and taken to hospital, where he eventually succumbed to his wounds. The third Battle was damaged by bomb splinters, but 142's remaining fourth aircraft was undamaged and the crew went ahead with their night mission despite the tragedy.

When Bob Bungey arrived over Montcornet, the town already appeared to be completely engulfed in flames. Those who had bombed before him had obviously done a thorough job. He carried out a dive-bombing attack from 5,000 to 2,000 feet (1,500 to 600 m), dropping two instant-fused bombs to add to the carnage. Five minutes later he dropped his remaining two bombs on the north-west entrance of the town. More fires broke out immediately. After this they searched for worthwhile targets to strafe but found none. Bob and Cpl Smith saved their ammunition. Then there were flashes on the ground to the west of the town. Gunfire? Flak? No anti-aircraft fire came in their direction. Bob landed back at Faux-Villecerf at 3.30 a.m.

One Battle from 226 Squadron failed to return on this night. It was aircraft K9176, Sgt Annan and his crew who had taken off shortly before Bob. Months later it was learned that Annan and his gunner had been taken prisoner, but the observer had perished.

On 21 May, Lord Gort, on the French 1st Army's left, sent an armoured British task force south to attack the German salient on the Arras heights but, after a favourable start, they were repulsed by Rommel's 7th Panzer Division and forced back to their starting line. Another effort was made in the direction of Cambrai by two divisions of the French 1st Army, but with similarly disappointing results.

The weather, which had been nearly perfect since the invasion began, was starting to change. In the evening, night operations were scheduled for the Battle squadrons and 226 Squadron dispatched a number of sorties before missions were suddenly cancelled by orders from AASF Headquarters. It wasn't because of the weather. Something serious was brewing – daylight missions at first light!

GHQ was panicking and had no idea where the Germans would strike next. It had requested that the Battle squadrons seek out and attack enemy tanks in the vicinities of Abbeville, Amiens and Arras. The instruction led Arthur Barratt to lodge a protest. He pointed out that this sort of mission was unsuitable for his light bombers, particularly because of the large area that had to be searched. Identifying vehicles was difficult enough, especially considering the poor view downwards from his low-wing light bombers. The chances of successfully hitting such targets were also poor, not only because of their small size but also because of the heavy ground fire that would be encountered at low level. It would be necessary to attack at low level to have any real chance of placing a bomb accurately on one of these vehicles and the costly attacks on the Maastricht bridges were painful lessons that should not be forgotten. Barratt's arguments fell on deaf ears. GHQ was unyielding and it was backed by the Air Ministry. The situation was desperate. Reluctantly, he had to comply.

At 5 a.m., the first Battles left Faux-Villecerf led by Wiggy Wight, who had been officially promoted to the rank of squadron leader. Wight's 142 Squadron, which had been held on standby all the previous day, rostered six aircraft for the task. No.103 Squadron, which now suddenly had a glut of thirty-one Fairey Battles on strength, sent four. The day before it had inherited the remaining aircraft of 218 Squadron, which had ceased operations owing to its heavy casualties. Its personnel were moving to Nantes on their way to return to England.

The morning's weather had worsened to rain and low cloud. Of Wight's six machines, one was unable to find a target and returned to Faux-Villecerf after having to land at Rouen to refuel. The last two machines away were recalled by radio because of bad weather. Another crew did manage to find a tank, which they bombed, but then became lost in low cloud and had to force-land near Paris. They returned by train the following day. One Battle from 103 Squadron was hit by light flak and had to force-land but the members of the crew were uninjured.

The whole effort was a fiasco. A couple of attacks had been made on tanks seen near Amiens, Bapaume and Doullens but none of the crews involved could report positive identification. They had attacked only because the vehicles had opened fire on their aircraft. Considering that by now most troops were firing at anything in the air that might be dangerous, they could have been anything – British, French or German.

Barratt was informed that in total, four Battles had aborted owing to bad weather, three had landed other than at their home base, one returned with its bombs and one had been lost – all this for the net result of one bombed tank, perhaps German. He was not surprised at these poor early morning results. They were so dismal that at 9.30 a.m. BAFF cancelled additional AASF missions. The brunt of the daylight bombing would have to continue to be carried out by Blenheims from No.2 Group in England.

In England, the newspaper headlines were cheering the uplifting exploits of the RAF's fighter pilots while informing the public of a 'strategic retreat' in Belgium and France. In reality, the 'strategic retreat' was deteriorating into a total rout. With the northern Allied groups cut off and pinned against the sea, General Guderian's armoured corps swept towards the British garrisons at Boulogne and Calais. To the south, the French were attempting to hold the line of the Somme and Aisne rivers, but General Weygand's attempt to co-ordinate a stronger Allied response was in tatters despite another supportive visit to France by Churchill. This was not helped by the death of one of his generals after a car accident. There would be no French offensive to cut off the German breakthrough. Nevertheless, the efforts at Arras enabled a large number of French troops and four divisions of the BEF to move back towards Dunkirk.

At least six Battles from 226 Squadron were up again that night (22/23 May) to attack a variety of targets. Bob and his crew took off at 11.25 p.m., on their way in aircraft P6601 to bomb the rail junction at Bingen. Weather conditions en route were poor with cloud, drizzle and sometimes rain. Nevertheless, the blackout below was not efficient so they were able to find the target without difficulty, although there were no searchlights and there was no obvious AA fire coming from the area. They made four dive-bombing attacks, each time descending from 4,000 to 2,000 feet (1,200 to 600 m) and releasing a single bomb. One was seen to explode on the railway line west of the town but the effects of other three were not observed. On the return trip the weather was just as bad, if not worse.

Gerald McLoughlin and David Crooks were among those who were up too. McLoughlin's objective was at Metz but he gave up trying to locate his target through the thick clouds and persistent rain. He returned to Faux-Villecerf with his bombs. Crooks had better luck. He flew through drizzle at 3,000 feet (900 m) but he too could not locate his target. Then, when he and his crew spotted a convoy moving north-west on a road north of Florenville and Neufchâteau, he dropped his four bombs on it instead. All the lights of the vehicles were extinguished immediately so the results of his attack could not be seen.

By Friday, 24 May, the German invasion of the west was two weeks old and the Allied armies had been cut in two. The main part of the BEF was surrounded with its back to the sea. In the south, the French and some British units faced the Germans across the Somme. British troops holding Boulogne had been evacuated overnight by the Royal Navy. Only the ports of Calais and Dunkirk remained in British hands, but Calais was already isolated and under siege. With this port blocked, there was only one place to go. To make an attempt to evacuate the BEF from Dunkirk looked like the only possible option.

The expectation was that General Guderian's Panzers would soon capture Calais too, but now, unexpectedly, something unusual seemed to be taking place. Aerial reconnaissance showed that his tanks were not pushing ahead. They were almost in Calais, and only 30 miles (48 km) from Dunkirk, but they had stopped. Were they out of fuel? Perhaps they needed maintenance?[3] Whatever the cause, there appeared to be a chance of some respite.

On the other side of the BEF to the north-east, the Belgians were under great pressure and possibly close to the point of collapse. Although Guderian's tanks had halted, German Army Group B commanded by General Fedor von Bock had not. During this day, his forces penetrated the Belgian lines above Courtrai and between Courtrai and Menin. The BEF's left flank was directly threatened.

Early in the afternoon, the AASF Wings were ordered to make every possible bomber ready for night missions. Bob carried out a test of the hydraulic system on Battle P2335, one of the machines he often flew. Urgent preparations were underway for the maximum effort but P2335 would not be ready in time. By 3.40 p.m., AASF HQ had a list of the number of aircraft that had been declared available for operations:

- 75 Wing: 88 Squadron had ten Battles at Les Grandes-Chappelles; 103 Squadron, eight Battles at St Lucien Ferme; and 150 Squadron, eight Battles at Pouan.
- 76 Wing: 12 Squadron had nine Battles at Échemines; 142 Squadron, six Battles at Faux-Villecerf; and 226 Squadron also had six Battles at Faux-Villecerf.
- Total: 47 Battles

Targets were widespread and included the towns of Givet, Dinant, Fumay and Bouvignes. The squadrons were ordered to cause maximum disruption to the enemy's lines of communication. They also had instructions not to bring any bombs back from over enemy territory. At Faux-Villecerf, 150 Squadron carried mixed bomb loads in their Battles for the first time. Most carried two 250-lb (113-kg) GP bombs with instantaneous fusing and eight 25-lb (11-kg) incendiaries but one aircraft carried the 250 pounders plus eight smaller 40-lb (18-kg) GP bombs.

For 76 Wing, seven out of 12 Squadron's nine aircraft (two aborted) flew their missions and all of these bombed in their allotted target areas. Some encountered moderate flak and searchlights. In the darkness, one crew saw an aircraft they identified as a Messerschmitt Me110 but it did not attack. From Faux-Villecerf, all the Battles of 142 and 226 Squadrons took off at various times during the night.

The early night departures were mostly made by 142 Squadron. Wiggy Wight targeted Givet in a high-level bombing attack from 10,000 feet (3,000 m). There was ground mist and his bombs straddled the road leading eastward out of the town. He encountered intense searchlight and anti-aircraft activity around Mézières and artillery fire could clearly be seen from the air. Other 142 Squadron aircraft bombed Mézières, Dinant and two machines unloaded on a convoy at Furney Cousey, but the sixth encountered a storm and had to return by D/F (direction finding radio) without dropping its bombs.

All six of 226 Squadron's Battles took off after midnight and they all made dive-bombing attacks. Bob Bungey and his usual crew flying Battle P6601 were the fourth to leave at 1.35 a.m. An hour and 10 minutes later they were over Givet searching for worthwhile targets. By now there was a great deal of intense searchlight activity and aggressive light and heavy AA fire especially in the area from Fomay to Givet. But they were in luck, as north of the town they could see a moving train.

Bob swooped after it and pulling out of his dive, dropped his four bombs from 1,500 feet (450 m). Two of them exploded not more than 10 yards (3 m) from the engine and the train ground to a halt. Whether it was damaged or not, if the tracks ahead were broken it was too dangerous for the train to continue on in case of derailment. Now it was a sitting duck. As if to give cover, concentrated AA fire broke out from east and west of the town as Bob brought his plane in low to strafe with his front .303-inch machine gun. Both he and Cpl Smith poured extended bursts of fire into it. It is not known if Battle P6601 was equipped with the lower gun, but if so Sgt Bingham would have been firing too. Stung into vigorous action, the flak coming from below became severe and remained so for 10 miles (16 km) both sides of the town. Despite this, Bob's aircraft was not hit and he and his crew were back at Faux-Villecerf by 4.20 a.m.

It had been a rare, satisfying night. The squadron had suffered no losses and besides Givet, railway targets had been successfully hit near Sedan, Dinant and Charleville. Gerald McLoughlin had bombed in a shallow dive west of Sedan but encountered an accurate, potentially deadly searchlight. It was extinguished very quickly when his gunner fired down the beam!

With daylight it was obvious the general situation had become far more serious. This prompted the AASF to send its available Battles out again late in the morning. Some of them bombed targets near Abbeville, including motor transport moving north along the Abbeville road. No.226 Squadron's daylight sorties were made by two aircraft, both of which returned safely.

Continuing the effort, the squadron put up seven aircraft that night, but three aborted with engine trouble. Bob and his crew left Faux-Villecerf half-an-hour after midnight in Battle L5419. Flying above the clouds, Sgt Bingham's reliable navigation located their objective, Nouzonville, without difficulty. Large fires were already burning at the target, and they counted about twenty-five searchlights very actively probing the darkness. Several other fires were observed to the south and east.

It was 1.26 a.m. when Bob dropped into a dive from 8,000 feet (2,400 m) and hurtled down to 5,000 feet (1,500 m) from where he released his four bombs. Exactly where they exploded on the ground was not seen, but the largest fire spread much further after the bombing. There was one burst of AA fire to the west. About 5 miles (8 km) south to south-west of Mézières they noticed an illuminated letter 'T' on the ground, but could see no obvious reason for it.

When morning arrived again, Guderian's tanks were still not pushing forward and this was giving the BEF the chance to hastily establish a 130-mile (200-km) perimeter around a corridor leading to Dunkirk. This corridor consisted of a 30-mile (48-km) stretch of coastline running from Gravelines through Dunkirk to Nieuport and extending inland almost to Lille, where six French divisions were surrounded by the Germans. The gap was very narrow and there were only two available roads running through to the port. The vital questions were how long could the corridor be kept open, and would the Royal Navy be able to rescue any of the troops already trapped in the port and on the beaches?

Meanwhile, quite some time had passed before the war correspondents at Rheims finally discovered where the AASF had gone. Late on the night of the 15th they had been informed by the RAF's service press officers (SPOs) that the German advance had reached within 20 miles (32 km) of Rheims, and to be prepared to leave at a moment's notice. They were told they would have to make their own way out, if the need arose. Noel Monks and four other reporters pooled their resources and bought a dilapidated old car in which to make their escape. They named it *Windy*.

When the AASF left, the bulk of the civil population went too. The correspondents reached Paris on the 16th, and remained there for several days before attempting to re-establish contact with the AASF. In fact, Rheims remained in Allied hands for nearly another month. A week after the evacuation when two of the SPOs made a return visit to the town to recover some equipment that had been left behind, they reported that apart from bomb damage near the station, the place seemed intact. The cathedral was certainly in an undamaged condition then. There were French troops in the town who said German tanks were sometimes coming up 'within spitting distance' but they always turned away again. Some had stationed themselves at Berry-au-Bac airfield for a time and captured a number of British troops who had returned to try to salvage abandoned equipment.

The correspondents found out where the AASF was almost a week after they arrived in Paris but their efforts to continue reporting met with frustration. Charles Gardiner recorded:

After we established contact with Bishop and the other SPOs at Troyes on May 22nd, we tried to work out a proper system by which we could continue to report the continual raids by the Battles, and the deeds of the Hurricane pilots. The roster system wasn't too good, since we felt that, in Paris, we were too far away from the Front to get any real facts about what was going on...

Our job was now virtually washed up. We were still dependent on hand-outs given by the SPOs. These scraps of information were hardly worth the sending – and certainly not worth getting all the way to Paris, and the paying up to a shilling a word for cable fees, via New York...

We did give it a trial for a time, but the copy which left Troyes for Paris by motor-cycle despatch rider at lunch-time (there was no phone) usually got held up somewhere en route, and never reached London in time to be used...

So with all communications gone, I decided to clear out and go back to London. This I duly did, and I managed to get a passage over on Air France (flying via Cherbourg and Poole) the day before Paris was first bombed...

Some of the correspondents were able to get out by air, but the majority had to take their chance at Bordeaux and the other Atlantic ports. Noel Monks managed to collect his wife from the South somewhere...

As for what was happening to the Fairey Battle squadrons: 'As soon as I got back to London I heard that the AASF was on the run again towards Nantes.'[4]

* * *

Operating at night had effectively reduced the AASF's casualty rate but the accuracy and effectiveness of night bombing was very much open to question. Were the right trouble spots being targeted and were they actually being found in the dark? If a necessity occurred, or opportunities presented themselves, the Battle squadrons still needed to be ready to fly during daylight. When they did so, the flak they encountered was invariably more accurate and deadly. If the Messerschmitts were about, the chances of suffering debilitating heavy losses were extremely high.

A special daylight raid was ordered on the 26th. Intelligence reported that there would be a meeting of senior German officers at Château Roumont, near Ochampes airfield. The job was assigned to six Battles from 142 Squadron, four from 103 Squadron, and two from 150 Squadron. The attacks were carried out in spite of driving rain and poor visibility, heavy anti-aircraft fire and, towards the end, the presence of four Me110s. Bombs were observed bursting all around the château, and direct hits were claimed. Initially, four Battles failed to return but one force-landed at Verdun and another crash-landed when its undercarriage would not lower. French troops reported one British plane shot down in flames by the Messerschmitts.

Returning British crews reported seeing numerous German aircraft on the ground at Ochampes aerodrome and the airfield at St Hubert.

Across the English Channel on 27 May, in an underground bunker deep within the cliffs of Dover called the Dynamo Room, the Royal Navy's Vice-Admiral Bertram Ramsay ordered the emergency evacuation of troops from the port and beaches of Dunkirk to begin. The room had housed an electricity plant during the First World War, hence the name. Ramsay felt that he might have two or three days in which to snatch perhaps 50,000 troops away from the Germans – just 50,000 out of 500,000! The mission was christened, Operation *Dynamo*.

Adolf Hitler issued orders on this day too. At last realising his mistake in halting Guderian's advance on Dunkirk to await reinforcements, he rescinded the order to delay. Calais still stood as a stumbling block between Dunkirk and the main German thrust. The British commander there had been told that his small force would not be withdrawn and must fight to the finish. Hitler now ordered a full-scale air and land assault on the Dunkirk corridor. Calais fell that day.

As for the BEF, to complete its retreat into the Dunkirk pocket, it was imperative for the British 3rd Division commanded by General Bernard Montgomery to pull back from its precariously exposed position in front of Roubaix. It was almost 50 miles (80 km) from Dunkirk and perilously situated in the middle of the German 6th Army. The aim was to reach a safer new position 25 miles (40 km) to the north of Ypres. To make it through they had to run a confusing gauntlet of refugees, tank traps, ruins and other obstacles, all in the dark and within range of the German guns. The darkness of the night of 27/28 May was illuminated by flashes of artillery fire, flares, and flames from ruined vehicles and buildings.

While this was happening, an armada of British naval vessels plus a flotilla of volunteer civilian boats and small craft slipped across the ominously gloomy waters of the English Channel to try to rescue as many trapped soldiers from Dunkirk as they could.

Worse was coming, however At four o'clock that morning, King Leopold of Belgium ordered the Belgian army to cease fire. The courageous Belgian troops, on whom the BEF had relied to block the German advance from the east for so long, had to surrender their arms. The collapse placed the BEF in the gravest danger. Lord Gort had no troops with which to close the gap and prevent an enemy breakthrough to Dunkirk. The situation which had become dire so quickly, now verged on the catastrophic.

Against the odds, Montgomery and his men did make it through before daybreak. They had walked and marched with as much of their equipment as they could, driving and pushing their overloaded trucks and vehicles through a corridor of hostile shellfire, perimeter outposts and refugee encampments to a place of safety of sorts, temporary though it might be. They had to hold there. Where else was there to go with the coming of dawn, except to the sand hills and the beaches?

Across the Somme, south of German Army Group A which included General Guderian's Panzer Corps, 226 Squadron at Faux-Villecerf was placed on standby for daylight bombing missions. Daylight again! The crews would have to wait tensely for the allocation of targets as they came to hand – if they came to hand, that is.

That morning when Bob Bungey checked the roster, he found that he and his crew, Sgt Bingham and Cpl Smith, were the first scheduled to take off. Weather conditions were far from promising, however.

6

The End of France

What do you do while you wait nervously on 'standby' or at 'readiness'? Check the plane? Bob Bungey, Sgt Bingham and Cpl Smith had been rostered to fly Fairey Battle L5461, a machine that had actually been built by the Austin Motor Co.'s shadow factory at Longbridge. Its engine was a slightly more powerful Rolls-Royce Merlin III, which made it a little faster, but it was apparently not fitted with the semi-fixed, rearward-firing ventral gun. Battle L6598, which was to be flown by Sgt Martin and his crew, did have this third weapon.

The bomb load was different this time. Bob's plane was loaded with sixteen 40-lb (18-kg) GP bombs instead of the usual four 250-lb (113-kg) bombs. These smaller bombs could be spread over a wider area when dive-bombing and would therefore be more effective against infantry and lighter vehicles such as cars, supply trucks and horse-drawn wagons. The aircraft to be flown by young Gerald McLoughlin, Battle L5305, another machine built by Austin Motors, was being loaded with the same. The others – P/O Heywood's P2161 and Sgt Martin's L6598 – were carrying the usual four 250 pounders. Periodically, the sound of aero engines being run up penetrated the air. The planes had to be kept warmed up ready for take off.

Time dragged by slowly – much too slowly. For many, waiting was the worst. Although everybody displayed a veneer of calm, the atmosphere was full of tension. Once a target was announced and the order for take off given, all that would change. Everyone involved would spring up and the place would turn into a hive of activity. Reactions would become automatic.

Perhaps Bob had time to write another letter to Sybil, or to his family back home in Adelaide. The mail was not very regular anymore.[1] Was it really only a month ago that he had asked Sybil to marry him and she had said yes? To choose an engagement ring, they had gone into London; Bob dressed in his civilian clothes. While they were there he'd had his photograph taken in Bond Street.

So much had happened since then. Les Clisby was dead, down in flames somewhere. It was a shock to realise someone so full of life could have gone so quickly – he and Bob would never again celebrate another birthday together. Doug Cameron was gone, Brian Kerridge too – both on the same mission. Bingham and Smith could have been killed then too because at the time they'd had to fly with another pilot. Howard Taylor had not lasted long either. Perhaps he should write a final letter – one to be opened if...

Despite such heavy losses, at least some Australians scattered among the Battle squadrons were still going strong. Alan Pitfield, who had taken Bob up in a Battle for the very first time back in January 1938, was now in 88 Squadron and had been recommended for a DFC. Wally Blom was up for one as well. Wiggy Wight and John Hewson were still in 142 Squadron. But there was always the question of who would be next? The odds were that this would happen during a daylight job, like today.

It was best not to ponder such things. It was far better to do something, anything, to distract yourself – perhaps play a card game, darts, chess, drafts, or maybe do a crossword, that's if there was an English newspaper to be found that somebody else had not got to first. What about reading a book, a novel, a Bible, a magazine – anything! Some seemed to just sit about catching up on some sleep, for a while anyway, until the order came ... if it came.

Some of the boys smoked cigarette after cigarette, others puffed on a pipe – pipes were very popular. Bob was not a smoker. The morning slowly dragged on. It was time to check on the weather yet again. The sky outside was mainly overcast and there were patches of low cloud and rain about, but some areas still seemed to be clear.

It was hard to know what was really happening. Obviously, the overall situation was far from good. The days of the British in France must be numbered. Most, if not all, of the Air Component's squadrons were moving back to England. How much longer before the AASF went too? At the moment, the Battle squadrons were staying south of the Somme preparing to fight alongside the French air force, or what was left of it, when the main German offensive against the rest of France began again. Would it degenerate into another bloody battle of the Somme lasting years, as it had in the First World War?

Most of the BEF had had it too; they were crammed inside a shrinking perimeter around the only available port on the coast of north-west France still not overrun by the Germans. How long could it survive there at Dunkirk? Perhaps the navy might at least get some troops out. Everything was happening so quickly!

Bob could not yet have known that during the day Prime Minister Winston Churchill would make a statement in Parliament to the effect that 'the BEF is fighting its way back to the coast under the protection of the RAF, and the Navy is embarking the troops'. At the same time he would announce that Belgium had surrendered. He would then warn, 'The House should prepare itself for hard and heavy tidings...'

Bob would not have known either that overnight about 11,400 men had already been evacuated from Dunkirk. He would have been aware though, from intelligence reports and reconnaissance sorties, that besides consolidating their southern flank facing the French, the Germans were moving large quantities of supplies and reinforcements northwards to crack the British perimeter and break through to the port, or what was left of it. How much more time did the BEF have left?

It was late morning when orders finally did come through for two of the Battles to carry out armed reconnaissance sorties. Bob's instructions were to search for enemy tanks, vehicles and troops along the length of the Amiens – Albert road. He lifted off at 11.30 a.m. followed 7 minutes later by Sgt Heyward and his crew who were to check from Amiens to Doullens and then make a follow up sweep along the Amiens – Albert road. Arriving over Albert an hour later, Bob found German mechanised transport consisting of about fifteen vehicles in a square within the town. They were contained in a confined area and so made good targets caught as they were. In a dive-bombing attack, he dropped eight of his 40 pounders on the surprised group and then swooped away to follow the road from Albert to Peronne.

There was another convoy ahead. It comprised about another fifteen vehicles, some of them horse-drawn. He dropped his remaining 40-lb (18-kg) bombs, which exploded in a ditch alongside the road creating havoc and confusion. Horses bolted in panic. To add to the chaos, Bob swung the Battle around and strafed using his front gun while Cpl Smith followed up in his turn with his rear machine gun. They kept this routine of going back and forth for 5 minutes before being satisfied with the destruction and moving on.

Flying through rain and low clouds from Peronne back along the road in the direction of Albert, Bob and his crew came upon a large concentration of enemy troops moving north-west towards Albert. They were somewhere between Maricourt and Clery. As the troops scattered, Bob and Cpl Smith attacked with machine-gun fire until they had exhausted all their remaining ammunition. The troops replied from the ground with light automatic and rifle fire but the Battle was not hit.

Bob and his crew were back at Faux-Villecerf at 1.30 p.m., landing just 3 minutes ahead of P/O Heywood's Battle P2161. Heywood and his crew had found no important activity between Amiens and Doullens and very little happening on Amiens – Albert road after Bob's devastating run. The Germans were keeping their heads down. Heywood's four bombs exploded in the middle of the road at La Houssoye and a machine gun opened fire from the village. Small numbers of troops found south of La Houssoye were strafed despite rain and low cloud.

The Fairey Battles of young Gerald McLoughlin and Sgt Martin were not there. They had taken off together at around the same time as Bob was plastering the German vehicles trapped in the square at Albert. The intelligence reports had been confirmed. The Germans were definitely moving large masses of supplies and reinforcements northwards, as well as building up their southern flank along the Somme.

Martin targeted a convoy leaving Albert on the Amiens road and dropped his four bombs after pulling out of a steep dive from 5,000 to 1,500 feet (1,500 to 450 m). His results could not be observed owing to low cloud. There was convoy traffic congestion, about thirty vehicles with covered trailers near Albert. These were machine-gunned from 1,200 feet (360 m) with rear and third guns and men were seen to fall from one of the trucks.

At an estimated distance of 2 miles (3 km) north-east of Albert on the Doullens road, Gerald McLoughlin dropped his sixteen 40-lb (18-kg) bombs on a convoy of 3-ton trucks but its position was not accurately known due to cloud and rain. At least one blast was observed on the road between two stationary lorries. He and his crew then machine-gunned the convoy from about 1,500 feet (450 m) and his gunner reported that the target was soon obscured by smoke.

Everybody had returned by 2.30 p.m. All of 226 Squadron's aircraft returned safely and their series of attacks had been very successful. Thankfully, there had been no sign of the *Luftwaffe*. The German Air Force was obviously busy somewhere else – Dunkirk!

The Belgian surrender took effect from 11.00 a.m., but British and French troops just managed to plug the gap left in the perimeter in time to prevent the Germans reaching Nieuport and the beaches. Despite deteriorating weather, a few Battles from 103 Squadron flew night missions to round off the day's bombing.

On the 30th, AM Sir Arthur 'Ugly' Barratt and AVM Philip Playfair visited a number of AASF units including 226 Squadron. They told everyone present that although the Germans were temporarily occupied, concentrating on attacking the evacuating BEF from Dunkirk, they were also preparing to launch an assault southwards across the Somme – it would not be long before the AASF was back in the thick of the action. They reminded everyone that the Germans had failed to reach Paris in the First World War and it was hoped the threat of this happening might yet galvanise the French into making another heroic stand.

Of course this would need to be done with RAF backing, and the support of some BEF units remaining south of the Somme. The AASF's Battle squadrons were to prepare to move soon to new locations so that, alongside the *Armée de l'Air*, they could cover what they called the 'Weygand Line' behind the Somme and Aisne Rivers. The French air force would be called upon to make a maximum effort by flying every serviceable aircraft of any type, including even its ancient slow night bombers that were previously considered only suitable for training.

Meanwhile, Wally Blom's DFC was recorded in the *London Gazette* on this day, and a rumour was circulating that the French were randomly handing out decorations to some AASF squadrons. It was known that 103 Squadron had been allocated at least three of them. The actual recipients of the awards were decided by tossing a coin! An Australian resident in 103 Squadron was Melbourne-born S/Ldr Harry Lee who had been one of the first pilots to carry out long operational flights at night. After he qualified at Point Cook in

December 1932 he joined the RAF early in 1933, and when his short service commission period was over he had been granted a permanent commission. In the event, the medals were never issued because of the collapse of France.

Late next morning, 31 May, the AASF called for twelve Battles to attack German aircraft seen parked on the aerodrome at Laon and on the nearby racecourse. At least six aircraft were able to take off but the weather was appalling with 10/10ths cloud down to 3,000 feet (900 m). This was supposed to give cover so that the attack was a surprise, but instead it completely thwarted the operation. Unable to find the targets, most Battles returned with their bombs, while others attempted to bomb a variety of targets by estimating their times of arrival (ETA). Records of the day are sketchy and conflicting, but twenty-four-year-old Cpl Gordon Jacobs of 226 Squadron from Norwich, England, was reportedly killed on this date in unknown circumstances.

That night three of 226 Squadron's Battles were prepared for night operations. The first took off after midnight. This was Bob Bungey and his usual crew leaving at 12.55 a.m. in Battle L6601.[2] The weather was clear but the ground was obscured. Bob spotted two rows of lights north-east of Conz, which could have been at Trier. They made a high-level bombing run, dropping their four 250-lb (113-kg) bombs from 10,000-feet (3,000 m) without encountering any flak or searchlights. The crew of the second Battle, which took off 5 minutes after Bob, saw a row of diffused lights as they reached their ETA and dropped their bombs. The third Battle, flown by Sgt Martin and his crew, aborted the mission. They took off at 1.30 a.m. but had to return 15 minutes later because the pilot's panel had blown out.

Mist and low cloud hung over Dunkirk when dawn broke on 1 June, but it dispersed as the sun rose in the heavens. Out of these clear skies a series of vicious *Luftwaffe* attacks developed against the shipping offshore until, mercifully, clouds rolled over again and the German effort dwindled away. Amid the carnage, ten vessels had been sunk, including three destroyers, and several others had suffered serious damage. Worse, German artillery was now covering the navy's newly swept central route to Dunkirk, as well as the direct and the eastern approaches. Confronted with the prospect of heavy losses from both enemy aircraft and these guns, Admiral Ramsay was obliged to call a halt to carrying out evacuations in daylight. From now on the work would have to be done only at night.

On 2 June, the embarkation of troops ceased at first light. Overnight, although the beaches were shelled and a trawler sunk in the harbour, loading continued according to plan. Early morning haze helped to cover the departure of the ships. When the *Luftwaffe* arrived at 8.00 a.m., it ran into five squadrons of RAF fighters. The German crews were kept much too busy fighting for their own survival to seriously molest the ships.

What had seemed at first to be a disastrous turn of events proved to have unanticipated advantages. It was soon realised that if the troops were only lifted off during the night, the demand for continuous air cover could be relaxed a little. The RAF could concentrate its fighters over the evacuation area in great strength during the two critical periods of dawn and dusk, when the ships were leaving and approaching Dunkirk.

In the meantime, the soldiers waiting in the sand dunes were in the safest place possible under the circumstances because the soft sand dampened the concussion from exploding bombs. It was realised at an early stage that casualties would be lighter there. Being sprayed by grains of sand was far less dangerous than being sprayed by shards of rock and metal. Bombs dropped on a rocky shoreline would have produced far more shrapnel with deadlier results. Throughout the day no ships were sunk and only two were damaged. They were hospital vessels which had courageously but rashly approached the harbour in daylight.

Before midnight, although the embarkation of the French Allies was going slowly because they failed to organise a continuous flow of men, a very welcome signal was able to be sent to Admiral Ramsay stating briefly, 'BEF evacuated.' But it was not over yet. French troops were still holding the shrinking perimeter and waiting in their thousands for rescue.

For two nights more the heroic rescue continued. On 3 June, as on the 2nd, embarkation ceased at first light and began again during the evening. Once more RAF fighter patrols were concentrated for the dawn period, but the mist was thick and the *Luftwaffe* stayed away. Around 7.30 a.m., there was a brush with some *Stukas* and then, mercifully, the weather closed in completely for the rest of the day.

News then quickly spread that Paris had been bombed at lunchtime. The night before, German planes had dropped warning leaflets and these had caused near-hysteria among the capital's population. Authorities claimed that when the raid did come, the city's anti-aircraft guns kept the bombers too high for them to bomb accurately but it was rumoured that 254 civilians had been killed nevertheless.

Meanwhile, at Faux-Villecerf, there was a fire in one of 142 Squadron's tents, which destroyed a great quantity of equipment including parachutes, flying helmets, maps and various instruments. As it was 142's turn to stage night operations, these items had to be borrowed from 226 Squadron and 105 Squadron, which was being withdrawn to Nantes. That night, five of 142 Squadron's Battles raided Trier. John Hewson, after releasing a parachute flare, scored a direct hit on the railway line.

In the early hours of 4 June, Major-General Harold Alexander patrolled along the shoreline of Dunkirk in a fast motorboat, searching to ensure that there were no more groups of British soldiers still waiting to be lifted off. When he returned to the quayside he boarded ship for Dover, the last Allied soldier to leave. It was 3.30 a.m. as the destroyer, HMS *Shikari*, departed.

Shikari left behind a backdrop of fire and thick oily smoke rising from burning vehicles and stores, and several thousand Frenchmen in a rearguard that continued fighting to cover the withdrawal. Fighting continued in the contracting bridgehead until later in the morning when the Germans were in the outskirts of the town and there was no other choice but to surrender. That morning, 26,175 Frenchmen that did escape were landed in England.

Finally, at 2.23 p.m. the Admiralty, with the agreement of French authorities, announced that Operation *Dynamo* had finished. In seven days 338,226 men had been evacuated under relentless enemy attacks from the air and on the ground.[3] Although the 112,000 Allied troops brought back were mainly French, there were also Belgian soldiers and a few civilians. Casualties numbered 68,000 killed, wounded or missing. A total of 222 naval ships had been involved plus around 800 civilian craft. Six destroyers and 243 other vessels were sunk. In the air, the *Luftwaffe* had been met and matched. Meanwhile, 40,000 troops, mostly belonging to the French 1st Army, who had fought the valiant rearguard actions on the perimeter, were marched into captivity.

While the evacuation from Dunkirk was going on, the remaining French forces and the few British units left over were trying to consolidate the 'Weygand Line' behind the Somme and Aisne Rivers. Their intention was to contain the enemy along this line, but in reality it was a hopeless task. The odds were heavily stacked against them. If 134 Allied divisions had not been able to stop the overwhelming German onslaught at the beginning, what chance did the last sixty-three under-strength and underequipped divisions really have?

Now that Dunkirk was over, the *Luftwaffe* had 975 fighters assigned to the Western Front redirected to operate against the southern flank. The Allies could only muster some 800 fighters, of which 300 were operating from England. There was a greater disparity in the bomber forces available. Germany could field 1,700 long-range bombers and 468 dive-bombers, but the RAF could only gather together 550. Of these, 400 were based in England. As for the AASF, its fighter force was only capable of mustering eighteen serviceable Hurricanes.

By the 4th, four AASF bomber squadrons that had been decimated while attacking the German spearheads, Nos.105, 114, 139 and 218, had been withdrawn to Nantes. Their surviving aircraft had been turned over to the remaining operational squadrons and many of their personnel, especially the air gunners and armourers, were in the process of receiving postings to other squadrons.

Bob's Log Book shows that on the night of the 4th, he and his crew flew Fairly Battle P2331 and carried out dive-bombing attacks on German convoys in the 'Hirson Area', the sortie taking 2 hours 25 minutes. The very next day, the Germans unleashed their overwhelming *blitzkrieg* again, this time pushing southward. Time was running out for France. The final event was on.

The dreaded Ju87 *Stuka* dive-bombers continued in their role as the terror weapon of the Battle of France, and the Germans had improved their techniques for even greater efficiency. After pin-point attacks opened up the Allied front at selected points, the Panzers roared through the gaps. Advancing troops had wireless contact with the *Stuka* control and by referring to a map grid, any strongpoint could be quickly neutralised before they again pressed forward. The *Stukas* pounded Allied troops and artillery, cut supply lines, bombed reserves and smashed any force that looked like making a stand. To those on the ground – soldiers and refugees alike – the sound of a *Stuka* in a steep dive was bad enough, but the sirens the Germans had fitted to the legs of the aircraft enhanced their terrifying effect. They were called the 'Trombones of Jericho'.

Although the German attack had been anticipated, what was not expected was that it would be so overwhelming and carried out over such a vast area. There were multiple crossings of the Somme and the Aisne. Most serious were the thrusts to the south-west from St Valery and Abbeville; south from Amiens by about 300 tanks; south-west from Peronne by another 400 tanks; south-west from Lafare-Chauny; and south-west from Laon. All were moving towards the Lower Seine – Paris!

The assaults were so widespread that it was difficult for the defenders to know where to bomb. It was well into the afternoon before the incoming intelligence information could be sifted and evaluated. AASF squadrons were on standby for most of the day, but as soon as tanks were reported on the Peronne, Roye, Amiens and Montdidier roads bombing missions were launched.

From Faux-Villecerf, No.226 Squadron was active over Roye where Bob Bungey and his crew in Battle P2161 found an enemy convoy, which they bombed and strafed. From Sougé at 7.30 p.m, Nos.12 and 142 Squadrons took off to attack tanks. They did not find any tanks or troop concentrations so they bombed two roads and an assortment of vehicles instead, but then there was a 'friendly fire' incident.

Several tanks were spotted heading towards Tricot, but it was not realised these were actually French vehicles. The German panzers had not yet advanced so far south. This led to three of No.12 Squadron's Battles being attacked by two *Armée de l'Air* Morane 406s. Two Battles were damaged and had to force land at Faux-Villecerf, fortunately without suffering any casualties.

Because of the enemy's rapid advances, Faux-Villecerf had to become an advanced landing ground chiefly manned by service units where the Battles could stand by for deployment against targets as threats materialised. Some units based there had to move back to safer fields to make room for flights coming in for standby duty. On paper, Wiggy Wight, John Hewson and 142 Squadron went to Houssay to join up with 150 Squadron but in practice they mainly stayed at Faux-Villecerf.

No.226 Squadron's move began on the 6th. Bob's Log Book shows that he touched down briefly at Orly on the way before finally landing at Sougé. At Sougé they joined up with No.12 Squadron whose personnel were in the process of settling in too. This squadron had transferred back from Échemines, a base which was also starting to be used as an advanced landing ground.

That night, the *Luftwaffe* came over the RAF airfields as the standby AASF Battles were operating. Fifty-three bombs were dropped on Échemines disrupting 103 Squadron as it launched sorties. The airfield itself received twenty-three hits and two aircraft suffered light damage. Just after midnight, Harbourville was raided and a Battle belonging to 88 Squadron was damaged by bomb splinters. Tragically, as one man raced for shelter he ran into the blades of a spinning propeller and was mortally injured.

Next morning, 226 Squadron pilots and crews flew from Sougé to Échemines where they landed for their standby duty. They only stayed briefly, however, probably because of the bomb damage, before heading for Faux-Villecerf and landing there to prepare for daylight missions in the afternoon.

After reconnaissance sorties flown early by Blenheims of the Air Component were studied along with other intelligence, it was obvious that the enemy thrusts were driving towards Paris. The Germans had failed to reach the French capital in the First World War, but it already seemed that there was little that could stop them now.

Nine Battles from 12 Squadron took off at 5.00 p.m. to bomb vehicle traffic, including tanks in the Poix area. They were attacked by Messerschmitt 109s. One Battle fell in flames.

The 226 Squadron crews left Faux-Villecerf with orders to return to Sougé after they had bombed their targets – and targets were not hard to find. They were plentiful. It was an exceedingly hot, dry day, and the German tanks and trucks stirred up substantial clouds of dust that attracted the attention of the fliers like moths to a flame.

Bob Bungey and his crew in Battle P2331 found a convoy of armoured vehicles in the midst of a dust cloud at Hornoy. They dive-bombed these, but the Messerschmitts were there too and Bob's aircraft drew the unwanted attention of at least one Me109.

Bob's Log Book reads simply, 'shot up by Me109.' There are no details on just how badly they were hit, but neither he, Sgt Bingham nor Cpl Smith seem to have been hurt. They landed safely at Sougé and were able to fly as a crew again the very next day. However, it does seem likely that the aircraft itself may have suffered a significant amount of damage.[4] Bob did not fly Battle P2331 again until the 15th, more than a week later, when he took it up for a 20 minute air test. The circumstances under which he did so were extremely dramatic.

At Sougé on the 8th, there was special news for 12 Squadron. For some it was cause for pride and celebration, despite the increasingly dire war situation. An announcement was made that F/O Don 'Judy' Garland and Sgt Thomas Gray had received Victoria Crosses for their self-sacrificing attack on the Maastricht bridges back on 12 May. These posthumous awards had been recorded in the *London Gazette* the previous day. With the squadron about to engage yet again in desperate and probably futile daylight bombing missions in hostile skies, just how morale-boosting and welcome this news of posthumous awards would have actually been for them must to be open to question.

That afternoon Fairey Battles from 226 Squadron, including Bob and his crew in aircraft L5037, flew forward to Faux-Villecerf again to stand by for ops. Overnight, they bombed Trier before returning once more to Sougé.

It was a night in which there seemed to be a lot happening. Searchlights were active in the vicinity of the River Aisne, and the areas around Soissons, Compiegne and Noyon were strewn with scattered fires. Meanwhile, the

Battles of 12 Squadron bombed Trier airfield and one crew dropped their load on a number of searchlights that were endangering the raiders to the north-east of Trier.

Nos.142 and 150 Squadrons were operating too, from Échemines. S/Ldr Wiggy Wight and his crew carried a bomb load of sixteen 25-lb (11-kg) incendiaries, which they released in two open sticks from 6,000 feet (1,800 m) on vehicles and troop concentration in Forêt de Saint-Gobain, west of Laon. They spent half-an-hour over the target area watching 'two large and several small fires burning merrily'. Afterwards, they returned via the beacons at Troyes and Orleans but, at Orleans, French ack-ack opened up with heavy fire despite being given the proper recognition signals.

On the 9th, although several Battle squadrons sent aircraft to Échemines for standby during the day, no sorties were flown because poor weather prevented the finding of targets. The only RAF bombers operating in daylight were Blenheims from No.2 Group that flew across from airfields in England. Unfortunately, communications between Britain and France were already breaking down badly. By the time the Blenheim squadrons had taken off and flown across to their target areas, the actual targets, usually troops and armoured vehicles, were often no longer present; they'd had plenty of time to move on.

The new so-called Battle of the Somme was quickly turning into a rout. It seemed that there could be a complete collapse of the front at any moment as German troops occupied Rouen, Dieppe and Compiègne, and reached the Seine and the Marne. Part of the French 10th Army, which included the British 51st Highland Division, withdrew to the coast at St Valéry hoping to be evacuated.

At least three of the Battle squadrons were able to fly that night. One aircraft failed to return. This was a Battle from 103 Squadron flown by S/Ldr Harold Lee and his crew. It was learned later that the plane's engine had failed and Lee, formerly from Melbourne and already the recipient of an AFC, had to give the order to bail out. His navigator and gunner were unhurt but Lee landed heavily and suffered a compound fracture of the right leg. He was evacuated to Le Mans.

For the Allies, over the next few days the struggle deteriorated towards disaster. The Germans crossed the Seine as the French retired in disorder to the Loire and General Weygand admitted officially that the front had been breached. With Paris increasingly threatened, the French government left the capital for Tours, where news reached them that Italy was about to declare war.

At 4.30 p.m on 10 June, the Italian Foreign Minister, Count Galeazzo Ciano, son-in-law of the dictator Benito Mussolini, received the French ambassador at the Palazzo Chigi in Rome and informed him, 'Italy considers itself in a state of war with effect from tomorrow, 11 June.' Fifteen minutes later, Ciano sent a similar declaration of war to the British ambassador.

France was in disarray. *Armée de l'Air* fighters normally concerned with defence on the border with Italy had long since been thrown into the battle in the north. Bitter disagreement broke out between the French military and political leaders. General Weygand considered that the French Army was virtually defeated and argued that they should surrender but Premier Paul Reynaud thought a final stand should be made in Brittany.

On the next day, the 11th, cut off as it was to the east and west by the enemy and considered impossible to defend by its military governor, Paris was declared an open city. For their part, the Germans announced by radio that if the French wanted them to recognise the status of Paris as an open city, they required the cessation of all French military resistance north of a line across Saint Germain, Versailles, Juvisy, Saint-Maur and Meaux. This condition was agreed to by the French so the capital would escape the devastation that had been inflicted on other major cities such as Warsaw and Rotterdam. Meanwhile, as the Germans advanced into central France, Rheims also fell into their hands.

At the same time, the French were pleading for more British support, particularly in the air, but Winston Churchill had to refuse. The RAF force's slender fighter strength needed to be carefully husbanded for the increasingly likely battle over Britain in the near future. Nevertheless a second BEF of two divisions, including the 1st Canadian Division which had been in Britain since December 1939, was promised to be sent Cherbourg to bolster the French with the idea of supporting a redoubt in Brittany.

To cross the Seine with its bridges blocked, damaged or destroyed, the Germans brought forward their highly successful pontoon bridges and began assembling them. It was against these, plus various troop concentrations and convoys, that the AASF Fairey Battle squadrons now had to launch attacks day and night. Pontoon bridges at Les Andelys, St Pierre and Le Manoir were particularly targeted but frequently the fliers experienced especially bad weather, fog and smoke from burning villages, sometimes all three.

With daylight attacks being made in the face of heavy anti-aircraft fire and patrolling Me109s and Me110s, there was a corresponding increase in AASF losses, and 226 Squadron was not spared. On the 11th, Battle K9176 crashed at Saint-Pierre-d'Autils, 2 miles (3 km) north-west of Vernon. This aircraft was flown by one of Bob Bungey's close friends, nineteen-year-old Sgt Gerald McLoughlin and his crew, who were all killed.

That night, Bob, Sgt Bingham and Cpl Smith took off in Battle L5452 and bombed woods near St Andelys where enemy troops and armoured vehicles were reported to be sheltering. S/Ldr Wiggy Wight of 142 Squadron was up as well to raid enemy concentrations in woods in the nearby Vernon area, but the weather turned bad and he had to turn back without bombing. One other 142 Squadron Battle failed to return and the crew was reported missing.

During the tragic Wednesday 12th, the British 51st Highland Division and four French divisions were forced to surrender at St Valéry after holding out for as long as possible. The AASF's bombing efforts for the day were mainly directed in support of these trapped troops, or against areas near the Seine crossings.

At dawn, nine Battles were ordered to attack a pontoon bridge reported to be south of St Andelys but when they arrived it could not be found so they bombed nearby roads and woods instead. Meanwhile, the French requested urgent attacks on bridges north of Senlis in the area of the Oise River. Several Battles, covered by *Armée de l'Air* fighters, found three pontoon bridges at Verberie Pont Pointe and to the south of Chevrières and claimed all of them destroyed, but not without cost. One Battle was shot down and another had to make a forced landing on a bomb-damaged French airfield at Mitry-Moray. Both planes were from 88 Squadron.

The French residents of the aerodrome were anxiously burning their remaining aircraft and preparing to evacuate, so the 88 Squadron pilot, P/O James Talmon, who would later receive the DFC, set fire to his crippled Battle and he and his gunner left with the French. He finally met up with 88 Squadron again at Brest on the 16th.

Talmon told what had happened to the other Battle. He described how he had seen the aircraft, Battle L5334 flown by F/Lt Alan Pitfield and his gunner, attack the northern end of one of the bridges. Then, amid an intense barrage of light and heavy AA ground fire, it had disappeared below the level of rows of trees nearby. Neither Alan Pitfield nor his gunner survived the resulting crash. So was killed the man who, back in January 1938, had taken Bob up in a Fairey Battle for the very first time. His DFC was recorded in the *London Gazette* of 30 June 1940.

No operations were flown owing to bad weather on the night of 12/13 June but daylight brought better conditions, which further improved throughout the day. The Fairey Battle units flew missions in the morning and the afternoon. Six aircraft from 142 Squadron flew an early armed reconnaissance of the Seine area including Vernon, Pacy, and Evreux, dropping bombs on forested areas believed to be providing cover for enemy troops.

At 10.45 a.m., three more of the squadron's Battles, led by F/Lt John Hewson, took off to attack armoured vehicles and troop concentrations seen moving along the Pacy – Vernon – Rouen roads. Hewson's crew members were Sgt Kitto and LAC Utteridge. Richard Kitto had been a member of John Hobler's crew back on 14 May when four out of eight Battles from 142 Squadron had failed to return from an attack on bridges between Sedan and Mouzon. Hobler had successfully crash-landed but suffered serious facial burns. Neither Kitto nor the gunner had been injured – at that time.

Led by Hewson, the three Battles found and attacked German columns and troops around Rouen. After bombing along the road, they were bounced by Messerschmitt 109s and 110s. All were shot up. One crashed, the second struggled home carrying a wounded crewman and the third, John Hewson's machine, burst into flames and he gave the order to bail out. Richard Kitto escaped by parachute but the gunner, LAC Utteridge, was wounded and unable to extricate himself. Realising that Utteridge could not bail out, Hewson ignored the fire and brought the Battle down to a successful forced landing. Utteridge, who was later awarded a DFM, was taken to Le Mans hospital but did not leave France. He was still in hospital when the Germans arrived and became a POW. After seeing his gunner safely into hospital, Hewson made his way back to the aerodrome at Faux-Villecerf. He received a DFC. Richard Kitto made his way to St Malo and was subsequently returned to the UK.

Later in afternoon at various times between 5.00 and 6.00 p.m., Battles from 12, 88, 103, 142, 150 and 226 Squadrons took off in a maximum effort to bomb tanks reported to be refuelling at a petrol dump in the woods near Montmirial. Existing records show that 12 Squadron contributed six machines and 142 Squadron five, and that the total number of aircraft involved was twenty-six, but how many of these actually came from each of the other squadrons is unclear. Bob Bungey and his crew were flying Battle L5419 in 226 Squadron's formation and all of the aircraft were carrying incendiary bombs.

By now the weather was fine and warm, with hardly a cloud in the sky but the Battles had to operate without escorts. No.88 Squadron was first away, despite receiving orders at midday for it to move and make its base at another airfield that evening. The Battle formation encountered Me109s. At least three Battles were attacked and one was shot down, its two-man crew escaping with wounds.

When 142 Squadron's aircraft were some distance from the target, at least a dozen Me109s dived on them from out of the sun. The Messerschmitts appeared to be armed with cannons and machine guns. The Battles scattered and one fell in flames. Others had varying degrees of damage. No.12 Squadron suffered most. No tanks were seen but incendiaries were dropped on the south side of the forest and on other woods nearby. The Battles were greeted by intense AA fire, and then the Me109s turned up. Out of the squadron's six Battles, three were shot down.

The loss of one aircraft, Battle P2161, has been recorded on this day for 226 Squadron and it is assumed that it occurred on this operation. It was shot down in the battle area near La Chapelle-Moutils, 18 miles (30 km) north-west of Provins. The members of the crew were apparently Sgt E. E. Hopkins, Sgt James Callaghan and Sgt Leslie Turner, all of whom were killed. Bob Bungey's Log Book shows that for him, the mission lasted 5 minutes during the 2 hours from beginning to end. He made a typically brief note in the book, just saying, '16 incendiaries dropped on petrol dump in wood at Montmirial.'

Out of the twenty-six Battles that had been despatched, seventeen succeeded in bombing. Considering the number of German aircraft about, and the intensity of the ground fire, it was obvious that the reports describing the enemy's location had been accurate. A large part of the forest was set on fire and, although few tanks were seen, something like an ammunition dump or fuel dump appeared to have been hit. It seems probable that some sort of an offensive was being prepared, possibly a final push. Altogether, six AASF Battles failed to return.

That day Prime Minister Winston Churchill was visiting Tours where he learned that General Weygand was pressing for an immediate armistice and even Paul Reynaud was pleading to be released from France's pledge to Britain not to treat separately with the Germans. The time had arrived for the British to start getting out of France before the country totally collapsed.

So far, British organisation in the south of France was still fairly safe from immediate threat from the German Army. In the brief lull before the enemy's new offensive on 5 June, Air Marshal Barratt had acted with great foresight by withdrawing his AASF from the south Champagne district to the region around Orleans and Le Mans. From this central position, and with its refuelling bases kept in south Champagne, the AASF had been well positioned to operate along the whole length of the battle line. But that all had changed when, on 11 June, the enemy broke through the French positions on the Marne, Oise and Seine. This had been the last line on which any realistic expectation of a successful defence could have been developed. Now every AASF unit was faced with mounting peril.

By 12 June, the Deputy Chief of Air Staff of the RAF, AVM Sholto Douglas, and A/M Barratt were communicating on preparing for a quick withdrawal from France. The next thing was to withdraw towards the west coast. New bases were obtained near Angers, Saumur, Rennes and Nantes, but as the enemy spread through France, the few remaining airfields became more and more congested. When the Hurricanes of No.1 Squadron moved to Nantes it was so crowded with aircraft that 'it looked like several Empire Air Days all at once'. To stay there for very long was to simply provide juicy targets for the *Luftwaffe*. Barratt reasoned that his bombers could operate from bases in England anyway, and it would be safer to do just that. Bearing this in mind, he instructed his Fairey Battle squadrons to fly home on 15 June.

Before this, on the 14th, Bob's squadron lost another plane and crew in the hunt for German tanks and troop concentrations. The Battle crashed at Breux-sur-Avre, 9 miles (15 km) south-east of Breteuil under unknown circumstances. Sometimes Battles were flown by a crew of two men instead of the usual three. The deaths of F/O Ken Rea, a New Zealander, and Sgt Frank Nixon have been recorded. If there was a third crewmember, his name and fate remains unknown. This was the day the Germans entered Paris.

Complying with A/M Barrett's orders, during the 15th all light and heavy anti-aircraft guns were removed from Sougé airfield leaving it to be defended by only a few mounted Lewis guns. At 7.00 a.m., a German reconnaissance aircraft circled the base. Its presence heralded the strong likelihood of air raids to follow and it stayed out of range of the Lewis gunners, much to their frustration.

Most of the ground staff of Nos.12, 103 and 226 Squadrons left, taking with them all the surplus equipment and spares that were possible. By stripping parts from other damaged and written-off machines, the skeleton ground staff that stayed behind endeavoured to patch up some of the u/s aircraft to make them flyable enough to reach England. These were the dramatic circumstances under which Bob had to test the airworthiness of Battle P2331.

It was thought desirable to move to an alternative site or withdraw. At 10.00 a.m., three Battles from 103 Squadron were despatched to carry out a reconnaissance of the area, searching for an alternative, secure landing ground. When they returned the crews reported that the airfield looked unoccupied from the air and so there was probably no immediate danger. They were wrong.

Wisely, orders were received from 76 Wing to destroy all remaining stores, equipment and damaged aircraft prior to imminent withdrawal to England. These instructions were carried out and the airfield's fuel dump was set on fire. Meanwhile, selected aircrews were instructed to fly the surviving aircraft back to England where they were to land at Abingdon in Berkshire. It meant a 3-hour flight away from German-held French territory across the English Channel before reaching home and safety.

By noon, twenty Battles from the three squadrons were considered able to be flown, but those who were rostered to take them up knew that it could be a risky business. Some planes were in questionable condition. Bob was not preparing to take off in Battle P2331. Instead he was at the controls of Battle K9351, one of the oldest machines on the base. Sgt Bingham and Cpl Smith were with him as usual. One by one, the aircraft taxied out and began taking off.

Most of the Battles had gone when Sougé was raided shortly afterwards by nine Do17s. Without any opposition save the paltry Lewis guns, the Dorniers were able to bomb with impunity and circle the airfield at will, machine-gunning everything in sight. Bombs exploded all over the airfield, destroying any damaged and u/s planes still on the ground. There were nine casualties among the ground personnel.

Another attack was made on Sougé later in the afternoon, but by that time the airfield was almost abandoned. The rear parties from 12 and 226 Squadrons had already left and a final inspection was in progress before the remainder headed for an evacuation port.

In the mid-afternoon, 3 hours after taking off, the surviving aircraft, including Battle K9351, reached Abingdon and began landing. For the AASF pilots and crews that touched down, the physical and mental relief was almost palpable. They had all flown and fought against overwhelming odds, and survived. Too many others had not.

The end of France was about to come and the RAF's Advanced Air Strike Force was almost no more.

7

145 Squadron RAF

By late afternoon on 15 June 1940, Bob could see that as well as those from 226 Squadron, there were Battles from 103 and 105 Squadrons scattered around the Abingdon airfield. Most of 105 had already moved on to Honington in Suffolk. No.103 was scheduled to go there too the next day. Meanwhile in Yorkshire, No.12 Squadron was down at Finningley and 88 Squadron, which had left France the day before, was already over at Driffield. No.142 Squadron had moved to Waddington in Lincolnshire. One Battle out of 142 Squadron's thirteen aircraft which had taken off for the UK had not arrived but it was known that it had force-landed safely at Rennes.

No.226 Squadron could not stay at Abingdon either. The airfield was far too crowded and much too busy. After being refuelled and checked, Bob (still flying Battle K9351) and the others took off and headed for Dishforth in Yorkshire, where they landed just over an hour-and-a-half later. It was here that the squadron would start to regroup and reorganise. There would also be time for some well-earned leave while waiting for the ground staff to rejoin them from France – those people who had transferred to the evacuation ports and those who had stayed behind at work until the last moment.

For these people, particularly if transfer by air could not be worked out, departure from France was far from easy. With the surviving Battles and Blenheims back in England, it was up to the remaining AASF fighters to cover the last British forces as they evacuated. Besides the leftover RAF ground staff, these included three British Army divisions under the command of Lt/Gen. Alan Brooke.

The problem was political too. Officially so far, a full evacuation had not yet been ordered. When the order did come – if it came – Barratt would need to cover seven French ports with just five squadrons of Hurricanes. There was now no conceivable military justification for retaining British forces in France, but there was a real fear that withdrawal would prejudice the French against continuing to fight on the British side from North Africa.

Meanwhile, on 16 June, France's ministers in desperation entrusted the fate of their country to Marshal Henri Philippe Pétain, the elderly statesman and victor of Verdun in the First World War. Pétain had been agitating for the premiership since 5 June. As soon as he was in power, he set out to negotiate a peace settlement with Germany. His approach to the Germans on the 17th was the signal for the British to totally withdraw the last of their forces.

To protect them from marauding *Luftwaffe* bombers while evacuating, the AASF had only its last Hurricanes and some anti-aircraft batteries. The Hurricanes flew at first from French airfields until they were in danger of being overrun, then from the Channel Islands. They were not completely alone. Fighter aircraft from southern England also helped over Cherbourg, while RAF Coastal Command planes protected the returning vessels at sea.

Meagre though these defences were, for the most part they were effective, but off Saint-Nazaire there was a major disaster. On the afternoon of 17 June, German bombers managed to elude the patrolling Hurricanes and sink the *Lancastria* with 5,000 troops and RAF personnel aboard. So serious was this tragedy that news of it was not revealed to the British public until after the war.

Nevertheless, by the afternoon of the 18th, the British forces had made good their escape. Nearly 200,000 men, mostly British, were evacuated to England. The Hurricane fighter pilots, most of whom had flown six sorties the previous day, could also now depart in whatever aircraft were still able to fly. As at Dunkirk, a great deal of equipment and stores had to be destroyed or abandoned. Of the 261 Hurricanes that had been committed to France, only sixty-six were able to be flown back to England in the middle of June. Altogether, RAF Fighter Command had lost a quarter of its existing strength.

Meanwhile, Pétain's plea for peace led to total surrender. In the Forest of Compiègne on 22 June, in the same railway carriage that had been used for signing the Armistice of 1918, when Germany had lost, the Treaty with Nazi Germany was signed. France was now defeated and Germany was the master of Western Europe.

Winston Churchill had been Britain's prime minister for little over a month when he announced on 18 June:

> What General Weygand called the Battle of France is over. I expect that the Battle of Britain is about to begin ... The whole fury and might of the enemy must very soon be turned on us. Hitler knows that he will have to break us in this island or lose the war. If we can stand up to him, all Europe may be free and the life of the world may move forward into broad sunlit uplands. But if we fail, then the whole world, including the United States, including all that we have known and cared for, will sink into the abyss of a new Dark Age made more sinister, and perhaps more protracted, by the lights of perverted science. Let us therefore brace ourselves to our duties, and so bear ourselves that, if the British Empire and its Commonwealth last for a thousand years, men will still say, 'This was their finest hour'.

Nearly a month later, on 16 July, three days before a bogus offer of peace, Adolf Hitler issued his top secret Directive No.16, 'Preparations for a Landing Operation against England'. It was to be an ambitious combined operation, involving the German Navy, Army and Air Force, code-named *Seelöwe* (Sea Lion). In his directive, the *Führer* said, 'The aim of this operation is to eliminate Great Britain as a base from which the war against Germany can be continued, and, should it be necessary, to occupy the country completely.'

The landing area was to be on a broad 200-mile (320-km) front along England's south and south-east coast. The army was to assemble and train the invasion troops. The navy was to sweep the English Channel free of mines and lay a protective minefield on each side of the invasion fleet's path. It was also to ferry the army and its supplies across the Channel to the beaches at Ramsgate and Folkestone, Hastings, Brighton, Worthing and the Isle of Wight, and as far away as Lyme Bay in Dorset.

This huge, widespread task was in reality far beyond the German navy's capability, particularly with the Royal Navy and Royal Air Force still intact. Hitler's admirals made more practical counterproposals for landings on a narrow front but still only under the security of an air umbrella. The success of any such operation depended on *Reichsmarschall* Herman Göring's *Luftwaffe*. The *Luftwaffe* needed to wipe out the RAF, as it had wiped out the air forces of Poland, Norway, Holland, Belgium and France, or at least be able to secure and maintain air supremacy over a portion of England's south or south-east coast.

The admirals also emphasised that the only vessels available to transfer troops across the English Channel were slow canal barges and river barges, commandeered from the Dutch and French. Tugs and motorboats would be needed to tow them across the open sea and push them onto the beaches.

In July, large numbers of barges began moving along the rivers and canals of Western Europe heading towards the English Channel and North Sea ports: Dunkirk, Calais, Boulogne, Le Havre and Cherbourg on the French coast; Antwerp and Ostend in Belgium; and Rotterdam in Holland. On reaching their destinations, their bows were removed, concrete floors were laid in their hulls and ramps were attached so that vehicles could be driven on and off them. Meanwhile, workmen busily repaired the roads and railways, cleared the canals and built storehouses for the enormous quantities of ammunition and supplies that were needed. Operation *Seelöwe* was swiftly turning into a real possibility. The *Führer* ordered the invasion fleet to be ready for launching by 15 August.

Also in July, aerial activity increased sharply over the English Channel as the *Luftwaffe* strove to close this shipping lane by sinking the commercial vessels sailing on it and smashing harbours from Dover to Southampton. This had the effect of drawing the defending RAF fighters into action. The destruction of Fighter Command was essential to obtain air superiority prior to any invasion attempt being staged so by drawing the Hurricanes and Spitfires up to intercept the attacks against shipping, the attrition had begun.

Losses began to mount on both sides but this was especially a matter of grave concern for Air Chief Marshal Sir Hugh Dowding, the officer in charge of Fighter Command. Dowding was fully aware that he could not afford to waste his fighter strength before the heavy attacks that obviously were to come in the near future. He needed every man and every plane and only grudgingly allowed them to be committed to battle. His instructions were that enemy fighter formations were not to be heavily engaged, the main defence effort was to be directed against bombers, and RAF fighters were forbidden to operate over France.

Fighter Command under Dowding was divided into four groups:

- Covering south-eastern England and to bear the brunt of the *Luftwaffe's* attacks was 11 Group, commanded by the resourceful New Zealander, Air Vice-Marshal Keith Park.
- Behind 11 Group, covering the Midlands, was AVM Trafford Leigh-Mallory's 12 Group.
- Covering the south-west coast and Wales was 10 Group under AVM Sir Quinton Brand.
- AVM Richard Saul's 13 Group defended northern England and Scotland against the *Luftwaffe* threat from Norway and Denmark.

Following *Reichsmarschall* Göring's orders, the emphasis on anti-shipping raids was continued. These attacks were carried out by *Luftflotte 2* (Air Fleet 2) from bases in Holland, Belgium and north-east France under the command of *Generalfeldmarschall* Albrecht Kesselring, and *Luftflotte 3* in north-west France, commanded by *Generalfeldmarschall* Hugo Sperrle. *Luftflotte 5* (Air Fleet 2) under *Generaloberst* Hans-Jürgen Stumpff threatened from bases in Norway and Denmark.

On 25 July, Kesselring's aircraft attacked a coastal convoy in the Straits of Dover after shadowing it from the Thames Estuary. At the same time, German surface craft also engaged, but were driven off. They returned again at night. Out of twenty-one ships, eleven were sunk or badly damaged. Next day the Admiralty suspended merchant traffic through the Straits in daylight.

At the end of the month, Dowding at least received some encouraging news. The aircraft industry under Lord Beaverbrook was making a maximum effort in the production of fighters. Hurricanes and Spitfires were rolling off the assembly lines at a rate well above official estimates. In May, output figures exceeded estimates by 23%; in June, output was up by an astounding 53%; and in July the output was still up by 51%. More than 1,200 fighters had been delivered since 1 May.

The pilot situation was far more difficult to remedy. Trained fighter pilots were urgently needed, but they took time to train – time for him to become proficient and time for him to become experienced in combat. The situation became critical as the battle progressed as the pilot loss rate exceeded the replacement rate. Lost experienced pilots from operational squadrons were being replaced by new pilots who only had 12–14 hours on Hurricanes or Spitfires.

And there was the sneaking, sinister problem of fatigue. This manifested itself in errors of judgement, frayed nerves and increased accidents, which could in turn lead to nervous breakdown. Dowding was well aware of the fatigue faced by his airmen and he ruled that pilots must have a minimum of 8 hours off duty in every 24 hours, and a continuous 24 hours off each week.

By the middle of August the situation was worse. Over a period of ten days ending on the 17th, more than 150 fighter pilots had been killed, wounded or were missing. If the same loss rate continued until the end of the month, Dowding would be down by 300–350 pilots. With only seventy to eighty replacements due to complete training by the end of the month, it was inevitable that his squadrons would be bled dry. To boost numbers in this emergency, it was agreed to cut operational training to a minimum, just enough to give the new young men some basic knowledge of the aircraft they would be flying into combat. The dangers of this measure were obvious but such risks had to be taken.

As another possibility, Dowding requested that pilots be transferred to him from Bomber Command. The Air Ministry pledged fifty volunteers. Five of them came from 226 Squadron. The squadron's Operations Record Book entry for 18 August recorded:

> Flying Officer R. W. Bungay [*sic*], Flying Officer Leggate, Pilot Officer D. A. Crooks DFC, Pilot Officer A. R Covington and Sgt Groves (all pilots) left at short notice to report to Fighter Command on posting.

No.226 Squadron, still flying Fairey Battles, had moved to Sydenham in County Down, Northern Ireland, just east of Belfast, on 27 June where it was retraining and flying a few patrols. It was well away from the dramatic events taking place over southern England. The keeper of the squadron's Operations Record Book frequently noted at this time: 'A quiet and uneventful day' interspaced with inspections, parades and training exercises. While there was relief in being safe, to aircrews accustomed to the danger and adrenalin rush of combat, this was dull and frustrating. They could not hit back and make the Germans pay for what they had done to France and for what they were now doing to England.

Other Battle squadrons were facing the same situation – training, parades and the inevitable frustration; however, stories were filtering through that some Battle squadrons were starting to retaliate. They were bombing barges in the Channel ports along the coast of France.

It was at the end of July that Bob Bungey heard shocking news: Wally Blom was dead! There had been a terrible accident. Wally's unit, 150 Squadron, was at Newton airfield in Nottinghamshire where the tragedy happened mid-afternoon on the 27th. As his plane, Battle L5528, was being made ready for operations, a flare suddenly dropped to the ground and burst into flames. With devastating speed, fire spread rapidly out of control despite every effort to quell the flames by those aboard the aircraft, the ground crews and headquarters staff. The bombs detonated. Six people were killed by the blast and five others were injured, one so severely that he died the following day. Included among the dead was F/Lt Walter Blom from Battery Point in Hobart. Wally was one of the Tasmanians in Bob's Point Cook class. Not only that, he had won the DFC for his courageous mission on the day the Germans invaded. Now he was gone. He had survived the fighting in France only to be killed in a wretched accident.

In truth, the young men who had come to England on the *Orama* after Point Cook were being decimated. Besides Wally Blom, Les Clisby, Bob's close friend from Adelaide who had shown so much promise, had been killed in France; Johnny Lewis from Sydney had been shot down on his first operation in a Wellington, a daylight job over the Heligoland Bight last December; John Sadler's Hampden flight from 144 Squadron had been completely wiped out in the same area two months earlier; Bill Edwards was still missing after four of 107 Squadron's Blenheims had failed to return on 12 May; Jack Kennedy's Hurricane had stalled and crashed when he swerved to avoid high power lines while trying to force land after disposing of a Do17 on 13 July; Stuart Walch, who was in the same squadron as Kennedy, was killed on 11 August when his section ran into a huge formation of Me109s – his Hurricane was last seen plunging into Lyme Bay; and two nights after that during a daring low-level, precision bombing attack on the vital Dortmund/Ems Canal, Rossy Ross DFC had been killed and Allan Mulligan was listed as missing.

As for the others, they were spread all over the place. Greg Graham who had flown Lysander co-op planes in France was somewhere back in England again; Neil Messervy was rumoured to be involved with secret, special high-flying Spitfires; and Bob Reed was flying Hampden bombers with 50 Squadron. Hunter had apparently been sent back to Australia under a black cloud before the war. And out of all the rest, Allan Farrington, Arthur Hubbard and Charley Fry were known to be somewhere in the Middle East or East Africa – God knows what was happening to them down there now, with Italy in the war.

At least the call to Fighter Command brought with it a chance to fight back. Bob and the others who volunteered were distributed all over the place to squadrons that were being 'rested' from combat. Percy Leggate was posted to an auxiliary squadron, No.615 at Prestwick in Ayrshire, Scotland; Aubrey Covington went to 238 Squadron at St Eval in Cornwall; Harry Groves, a Londoner, joined No.3 Squadron at Wick in Scotland; and John Hewson went to 616 Squadron; but Bob lost track of David Crooks, the pilot who had been interviewed with him in France during mid-May by the BBC reporter Charles Gardiner. Bob's transfer on 18 August was to 79 Squadron at Acklington near Alnwick in Northumberland, but the following day that posting was changed to 145 Squadron at Drem near Edinburgh – he would be going further north, back to Scotland again.

No.145 Squadron had been originally formed late in the First World War in Palestine and it became operational with SE5 Scouts during the final offensive of September 1918. Its role then in co-operation with No.111 Squadron and No.1 Squadron, Australian Flying Corps, was to maintain standing patrols over the enemy airfield at Jenin to keep the German aircraft grounded. It was disbanded on 6 September 1919. The squadron reformed at Croydon on 10 October 1939 as a day/night-fighter unit equipped with Blenheim Ifs. In March 1940, it started converting to Hurricanes and in May became operational, ferrying Hurricanes to France and supporting the squadrons there. Its first action took place over France on 18 May when it engaged twelve He111s.

During June and July, flying from Tangmere and Westhampnett in Sussex, 145 Squadron was one of the units bearing the brunt of the fighting over coastal convoys moving through the English Channel. Its heaviest combats took place on 8 August when it engaged three large *Luftwaffe* raids on Convoy *Peewit* off Portland and lost four planes and four pilots in the process. Despite these losses, its pilots claimed nine Ju87 *Stukas*, two Me110s and four Me109Es destroyed. Since the beginning of August the squadron had lost thirteen aircraft and eleven pilots killed. Six days later it was withdrawn north to Drem to rest and rebuild.

There were many new replacement pilots coming in. On the 17th, the same day Bob was flying his last Fairey Battle patrol over Ireland with 226 Squadron, three Belgian pilots arrived at Drem and reported to the station adjutant. They were P/Os Jean Offenberg, Baudouin de Hemptinne and Alexis Jottard, all of whom had made dramatic escapes from the Continent making their way to Britain to join the RAF. After the usual introductions and entering their names in the Arrivals Book, the adjutant informed them, 'You are now attached to the station at Drem, No 145 Squadron 'B' Flight.'

Jean Offenberg, who was acting as spokesman because of his better English, asked, 'Who's in command of 145?'

'Adrian Boyd,' he was told.[1] F/Lt Adrian 'Ginger' Boyd had been posted to 145 Squadron as a flight commander in October 1939 and he saw action over the French coast and Dunkirk late in May. He was awarded a DFC on 21 June, and while flying three sorties during the big air battles on 8 August he claimed five enemy aircraft destroyed and one damaged. A bar to his DFC was awarded on the 13th, just two days before the squadron withdrew to Scotland. Boyd had taken over when the CO, S/Ldr John Peel (who was also awarded a DFC on the 13th) was injured and temporarily posted to command RAF Hunsdon in Hertfordshire. Boyd's first task as acting CO's was to oversee the squadron's build up back to strength. The adjutant also informed the Belgians that they would not be meeting their new comrades just yet because they were all on well-deserved leave.

'Who's in command of our Flight?' asked Offenberg.

'"B" Flight, wait a minute.' The adjutant rummaged in one of his drawers and brought out a bundle of papers. He pulled out a sheet on which was typed a list of names.

'"B" Flight – let's see. Oh yes. Boyd. No, I'm wrong. Boyd's in command of the squadron now since he replaced Johnny Peel who was wounded and brought down on the 8th. I don't think there's a flight commander yet for "B" Flight. But never mind,' he said philosophically, 'they'll choose the best fellow they've got.'

The newcomers were accustomed to the rigid regulations of the Belgian Air Force. Baudouin de Hemptinne, remarked, 'They've only got to appoint the senior in rank.'

'You're wrong there,' said the adjutant, 'It's wartime and a man's rank has nothing to do with it, unless he happens to be the best. You'll see, it will be the best pilot who will be given "B" Flight.'

He also told the Belgians with a smile, 'The squadron as a whole has a scoreboard with forty swastikas. They're terrific fellows, the boys of 145. A bit rough, but you'll soon find that they're a fine bunch.'

Two days later, on the 19th, there was another new arrival, F/O Paul Rabone, a New Zealander from Auckland who would, perhaps intentionally, be called 'Rawbone' by Offenberg. Formerly with 88 Squadron, he, like Bob, had flown Fairey Battles in France. On one occasion while returning from a raid on the Maastricht Bridges, his aircraft was severely damaged by flak. He and his crew bailed out but landed behind enemy lines. In the confused situation, they managed to acquire civilian clothes, join a refugee column and reach Dieppe after a five-day trek. From here they flew back to England and rejoined 88 Squadron in France again three days later. On 12 June, while attacking a bridge on the Seine, Rabone's Battle was shot down by a Messerschmitt 109. He and his crew successfully bailed out again and were able to rejoin the squadron before it evacuated on the 15th. Back in England, he too had answered the call for volunteers to join Fighter Command.

While Rabone and the Belgians were settling in to their totally new surroundings (Alexis Jottard even found time to go trout fishing) and enjoying the sights of nearby Edinburgh, F/O Bob Bungey arrived at Drem on the 20th. He found it a pleasant village nestled in the foothills on the south shore of the Firth of Forth Estuary. It felt like he was coming to a peacetime airfield on a fine summer's day. Heather covering the slopes of the hills in the distance painted the landscape 'a velvety purple beneath the sunny August sky'. Arriving the same day was another new pilot, Sgt Duncan Sykes.

Bob was attached to 'A' Flight which had recently been put into the capable hands of Acting F/Lt Richard Rowley, pending his promotion to full flight lieutenant. Dick Rowley had joined the Auxiliary Air Force in 1937 and like so many of the RAF's 'weekend fliers' had been called up for full-time service in August 1939, just before hostilities began. His current job was checking out the newcomers and assessing their ability to fly Hurricanes.

There were advantages in having former Fairey Battle pilots coming into Fighter Command to fly Hurricanes, Spitfires or even two-seater Defiants. All these types were powered by the same Rolls-Royce Merlin II or Merlin III engine. The newcomers were already familiar with it. But the engine did not have to work so hard in fighters until combat. Instead of needing to carry a Battle's three-man crew, fuel, two guns and a load of bombs; a Hurricane carried just one man, fuel and eight machine guns. Instead of lumbering heavily along at only 200 mph (320 km/hr), a Hurricane could hurtle along at more than 300 mph (480 km/hr).

Bob's Log Book shows that he flew a Hawker Hurricane for the first time on Thursday the 22nd. This was Hurricane Mk I R4177, a machine that was powered by a Rolls-Royce Merlin III engine and had actually been built under contract by Gloster Aircraft Co. Ltd at Brockworth. The Hurricane looked big and strong, but after the Fairey Battle Bob found it was easy to fly and the controls were light. He spent the day getting the 'feel' of his new mount by carrying out three sessions of circuits and bumps. On Friday, after another session of circuits and landings, he commenced a busy schedule of formation flying practice in the No.2 and No.3 positions.

The squadron's other pilots had arrived back from leave by the 21st and the first unit get-together was noted in Jean Offenberg's biography, *Lonely Warrior*:

On the 21st of August the whole squadron was present in the mess when the three Belgians came in to lunch. They were exactly as Offenberg had imagined them – young, noisy and gay. They wore their tunics over pullovers without collar or tie and flying boots. The introductions were quickly made. Jean could not catch all the strange sounding names as he shook hands: Storrar, Dunning-White, Sykes, Honor, Weir, Newling, Faure ... A young fair-haired rather short youth came up to Offenberg, put out his hand and said: 'I'm Franck Weber,' and added in rather halting French 'Welcome to 145. I am Czech and I served in France.'

Offenberg's notes – narratives that he wrote down in three old dog-eared notebooks such as 'one buys in a general store in the suburbs of a great city' – were based on his memory and it seems to be faulty here. Bob may or may not have been present, but if he was the Belgian did not refer to him. He did, however, mention Duncan Sykes who had arrived on the same day as Bob. It could well be that the name 'Bungey' was among 'all the strange sounding names' that Offenberg 'could not catch' on this lively occasion. However, in mentioning Franck Weber at this juncture, Offenberg's memory is definitely faulty. Records show that the Czechoslovakian, P/O Frantisek Weber, could not have been present as he actually joined 145 Squadron at Drem three weeks later, on 11 September. Possibly adding further to Offenberg's confusion, an Englishman with the same surname, Sgt Jack Weber, joined 145 Squadron at Tangmere two months later on 13 October.

Likewise, F/O Dudly Honor, an Anglo-Argentine, could not have been present either as he actually joined 145 Squadron after the get-together too, on 28 August. He was, in fact, another pilot who had flown Fairey Battles in France. He had been with 88 Squadron, the same unit as the New Zealander, Paul Rabone. He too had volunteered to join Fighter Command and finally turned up at Drem.

The occasion of the first get-together after leave which Offenberg described was undoubtedly lively as there was plenty of cause for celebration. F/O Jim Storrar's award of a DFC had just been announced and P/O Nigel Weir was back and had been recommended for a DFC as well. Storrar had joined 145 Squadron in October 1939 and since Dunkirk, he had claimed at least nine destroyed and shares in a couple of others, plus a couple of probables and damaged as well. Nigel Weir had learned to fly at Oxford University and was another of the Auxiliary Air Force officers who had been called up in August 1939. During the heavy engagements on 8 August, he claimed two Me109s and a *Stuka* destroyed, but three days later he had to force-land his damaged fighter after combat near Swanage. His DFC came through on the 30th.

P/O Mike Newling was a survivor. He'd had to bail out east of Brussels back on 18 May but managed to rejoin 145 Squadron again two days later. After sharing an Me109 and destroying an Me110 over Dunkirk, he shared a He111 on 19 July but his Hurricane was shot up and he had to force-land on Shoreham airfield. On this occasion, he suffered concussion and was admitted to hospital.

The threat for northern England and Scotland was long distance from *Luftflotte 5*, based in Norway and Denmark. Back on 15 August, believing that the RAF's fighter squadrons were concentrated in the south, *Luftflotte 5* had mounted strong assaults across the North Sea but had run into a hornet's nest of 'resting' Spitfire and Hurricane squadrons. The Germans were badly mauled, losing sixteen bombers and seven Me110 fighters. No.145 Squadron had not taken part because at that stage it was in the midst of moving up from the south. So far since then, *Luftflotte 5* had not made any more major daylight attacks, confining its activities instead to irregular light nuisance raids at night and a few sporadic daylight reconnaissance sorties by single aircraft.

As Bob Bungey's first week wore on, his orientation moved from sessions of formation flying to practicing set-piece attacks and beam attacks. Then he took part in alerts to intercept 'bogeys'. These were unidentified aircraft, possibly German reconnaissance planes, near the Scottish coast. There were two alerts on the 28th. In reaction to the first, the Hurricanes were recalled after only 5 minutes, and on the second ground control directed Bob's section over St Abbs but no contact was made.

Bob was particularly busy on the 30th. At first he flew in a Hurricane detachment to his old stamping ground across the Firth of Forth Estuary and up to Montrose where, nearly three years before with No.8 FTS, he'd had his very first flight in an RAF aircraft. During the day there was another alert with the same fruitless result – no interception. Finally, after dark, he practised night flying again for the first time since operations in France, concentrating particularly on 'head lamp landings'. His night flying experience stood him in good stead.

On the last day of the month the Hurricanes took off to intercept more reported bogies and this time three of them were found. They were twin-engined types but as the fighters closed in Bob could see that they did not have German markings. They turned out to be RAF Avro Ansons, probably from a local flying school.

* * *

Down south at the end of August and beginning of September, the Battle of Britain was reaching crisis point. After a month of attacking British coastal shipping and ports throughout July and early in August, the Germans had launched massive daylight air raids on the airfields and coastal defences of south-east England. By the end of the month, No.11 Group, commanded by AVM Keith Park, was fighting for its life – and losing!

The situation was not helped by friction between the key British commanders. Covering south-east England as it did, 11 Group was bearing the brunt of the *Luftwaffe's* attacks and being battered into submission. Behind 11 Group, covering the Midlands, was AVM Trafford Leigh-Mallory's 12 Group, which was the back-up group, but Park and Leigh-Mallory were constantly at loggerheads over tactics. Leigh-Mallory advocated employing 'Big Wings' consisting of from three to five squadrons of Hurricanes and Spitfires against the enemy formations, but it took time for so many fighters to take off and assemble in formation.

Time was a luxury Keith Park did not have – the enemy was much too close, just across the English Channel. His squadrons had to scramble singly or in pairs within minutes and claw for height before the *Luftwaffe* arrived to bomb their airfields. Leigh-Mallory's fighters were supposed to come south on request to cover these airfields but they were often too late and sometimes did not arrive at all. The two groups were operating under completely different conditions, and the *Luftwaffe* raids mounted daily allowed for little respite.

By the evening of 6 September the situation was grim. Between 24 August and 6 September, Fighter Command had lost 295 fighters and 171 were badly damaged. Only 269 new and repaired Hurricanes and Spitfires had come on strength. At the same time, 103 fighter pilots had been killed and 128 wounded, resulting in the average number of pilots per squadron sinking from twenty-six to sixteen. So dire were the circumstances that HQ Home Forces issued its Alert No.3: 'Invasion probable within three days'.

Next day, anticipating the usual airfield attacks, the British defences were taken completely by surprise when the *Luftwaffe* launched massive daylight assaults against London. The docks, warehouses and London's East End were set ablaze and the sky was prematurely darkened by a massive pall of smoke. As night fell, the first of 318 German bombers approached, guided by the fires. By morning, 306 civilians were dead and 1,337 badly injured. It was the beginning of a series of violent attacks on London over the next fifty-seven consecutive nights – the Blitz had arrived.

That night, the British Chiefs of Staff (COS) issued the code word 'Cromwell' for Alert No.1 – 'invasion imminent and probable within twelve hours'. It was received in some places with panic and false alarms. Numerous Home Guard and army units ordered the ringing of church bells, the signal that an invasion had already started. Meanwhile, Bomber Command concentrated on attacking the invasion barges that the Germans had assembled in ports on the Channel coast.

At Drem and Montrose, the only ways to keep informed of what was happening down south were via the newspapers and BBC radio communiqués. These, of course, were laced with propaganda. They reported that RAF fighters were more than holding their own against the *Luftwaffe* by fighting brilliant actions all along the south and south-east coasts. According to them, formations of hundreds of German bombers escorted by Messerschmitts were being intercepted each day and broken up by the defending Hurricanes and Spitfires which made them pay dearly for every bomb they dropped on British soil.

It was as if the two sides were playing a huge game of cricket, a vital home test! Scores were announced daily telling of the enemy aircraft destroyed compared with RAF losses. On 15 August, 180 German aircraft had been shot down for the loss of only thirty-four British fighters. On 31 August, ninety-four German aircraft had been destroyed for the loss of just thirty-seven British fighters. On the day they bombed London, 7 September, 103 German aircraft were destroyed for the loss of just twenty-two British fighters. Then came news of an even greater victory. On 15 September, 185 German aircraft were shot down for the loss of a meagre twenty-five British fighters. On these random days alone, therefore, the Germans had apparently lost 562 aircraft and the British 118 – in other words, it was nearly a 5:1 ratio in favour of the defenders. Clearly, the squadrons being 'rested' up north were out of the 'game' and missing all of the 'fun'![2]

Bob flew two patrols from Montrose on the first day of September in a section with Mike Newling and Sgt Thorpe. Peter Thorpe was another newcomer to 145 Squadron, having arrived at Drem two days after Bob. The trio stayed together flying as a section on alerts and patrols for the first half of the month. When they weren't on these vain searches for bogeys, the normal training continued. On the 7th, Bob took on the role of leader for the first time for formation flying and practicing R/T procedures. On the 10th, there was air-to-ground firing practice (into the water offshore) and two days later, Bob and Peter Thorpe spent time mock dogfighting.

Meanwhile, 145 Squadron had been spread out even further with Adrian Boyd taking a detachment, 'B' Flight, up to Dyce in Scotland's north-east not far from Aberdeen. In this area on 8 September there was a rare encounter with a German reconnaissance bomber. A section of Hurricanes flown by Jim Storrar, Jean Offenberg and Duncan Sykes found an intruder, which they identified as a Dornier Do215, dodging from cloud to cloud. They pounced on it and hits were scored before it managed to disappear back into the ample cloud cover. For 10 more minutes they searched in vain without any luck. The Dornier was counted as 'damaged'.

The squadron's Operations Record Book entry for 19 September reads:

Weather. Fine all day. No operational occurrences to report.

Information was received from No.14 Group that Flight-Lieut A. H. Boyd DFC had been promoted to the rank of Acting Squadron-Leader and appointed to command the Squadron with effect from the 16th September 1940.

Now that Boyd, who was the officer commanding 'B' Flight before CO John Peel had been injured, was finally officially in charge of the squadron, it was time for 'B' Flight's new flight commander to be chosen.

The previous day, the Belgian pilots in the squadron had received a letter with news of their comrades – fliers like them who had escaped to England and joined the RAF, who were, unlike them, in the thick of the fighting down south. Many were close friends, and there had been casualties. It was too much. They felt guilty. Jean Offenberg wrote down in one of his note books, 'Of all the squadrons of Fighter Command we had to be posted to one stationed in the quietest sector of the British Isles while our pals get themselves killed in the South...'

They immediately approached Boyd and asked for a transfer to join their comrades fighting in the south.

Boyd told them not to worry: 'A transfer isn't necessary. In a fortnight we're going back to the old fighter territory.'

'We're leaving for the south?' asked Jean Offenberg.

'Yes, to 11 Group.[3] Does that satisfy you?'

'Yes sir.'

'Well, in the meantime, I've been bequeathed a new commander for "B" Flight ... An Australian named Bungey ... In a day or two you'll fly a Hurricane to Drem ... That one,' he said to Offenberg, pointing to one of the machines.

'No.2683. You'll leave it there and I'll send a Fairey Battle to pick you up. On the way back you'll stop at Montrose, meet Bungey and bring him back here. OK?'

The squadron's Operations Record Book entry for 24 September reads:

Weather. Fair but cloudy. No operational occurrences to report.

Flying Officer R. W. Bungey assumes command of 'B' Flight as he is being promoted to the rank of Flight Lieutenant.

At Montrose that day, it was late in the morning when Bob saw the Fairey Battle he was expecting to take him to Dyce touchdown and taxi off the runway. As it rolled to a halt, he could see two men on board. The pilot was Paul Rabone, the New Zealander, and the other was Jean Offenberg. As ordered by Boyd, the Belgian had delivered Hurricane P2683 to Drem and had to wait there for two days before being picked up. As soon as Rabone and Offenberg stepped down, the Kiwi began insisting that he knew of a nice restaurant for lunch, the George Hotel, but Offenberg was impatient to return to Dyce. Then, he recalled:

An officer in a leather jacket came up, dumped his pack and introduced himself. 'I'm Flight Lieutenant Robert Bungey and you've probably come from Dyce to fetch me. Well I'm all set.'

Rawbone [*sic*] looked at me and I felt that he was going to say that he wasn't by any means ready. But he changed his mind.

'All right. Let's get going then.'

As we walked towards the control tower Bungey, who was walking next to me, said in his odd drawling Australian accent, 'Are you from 145 Squadron?'

'Yes, sir, "B" Flight, yours.'

'By your accent I can tell you're not English,' he said, shifting his valise to his other hand.

'No, I'm Belgian. There are three Belgians in "B" Flight.'

'Have you been in action yet?'

'Yes, I have one German confirmed and a second damaged.' Wishing to change the subject, I added, 'There are also a Czech and an Anglo-Argentine in "B" Flight...'

'Well that's fine. I'm a Digger. We shall be a fine bloody Russian salad and there won't be any chance of getting bored. You can call me Robert or Bob if you like. What's your name? I thought I heard Offenberg just now.'

'Yes, but everyone here calls me Pyker.'

'That's an odd name. What does it mean?'

How difficult it would be to make him understand all the nuances of the Brussels street kids' jargon.

'Oh, I've never really found out,' I replied. 'It's a name they sometimes give in Brussels to boys who are born there. It's unimportant.'

Rawbone flew us to Dyce for lunch despite his desire to visit the *George Hotel* in Montrose. He even managed to put the Battle down as lightly as a feather. A perfect three-point landing...[4]

Late that afternoon, Bob flew a brief orientation patrol with Offenberg and Baudouin de Hemptinne as wingmen.

The 26th was a busy day in which he flew two more patrols with Offenberg and de Hemptinne, and then for good measure he finished off with another patrol of his own at night. All of these sorties were in Hurricane P2696 which carried the identification letters SO-P.

While Bob was catching up on his sleep the next day, more heavy daylight fighting took place in the south with air battles ranging from London to Bristol. Once again the *Luftwaffe* suffered heavy losses. News reports announced that 133 German planes had been brought down for a loss of just twenty-eight RAF fighters.[5] Surely the Germans could not afford such a rate of attrition for much longer.

But there were other reports that were depressing. In Berlin that day representatives of Germany, Italy and Japan signed the Tripartite Pact, a military alliance that recognised the right of the Germans and Italians to establish their 'new order' in Europe and of the Japanese to impose their 'new order' in Asia where there was a risk of clashing with British and American interests.

News of the pact reached Britain while there was a meeting of the War Cabinet. Prime Minister Churchill was quick to point out that the terms of the agreement seem to be designed to safeguard against the possibility of the United States intervening in the war. Britain and the Commonwealth were now even more alone.

September finished. October arrived. Then, at last, it was time. At Dyce early on the morning of Thursday, 10 October, the Hurricanes of 145 Squadron lined up and began taking off. The squadron was going south again – to Tangmere.

8

Tangmere

Construction of an aerodrome near the village of Tangmere in Sussex, 3 miles (5 km) east of Chichester, began during the First World War in 1917. Ironically, the work was carried out with the help of German POWs that were drafted in as labourers and despite opposition from the local population.

At first it was used for training. Three operational squadrons arrived in March 1918 and during the months before the Armistice, Tangmere was loaned to the US forces for flying training. After the war, early in 1919, the aerodrome was closed but the property was retained by the Air Ministry. It was re-opened in June 1925 and No.43 Squadron took up residence in December 1926. No.43 was joined two months later by the newly re-formed No.1 Squadron. Apart from replacing the various types of aircraft being flown there, little changed at Tangmere over the next eleven years.

From 1937 onwards, Tangmere grew as the RAF expanded. New workshops, buildings and barracks were started and 1938 saw the beginning of blast-protection pens around the newly laid perimeter track. As well, construction started on two permanent 1,600- by 50-yard (1,463- by 46-m) runways shaped in the form of a crossed 'T' running north to south and north-east to south-west. These were completed during the autumn of 1939.

In the last week of August 1939, No.217 Squadron, which had arrived with Avro Ansons in 1937, left for Cornwall and in September 1939, No.1 Squadron went to France as one of the two Hawker Hurricane units of the AASF. No.92 Squadron formed at the station with Blenheim fighters and No.43 moved to Acklington the following November. The first winter of the war passed quietly with Nos.501 and 605 Squadrons in residence.

Tangmere had little to do with the fighting in France during May 1940 but the airfield became busier during the evacuation of Dunkirk. Late in June, some *Armée de l'Air* Curtiss P-36 Hawks flew in after the collapse of the French armed forces.

During July 1940 the Tangmere squadrons, at various times Nos.1, 43, 145 and 601, were engaged in the preliminary skirmishes over the English Channel prior to the all-out attacks the *Luftwaffe* launched on *Adlertag*. The 8th of August was No.145 Squadron's day of glory shared throughout day-long battles over the westbound Convoy *Peewit* to a lesser extent with Nos.43 and 601 Squadrons. That same day, 145 Squadron transferred to the satellite aerodrome at Westhampnett.

At 1.00 p.m. on Friday, 16 August, the day after 145 Squadron had departed from Westhampnett for its 'rest and recovery' in the north, Tangmere was the target of a heavy raid by Ju87 *Stuka* dive-bombers. In the space of a few minutes those attackers that reached the aerodrome had inflicted extensive damage. Two hangars were totally destroyed, one of them by fire, and the other three damaged. Seven Hurricanes, six Blenheims and one Magister were either destroyed or damaged, together with nearly forty vehicles. The station's workshops, fire hydrant pump house and a nearby air-raid shelter received direct hits. Also severely damaged were stores, the sick quarters, the Y-service hut, the officers' mess and a Salvation Army hut.

Despite a multitude of craters in the surface of the aerodrome, all the airborne Hurricanes of Nos.43 and 601 Squadrons landed safely and Tangmere remained operational. The repairs and inspections normally carried out in the hangars were switched to dispersals and the squadrons based there continued to give a good account of themselves throughout the Battle of Britain.

As for the damage done to the airfield that day, it is on record that the personnel at Tangmere watched with approval as the station commander set one of the captured German crews to sweep up the remains of the hangars!

* * *

On Thursday 10 October, the Hurricanes of 145 Squadron arrived back over Tangmere and began touching down at 12.40 p.m. They had covered the stretch from Dyce to Tangmere in 3 hours and 5 minutes flying time, including a brief stop at Church Fenton in Yorkshire. Everyone landed safely and most of the pilots who had been with the squadron for some time felt as though they were coming home.

As a peacetime air base, and in spite of the earlier bombing, Tangmere had comforts that were not to be found on all of the RAF's airfields. There were individual rooms for the officers in a building that was situated only 100 yards (90 m) or so from the mess where they went for meals.

While most of the others searched to find their accommodation and settle in before taking a look around, Bob merely selected an armchair in a corner of the dispersal hut, put down his valise and installed himself there as though he had never been anywhere else. In front of him was a charming rural scene – a huge field stretching as far as the eye could see, dotted with grazing cattle and in the distance he could see the roofs of some farmhouses behind a screen of trees. Jean Offenberg noticed him sitting there.

'Do you know this part of the world, Bungey?' he asked.

'Me? I've never been here before,' Bob replied.

'And yet you settle down like a lord in your armchair and look completely at home. Aren't you going to take a look round the joint? At least come to the mess and bring your precious goods and chattels.'

'Not worthwhile,' Bob grumbled, 'There'll be a scramble as soon as we're filled up. Take a pew,' he said, pointing to an armchair. 'We can settle down this evening.'[1]

Bob was right. There was just time for a quick lunch and soon afterwards the order came: 'Scramble!'

There was a rush to each waiting, warmed-up Hurricane and to strap in (helped by the mechanic). Contact! Self-starters pressed. The propellers turned slowly and jerkily at first and then whirred into action as a dozen Rolls-Royce Merlin engines coughed into life. They threw back a huge cloud of dust. Soon the twelve fighters were lined up, wing to wing, on the extreme north of the main runway.

It was vital to be quick. 'B' Flight was in two sections. The first section led by Bob consisted of Dudly Honor and Nigel Weir; the other Pyker Offenberg, Alexis Jottard and Duncan Sykes. Offenberg's section of three was the last to leave and Bob's Hurricanes had not yet reached the centre of the runway before the Belgian and his wingmen released their brakes and gave their engines full throttle. Once airborne, Boyd ordered them all to form up. Following orders from Tangmere ground control they climbed swiftly and flew eastwards along the coast as far as Beachy Head.

Over Beachy Head, Tangmere Control ordered the Hurricanes to turn south. Nervous eyes tensely searched the sky. Where was the enemy?

The control officer at Tangmere had a composed BBC announcer's voice and after a time he announced calmly that the squadron could return home. It was probably a false alarm. It was also an anticlimax, a letdown. Boyd was 'irritated'. Some pilots expressed 'a torrent of abuse' which must have burst over the loudspeakers in the operations room for anyone who happened to be there to hear.

Shortly afterwards, back at dispersal, Bob finally picked up his valise and went in search of his accommodation. The real war would start again tomorrow.

The next day was busy, but uneventful. It started with Bob leading the six Hurricanes of 'B' Flight on an hour-long dawn patrol out over the Isle of Wight to cover a convoy just offshore. There were large areas of covering fog. They made no contact with the enemy and returned to Tangmere at 7.45 a.m. – in time for breakfast.

Bob led off a second patrol at 11.50 a.m. which lasted just 25 minutes.

Adrian Boyd took the squadron up again at 2.35 p.m., this time up to 30,000 feet (9,100 m). There was no heating in the Hurricanes and the pilots felt almost frozen. Their controls were difficult to use and ice soon formed on the windscreens so they were obliged to lose some altitude. Long vapour trails were noticed far away to the west but there was no chance to engage them. Boyd requested to take a closer look but Tangmere Control denied permission because they were in another sector. It was someone else's job. They landed at 3.45 p.m.

This was a pattern being repeated all over southern England. At times large formations of Me109s could be seen but they were always high above and unable to be engaged in combat. Bob was up for the fourth time at 4.25 p.m., this time with Pyker Offenberg as a pair on patrol looking to find stray German reconnaissance aircraft. The result was the same – no contact.

The nature of the air war had changed. German bombers were coming over after dark now and night defence was the Achilles heel of both sides. At this stage of the war, bombers prowling at night could wander almost at will over the opposition's territory without suffering the prohibitive losses that plagued attacks in daylight. The RAF had learnt that lesson early in the war and by now in the Battle of Britain so had the *Luftwaffe*. The night Blitz on London had started after dark on 7 September and it was still going on every night that the weather permitted.

During the day, the tactics the Germans had adopted at the beginning of October posed serious new problems for the defending Hurricanes and Spitfires of Fighter Command, which forced them to fly many fruitless sorties. They were obliged to do so because mixed in with the *Luftwaffe's* fighter formations were groups of bomb-carrying Me109s. A third of the German fighter force was in the process of converting its aircraft into fighter-bombers. Me109s could carry a 250-kg bomb and Me110s were capable of carrying a total load of 700 kg. Although the change was far from popular with the Messerschmitt pilots, the new problems they created for the RAF were difficult to solve. In the morning bomb-carrying Me109s with high-flying fighter cover had dropped their loads on Ashford, Canterbury and Folkstone inflicting more than fifty casualties.

It was the presence of fighter-bombers mixed in with the fighters which made it essential for the RAF try to intercept every enemy raid. No longer could formations that were apparently all fighters be allowed to roam unmolested. Unfortunately, the Hurricanes were unable to climb high enough or fast enough to intercept effectively, and at high altitude they were no match for the Messerschmitts. The Spitfires, unless they were scrambled early enough, were having difficulty reaching the high-flying enemy planes too. Once the Me109 formations were across the coast inland behind the radar wall, it was up to the Observers' Corps alone to plot their movements. To do this accurately could be exceedingly difficult because the presence of any haze or cloud, combined with the raiders' extreme height, made them very hard to spot.

On 12 October, during a squadron patrol at 30,000 feet (9,100 m) led by Adrian Boyd, Tangmere Control reported bandits 20 miles (32 km) from 145's position. They were over Hastings. Bob was weaving on the starboard flank as the Hurricanes banked eastwards into the sun but at the same time Offenberg's voice suddenly crackled over the intercom: 'Red 1, I think I can see aircraft in the sun.'

The Hurricanes scattered in all directions as, in the same instant, bouncing Messerschmitt 109s hurtled through the formation.

The next 10 minutes were chaotic. There was uproar – urgent cries over the radio: 'Break away, break away...' The Hurricanes had scattered only just in time. Despite the icy temperature at that height the pilots sweated and their muscles ached as they twisted their machines in all directions. The Messerschmitts were much faster and more manoeuvrable than the Hurricanes at such high altitudes. A parachute floated down. The 109s dived away and sped off far below.

Boyd, whose call sign was 'Red 1', calmly ordered everyone to rendezvous over Selsey Bill. As they did so reports came flooding in.

'Red 1 from Yellow 1. My No.2 has gone down in a spin. I didn't see anyone firing at him.'

'Probably passed out.'

'Red 1 from Blue 3. Blue 2's been shot down and bailed out.'

'That's Thorpe.'

'He'll be okay.'

Peter Thorpe, Blue 2, bailed out and came down at Coghurst. He was injured and taken to Buchanan Hospital in Hastings.

The Hurricane flown by Yellow 1 crashed at Courseham Farm, Chittenden, near Cranbrook; twenty-one-year-old Sgt John Wadham had not passed out. His body was recovered from the wreckage. He had been shot in the head and must have died instantly.

There was a measure of revenge later in the afternoon when Boyd and Dudley Honor found an Arado 196 and shot it down into the sea and the New Zealander, Paul Rabone, downed a Me109. Mike Newling scored a few hits on a second Messerschmitt and saw a trail of smoke as the German dived away. He did not try to follow it down to make sure. After landing back at Tangmere, Rabone counted thirty-two bullet holes in his Hurricane.

A characteristic of the Me109E's fuel-injected Daimler-Benz DB601A engine was that when suddenly pushed to full throttle it emitted thick, black smoke. This feature led to many Allied pilots unintentionally claiming Me109s were 'destroyed' after they were last seen going down streaming black smoke. It was also an attribute that enabled many German fighter pilots to escape to live and fight another day.

These were dangerous skies. October was fast becoming known as 'Messerschmitt Month'. They were always there somewhere and they were always somewhere above, just waiting to pounce.

On the 15th, over Christchurch on the mouth of the Avon River near Bournemouth, 145 Squadron was taken completely by surprise. The Me109s dived on the Hurricanes from out of the sun in a hit-and-run attack before anyone was aware of their presence. In just a couple of seconds 'they swept past like meteors, preceded by a jet of tracer bullets'. The RAF pilots were left with impressions of yellow noses, black crosses, and a white parachute floating in the sky. Only Adrian Boyd, flying this day with Bob's 'B' Flight, and Dunning-White were quick enough to fire. There was no hope of catching up with them as they dived away.

On returning to Tangmere, one Hurricane was missing. It was the Czech, P/O Juri Machacek. He had joined the squadron at Drem back on 11 September. No one saw what happened. He was flying as tail-end charlie, the aircraft guarding the squadron's rear. Fortunately, news was quick to come in that he had bailed out, wounded with shrapnel splinters in his legs. He was in Lymington Hospital and would be alright in a few weeks. There was no crash site. The Hurricane must have plunged into the sea.

Late that afternoon Bob led Dudly Honor and Peter Dunning-White on a patrol. They took off at 6.15 p.m. under direction from Tangmere Control for course and height. It was uneventful – no contact – and they returned at 7.40 p.m.

There was the same routine on the 16th, Bob leading patrols in the morning and early afternoon – no contact. The next day, it was a mid-afternoon patrol with Adrian Boyd again taking a turn to fly in 'B' Flight. He was with Dunning-White and Pyker Offenberg. Bob had Dudly Honor and Duncan Sykes in his section – no contact.

The squadron's Operations Record Book shows that after Bob flew his sortie on 17 October he did not fly again until the 20th.[2] This was most likely the time that he and Pyker Offenberg decided on some leave. Offenberg wrote:

My flight commander, Bob Bungey, having suggested that a couple of days' rest would not come amiss, we went to see Boyd to get his blessing.

'Where do you think of going?'

'To the Old Ship at Bosham to sleep for forty-eight hours.'

'And you won't stir from there?'

'No, but in the event of Mr Churchill needing Offenberg or myself,' said Bungey, already looking very holiday-like in his sun glasses, 'don't hesitate to give us a ring.'

And so we spent two marvellous days in that old inn which the years seem to have forgotten at the edge of a creek, into which the waters of the Atlantic do not dare to thrust their waves. In front of the inn there was a porch and a small garden with a crazy pavement path and a few dying asters.

It is very 'Olde English' with its oak beam, blackened walls and a few lanterns from caravels which have been cast up on its beaches.

In the old days the sailors came to quench their thirst here after their privateering – pirates or corsairs with faces bronzed by the sea wind. Today the inn is the rendezvous of the Tangmere fighter pilots, who come to drink a pint or two when dusk falls on their airfield. The old walls then hear stories which must thrill their 300-year-old plaster to the marrow and remind them of the good old days of piracy...

Jean Offenberg's writings provide personal glimpses of Bob Bungey as a man and a flight commander. Of him, the Belgian wrote: 'He is fair-haired and has the face of an obstinate woodcutter.'

Back at Dyce shortly after they had first met he had noted:

I was in the mess with Dunning-White and Bungey. Leaning against the bar we listened to the wireless blaring out an old dance hit. Dunning-White knew it and hummed the words:

'My honey and me,

And baby makes three,

We're happy in my blue heaven...'

'Good dance tune, eh, Pyker?' said Bungey, doing a few steps. 'Why don't you go dancing tonight at the Caledonian?'

'We can't buzz off to Aberdeen at nine in the evening,' I grumbled. 'Anyhow, I'm on ops at six tomorrow and I want to be fresh and fit.'

'Don't be such a mutt, Pyker,' advised Bungey. 'You don't go out and you take things too seriously. You never drink much either...'

'And when he does he always takes a big dose of *Eno's* afterwards,' interpolated Dunning-White, 'It may be wonderful for the health but I'd rather die a slow death.'

On another occasion he wrote:

Patrol with Bungey. He's a grand chap. I should like to fly as a pair with him for good. Perhaps he has inherited it from his Australian ancestors, but I can feel that he likes killing; this is not the case with the other members of the squadron. I think he loves a scrap and to spray the enemy planes with his tracers. I should like to bet that he laughs himself sick when a Jerry aircraft is blown to smithereens in front of his eyes.

But he is a marvellous shot and after all ... we're at war.

And, of the short leave the pair spent at the Old Ship at Bosham:

I spent two days of complete rest putting my ideas in order. Bungey spoke of his native land, Australia, to which he wishes to return one day 'unless one of those bloody Huns pumps an explosive bullet into my guts'.

His advice is very precious, for he has many combats to his credit, and last night, leaning on the bar where the beautiful Nancy presides, we discussed fighter tactics and the respective performances of Hurricanes and Messerschmitts.

'What we ought to avoid,' said Bungey, his face cupped in his hands and his elbows on the counter, looking at Nancy, who seemed to smile at him, 'is flying in sections of three. We ought to fly in pairs like the Germans do. The leader can then fire, knowing that his rear is protected.'

'We must try and convince Boyd, that's all,' I replied.

'Yes, that's all. But ... there you are.' He changed the subject and said to the barmaid: 'Same again, Nancy, please.'

Bob Bungey's seemingly casual remark was, in fact, a perceptive assessment of tactics in the air in 1940.

As a basic element, the *Luftwaffe* had its fighters fly in pairs, each called a *Rotte*. About 200 yards (180 m) separated each plane and the main responsibility of the wingman, or Number Two, was to cover the leader from quarter or stern attacks. The leader looked after navigation and covered his wingman.

Two *Rotten* made up a *Schwarm* (Flight) of four aircraft. This combination improved a *Schwarm's* all-round vision, combat flexibility and gave mutual protection.

Two or three *Schwarm* made up a *Staffel* (Squadron). During the early part of the war the *Staffel* (plural *Staffeln*) had a nominal strength of nine aircraft, and was commanded by a *Staffelkapitän* with the rank of *Oberleutnant* or a *Hauptmann*.

Next was the *Gruppe*, which was established at three *Staffeln* each with nine aircraft, plus a *Stab* (headquarters) unit with three, making thirty aircraft in all. The *Gruppe* commander carried the title of *Kommandeur* and was usually a *Hauptmann* or a *Major*.

The *Geschwader* (plural also *Geschwader*) was the largest flying unit in the *Luftwaffe* to have a fixed nominal strength. Initially it comprised three *Gruppen* with a total of ninety aircraft, and a *Stab* unit with four, making a total of ninety-four aircraft. The *Geschwader* commander had the title of *Kommodore* and usually held the rank of *Major, Oberstleutnant* or *Oberst*.

A *Jagdgeschwader* (abbreviated to *JG*) was a day fighter wing; *Zerstörergeschwader* (*ZG*) a wing of twin-engined fighters; a *Kampfgeschwader* (*KG*) a wing of bombers; *Stukageschwader* (*StG*) a wing of single-engined dive-bombers and so on.

On the other hand, the RAF's flying tactics early in the air war were a leftover from peacetime. At the outset Fighter Command squadrons flew in the tidy tight formations that undoubtedly looked good at air displays, but were completely wrong for combat flying. The aircraft were packed in so close that only the leader could see where the squadron was going and what was happening. The other members of the fighter formation had to concentrate mainly on keeping in position instead of being able to search the sky for the enemy escorts. The disastrous result was that many unsuspecting pilots were 'bounced' – taken by surprise – and shot down.

As a basic element, the RAF had its fighters fly in a section of three in a tight Vic ('V') formation; two sections of three made up a flight of six; and two flights of six made up a squadron of twelve. In practice, a section of three was far more cumbersome than a pair. Turning in to attack a bomber, for example, the formation leader would have to call, 'Aircraft, line astern, go' before leading his wingmen around. On finishing the manoeuvre he would say 'Aircraft, form Vic, go' to re-align his wingmen back into position for a co-ordinated attack. It was all very time consuming and based on the assumption that the target would oblige by continuing to fly straight and level waiting to be attacked.

Bob and Pyker Offenberg returned to Tangmere by at least the late afternoon of Saturday the 19th. Bob's Log Book shows that he flew a sortie that night that lasted 1 hour 30 minutes. The German bombers were active over London, Liverpool, the Midlands and Bristol but they remained elusive in the darkness.

Adrian Boyd was willing to try Bob's idea of flying in pairs. Offenberg commenced training with Dunning-White. On occasions over the next few days, Tangmere Control vectored the pair after bogeys reported over the Isle of Wight, but each time they did not manage to make contact. When the whole squadron flew, 'A' and 'B' Flight together, they reverted to flying in the usual Vics of three.

Boyd, following his normal practice of alternating between flights, led the squadron at the head of 'A' Flight on the morning of 25 October, with Bob leading his 'B' Flight. At 30,000 feet (9,100 m), Dunning-White spotted black specks on the horizon, coming in from the south. They were undoubtedly Messerschmitts and for once the Hurricanes had the advantage. Bob's wingmen were the Belgians Pyker Offenberg and Baudouin de Hemptinne. All the squadron had to do was turn eastwards and cut them off, but when Boyd reported the bandits to Tangmere Control permission to intercept was refused. Instead, Tangmere called another squadron in the sector to attack but the other squadron lost sight of them. A rare opportunity was wasted.

The squadron landed but was only on the ground for just over half-an-hour when it was scrambled again at 11.40 a.m. Tangmere Control reported bandits at 30,000 feet (9,100 m), 40 miles (64 km) south of the coast. The Hurricanes climbed frantically as they strove to reach 29,000 feet (8,850 m) in the hope of being in position above the raiders when they were intercepted.

Unfortunately, when the bandits were spotted they were still well above. There were at least 15 of them – Me109s – up at around 32,000 feet (9,800 m).

Boyd reported to Tangmere, 'Red 1, we're too low and too late. We shall engage at a great disadvantage.'

He concluded his transmission with a warning to Bob Bungey: 'Blue 1, watch the sun. That's where they'll come from.'

'Blue 1, okay,' Bob acknowledged.

The widely spaced Germans slowly circled above, apparently not knowing the rising British fighters were coming. What were they doing? They had the advantage of height and would have to be blind not to have spotted their opponents.

The Hurricanes continued climbing towards them, but then a voice suddenly cried out over the R/T, 'Red 1 from Yellow 3. I've got three on my tail!'

'It's Yule. Where the hell is he? Red Section follow me.'

The three leading Hurricanes, Boyd's Section, half rolled to turn but it was too late. Yule called again, 'They've got me. I'm bailing out. Cheerio.'

Bob Yule was the tail-end Charlie meant to be guarding the rear. He was not able to keep up in the climb and, with his attention focussed on keeping his companions in sight, did not notice his danger. In fact, nobody had noticed his danger. Only the pilots of the German *Staffel* were aware of what was happening. While they remained above playing the role of decoy and refusing to attack, a *Rotte* or *Schwarm* of their number had carried out an ambush on the hapless New Zealander.

After this the two sides watched each other warily, like a pair of boxers waiting to punch or counterpunch whenever there was a chance, until the German pilots, ever conscious of their fuel situation, decided it was time to depart.

As the remaining Hurricanes flew home over Selsey Bill, Baudouin de Hemptinne reported engine trouble – a glycol leak? The Rolls-Royce Merlin was overheating and about to seize. De Hemptinne managed to force-land his Hurricane at High Beeches, Haywards Health Golf Course. The Belgian was uninjured. He leaped out of the cockpit and ran clear. Just 2 minutes later the aircraft erupted in flames.

Meanwhile, despite his transmission, Bob Yule did not bail out. Thanks to his skill as a pilot he managed to put his Hurricane down on the field of a farm near Brightling. The New Zealander from Invercargill had been wounded in the leg and was admitted to Pembury Hospital. His Hurricane was a write-off.

* * *

Two days later on Sunday the 27th and the whole squadron took off on patrol at 10.45 a.m. 'B' Flight consisted of Bob with Pyker Offenberg, Alexis Jottard, Dudley Honor, Duncan Sykes and the Irishman, Sgt Bill McConnell.

It was cloudy with plenty of places for the Messerschmitts to hide. As they reached 15,000 feet (4,500 m) while climbing, bogeys were spotted to starboard much higher up. Adrian Boyd reported their presence to Tangmere Control and was assured that they were actually patrolling Spitfires.

The Hurricanes clawed their way up to 32,500 feet (9,900 m) where the rarefied air was bitterly cold. Over Halton, Boyd noticed about a dozen Me109s a few thousand feet lower down. He dived with his section and a split second later Bob followed with Blue Section. As the Hurricanes came into range, the 109s scattered and zoomed up in a rapid climb at full throttle. The Czech, Frantisek Weber, who was Boyd's No.2, fired at a Messerschmitt that half rolled and went spinning down out of sight.

Bob chased after the German fighters but after losing the speed he had built up from the momentum of his dive they soon pulled away. Hurricanes simply could not keep up with Me109s at high altitude. From long distance, Offenberg fired a hopeful short burst from his machine guns. No luck!

As 145 climbed back to 30,000 feet (9,100 m), Alexis Jottard expressed his opinion with some venom of what he thought these 'bloody Hurricanes'. Some way off the 109s clashed with Spitfires and a dogfight was going on as the Hurricanes set course for home.

They were cutting it fine as they were down to their last fuel reserves. Two from 'B' Flight did not make it. Having used up their reserve tanks, Dudley Honor force-landed near Halton and Duncan Sykes was obliged to land near Amersham. Both of the aircraft suffered some damage but both pilots escaped injury.

The *Luftwaffe's* hit-and-run fighter and fighter-bomber raids continued all day, and at 4.30 p.m. the squadron took off on patrol again. 'B' Flight was only five aircraft strong. Bob, Pyker Offenberg and Alexis Jottard were up again and they had been joined by Peter Dunning-White and Nigel Weir.

They climbed to 25,000 feet (7,600 m) over the south coast east of the Isle of Wight, but had not been there for more than 5 minutes when Me109s suddenly attacked them from out of the sun. Tangmere Control had not warned of the enemy's presence and nobody had spotted them coming. An aircraft pouring a long trail of smoke from its tail went down in a vertical dive.

All of a sudden a formation of three 109s shot overhead at full speed and Bob immediately gave chase. At the same time, Pyker Offenberg dived steeply and pulled up in a zoom. The radio was in an uproar.

Somebody, probably Bob, shouted, 'Your bird, Pyker! To port!'

Offenberg was about 200 yards (180 m) away when he fired. Black smoke came from the Messerschmitt's starboard wing. The Belgian blacked out then and did not see what happened next. Nor did the others.

Three Hurricanes failed to return to Tangmere. 'A' Flight had been hit hard, with Sgt John Haire and the Czech, Frantisek Weber, missing. Alexis Jottard was missing from 'B' Flight too. It had been a bad day with five aircraft lost. At least the two pilots, Honor and Sykes who had force-landed in the morning, were safe. Now all everyone could do was wait for news of the others.

At 7.00 p.m., No.11 Group notified the squadron that John Haire had ditched in the sea offshore of Bembridge and walked ashore. He was not injured. Frantisek Weber was okay too. He had bailed out off the Isle of Wight and been rescued from the sea by an MTB. His Hurricane had crashed into the Solent.

There was still no news of Alexis Jottard. Jean Offenberg became distraught when Jottard's name was removed from the board. Offenberg was credited with a Messerschmitt 109 probably destroyed, but that was no consolation. The two were the closest of friends; they had been through a lot together.

They had both been in the Belgian Air Force when the Germans invaded their country on 10 May 1940, and Offenberg had shot down a Dornier Do17 that day. When their country was overrun, they escaped with others to France to fight on in the *Armée de l'Air*. After France collapsed too, he and Alexis Jottard took two Caudron Simouns on 20 June and flew to Corsica. From there they flew to Philippeville in Algeria, then on to Oujda, where a Belgian training school had been set up. Unimpressed by the poor morale they found there, the pair went by train to Casablanca where they met up with some other Belgians, who were trainee pilots, and some Poles. The Poles already had permission to sail that evening in a cargo ship bound for Gibraltar. The Belgians and some escaping Frenchmen slipped on board with them.

At Gibraltar they transferred to a British vessel, which berthed at Liverpool on 16 July. Offenberg and Jottard stayed together when they disembarked and on the 30th went to No.6 OTU, Sutton Bridge, before joining 145 Squadron on 17 August. Now, after so much, Jottard was missing.

Alexis Jottard would not return. His Hurricane had plunged into the sea 5 miles (8 km) south-east of the Isle of Wight and he was never found. His name is listed on Panel 8 of the Runnymede Memorial and he has a memorial grave in the *Pelouse d'Honneur* at the Cemetery of Brussels at Evere.

The 27th of October had been an extremely busy day for Fighter Command. The *Luftwaffe* had made an early start by raiding London and convoys in the Thames Estuary with formations of as many as fifty aircraft. London suburbs were hit and the docks damaged. More fighter-bomber and fighter sweeps were flown later in the morning and early afternoon with simultaneous raids on Southampton, London and Martlesham Heath later in the afternoon.

To ward off the attackers, Fighter Command's pilots flew 1,007 sorties and lost ten aircraft shot down, but five of the pilots survived. Germans losses were put at fifteen. This RAF effort was greater than that made back on 15 August when 180 German aircraft had been claimed shot down for the loss of thirty-four British fighters. On that occasion, in the days of the massed escorted bomber raids, Fighter Command had flown only 974 sorties.

It would be wrong to suggest the Germans had relaxed the pressure on Fighter Command or that the fighting in October was an anticlimax. In many ways the RAF fighter pilots were being subjected to one of the most severe tests of the period which the world knew as the Battle of Britain. The physical strain of fighting at great heights was demanding and the seemingly never-ending German fighter-bomber attacks and fighter sweeps required great vigilance and meant increased operational activity.

When the weather was clear the *Luftwaffe* multiplied its attacks so RAF fighter squadrons of twelve aircraft usually averaged 45 flying hours a day and sometimes as much as 60 hours. This volume of operational flying was also increased by the need to keep up with standing patrols. It was relentless exacting pressure.

On the 28th, Bob flew two patrols starting with an early morning pairing with Peter Dunning-White. Next day, he flew a gruelling of four sorties including an early morning patrol, again with Dunning-White, and another in the mid-afternoon paired with the Irishman, Bill McConnell. The others patrols involved the whole squadron. On the 30th, despite low cloud and continuous drizzle everywhere, the squadron, Bob and 'B' Flight included, patrolled twice at full strength during the day as the *Luftwaffe* persisted with its nuisance raids, albeit on a reduced scale. The last day of the month brought rain with drizzle in the English Channel and haze in the Dover Straits and Thames Estuary. Bob flew one sortie, a morning patrol with the Anglo-Argentinean, Dudley Honor, who had returned to the squadron a couple of days earlier.

According to Air Ministry Orders issued later, when eligibility for the awarding of campaign medals was being decided, to receive the much prized Battle of Britain Clasp on the 1939–1945 Star an airman must have served with RAF Fighter Command and flown at least one operational sortie between 00.01 hours on 10 July 1940 and 23.59 hours on 31 October 1940. These dates and times have been generally accepted over the years, but not universally so. To those who were involved, the finish was far from clear cut. Many days in November brought more combat activity than some of the early days in the battle. The scale of air fighting over Britain during the latter part of the year simply tapered off gradually with the onset of winter's more hostile weather.

There was certainly no slackening of effort on the first day of November. Bob and 'B' Flight notched up three patrols. During the first, while the squadron was climbing at 10,000 feet (3,000 m) over the coast east of Portsmouth, Adrian Boyd had engine trouble. He came down in a slow glide and landed back at Tangmere 10 minutes ahead of the others. Baudouin de Hemptinne and Bill McConnell were next down together, followed by Pyker Offenberg, and then finally Bob and Nigel Weir.

During the 3.15 p.m. patrol, Bob led 'B' Flight detached from the rest of the squadron. At 20,000 feet (6,000 m) above a layer of scattered clouds, bandits appeared overhead at two o'clock high. Warily, Bob banked the Hurricanes to move closer. Were they just acting as decoys, diverting attention, trying the same trick as before?

Suddenly, a lone Me109 swept in attacking from behind. It broke away underneath the formation. Offenberg was the quickest to react. He immediately dived onto its tail and fired. The 109 fell away towards the sea with glycol streaming from its engine and pieces of cockpit breaking off. Offenberg followed, still firing to finish it off, but he lost sight of it in low clouds over Selsey Bill. The third patrol for the squadron that day involved searching for enemy aircraft reported south of Brighton, but none were found.

There was good cause for celebration in the mess that night when news arrived that Pyker Offenberg's Messerschmitt had been found. It had crash-landed intact in open country near Selsey Bill and the pilot had been captured uninjured.

Next morning, Offenberg was driven by Dudley Honor in his ancient Austin to find the field where the Me109 had come down. It was still there and seemed quite undamaged except for hits on the engine. The village policeman presented Offenberg with the pilot's parachute, flying helmet and Mae West as a war souvenirs. Honor had his camera and took a 'victor and vanquished' souvenir photograph as well.

Meanwhile, Bob flew a fruitless early morning scramble with Baudouin de Hemptinne, and in the afternoon he had an errand of his own to perform. The squadron's Operations Record Book shows that he flew Hurricane 2924 to Benson and back on the 2nd, the flight lasting an hour: 'Time Up 13.10'; 'Time Down 14.10.'

However, this does not tally with the entries in Bob's Log Book. According to these, although he did fly Hurricane 2924 to Benson on the 2nd (flight time 20 minutes), he did not fly it back to Tangmere again until the next day, the 3rd (flight time 40 minutes). Bad weather severely curtailed *Luftwaffe* operations over Britain during the 3rd and 145 Squadron's Operations Record Book does not record any sorties at all for 'B' Flight on that day. It is likely that because of the weather, 'B' Flight was stood down from operations for the day. While he does not note a time of day for his return flight, Bob wrote in his Log Book 'Cloud less than 100 ft over sea (in cloud from Readg [presumably Reading])' corroborating that flying conditions were poor. This was probably why the return flight took longer.

Sometimes what goes into official documents may not actually record all the facts. It does not stretch the imagination to suggest that something unofficial might have been going on. Perhaps it was a co-incidence that the location of RAF Benson airfield happened to be only a couple of miles away from a picturesque old country town in the upper Thames Valley called Wallingford – reputedly the best example of a preserved Saxon town in England. Not only did Wallingford have a 900-foot-long medieval stone bridge built over the river, and a castle, both easily recognisable from the air, there was also a particularly attractive dark-eyed girl who lived there. Sybil. Locals do, in fact, tell of a girl standing on the bridge and waving at a low-flying Hurricane waggling its wings and sweeping past – another co-incidence?

The squadron's Operations Record Book shows that Bob's next sortie was on the 4th between 4.40 p.m. and 5.35 p.m., apparently in a section with Jean Offenberg and Baudouin de Hemptinne, although the two Belgians had recently been experimenting with flying as a pair. Bob's Log Book entry corresponds listing one sortie for that day.

On 5 November, Bob flew a weather test in Hurricane 6889 and later two patrols in the same aircraft. Messerschmitts were seen overhead, but they were far too high for 145 Squadron to do anything about them.

Bob flew two more sorties on the 6th but it was Pyker Offenberg who again proved himself a rising star. During a series of clashes Offenberg shared in the destruction of another Me109. He thought that the other Hurricane which had attacked the Messerschmitt was flown by Adrian Boyd, but Boyd declared that it was not him – he had not fired at all. It seems likely that the other Hurricane involved was flown by P/O Thomas Guest of 56 Squadron who was in the area and claimed a 109 at around the same time.

The 7th of November was ill-fated for 145 Squadron. On this day, *Stuka* dive-bombers were reported to be after shipping near Portsmouth. Eleven Hurricanes were scrambled at 1.50 p.m. and ordered to patrol near the Isle of Wight. As usual, Bob was leading 'B' Flight. The other members of the flight were Nigel Weir, newcomers P/O John Ashton and Sgt Hick, Bill McConnell and Duncan Sykes.

After a short time over the Isle of Wight they were instructed to return to base and patrol at 20,000 feet (6,000 m), but as they did so there was a chilling realisation that that they were not alone – enemy fighters were appearing all around them. Three formations of fast and deadly Messerschmitt 109s were shadowing them: one group ahead, one astern, and the third flying on a parallel course to the south.

They were caught in a trap!

There were about fifty of them!

Eleven against fifty!

The Hurricane pilots could not try to engage any group without putting themselves at the mercy of the other formations. All they could do was stay alert and keep gaining more height as they waited for the 109s to make the first move. And they did.

Breaking formation in pairs, they began an attack on the Hurricanes of 'B' Flight at the rear. They came in fast.

The squadron's Operations Record Book shows that only one Hurricane from 'B' Flight returned to Tangmere that day. It was Hurricane 6979 flown by Sgt Hick.

9

Hurricane Winter

The Me109s were from the *Luftwaffe's* elite *JG2*, the fabled *Richthofen Geschwader* which had been named after the renowned 'Red Baron' of the First World War, Manfred von Richthofen. That day, No.145 Squadron's eleven Hurricanes had the misfortune to run into the entire *Geschwader* on an offensive sweep over the Isle of Wight.

Most leading German fighter aces wanted to equal or better the Red Baron's score of eighty enemy aircraft shot down, and nobody more so than Major Helmut Wick. He was one of Germany's rising stars and a favourite of *Reichsmarschall* Herman Göring. It was he who led the *Richthofen Geschwader* that day.

The youngest son of a civil engineer, Helmut Wick had joined Germany's new *Luftwaffe* in 1936 and, under the instruction of skilled pilots such as the renowned Werner Mölders, he soon demonstrated exceptional flying talent. He scored his first kill, a French Curtiss P-36, in November 1939 during the so-called 'Phoney War' period. When the Battle of France began in May 1940, his tally mounted rapidly.

Described as 'aggressive and impetuous', Wick's score at the end of October 1940 stood at forty-nine. He was ambitious and eager to catch up to Werner Mölders' score and, if he could, surpass it. At the age of twenty-five, Wick was commander of the *Richthofen Geschwader* and just two days ago, on 5 November, at a meeting of fighter and bomber commanders with Herman Göring, the obese air force chief had presented him with a large gold ring bearing the *Luftwaffe* emblem.

As if in celebration, yesterday he claimed to have shot down two Hurricanes and two Spitfires during a fighter sweep over the Southampton area. Today, he claimed one of 145 Squadron's Hurricanes for his fifty-fourth victory, but fate would decree it to be his last.[1]

Four other pilots claimed Hurricane kills as well: *Oberleutnant* Erich Leie (two) and one each by *Oberleutnant* Rudolf Pflanz, *Leutnant* Siegfried Schnell and *Leutnant* Heimberg. A total claim of six Hurricanes shot down without loss!

Actually, five Hurricanes had gone down. No.145 Squadron's Operations Record Book noted, 'F/Lt R.W. Bungey was shot down in the sea off St Laurence,

Isle of Wight. He was slightly injured. P/O A. N. C. Weir went down near Ashey Down, Isle of Wight, and was uninjured. P/O J. H. Ashton went down in the centre of the Isle of Wight and was uninjured (except for a bruise on his head). Sgt-Pilot D. B. Sykes went down near Ventnor and was slightly injured. Sgt-Pilot J. McConnell was shot down near Wittering and slightly injured.'

'Whilst continuing the climb', it went on, 'F/Lt Riley seized an opportunity to attack one detached Me109 which he pursued towards France. When about 20 miles South of the Isle of Wight, he sighted a Squadron of twelve enemy aircraft (Ju87s) flying West at a height of 13,000 feet in line astern. He immediately attacked and shot down one (probable). The Me109, which he had originally chased had now turned to attack him so he broke off the action and returned to his base. The Squadron (less five aircraft) landed at approximately 1500 hours.'

The two Belgians, Jean Offenberg and Baudouin de Hemptinne, missed the fight because they were off duty and had taken themselves to the cinema in nearby Chichester. The account in Offenberg's biography tallied with the squadron's record book:

> On our return I learned that 145 Squadron almost in full strength had been attacked by fifty Mes west of Plymouth. A spectacular dog-fight ensued in which five pilots of 'B' Flight were shot down: Nigel Weir, MacConnell, Ashton and Bungey the Australian are unhurt for they managed to bail out in time; my pal Sykes crash-landed and is only slightly wounded.
>
> The results are not particularly good for such a show since the only Jerry shot down was a Junkers 87, easily accounted for by Pilot Officer Riley of 'A' Flight.

But despite what the ORB and Offenberg's biography stated, something was not right. One of the RAF pilots had, in fact, been killed. Three days later, on the 10th, 145 Squadron's ORB corrected the earlier entry:

> On this day it was also ascertained from the Military Brigade Headquarters, Chillerten (Isle of Wight), that the report made on 7/11/40 to the effect P/O A. N. C. Weir had landed safely on the Isle of Wight was incorrect. They had apparently mistaken him for P/O J. H. Ashton...[2]

For some reason Nigel Weir had not flown his usual aircraft, Hurricane P2683, on the 7th. This was being flown by Ashton but in the aircraft there was a bullet-proof cushion with Weir's name on it. Weir's uncle had given it to him. When Ashton crashed in the centre of the island near Ashley, it was at first thought that he was Weir.

Hurricane P2720, which Nigel Weir was flying, was seen to dive straight into the sea south-east of Woody Point off Ventnor where it sank immediately. He had no chance.

Accounts of what happened to Bob Bungey vary too. Several have written that he bailed out, but that was not the case. Bob's instrument panel in front of him was suddenly shattered by a of hail bullets. One of the Messerschmitts had swept in from behind. There is a one-in-five possibility that Bob may have been Helmut Wick's 54th, and final, victory. Bob was probably saved from death by the armour plate behind his seat but his aircraft, Hurricane V6889, was crippled. While he still had some control, he had to try and ride it down to force-land or ditch in the shallow water off the Isle of Wight

Twelve-year-old Ray Fairminer was at school when he heard that an RAF Hurricane had been shot down near his home. Excited by the news, he rushed home to tell his parents. Ray's father was a maintenance engineer at the local hospital. Perhaps he would know more about it.

The youngster had a surprise in store. Drinking tea with his parents he found a total stranger – a pilot. He was a genuine Battle of Britain fighter pilot, and an Australian. Ray had never met an Australian before. Bob Bungey had been rescued from a sandbank at Littlestairs near Shanklin and taken to the hospital where Ray's dad had met him and invited him home 'for a cuppa' while he waited for transport back to his squadron.

Bob introduced himself to the excited young lad and soon they were deep in conversation. Before he left to return to Tangmere, Bob told Ray that he had been flying along and suddenly his dash had blown up in front of him. A Messerschmitt had got him from behind.

Next morning Bob visited Shanklin again and he gave Ray a half-crown to share with his classmates at the tuck shop. He said to the youngster, 'I'll be back.'

At Tangmere that evening a big dance was held in the mess. Probably not wanting to place stress on his knee, which had been injured, Bob went to the pictures in Chichester with Offenberg and de Hemptinne. It seems likely that his injury was actually an old football wound suffered years earlier at school, which had been aggravated by his forced landing in the water. Ray Fairminer had apparently not noticed Bob limping and thought him uninjured. Bob may have made sure of that.

The weather on 9 November was described as poor and very cloudy, but there was flying nevertheless. At 9.20 a.m., Bob and Pyker Offenberg took off as a pair and as they climbed through the mirk they were vectored to south of the Isle of Wight. They climbed to 22,000 feet (6,700 m). Above 20,000 feet (6,000 m), the Hurricanes were very sluggish and could only gain more altitude slowly by flying in a straight line or a very gentle curve. Turns, if they were needed, had to be made very gently otherwise no height would be gained or could even be lost. At 22,000 feet (6,700 m) visibility was very poor. There were clouds from 1,000 to 22,000 feet (300 to 6,700 m). It was silly to try and intercept anything in such conditions. A whole formation of enemy aircraft could have been hidden in the cloud blanket. They started to loose height.

As they came down to 13,000 feet (4,000 m), they suddenly spotted a Ju88 only 200 yards (180 m) ahead on their starboard quarter. The Junkers was flying due south. They were on a course of 190°.

Pyker Offenberg called, 'Bungey, tally ho, get cracking.'

'Wade in,' Bob ordered as he manoeuvred to cut off the enemy aircraft's escape route – but which way? It was impossible to tell. There was thick cloud about everywhere – plenty in which to hide!

Offenberg dived after the bomber and as he closed in from the left and slightly below, gave it a burst of .303-inch machine-gun fire at about a 200-yard (180-m) range. The Ju88 pilot reacted quickly and dived with the Belgian trying to follow in hot pursuit close behind on its tail. Even so, by pushing forward into a dive the Ju88, with its fuel-injected Junkers Jumo engines, gained precious seconds. To follow in a dive, first the Hurricane had to half roll onto its back. The carburettor system feeding fuel into the British fighter's Rolls-Royce Merlin engine was subject to centrifugal forces – if the pilot simply pushed the control column forward to dive, the engine would cough and splutter and briefly lose power.

As the bomber gained speed, Bob saw Offenberg fire again while performing a half roll. This time he missed. Then they both disappeared into the clouds below and were gone.

To try and pursue them was pointless. There was little likelihood of finding them again by stooging around blindly. The encounter had been a fluke in the first place. What were the odds of meeting by chance an enemy plane where the clouds were only slightly less dense? Bob turned away to return to Tangmere alone. Besides, he had a promise to keep.

At Shanklin, young Ray Fairminer was 'thrilled to bits' to see a lone Hurricane appear overhead and stage a private aerial display. It was Bob Bungey. The show lasted for maybe a minute or so. For a finale, Bob swooped the Hurricane low over the ground, zoomed up into the air for a victory roll and was away as fast as he had arrived. It was a show the boy would never forget.

Jean Offenberg landed back at Tangmere just after Bob touched down. In fact, the squadron's ORB logged them both down at 1020 hours.

At debriefing, the Belgian excitedly described how he had followed the Ju88 in its steep dive and continued firing until it eventually disappeared into low cloud. Bob, for his part, insisted that flame was coming from the fuselage. Offenberg was allowed a 'probable' victory.

A Ju88 from I/KG51 was damaged in combat during the day and subsequently crash-landed at Villaroche. It seems likely this was in fact the aircraft intercepted by Bob and Pyker Offenberg.

Euphoric over his success, it was after this that the Belgian wrote down in one of his precious notebooks: 'Patrol with Bungey. He's a grand chap. I should like to fly as a pair with him for good...'[3]

The squadron only flew two more patrols in the morning and none in the afternoon. Each time formations of three aircraft were used.

From 10 November onwards, although the Tangmere squadrons flew numerous patrols and attempted to intercept single German reconnaissance aircraft in poor weather, clashes were fewer and fewer. For the *Luftwaffe* during the shortening daylight hours, fighter sweeps and reconnaissance sorties were the order of the day and the bombers ventured out only at night. When 145 Squadron happened to encounter the Messerschmitts, they were usually well above and refused to fight. The intense air battles of the summer months were over.

Bad weather made it equally hard for the enemy to operate. If there was a clash, the dangers involved in safely finding the way back to base were very real for both sides. Frequently the clouds were extremely low, reducing visibility to only about half-a-mile. With high ground in the vicinity, low flying alone could be very hazardous.

Meanwhile, changes were in the wind at the highest level. The 25th of November marked the end of an era for RAF Fighter Command when ACM Sir Hugh Dowding was replaced as AOC-in-C by ACM William Sholto Douglas. Dowding would be ultimately acknowledged as the architect behind the RAF's victory over the *Luftwaffe* in the Battle of Britain. Less than a month later, on 18 December, Dowding's former right-hand man, New Zealander AVM Keith Park, whose brilliant defence tactics had won the Battle of Britain, ceased to be AOC of No.11 Group. He was replaced by AVM Trafford Leigh-Mallory, former commander of 12 Group. Ignominiously, Park was transferred to No.23 Training Group.

Towards the end of November, a new Spitfire squadron arrived at Tangmere. No.65 Squadron came south from Turnhouse in Scotland to replace 213 Squadron, which had departed, taking its Hurricanes north to Leconfield. No.65 had been in action over Dunkirk and taken part in the early stages of the Battle of Britain until the end of August when it had been withdrawn to rest and rebuild. An hour after it arrived on the 29th, it was in the air at 30,000 feet (9,100 m), the pilots half frozen while searching in vain for enemy fighters that were supposed to be in the vicinity.

High altitude flying was extremely cold and uncomfortable. By far the worst problem was poor visibility because of fogging up. Water vapour from the pilot's breathing would continually ice up the Perspex canopy. To see out, it was necessary to scrape the ice crystals away, but as soon as they were brushed off new ones began forming to fog vision again. After an hour of intense cold and misery and descending to land, during the last few minutes at the lower, warmer altitudes the ice crystals melted. The inside of the cockpit would become a mass of dripping water as if there had been rain. The only area that stayed frozen was the armoured glass at the front, which was very thick. It took much longer to warm up, retaining its frost usually until just before landing.

The 145 Squadron boys were envious of 65 Squadron's Spitfires, but Bob was delighted to see a familiar face among the newcomers, another Australian, F/Lt Gordon Olive. Gordon Olive was a Queenslander and one of 65 Squadron's flight commanders. He had been at Point Cook in the senior course when Bob was there. Gordon, who was equally pleased to see Bob, recalled later:

> It was good to see him as I always had a great admiration for him. It was quite a surprise to see him on fighters, as, before the war Bob had been one of the Bomber Command boys and it was seldom that a pilot turned from bombers to fighters.
>
> I knew that Bob had flown Fairey Battles in France and had been one of the few survivors of ... the most heroic and desperate air fighting of the French campaign... Bungey's spirit was such that he applied for service in Fighter Command when we were so hopelessly short of pilots. He could fly and he knew all about the Merlin engine which powered the Hurricanes as well as the Fairey Battles.
>
> So he came in to fight in the last desperate days of the Battle of Britain where he gave a very effective account of himself and in the process was shot down again trying to outfight too many of the enemy. On this occasion

he damaged his knee and was as a result very lame. This did not seem to discourage him, nor did it stop him from flying at every opportunity...

As our squadrons took it in turns to stand by at 'Readiness', I saw Bob only at meal times and when we were off in the evenings.

During the day we sat out in the little wooden hut on the aerodrome trying to keep out of the drafts and to get some heat out of the little stove. We read, chatted or played cards according to the mood and now and again we would fly. Operational sorties were down to once a day or ever less and frequently that was against a single intruder or a small formation of enemy planes. It seemed impossible that the great clouds of bombers and fighters were a thing of the past. In their day they had seemed so permanent...[4]

One of the promising pilots in 65 Squadron who Bob met for the first time was an outgoing young Irishman, F/O Brendan 'Paddy' Finucane. He already had a brace of Me109s and Me109 probables to his credit. Although neither realised it then, their stories were fated to become closely linked.

But oh those Spitfires! They were smaller, smoother and more streamlined than the Hurricanes. The Hurricanes with their wider-apart wheels were more stable for landing on rougher grass airstrips whereas the narrower outward-swinging Spitfire undercarriages seemed much more fragile and less stable. But in the air, the Spitfires were the thoroughbreds and much faster; the Hurricanes were the work horses.

The next day was tragic for 145 Squadron when Hurricane P3704 crashed in flames near Chichester, Sussex, and was destroyed. The twenty-four-year-old Polish pilot Sgt Wilhelm Sasak was killed. An inquiry into the crash began on 1 December. It established that while the squadron was returning to Tangmere from a patrol, the engine of Sasak's Hurricane suddenly caught fire for some unknown reason. Sgt Sasak broke away from the formation but did not bail out. It was assumed that he may have been overcome by fumes from the engine.

Fine weather greeted the beginning of December and during the first couple of days Bob led three-aircraft patrols searching for single 'bogies', but there were no intercepts.

Early in the afternoon of 8 December, a section of three Spitfires from 65 Squadron led by Gordon Olive intercepted a Messerschmitt Me110 in clear blue sky above Portsmouth. The twin-engined German fighter was undoubtedly on a reconnaissance mission, probably checking for shipping targets in the area. Olive closed in and shot off its twin-finned tail. The three Spitfire pilots watched as it plunge down on fire vertically into the blue-black water of the English Channel.

Three days later it was 145 Squadron's turn. The weather was fine all day but with thick heavy clouds at around 6,000 feet (1,800 m), and there were very gusty winds. Flying as a pair again, Bob and Pyker Offenberg took off at 1715 hours and were ordered onto a course of 100° until they reached Brighton. They orbited there as they climbed slowly to 12,000 feet (3,700 m). After about 5 minutes, Control ordered, 'Vector 240, Angels 14.' (Change course to 240° and climb to 14,000 feet.) Suddenly, they noticed a black dotted contrail heading north-west. They continued climbing and at 18,000 feet (5,500 m), just off Littlehampton, saw an aircraft 2,000 feet (600 m) above and about 1,000 yards (900 m) ahead. It was still maintaining a north-west heading.

They immediately closed in and Offenberg attacked from below on the starboard side. As they did so they could clearly make out the shape of the trailing edge of the wings in the fading light. It was a Heinkel He111. They were off Selsey Bill when Offenberg opened fire at a range of 150 yards (140 m) giving it a 5-second burst. Grey smoke immediately trailed from the Heinkel's port engine and it began to dive, turning to starboard and heading south. As the enemy aircraft turned, Offenberg fired the rest of his ammunition from dead astern at 200–250 yards (180–200 m) as he was afraid of losing the enemy aircraft in the darkness.

Meanwhile, Bob had been attacking from dead astern while Offenberg was still below. He opened fire from 300 yards (270 m), closing in to 25 yards (23 m) giving short bursts. The gunner stopped firing, possibly killed or wounded. The port engine continued trailing smoke and then a large fire broke out between it and the fuselage. Flames burnt brightly for about 2 minutes as the aircraft went into a slow shallow glide, and then they appeared to go out. By then the port engine had stopped and the starboard engine seemed to have stopped too, but now both Hurricanes were out of ammunition. They could not deliver the *coup de grâce*.

Bright moonlight helped to keep the Heinkel in view. It looked to be finished anyway. No evasive action was taken, it merely continued in its shallow glide. They followed it for about 20 miles (32 km) out to sea in the semi-darkness. At 2,000 feet (600 m) and still in a shallow glide, it finally disappeared into low cloud. Control reported that it had vanished off their screens.

In their Combat Report, Bob and Pyker Offenberg claimed one 'He111 destroyed' and the intelligence officer wrote, 'Assessment ½ each pilot'. The report was altered later to read one 'He111 Probable' because they had not seen it crash.

In fact, the He111 that they had attacked in the gathering twilight was a machine from *II/KG27* and it was heavily damaged in the engagement. The pilot, *Leutnant* Edmund Tremel, managed to coax the crippled bomber back as far as Le Havre, but on reaching there he lost control and crashed. Tremel and two of his five-man crew were killed. The Heinkel was destroyed, but this would not be known until after the war.

Air combat is a double-edged sword. On the afternoon of 12 December, another engagement brought disaster to 65 Squadron. At 14.20 hours, 'B' Flight was headed towards Selsey Bill when the pilots sighted a Junkers Ju88 despite heavy clouds. Blue Section went into line astern and engaged the German aircraft, but as each Spitfire closed in it was subjected to heavy and accurate return fire. The Ju88 was an aircraft of *4(F)/121* and it managed to escape into the clouds unscathed, the crew claiming two of the Spitfires shot down. The claim was accurate. P/O Bill Franklin and Sgt Merrick Hine failed to return. Tangmere received a report that one of the Spitfires was seen breaking up in the air and crashing into the sea.

While a sergeant pilot, Bill Franklin DFM and Bar had been one of 65 Squadron's rising stars with numerous successes in the actions over Dunkirk and during the Battle of Britain. He had been commissioned in September and modern research has credited him with at least thirteen enemy aircraft destroyed plus three others shared. His name, and that of Sgt Hine, can be found on the memorial at Runnymede for those RAF airmen who lost their lives but have no known grave.

With the German bombers coming in force by night, Britain was staring blindly into the dark reality of facing disaster after disaster, like the night of 14/15 November. That night the *Luftwaffe* had carried out Operation *Moonlight Serenade Corn*, highly accurate spectacular attacks upon the city of Coventry. Using the *Knickebein* blind navigation aid, 437 German aircraft ravaged the city. Some 60,000 out of 75,000 buildings were destroyed or badly damaged. The magnificent 14th-Century cathedral and many ancient structures in the historic centre of the city were reduced to rubble. There were 568 men, women and children killed and 1,200 injured. Among the fatalities, 420 people who were never identified had to be buried in a communal grave.

Fighter Command's night defence was impotent. Of the 124 nightfighters sent up not one was successful. Just one Blenheim managed to intercept a bomber but it quickly merged back into the darkness when attacked. It was claimed as 'damaged'. A second Blenheim fired without any visible effect on a He111 that passed underneath it, but that was it. In fact, only one German bomber was lost, a Do17 of 6/KG3 shot down by AA fire.

Despite British propaganda asserting that this was purely a 'terror raid', the actual targets were the numerous small factories situated within the precincts of the old city of Coventry. These were all devoted to producing various aircraft parts and other military equipment. More than twenty of these were destroyed. To reach them the *Luftwaffe* bombers crossed the British coastline in three waves; one between Portland and Selsey, another between Selsey and Dungeness, while the third crossed in over Norfolk and Lincolnshire. The first two routes fell within range of Tangmere's fighters.

After this successful bombing of Coventry, the Germans willingly added to the idea of it being a 'terror raid' by coining the word *Koventrieren,* meaning to 'annihilate, raze to the ground', and using it for their own propaganda. The *Luftwaffe* began aiming attacks at various other larger cities, as well as on London.

The challenge for the RAF and British science experts was to somehow effectively combat this widening night assault. At this stage, airborne radar carried in nightfighters – called 'Magic Mirrors' by the crews – was far from efficient, but it was improving. So too were the night fighter types. Slow Bristol Blenheims and single-engined Boulton Paul Defiants were being supplemented by the new heavily armed Bristol Beaufighters coming into service.

In the interim, one attempted RAF countermeasure was to send up day fighters, Hurricanes and Spitfires, to patrol in the pathway of the incoming bombers on bright moonlit nights. It was a long shot. By following instructions from the ground RDF, the fighter would be guided into a position where there was some hope of making a visual contact. Using this method, from time to time there were the occasional successes, but these were very few and far between. In reality, it was a hopeful 'trying to find a needle in the haystack' effort.

To this end, 145 Squadron's 'B' Flight started practicing takeoffs and landings at dusk and began flying at night on the 12th. It was 'A' Flights turn the following day. Because of his previous night flying experience, Bob flew one of the squadron's first nocturnal patrols on the 13th/14th, not unexpectedly without achieving a contact.

On the night of 22/23 December, 299 *Luftwaffe* aircraft bombed Liverpool and Birkenhead. By midnight German crews could see the glow of fires from 155 miles (250 km) away. Casualties were heavy: 218 people killed and 173 injured. The RAN cruiser, HMAS *Australia*, which was undergoing a refit in Liverpool Harbour, had her replacement Walrus amphibian damaged by shrapnel.

Meanwhile by day, as Christmas approached and the weather worsened, *Luftwaffe* activity over southern England slackened off even more.

Christmas Eve arrived. The Tangmere sector was exceptionally quiet. No German aircraft were seen by 145 Squadron for a week. Pyker Offenberg spent his first Christmas away from his own home with an English family in Dunmow, Essex. He was taken there by Eric Faure, one of the pilots going off on leave. The two days he spent with them in Dunmow seemed all too short but he was glad to be back in the officers' mess at Tangmere with his old friends, the pilots of 145 Squadron.

At this stage in his narrative, Jean Offenberg's biographer included an unusual and puzzling comment concerning Bob Bungey:

Pyker loved and admired all these men with whom he lived at such close quarters.

Each time he left the station, even for a few hours, something seemed to be missing. Then he was happy to find Dunning-White again in flying boots, sitting on the steps of the hut which served as the squadron office. *He was delighted to find that Bungey had not been shot down despite the mistakes he was bound to have made on his last mission.* [Author's italics] Sitting on the Squadron commander's desk Dudley Honor, in far from regulation kit, was singing an Argentine air. He stopped when Pyker came in:

'Hullo, Pyker. Back at last, eh? Go hide your head. We've been in a murky scrap with fifty Jerries over Plymouth and you weren't in the party.'

'You had a scrap?'

'Sure. A scrap, and I nearly got shot out of the sky. I'm sorry you weren't with us.'

'So am I, Dudley. You can be quite sure of that.'

Offenberg spoke fluent English by this time. He had no need of books or special courses. His highly unorthodox English, full of slang expressions, would have made an Oxford don shudder. He had learned it in 145 Squadron, sitting in old weather-beaten armchairs, by the Hurricanes when his section was in readiness for a 'scramble'.

'Bungey had not been shot down despite the mistakes he was bound to have made on his last mission...' What mistakes? Was Jean Offenberg making

reference to the fact that Bob was continuing to fly despite his knee injury? If so, the comment still does not ring true when it is compared with the Belgian's other comments about Bob. Very puzzling – it does not make sense.

Nor does Dudley Honor's comment make sense. During the Christmas/Boxing Day/New Year period no such air battle 'with fifty Jerries over Plymouth' took place. Nor did such a battle occur anywhere else. The last time 145 squadron encountered 'fifty Jerries' was over the Portsmouth area back on 7 November – and Pyker had missed that particular scrap because he was away from Tangmere for the day.

However, it does start to make sense if it is realised that these were merely typical examples of high-spirited banter between fighter pilots – banter which Pyker Offenberg jotted down in his notebooks as he was teaching himself English. He did this while he was 'sitting in old weather-beaten armchairs by the Hurricanes when his section was in readiness for a "scramble"'. They were typical of the 'stirs', 'teases' and 'sling-offs' that regularly took place among friends and comrades-in-arms.

Knowing how keen Pyker was to be in every battle, and how disappointed he had been when he missed the fight on 7 November, it would have been perfectly natural for Dudley Honor to greet the Belgian in the way he apparently did after Christmas. It was Dudley who had driven Offenberg in his ancient Austin to find the Me109 he had shot down on 2 November, and it was Dudley who had taken a 'victor and vanquished' photograph for Pyker as a souvenir.

To Jean Offenberg these men were 'his pals'. Dunning-White 'in flying boots, sitting on the steps of the hut'; Dudley Honor 'sitting on the Squadron commander's desk, in far from regulation kit, singing an Argentine air'; and Bob.

'*Bungey had not been shot down despite the mistakes he was bound to have made on his last mission…*' Even as high-spirited banter among friends, the statement suggests a lot about Bob. Far from being a person who was always making mistakes, the opposite was true. He was a person who prided himself on not making mistakes. Bob was a steady and meticulous individual – a former accountant and former bomber pilot – who carefully dotted the i's and crossed the t's. He rarely made an error. Just as Pyker Offenberg was mockingly chided for missing another battle, Bob was teased for apparently being always right.

It must be asked, however, could such boisterous backhanded compliments, while meaning to be simply loud, humorous and harmless, be taken seriously by a person who was, in reality, very sensitive? Could they have a detrimental effect on someone who was really inwardly reserved and overly conscientious about his responsibilities? How hurtful could they be? While outwardly laughing off such banter, what if he happened to be involuntarily storing what was said into his subconscious, and into his heart and soul?

What if he, through no fault of his own, had been ambushed by odds that were overwhelming, had been shot down and had almost lost his flight with one man killed? Although the circumstances were totally beyond his control, could he have inwardly regarded what happened as his personal responsibility, his fault, his mistake? Could it be that these were his private thoughts?

What could he do in the face of such banter? He could hide the hurt. He could banter back, of course, but unknowingly and unwittingly he might be storing within the seeds of his own destruction.

The comments about Bob by Jean Offenberg's biographer may or may not be valid, but his description of the Belgian pilot's return to Tangmere after Christmas and of him being greeted at that time in the way he was by Dudley Honor is fiction. It may have been the way Dudley Honor greeted Offenberg back to Tangmere after the big battle on 7 November – but not after Christmas.

On the second day of December 1940, a revealing entry was made in 145 Squadron's ORB. It said: 'Flying Officer D. S. G. Honor DFC was posted for duty in 85 Squadron, Gravesend, 3rd Dece.' Not only was there no big dogfight, Dudley Honor was not even a member of the squadron by Christmas!

The last time the ORB records him flying with 145 Squadron was way back on 27 November. The ORB does show that Bob, Pyker Offenberg, Dunning-White and the other pilots were actively carrying out practice flights, gun camera practice and engine tests on 27 and 28 December, and Bob flew an individual dusk patrol on the 27th. Dudley Honor's name does not appear anywhere.

Then 1941 arrived, bringing with it very cold, to intensely cold, weather and wind. Bob and Pyker Offenberg carried out a dusk patrol on New Year's Day, and four pilots were held available for night flying. During the 2nd, there was no operational flying and some snow fell in the afternoon.

It was fine but very cold on 4 January. Between 1320 and 1405 hours, Bob, Dunning-White and Jean Offenberg were scrambled and vectored after an enemy aircraft was picked up flying south by RDF. They were unable to get within sight of it despite being informed by Control it was only a short distance in front. Perhaps it was one of those Ju88s, which were able to fly just about as fast as their poor old Hurricanes. Flying south, it would have been heading for home and safety as fast as it could.

The 5th arrived with ten-tenths of cloud beginning at 2,000 feet (600 m). Severe icing conditions were reported between 2,500 (760 m) and 4,200 feet (1,300 m).

Owing to adverse weather, there was no flying of any kind the next day but some exciting news was recorded in the ORB: 'Information received from Headquarters, Fighter Command that the Squadron is to be re-equipped with Spitfire Aircraft, Mark 1...'

The response was enthusiastic: 'Signal sent stating Squadron prepared to accept same immediately.'

Spitfires! They were going to get Spitfires!

10

Spitfire Spring

Change was in the air – the pendulum of daylight warfare was starting to swing the other way.

Back on 20 December, two Spitfires from 66 Squadron at Biggin Hill had slipped across the English Channel to France and strafed the *Luftwaffe* airfield at Le Touquet. It was RAF Fighter Command's first offensive operation – a small-scale harassing raid by fighters. This type of low-level strafing mission was originally code-named *Mosquito* but it would soon be changed to *Rhubarb*.

It happened again just after Christmas. Fighter Command's new C-in-C, Air Chief Marshal Sholto Douglas, was well aware that the morale of both the public and his command needed to see change towards a more offensive attitude. He ordered his pilots to adopt a policy of 'leaning forwards into France'. At 12.47 p.m. on the 27th, two Spitfires from 92 Squadron at Biggin Hill flew across to Abbeville at low level where one strafed a staff car and lorry convoy before returning home safely. Having become separated, the other Spitfire returned without finding a target.

Early in the new year, the 'buzz' running around Tangmere was that the fighters would soon be going onto the offensive. Training for sweeps over the Continent was to be organised. The new Spitfires that the pilots of 145 Squadron were expecting would come in very handy for this, but they were not due to start arriving until the 10th.

Air Vice Marshal Leigh-Mallory came to Tangmere one lunchtime to give the squadrons there a 'pep talk'. In his opinion, the Battle of Britain had been fought on the wrong principle. Instead of employing single and paired squadrons, the fighters should have been massed together into huge multiple formations and then attacked the bombers in strength. After the Battle of Britain, Sir Hugh Dowding had been retired and Leigh-Mallory had replaced AVM Keith Park. Air Chief Marshal Sholto Douglas was now in charge of Fighter Command and many changes were being made. To show that this was the way, Leigh-Mallory proposed to send many wings of fighters in huge formations over France to tackle the Germans on terms favourable to the RAF. This time, Leigh-Mallory promised, the RAF would have the superior numbers and the Germans would have a taste of the Battle of Britain in reverse.

Rousing though Leigh-Mallory's words may have been, particularly to the newer pilots, they were not greeted with enthusiasm by everyone present, especially some of the veterans. No record has been found of Bob Bungey's thoughts on Leigh-Mallory's visit and opinions, but his mate from Point Cook days, Gordon Olive, who was a flight commander in 65 Squadron, was there and wrote later:

> I did not like this idea. Had Leigh-Mallory implied less criticism of Park and Dowding, I still would not have liked it.
>
> I had learned that large formations of fighters had big disadvantages and small ones big advantages. Large formations could be seen too easily and from too far away; they could be stalked and taken advantage of tactically. They were also very unwieldy and as all the pilots were busy keeping station in their formations, only the leaders had any time or opportunity for effective search. This made the big formation a liability rather than an asset.
>
> From the start I felt that the only result would be that we would fly over enemy territory where we would meet, not the great massed formations of 1940 but small elements of twos and fours which would dive out of the sun or other positions of advantage and destroy our large formations aeroplane by aeroplane just as we had done the summer before...

Olive's thoughts turned out to be prophetic on Thursday, 9 January 1941, three days after the rumours started, and the day before 145 Squadron was to begin the change over from Hurricanes, orders were received for it to take part in one of the first major sweeps over the occupied Continent.

The pilots were enthusiastic, especially the Belgian Jean Offenberg, but he was disheartened to find that he had not been named among those who were to fly.

'Sorry, Pyker, it's not for you,' Bob Bungey had to tell him.

'Why?' Offenberg snapped back.

'Continentals are not allowed to take part in missions of this type – Air Ministry orders. It's too dangerous for you should you happen to be shot down. Sorry, Pyker, old man.'

Bitterly disappointed, Offenberg and his comrade Baudouin de Hemptinne could only watch as the others climbed into their Hurricanes, possibly for the last time. Perhaps significantly, according to Offenberg's biographer, they took off in pairs, not the tired old Vics – in-house tactics might be changing too. They all gained height and manoeuvred into formation with 65 Squadron's Spitfires and 610 Squadron's Spitfires from nearby Westhampnett. Then they disappeared into the clouds still climbing towards the south out to sea on the way to France.

Later, in his Log Book, Bob noted the route they followed: Le Touquet; St Omer; and Dunkirk before turning for home.

Pyker Offenberg was watching as they returned. They were all there. Nobody was missing. Bob greeted him.

'Well, Pyker, old man. It's a piece of cake. We didn't see a thing the whole trip. We met nothing.'

'Nothing at all?'

'No. Not even ack-ack ... all over Brittany. An absolute picnic...'

This type of operation, a fighter sweep over enemy territory without escorting bombers, would become known as a *Rodeo*.

Besides *Rhubarb* and *Rodeo*, more new code words were starting to surface. These included:

- *Circus* – an operation by bombers, or fighter-bombers, escorted by fighters which was primarily and designed to bring enemy fighters into action.
- *Ramrod* – an operation similar to a *Circus*, but this time priority was given to the destruction of the target. Fighter *Ramrods* would also be flown using cannon-armed fighters such as the new Westland Whirlwinds that were being talked about instead of bombers.
- *Roadstead* – an operation to escort bombers making diving or low-level attacks on ships, whether at sea or in a harbour. Fighter *Roadsteads* would be also flown.

The RAF launched its very first *Circus* operation the next day, Friday 10th. It marked the beginning of a reversal of roles for the opposing sides since the evacuation of Dunkirk. For the first time since the middle of 1940, an escorted British bomber force was ordered to penetrate into enemy-held airspace.

Circus No.1 involved sending six Blenheims of 114 Squadron to bomb ammunition dumps at Fôret de Guînes in France. The escort was huge with no less than nine squadrons of fighters, plus there were two more squadrons used for forward air support. The *Luftwaffe's* response was minimal and the RAF actually came off second-best. For the loss of two British fighters and two more damaged, not one German fighter was shot down, despite of some over-enthusiastic claiming at the time. Nevertheless, this was the start of the daylight air offensive from England, a campaign that was destined to last for more than four years.

The squadrons at Tangmere were not involved in *Circus No.1*. During the 10th, the first five Spitfires were flown in for 145 Squadron, much to the excitement of 145's enthusiastic pilots who took turns to sit in them and fly them. Bob was one of the first to go up in a Spitfire for a local 20-minute hop at 11.35 a.m. After his turn later in the day, Pyker Offenberg had to be chastised for performing aerobatics only 30 feet (9 m) above the ground!

The machine that Bob flew that Friday morning was Spitfire Mk I, N3127, which actually carried the identification code letters 'YT'. This revealed that it was really an aircraft belonging to 65 Squadron, which was also stationed at Tangmere. The codes allocated to 145 Squadron were 'SO'. This particular aircraft had been in service for some time. It was first delivered to 266 Squadron in February 1940, before coming into 65 Squadron's hands at Turnhouse in Scotland the following October, prior to 65's transfer south to Tangmere. As 65 Squadron was about to receive new Mk IIA Spitfires, Spitfire N3127 was eventually officially turned over to 145 Squadron later in January.

The word was that 145 would be using Spitfire Mk Is for familiarisation and training on the new type before it too would be re-equipped with the newer Spitfire Mk IIs.

Meanwhile, for 145's Hurricanes it was business as usual. Bob in Hurricane V6988, Pyker Offenberg and Sgt Gardiner, a newcomer whom Pyker called a 'martyr', took off from Tangmere at 1.45 p.m. and carried out a patrol but made no contact with the enemy.

Peter Dunning-White, Sgt Russell and Sgt Turnbull who took off 5 minutes after Bob and his section, had better luck. Patrolling over Littlehampton at 15,000 feet (4,600 m) they intercepted a Ju88. Despite intense return fire, Dunning-White closed in and fired a 3-second burst causing flames to flow back from one engine. The gunner stopped shooting, probably either wounded or killed. Turnbull then gave chase for about 35 miles (56 km) before losing contact when the Ju88's smoke trail thickened and it dived towards the sea. They claimed a probable kill.

Bob's day was not yet over. At 5.35 p.m., he was at the controls of Hurricane V7003 after its maintenance inspection and performed a standard routine engine test flight. It was the aircraft he had been using for most of the week.

Bob had leave due for the weekend and on Saturday morning he flew the squadron's hack Miles Magister R1875 up to RAF Benson, the first stop on his way to visit Sybil at Wallingford. By now he had a quite well-established routine – the telephone call, the 30- to 40- minute flight, the low approach, and later a departure over that familiar waving figure that looked so small and vulnerable on the bridge across the Thames at the edge of the village.

He flew the Magister back to Tangmere on Monday morning, the 13th. Then he had another short familiarisation flight in Spitfire N3127. He was lucky to fly at all as the weather that day was poor. It deteriorated even further over the next few days. In fact, inclement weather curtailed operational flying by both sides during much of the rest of January.

The whole month passed uneventfully. There was no way the Germans could launch an invasion now despite their propaganda threats. Between a couple of periods of really bad weather, Bob either flew patrols over the south coast or trained with Pyker Offenberg and Gardiner the Martyr.

Squadron Leader Johnny Peel left after a short period of command. His leadership had been very much an on-again, off-again affair. Slightly injured, he had made a forced-landing on the Isle of Wight back on 8 August 1940 and been awarded the DFC. A month later he had left the squadron but returned to command again on 18 November. Now, early in the New Year he was posted away again. (In March he would be appointed wing leader at RAF Kenley.)

Peel was replaced by the newly promoted S/Ldr Bill Leather, a former RAuxAF pilot who had joined 611 Squadron in May 1936, and been called to full-time service with that squadron on 26 August 1939. He served with distinction during the Battle of Britain and had been awarded a DFC in October 1940. Leather's approach to training and tactics was rigid and traditional and this meant continuing to fly in sections of three. He would lead 145 Squadron for the next three months until mid-April.

Adrian Boyd, who had been in temporary command when Bob had joined 145 Squadron in Scotland, had been posted to an OTU in December after Johnny Peel's brief return. In August 1941, he would be appointed wing leader at RAF Middle Wallop.

Frantisek Weber, the Czech from Prague, left Tangmere on 26 January, was promoted to flight lieutenant and in June 1941 he was placed in command of No.310 (Czech) Squadron. As the old hands departed, new pilots arrived and had to be trained. The veteran Mike Newling received a well-earned DFC, recorded in the *London Gazette* on 4 February.

Early in his reign, Bill Leather invited all the officers of the squadron to a night out at the nearby market village of Midhurst. Commandeering all the cars available, this bunch of brigands burst into the Old Spread Eagle pub where, noisy, happy and excitable in their smart uniforms, they commandeered the tables. The only others present were those men who were too old to fight, and these became eager listeners as they were regaled with tall tales of Messerschmitts, tracers, smoke trails, weavers and other stories which only fighter pilots could tell. The boys flirted with the barmaid as she served them with drinks. Bob, who was not a drinker, and Pyker Offenberg challenged the locals to games of darts. It was a good night, a very happy night – and a very late one. If the locals were not awakened by the throbbing engines of *Luftwaffe* bombers passing overhead to London, their slumbers may have been shattered by the merry singing of the RAF boys as they loudly made their way home in their rattling old vehicles.

Nevertheless, despite having a heavy night, six fighters from 145 Squadron were in the air again over Sussex on dawn patrol at 25,000 feet (7,600 m) as per usual. With the weather gradually improving, the new chapter in the air war began. There were four *Circus* operations in February.

During the afternoon of the 2nd, *Circus No.2* made up of five Bristol Blenheims supported by no less than six squadrons of Spitfires and Hurricanes targeted Boulogne Docks. Three more squadrons of fighters carried out a supporting sweep of the Channel. Seven Me109s were seen in the target area, but they made no attempt to intervene. Then, in a diving attack on the bombers by two Messerschmitts just as the force was leaving Boulogne, both were damaged by the escorts, one crash landing wrecked near the port. In other clashes, two 109s were claimed destroyed, and another a 'probable', but one Spitfire was lost and one force-landed damaged. Three others almost out of fuel were obliged to force-land at various places.

Although the weather was fair in the morning on 5 February, it started to deteriorate after midday. *Circus No.3* to St Omer/Wizernes began shortly after noon and consisted of twelve Blenheims, six each from 139 and 114 Squadrons, escorted by six squadrons of fighters plus three more squadrons flying target support. This time units from Tangmere Control, Nos.65, 302 and 610 (the latter two from Westhampnett) flew as top cover. As several Me109s made diving attacks, 65 Squadron separated from the rest of the top cover wing and chased them down. F/Lt Paddy Finucane claimed a 109 shot down at low level, but two of 65s Spitfires failed to return. A No.610 Spitfire went down burning west of Wizernes, and another was badly shot-up – although wounded, the pilot managed to bring the battered fighter home. In all, the operation cost the RAF seven fighters lost, plus one badly damaged.

No.145 Squadron was not involved. When the weather cleared and flying was possible, new Spitfires were ferried to Tangmere and delivered to the squadron. Bob, Pyker Offenberg, P/O Ashton and Sgt Turnbull proceeded to Duxford where they picked up four Spitfires that formerly belonged to 92 Squadron and flew them back to Tangmere. The rest of the pilots carried out formation and cloud flying practice in their new machines, plus some 'sea-firing'. As some wit has remarked, 'You can't really miss the ocean, can you?' A section of three Hurricanes patrolled over the base in the afternoon.

At noon on 10 February, six Blenheims and thirty Hurricanes flew a *Roadstead*, a low-level attack on shipping in the harbour at Boulogne, which drew no reaction from the *Luftwaffe*. At almost the same time, *Circus No.4* consisting of six Blenheims escorted by four squadrons of fighters was on its way to Dunkirk Docks. One Hurricane was lost and two damaged for two Me109s claimed destroyed.

Another *Roadstead* made up of six Blenheims escorted by twenty-six Hurricanes and sixteen Spitfires attacked Calais later in the afternoon. The bombers hit their target but this time the Hurricane escorts were badly mauled. No claims were lodged by the RAF pilots but four Hurricanes were lost and several others damaged. Again 145 Squadron was not involved. It was still accumulating Spitfires and new pilots.

There was news for the Belgians on 21 February. The group captain in command of Tangmere announced that in future foreigners would be allowed to participate in offensive sweeps over the Continent. For the aggressive Jean Offenberg, this was very welcome. His biographer wrote: 'Life was good. The grey English sky with all its clouds and cloying mists had cleared for him … With Bungey he played at war in mock air battles, "chasing each other", as he writes, "round big clumps of cumulus"'.

As the Spitfires arrived and became available for squadron training, 145's Hurricane numbers were reduced. On the 22nd, four were ferried out, three of them by Bob. Each time, this involved him in flying one aircraft across to Westhampnett satellite airfield, just a direct 2 miles (3 km) away – 5 minutes flying time – down the road, and leaving it there. Then he would be driven back for the next machine.

Four days later on the 26th, *Circus No.5* began at midday. Twelve Blenheims from 139 Squadron escorted by sixty-four RAF fighters set out to bomb Calais. From the point of view of stirring a strong reaction from the *Luftwaffe*, the raid was a dismal failure. The bombing was carried out without interference, apart from heavy flak. As the force turned for home, a Spitfire pilot of 54 Squadron followed his leader down after a lone Me109 but then lost contact, only to be caught and shot down by another Messerschmitt near Calais. He was captured without injury.

With the Hurricanes gone, it was time for action in the Spitfires. As if to celebrate his DFC, the veteran Mike Newling scored 145 Squadron's first victory in a Spitfire on 1 March. At 7.15 p.m., he led his section of three Spitfires off the

Isle of Wight and intercepted a Ju88 on its way to bomb Cardiff. Their combined fire shot the German bomber down into the sea off St Catherine's Point.

On Monday, 3 March, after Bob returned from another weekend of leave at Wallingford, he flew a Mk II Spitfire for the first time. This was Spitfire P7975, one out of a pair that had been delivered the week before. Originally, it came from the Vickers-Armstrong Ltd factory at Castle Bromwich out of the first contract for a thousand Mk II Spitfires. As the commander of 'B' Flight, Bob could choose it as his regular aircraft.

Of interest is the fact that just a couple of machines ahead on the Castle Bromwich production line there was another Spitfire, which the RAF gave the serial number P7973. The ultimate destiny of this particular aircraft would place it into the hands of the Australian War Memorial in Canberra. It can still be seen on display there in the museum, but a great many things would happen to it before that would come to pass.

Bob flew his new Spitfire P7975 a week later, on Monday 10 March, when patrols were ordered to provide air cover for a convoy of coastal steamers off the south coast. It had been a long time since 145 Squadron had been fully committed to operations. Everybody watched in silence as Bill Leather appeared in the crew room to write up on the blackboard in chalk the names of those who were wanted. It would still be a formation of three. In capital letters he wrote: 'No.1 PYKER; No.2 MACCONNELL; No.3 SYLVESTER' – two veterans with one of the newcomers. The trio departed immediately to get ready.

The next names to go up on the blackboard were: 'No.1 BUNGEY; No.2 DEHEMPTINNE; No.3 GUNDRY' – again, two veterans and a newcomer but they would not be needed for another hour or so.

Offenberg located the convoy south of the Isle of Wight. There were about twenty-five coastal vessels – the brave little ships of the Coal Shuttle Brigade. The weather was good with fairly clear visibility but there was no trade in sight. After circling above the convoy for a fruitless hour, the Belgian led his section back to Tangmere.

As they landed, Bob's section of Spitfires took off. When they arrived over the ships dense clouds were forming and the sky to the south was completely overcast. They circled, cruising at 15,000 feet (4,600 m), but the voice of the sector controller warned of a bandit at Angels 10, i.e. 10,000 feet (3,000 m). It was flying along the south coast about 25 miles out to sea. They were vectored to intercept.

Bob and his wingmen scanned the darkening sky carefully and at first could see nothing. Then suddenly, lower down at two o'clock, the dark shape of an aircraft emerged from the clouds. It was about 3,000 feet (900 m) below and looked like a Junkers Ju88. German records indicate it could have been a machine from *Kampfgeschwader GR.806* based at Caen.

'Green leader, tally-ho!' Bob and his section were about to attack. They manoeuvre into position as they had practised many times.

The *Luftwaffe* crew was alert. The three Spitfires had been seen and the bomber pilot immediately turned south, diving slightly to gain speed. De Hemptinne attacked the bomber at the instant it turned. He fired while closing in to 100 yards (90 m). As he broke away, Bob came in from three-quarters astern. During his attack the enemy's rear gunner stopped firing – perhaps he had been killed or wounded, or perhaps the gun itself was damaged or jammed, but the two Spitfires were out of ammunition.

The German plane continued diving to the south and finally straightened out at 1,500 feet (460 m). Bob and de Hemptinne re-formed to sit above and behind on the bomber's tail. They would have made easy targets for any capable rear gunner. The aircraft seemed defenceless, unable to return fire, but it was still flying. It needed to be finished off. Now was a good time for Gundry the newcomer to be blooded.

According to the account told later to Jean Offenberg in the crew room, De Hemptinne then called Gundry on the intercom to face his baptism of fire: 'Green 3, wade in. Push your attack home and fire when you're certain of hitting him. Don't be scared: he can't fire.' He and Bob would have then moved out of the way.

The novice dipped his wings and came down in a magnificent sweep, finishing on the tail of the Ju88. He fired a long burst – far too long – making his break so near the enemy's tail unit that he nearly ran into it. When he pulled out he was only 50 feet above the water.

At this moment, in a fight which had only lasted a few seconds, the Junkers flew into the clouds near the coast, to reappear a little lower down, and crashed into the sea.

Green Section re-formed and returned for home a few feet above the waves.[1]

No.145 Squadron's records for 10 March reveal doubts about Gundry's 'kill':

Weather fine. Convoy patrol in the morning. In the afternoon a sweep carried out over Hastings, Boulogne, Cap Gris Nez and Calais. Earlier in the afternoon a Ju88 was attacked over the Channel by F/Lt Bungey, P/O De Hemptinne and P/O Gundry. In spite of firing all their ammunition, it could only be claimed as damaged, and was last seen climbing for cloud cover.

Gundry's attack had apparently not been fatal and indeed *Luftwaffe* records show that Ju88A5 No.4157 of *Kampfgeschwader Gr.806* later crash-landed at Caen. It had suffered 40% damage in combat but there was no mention of the presence of any casualties among the crew. Obviously, it had not crashed into the sea, as was suggested.

However, there were other German aircraft operating in the same area that day. The *Luftwaffe* sustained another loss when a Messerschmitt 110E-3, No.2316/4U+XL, from *3.(F)/123*, failed to return. This was a *Luftflotte 3* reconnaissance unit equipped with a mixture of Ju88s, Do17Ps and Me110s based at airfields in the Paris area, and the aircraft was reported missing somewhere south of Portsmouth, believed to have crashed into the sea. Of its two-man crew, *St.Fw* H. Zeigenbalk was listed as missing and *Fw* W. Ruschenburg was listed as killed.

Was it actually this Me110, not the Ju88, which Green Section had seen crashing down into the water? As Ju88 No.4157 made good its lucky escape from the Spitfires hidden by cloud cover, could it have been Me110 No.2316 that appeared 'a little lower down, and crashed into the sea'? Or, could it have been the Me110 that the three Spitfires attacked, not the Ju88? Mistakes in aircraft recognition were not rare.

The weather improved the next day and 145 Squadron was committed to patrols over the Portsmouth area to try to intercept more possible German reconnaissance machines, but no contacts were made. Again on the 12th, the weather was fine but this time the day was occupied with a full programme of practice flying. That night, the *Luftwaffe* paid Tangmere aerodrome a visit. About twenty bombs were dropped, including a large one that fell on the corner of the officers' mess. Five people were killed.

Circus No.7 was flown in the early afternoon of 13 March. Six Blenheims of 139 Squadron attacked Calais/Marck airfield under heavy fighter protection. This included the Tangmere Spitfires flying top cover. Nos.610 and 616 Squadrons from Westhampnett were employed with 145 capping as top squadron, Mike Newling leading 'A' Flight and Bob leading 'B' Flight.

After the bombers unloaded, they withdrew towards Boulogne where the escorts were hotly engaged by Me109s flying in pairs. No.610 Squadron fought off the main assaults and in the process claimed one Messerschmitt destroyed and two probables for the loss of one Spitfire and pilot. Bob and the 145 squadron pilots could see the dogfight below, but there was little they could do to intervene. They were busy themselves. With the exception of Sgt Sykes who had to return to Tangmere early, 145 landed without loss between 3.10 and 3.15 p.m. Tangmere was on the receiving end of more bombs, a further twenty-three of them during the night. Four Spitfires were damaged.

The next day brought fine weather and more practice flying. It clouded over after dark and no bombs were dropped during the night.

Meanwhile, No.65 Squadron, 145's sister squadron at Tangmere, approached the end of its third tour of front-line duty. It had operated over Dunkirk, during the frantic August days of the Battle of Britain and joined 145 Squadron at Tangmere last November. It was due to be relieved. Gordon olive noted with some pride:

> During this time our squadron had lost some twenty two pilots killed due to enemy action and our claim of kills, though conservative in the extreme, stood at about seventy five...
>
> Douglas Bader, the great exponent of these new tactics which I disliked so much, was coming down and he would show us how it was done...

The irrepressible Douglas 'Tin Legs' Bader, who had lost his own legs as the result of a pre-war flying accident, was already an RAF legend. After recovering and being fitted with experimental artificial legs, through sheer determination and his own force of personality he was able to return to flying. During the Battle of Britain he commanded 242 Squadron and ultimately led No.12 Group's Buford Wing of up to five squadrons of Hurricanes and

Spitfires. He was a loud exponent of using fighters stacked in large numbers in 'Big Wings' and an avid supporter Air Vice Marshal Leigh-Mallory's ideas. No.65 Squadron's place in the line would be taken by Bader's 242 Squadron, and Bader himself would take over command of the wing. Prior to his appointment, there had been no formal position of wing leader at all, the lead was usually taken by the senior pilot in the formation.

Olive continued:

Further news angered us more. Not only was it to be the end of our third tour in the front line, the squadron was to be completely broken up. Perhaps the 'new order' had reason to think that we were critical of their magnificent new tactics. Perhaps they felt we were too tired to appreciate brilliance when we saw it, or perhaps we were too set in our ways... Sam[2] was to go to an operational training unit. MacPherson[3] was to go to another. Wigg[4] was to go for a rest too, as were all the others who had completed the last tour. I was to be promoted to squadron leader and stay on at Tangmere as a Controller in the Operation's Room for three months. At the end of the rest I was to take over command of another squadron...

MacPherson and Wigg were morose, Sam was even more remote than ever, and Twitching Whiskers drank so much whisky that he was incoherent. Paddy Finucane and Dave Glaser[5] were the only ones not visibly affected, nothing ever worried them... We were not tired this time, we felt we could go on indefinitely at the present tempo. We were getting plenty of sleep and the operations were nothing like as hazardous as the previous summer. However, that was it.

We had a somewhat sad series of farewells and the squadron flew off to its rest area leaving me at Tangmere. I never saw Wigg again. Sam Saunders I was to see twice ... Mac, my dear friend Mac, I would see only once more.

It would have been a very lonely time for me but for Bob Bungey. His unit, 145 Squadron, stayed on for a few more weeks.

But Bob's time at Tangmere was coming to an end too. His damaged knee, whether it had been caused by his forced-ditching near the Isle of Wight back in November, or had been an old football injury aggravated by what had happened, was giving him more and more discomfort. Walking around now, he was very lame but he continued to fight off the idea of giving up flying. In the end, his decision for surgery was one in which he had no real choice – the knee had to be fixed or he would only be suitable for a desk job.

No.145 Squadron was about to be moved out of Tangmere too, but only a few miles south to the other satellite airfield at Merston. Once there, there would be another 'changing of the guard'. Bill Leather would be replaced by the newly promoted S/Ldr Percival Stanley Turner DFC.[6] An English-born Canadian, Stan Turner had been a flight commander in Bader's 242 Squadron during the Battle of Britain and was therefore a staunch supporter of Bader and Leigh-Mallory, and their ideas.

Bob had to make his own series of sad farewells. Because of the estimated time he would need for medical treatment and recovery, regulations required the squadron to appoint a new commander of 'B' flight in his absence. This meant that even if all went well, it was unlikely he would come back to 145 Squadron.

He would miss them, his family of friends. There were the two Belgians with whom he got on so well, good old Jean Offenberg[7] (Pyker) and Baudouin de Hemptinne;[8] the very capable Mike Newling;[9] and Peter Dunning-White[10] had already been posted away to 615 Squadron at Kenley as a flight commander on the 18th; and, of course, the other Aussie on base, Gordon Olive[11] – would he meet up with any of them again? Bob left Tangmere on the morning of 30 March to go to a hospital near London.

Meanwhile to the north at Kirton-in-Lindsey in Lincolnshire, at the same time as Bob was undergoing treatment, a new squadron was being formed. Although it was a Royal Australian Air Force squadron, it had been allocated a Royal Air Force number and it was meant to be part of the Royal Air Force.

The new unit was No.452 (RAAF) Squadron.

11

452 (RAAF) Squadron

No.452 Squadron was the first RAAF squadron formed to serve in RAF Fighter Command in England, and the first to be equipped with Spitfires. It was created under Article XV of the Empire Air Training Scheme (EATS).

This agreement that brought the EATS into existence was signed at Ottawa in Canada on 17 December 1939 by British and Commonwealth representatives. According to its terms, Britain would supply nearly all the aircraft and a nucleus of skilled personnel, and the Commonwealth dominions would fulfil the other requirements. The Australian government committed to the creation within Australia of nine Elementary Flying Training Schools, seven Service Flying Training Schools, four Air Observer Schools and four Bombing and Gunnery Schools.

Australian government approval was also given to a plan for the progressive formation of RAAF squadrons under Article XV. Two were to be formed by March 1941; six by July 1941; nine by September 1941; twelve by December 1941; fifteen by March 1942; and eighteen by May 1942. Canada and New Zealand were similarly committed. RAAF, RCAF and RNZAF units created under this system were to be under the command of the RAF and allocated RAF squadron numbers ranging from 400 to 499. The Australian numbers were to start at 450. The first to form, Nos.450 and 451 Squadrons, were committed to the fighting in the Middle East. Technically, they should be labelled by the RAF squadron number; country of origin service; Squadron RAF. In other words they should be No.450 (RAAF) Squadron RAF and No.451 (RAAF) Squadron RAF, and so on.

No.452 (RAAF) Squadron began forming at Kirton-in-Lindsey in Lincolnshire on 8 April 1941 under the command of S/Ldr Roy Dutton DFC and Bar. Dutton was an experienced pilot, a pre-war air drill flyer at Hendon, and he had nineteen enemy aircraft destroyed to his credit. He had been posted in from his flight commander's position in 145 Squadron at Tangmere.

On the other side of Kirton-in-Lindsey, No.65 Squadron was settled in after its arrival from Tangmere at the end of February. The fighting Irishman

Paddy Finucane was still a member of the squadron but on 14 April he was promoted to flight lieutenant and appointed to command 'A' Flight in the new Australian unit.

To end his successful first tour, Finucane flew one more sortie with 65 Squadron on the 15th, a wing sweep over Boulogne with 266 and 402 Squadrons. On the way back at 14,000 feet (4,270 m) midway between Calais and Dover late in the afternoon, he shot a Messerschmitt 109 down into the Channel. He was recommended for the Distinguished Flying Cross and his logbook was signed with a fighter pilot rating of 'exceptional'. His DFC was awarded ten days later on 25 April. The citation said he had shown great keenness to engage the enemy and destroyed five enemy aircraft. 'His courage and enthusiasm have been a source of encouragement to other pilots of the squadron.'

Brendan Eugene Finucane was an inspired choice for the new Australian squadron.

The first groups of Australian pilots had already arrived at Kirton-in-Lindsey, mostly from No.57 OTU, a Spitfire training unit. The first to turn up on 12 April were Sergeants Alex Roberts and E. B. 'Pat' Tainton, posted in from 607 (County of Durham) Squadron. They were followed over the next month by others who were mostly posted in from operational training units.

Next came P/O Ray Thorold-Smith (from Young, NSW) and eleven sergeant pilots. From South Australia: Paul Makin (Adelaide), transferred from the RAF, and Ian Milne (Wirrabara); from Victoria, Ed Walliker (Warrnambool). From NSW: Dick Gazzard (Sydney), Jim Hanigan (Sydney), Arch Stuart (Grafton), Pat Tainton (Sydney), Alex Roberts (Lismore). And from Queensland: Andy Costello (Charters Towers), Raife Cowan (Brisbane) and Barry Haydon (Brisbane).

The second batch of Spitfire-trained pilots to arrive was made up of: Keith 'Bluey' Truscott (Melbourne, Victoria), Jay O'Byrne (Launceston, Tasmania), Ray Holt (Cracow, Queensland), Bill Eccleton (Sydney, NSW), Don Lewis (Melbourne, Victoria) and Don Willis (Melbourne, Victoria) who were pilot officers. Fred McCann (Hobart, Tasmania), Barry Chapman (Charleville, Queensland), Keith Chisholm (Manly, Sydney) and Ken 'King Kong' Cox (Melbourne) were sergeant pilots.

With the arrival of the first Mk I Spitfires on 17 April, training began in earnest. By the end of the month the Squadron had an establishment of sixteen Spitfires, seven officers (four of whom were non-flying), eleven sergeant pilots and eighty-three other ranks.

Ian Milne's memories of these early days were vivid:

Early in April 1941, I arrived at Kirton Lindsey to find that the squadron consisted of Paul Makin and myself from the new intake, Paddy Finucane the officer in charge, an engineering officer, a senior NCO, and that appears by my memory to be the sum total. Quite soon afterwards, Tainton and Roberts appeared, who were with me on the first course, and we commenced flying.

My first flight was on April 20th with Paddy Finucane in a Magister doing a check duel for some fifteen minutes and then into the air for my first flight in a Spitfire Mk I. This amounted to circuits and landings and turns and general familiarisation, and then sector reconnaissance to get familiar with the countryside.

Then we proceeded with routine training until our commanding officer appeared and his name of course was Roy Dutton. He was an RAF officer of considerable ability and service record.

It was early in June when 452 Squadron was required to assist in a fund raising effort by low flying a formation of four aircraft over a nearby village where a War Weapons Week function was being conducted to hopefully raise £5,000 which would enable a Spitfire to be named after the village. The Mk II Spitfire that I flew actually wore the Coat of Arms of the city of Hull.

The day that was selected for the flight was marred by impossibly rough weather for close formation flying and we all expected that the people upstairs would decide to abort the flight. However, no scratching was forthcoming and Roy Dutton escorted by Andy Costello and Dick Gazzard formed the vic and Paddy flew in the box in line astern of the CO.

Over the village they flew through some particularly turbulent air. The CO's aircraft dropped downwards suddenly while Paddy's aircraft remained level and this brought Paddy's airscrew into collision with the CO's tail unit. The CO was only able to force land straight ahead, fortunately on the village green without hurting anybody except himself. He was removed to hospital for an indefinite period of repair and recuperation.

Paddy managed to fly home with a very ropey motor and about a foot having been removed from each propeller blade. To make the formation tidy, Paddy would have been doing his best to match the pattern of Andy and Dick. I often led Andy and Dick in formation. They always flew tight formations very precisely.

Roy Dutton returned from hospital and was back at Kirton-in-Lindsey by 4.30 p.m. When Paddy Finucane came into the officers' mess, he found George Potter, the station adjutant, with his battered but otherwise intact CO slumped in an armchair in the ante room. Finucane stared at Dutton and exclaimed, 'God, sir, I thought I'd killed you.'

According to George Potter, Dutton replied, 'You won't get my job that way, Paddy.'

Although Dutton was back, he was not in good shape. Outwardly, he was wearing only a small bandage on his forehead but his face was swollen where an eyebrow had been stitched together and he had cracked ribs. When he walked, he could only do so with difficulty. In the crash, he had been knocked unconscious when his restraining straps broke on impact, and at Halifax Hospital they had dosed him up with rum as they treated his wounds. He had also sustained a back injury, which would plague him with trouble later when he was serving as SASO with the RAF's No.249 Wing in Italy.

Paddy Finucane did, in fact, get Roy Dutton's job – temporarily at least. Dutton had to take the obligatory sick leave and that left his senior flight commander as temporary squadron commander in full charge of 452 Squadron's training programme. In three weeks, the young Irish ace had suddenly gone from being a new deputy flight commander to a temporary squadron commander charged with being responsible for twenty-three pilots and sixteen Spitfire Mk Is, plus around 130 ground crew including NCOs and airmen.

There was always banter and rivalry between the pilots of 452 Squadron and 65 Squadron, Paddy Finucane's old unit, and after Dutton's crash one of 65 Squadron's humourists placed a sign up: '452 yards to Bend 'em Brendan and his demolition squad'.

There was a spate of minor accidents during training, mainly while taxying and landing. Bluey Truscott's aircraft clipped the top of one of 65 Squadron's Spitfires at its dispersal. Alex Roberts damaged a Spitfire while taxying. Ed Walliker had to belly-land with an undercarriage problem. Jay O'Byrne and Andy Costello both crashed, and Raife Cowan undershot on his approach and ended up in hospital with a broken arm. Finucane let the sign stay where it was as 'Bend 'em Brendan's demolition squad' seemed to be turning into a reality.

Finucane was joined on 8 May by a thirty-four-year-old Scotsman, F/Lt Graham Douglas, who was a former flying instructor. Douglas became the commander of 'B' Flight. Although he had spent a few weeks with No.74 Squadron, his experience as a fighter pilot was very limited, so the responsibility for 452's training stayed with Finucane. It was a case of the right man being in the right job at the right time. The Irishman was the only pilot among the twenty-five on strength who had combat experience.

'Paddy was just what was needed to get the squadron on its feet', recalled Graham Douglas. 'He was a terrific morale booster...' There was such a natural affinity between Finucane and the Australians that he came to regard 452 as 'his' squadron.

'We finished using our Mk I Spitfires,' recalled Ian Milne. 'May the 18th was the last flight I had in a Spitfire Mk I. We then received time expired aircraft for front line action supposedly from a Polish squadron which we collected from Northolt and flew back to Kirton.'

Finucane's new Spitfire Mk II carried the serial number P8038. It was the first of four Spitfires that would feature his own personal shamrock emblem.

By the third week in May, the squadron was fully re-equipped with the Mk II Spitfires that had been collected on 21 May from No.303 (Polish) Squadron, and after solving some ground crew servicing problems, Finucane gave his whole attention to improving 452's proficiency in the air. His training was intense with practice dogfights, formation flying, air drill, a battle climb to 32,000 feet (9,750 m), practice interceptions and gunnery training at the Sutton Bridge and Manby firing ranges.

RAF Fighter Command declared the Australian squadron fully day operational on 2 June, much to Finucane's satisfaction. Because of

Roy Dutton's injuries and the obligatory length of time he needed to recover properly, standard RAF procedure dictated that he be replaced as commanding officer. The Australian government had requirements too, primarily that Australians should be in command of their own EATS squadrons as soon as that was possible to be achieved. Accordingly, pressure was exerted from Australia House for 452 Squadron's new CO to be an Australian.

The new CO arrived on 10 June. He was described as being 'twenty-six, lean and hawk-faced with the healthy tan of the Australian open air type'. It was Bob Bungey with the new rank of squadron leader, and he was no longer limping.

Bob and Paddy Finucane knew each other from Tangmere days through Gordon Olive, and thanks to Paddy's outstanding effort Bob was able to take over a squadron that was already well on the way to being moulded into a fighting unit. Ian Milne recalled:

> There was a short period during the squadron's progress that we operated with Paddy Finucane in command in lieu of a new commanding officer, and then we were delighted to be informed that our new CO had arrived, and further more delighted to find that he was an Australian and particularly for Paul Makin and myself that he came from Adelaide. Bob Bungey was with us.
>
> Then the procedure went on as everybody expected to raise the squadron to readiness for combat and this was done with a great deal of attention to detail and discipline. Bob was quick to react to any suggestion of slackness and substandard performance and as was necessary he corrected the errors that were threatening to the performance of the job in hand.

Next day, the 11th, Bob flew the squadron's Magister with Jay O'Byrne as passenger to Tangmere to pick up a Spitfire. O'Byrne flew the Magister back while Bob brought the Spitfire. Initially, he entered this in his logbook as Spitfire 7973 (P7973), but the book shows a correction. The numbers 7973 are crossed out and 8038 written in just above. If this is right it would have been Paddy Finucane's Spitfire P8038, although what it was doing at Tangmere is unknown. If Bob's original entry is actually the correct one with the serial number P7973, this was the aircraft which would ultimately reside in the Australian War Memorial's collection in Canberra. Spitfire P7973 did, in fact, become Bob's regular machine during June and July 1941.

Although the pilots would lay claim to a particular aircraft that they flew regularly, it did not mean that was the only machine they flew. Routine maintenance and servicing governed which aircraft were available at any given time. Bob did fly Paddy Finucane's Spitfire P8038 again on 14 June to practice cloud flying and for a night flying test. The last time he flew Spitfire P7973 was while leading a 'Squadron Balbo' on 7 July.[1] This required intense practice of combat manoeuvres in large formations until every pilot was competent and ready to take part in front-line fighter sweeps and *Circus* operations.

Bob was quick to realise that, as well as Paddy Finucane and Graham Douglas, there were numerous other promising fliers as well as outstanding characters in 452 Squadron. They were a varied lot.

Thickset, red-haired and so naturally called 'Bluey', Keith Truscott from Melbourne was an imposing, outgoing, all-round sportsman and former Aussie Rules star who had a high-pitched voice, especially when he became excited. He had nearly failed the basic flying course on Tiger Moths at Essendon in Victoria, but his qualities clearly marked him out as a fighter pilot during his later flying training at Calgary, Canada. After reaching England, as his group travelled to Hull by train, he and Jay O'Byrne won all the money at pontoon and poker on the way down to the changeover at Manchester. Then, as the others searched around for tea, Truscott vanished and reappeared shortly after with a bottle of scotch which was emptied well before they ultimately reached Kirton-in-Lindsey.

Another was Ray 'Throttle' Thorold-Smith. Although he was born in Sydney NSW, his school days were spent at Xavier College at Kew in Victoria, and then back in Sydney at Christian Brothers Colleges at Manly and Waverley. Before joining the RAAF on 27 May 1940, he had completed his fourth year at the School of Medicine at Sydney University. He had been commissioned in March before joining 452 Squadron. Keith Chisholm was from Petersham in Sydney and he had been studying dentistry until he joined the RAAF on 24 June 1940. He was posted to the United Kingdom and joined 452 Squadron as a sergeant. One of the quieter types was the tall South Australian Ian Milne, whose background was the land and who stood head and shoulders over most of the others. For him the cockpit of a Spitfire must have been a very tight squeeze. Andy Costello was from Queensland and had already flown privately before the war. He stood out as exceptional and demonstrated outstanding skill in close formation flying.

Taken as a whole, they all seemed so confident – boisterously over confident, in fact. For one thing, the squadron's R/T discipline left a lot to be desired and was the cause of some irritation. Bob realised it would need to be stressed that on fighter sweeps and *Circus* operations strict R/T silence needed to be maintained except for the instructions coming from controllers and the brief acknowledgments by wing leaders.

Ever a tactical thinker, Bob worked out a routine for the squadron Balbo in the air in line with the idea he had expressed to Jean Offenberg earlier at the Old Ship at Bosham. It would be trained to take off in threes so that the section and flight leaders could lead while taking off, then on order as they crossed the English coast they would manoeuvre into a battle formation made up of three sections of four, with two pairs in each section. It would require discipline and practice, but Bob was sure it would work.

Some of the pilots reckoned they were ready for combat already and week after week of endless practicing seemed frustrating. Ian Milne remembered Andy Costello especially!

Andy was a boy from an old pastoral family in Queensland who had been flying privately before the war. When he came to the squadron we found he was a pilot of extraordinary ability and in company with Dick Gazzard – I had the privilege of flying leader to these two boys and I found them remarkable in their ability to fly close flawless formations.

As time passed, Andy particularly became impatient. He felt he was ready to fly in combat and he was being unduly deprived. This aroused a certain amount of resentment.

We were particularly forbidden to undertake unnecessary low flying particularly around the aerodrome because of the fact there was an element of danger there – not merely an individual breaking the rules but there was a nightfighter squadron using the same aerodrome and another Hurricane squadron forming on a third side of the aerodrome. There was a considerable amount of traffic which was not required to monitor each other's progress except by proper procedure around the aerodrome.

So, when Andy suddenly gave vent of his feelings in a beat up of the aerodrome, he came back and landed and was pretty quickly taken to the commanding officer's private office by the ear and Bob gave him the dressing down that he was entitled to. Andy accepted that with some reservation, but fortunately with enough understanding to see that it was a pattern of behaviour that Bob could not suffer in the squadron for the risk of creating a split or division of loyalty – intolerable especially in a fighter squadron...

...Bob's concern for avoiding unnecessary and tragic losses through breaches of discipline was well based. He justly and consistently demanded following rules and procedures. Dangerous situations could arise unintentionally and if you were fortunate enough to avoid tragedy through failure to comply with laid down procedures you were lucky.

There was a case in point when we were returning from a babysitting operation at Leconfield while the home squadron there was away doing a sweep in the south west of England and we were covering their responsibility with half a dozen aircraft. We were returning to Kirton Lindsey led by Paddy Finucane with myself leading the second section of three and when we returned to the aerodrome Paddy instructed us to split up and land independently.

I took my section away and waited for him to bring his section down independently, but they didn't come so I proceeded to split up my section over the aerodrome in a Prince of Wales feathers pattern, as was normal, and announced that we would land independently following my lead.

As I completed my run, or was about halfway through my landing run, I found myself in a position where I passed between Paddy's aircraft and his No.2 coming head-on, the impact speed being between 150–180 mph!

However, nobody touched anybody, we'd cleared each other.

When I arrived back at the dispersal pen, Paddy was there very, very cross and disturbed and launched an attack on my failure to land into the wind. I said that I'd landed according to the landing 'T' laid out by the duty pilot in front of the control tower and then pointed to it. I pointed out that he'd condemned my action without checking with the duty pilot. He came back from the phone to me abjectly apologetic.

This of course could have had two results. One, a heap of burning aircraft with several pilots either killed or badly injured, or on the other hand a screaming warning to everyone to pay attention to the details that Bob was insisting on and make sure there was no landing 'T' out and you could still obey the wind. When the wind became indecisive, it was important for the duty pilot to supercede and override the wind and demand that everybody land in the same direction...

Meanwhile, more Australian EATS squadrons were being established in England. On 6 June, 455 (RAAF) Squadron, Australia's first medium bomber unit, was formed and began its official existence at Swinderby, also in Lincolnshire about 20 miles (32 km) south of Kirton-in-Lindsey. At this stage, though, it had no crews and more than a month would pass before it received its first Handley Page Hampden. However, the instructions between the UK and Australia had become confused somehow – the ground staff personnel being assembled at Williamtown in New South Wales were for a squadron that was going to operate two flights of Vickers Wellingtons, not three flights of Hampdens.

On 16 June, 457 (RAAF) Squadron, Australia's second Spitfire squadron in RAF Fighter Command, formed at Baginton in Warwickshire. Its CO, S/Ldr Peter Brothers, and two flight commanders were RAF pilots, while most of the others were EATS trained Australians.

Four days later on 20 June, Bob's mate from Point Cook and Tangmere days, S/Ldr Gordon Olive DFC, was appointed to command and form 456 (RAAF) Squadron at RAF Station Valley on the Isle of Anglesey in Wales. This was to be Australia's first night fighter squadron and its initial equipment would consist of sixteen Boulton Paul Defiants. The new unit came into existence officially on the 30th.

Suddenly, in the early hours of 22 June 1941, the war situation changed dramatically when the German forces launched a massive invasion of the Soviet Union. At 4 a.m. Berlin time, the Soviet ambassador in Berlin was called to the *Wilhelmstrasse* and told that Germany had entered Russia in response to 'border violations' Adolf Hitler had used the same lie to justify his invasion of Poland in September 1939. In fact, this was the culmination of months of planning by the German general staff in response to Hitler's orders. The plan was called Operation *Barbarossa*, and it began along a 1,800-mile (2,880-km) front from the Baltic to the Black Sea. There were 151 Germans divisions, just over 3 million troops, thrown into the battle. They were using the now-familiar overwhelming armoured punch of *blitzkrieg* tactics with tanks, artillery and aircraft. The objective was to destroy the Soviet Union and Bolshevism once and for all.

From the outset the Germans achieved phenomenal, crushing successes, both on the ground and in the air, thanks to the technical superiority of their equipment and their combat experience. By nightfall the panzers had penetrated deep into Russian territory inflicting heavy losses and the Soviet Air force had lost 1,811 aircraft, 1,489 of them on the ground. The *Luftwaffe's* losses amounted to just thirty-five aircraft, including a Messerschmitt Me110 that was deliberately rammed by a Russian pilot.

Britain's first official reaction came that same night in a broadcast from London by Prime Minister Winston Churchill. In it he promised the Russians 'any technical or economic assistance in our power'.

In practical terms for RAF Fighter Command, this meant that its *Circus, Rhubarb, Rodeo, Ramrod,* and *Roadstead* missions had to be intensified. Now there was the additional motivation of keeping as many enemy aircraft as possible pinned down on the Channel coast to prevent them reinforcing the *Luftwaffe* on the new Eastern Front.

Obviously, 452 Squadron would soon be committed to the fighting, but before that could happen Andy Costello's continuing impatience led to tragic consequences on the night of 4/5 July. Interviewed years later, Ian Milne recalled:

> Andy continued with his normal duties until one night we were required to do some night flying. Ray Thorold-Smith, Andy and myself were airborne that night when towards midnight the controller called us up and said we were required to pancake back on the station and give our exercises away because they had plots coming in from over the North Sea of enemy bombers apparently to attack Hull or the London Steel Mills nearby.
>
> We decided to go ahead and follow instructions so Ray Thorold-Smith and I were in the process of landing when we heard Andy call up and ask permission to investigate an unidentified aircraft over the coast about North Coates city south of Grimsby. The controller forbad that and said proceed according to orders and land back at base. Andy being an independent soul to a degree proceeded to follow this aircraft which he apparently lost and then found he was short of fuel. He asked for an airstrip to be lit at North Coates city.
>
> He did a dummy run across the field to check the lights, the runway and the drift and then the people on the ground realised that as he went over on the dummy run he was being followed at very close range by a Junkers 88. As he cleared the end of the strip, the Junkers 88 blew him out of the air, and we lost Andy...

Andy Costello's aircraft, Spitfire Mk IIA P8085, crashed at Fen Lane Farm, North Somercotes. He was the victim of *Ofw* Peter Laufs, an experienced Ju88 intruder pilot of *I/NJG2*. Laufs claimed that he shot down a single-engined aircraft that was preparing to land at North Coates, but he erroneously identified it as a Defiant. He had been flying night intruder missions over England since July 1940 and this was his fourth success.[2]

If only Costello had waited. The Australian squadron was only a week away from its first action. Ian Milne again:

> It wasn't until July 11th that we were considered suitable to go into combat. This was a sweep over France which was launched from West Malling just

south of London. We launched from West Malling because we were able to refill our tanks and take off for St Omer escorting bombers, covering the retreat from that area of France.

The operation 452 Squadron was involved in on 11 July was *Circus No.44*, which was actually a diversionary raid carried out shortly before the main bombing attack, *Circus No.45*. Their job was to protect a single Bristol Blenheim, which was playing the dangerous role of decoy. The mission was mandatory for the CO and the flight commanders – Bob Bungey, Paddy Finucane and Graham Douglas – but competition was so fierce among the others wanting to fly 452's first *Circus* that they had to draw lots out of a hat. Bob and Paddy were still the only pilots with combat experience.

The nature of *Circus* operations had changed since they were defined in back in February, as experience had shown the original sweep formations were completely inadequate for the task. A letter from the chief of Fighter Command, Air Marshal Sir William Sholto Douglas, to his group commanders had outlined new fighter components. These were now Escort, Escort Cover, Target Support, Freelance, Forward Support, and Rear Support.

Each of these roles now had a full fighter wing of three squadrons assigned to the task. Instead of one squadron for close escort as defined earlier, now there were three, and the original concept of using six Spitfire squadrons on a sweep had now ballooned to a minimum of eighteen squadrons considered necessary for the same job.

There were two wings from 11 Group: Biggin Hill with 72, 92 and 609 Squadrons; and the so far incomplete Kenley Spitfire Wing of 485 (RNZAF) and 602 Squadrons. The three squadrons in the 12 Group Wing were 65, 266 and 452 (RAAF).

The 12 Group Wing refuelled at West Malling and rendezvoused with the others over Mansion at 2.35 p.m. The Biggin Hill Wing was there but there was only one squadron from Kenley – 485 Squadron, the New Zealanders. They could not wait around for 602 Squadron, which failed to make contact. They all crossed the French coast east of Dunkirk at 2.45 p.m. The weather was good, except for Channel haze and some scattered cloud.

The positioning within the 12 Group Wing was: No.266 Squadron leading at 17,000 feet (5,200 m), 452 Squadron in the middle at 18,000 feet (5,500 m), and 65 Squadron top cover at 19,000 feet (5,800 m). As ordered, 452 Squadron split into fours over Poperinghe and headed towards Cassel.

As they started their sweep inland, the pilots of the Biggin Hill Wing spotted black specks coming from the east. There seemed to be a considerable number of fighters already up over enemy territory when the wing arrived. The specks were Me109s flying in no evident set formation, but they were obviously trying to manoeuvre into a position up-sun of Gravelines in order to intercept the British Balbo on its way out.

The Biggin Hill wing leader decided to head straight to Gravelines and reach there before the 109s were properly ready. As the wing flew out across the English Channel several pilots noticed that three enemy aircraft were shadowing them, cruising just out of reach behind. When the wing approached the coast of England again three enemy formations, each made up of ten Me109s, suddenly appeared. The first two formations were allowed to go by, but the third was engaged. In the ensuing dogfights the RAF pilots claimed six Messerschmitts destroyed, two probably destroyed, and seven more damaged. One pilot failed to return.

The pilots of Kenley's 485 Squadron nearing the coast towards Gravelines at 23,000 feet (7,000 m) saw six Me109s. Short bursts were fired at two of them but with no obvious results. One pilot from the New Zealand squadron failed to return.

Five miles (8km) west of Lille at 3.00 p.m., 452 Squadron was flying in fours in line astern when it encountered trouble. Paddy Finucane was leading the starboard section and as he looked behind he noticed ack-ack fire. Immediately above the AA fire he spotted eight enemy aircraft. They dived to attack Finucane's section but he turned to starboard away from their line of approach. The leading attacking Me109 overshot and as it passed, Finucane cut inside its turn and followed it down. When about 150 yards (135 m) behind, the Irish ace gave the 109 a short burst of 3 seconds from quarter astern. He saw the enemy pilot bail out. Hanigan and Truscott saw the 109 diving straight down at high speed to within about 1,000 feet (300 m) of the ground.

While Finucane's Red Section was busy, Bob kept the rest of the squadron, Blue and Green Sections, back at 18,000 feet (5,500 m) staying on the alert for any more surprises until it was time to withdraw. They were peppered by AA fire, which they described later as 'extremely accurate'. Finally, the squadron made for home over the French coast passing over Gravelines where more enemy fighters were seen, away off in the distance. They were too far away to be engaged.

Down at 1,000 feet (300 m), Finucane led Truscott and Ian Milne back across the Channel and landed at Manston to refuel at 3.25 p.m., before then proceeding to West Mailing. Red 3, Jim Hanigan, lost contact with the section in the Channel haze. He reduced the height down to almost 0 feet but missed the coast of Kent and forced landed in Essex out of fuel.

Bob and the others landed at West Mailing at 3.25 p.m., the same time as Finucane, Truscott and Milne were touching down at Manston. Paddy Finucane flying Spitfire P8038 was the only member of 452 Squadron who had the chance to open fire, and he claimed 452's first enemy aircraft destroyed.

Circus 44 was considered a success with seven enemy aircraft claimed destroyed, two probably destroyed, and seven damaged. *Circus 45* with bombers took place 40 minutes later and achieved maximum surprise with a minimum of interference from the enemy. However, of the three RAF pilots admitted lost, one was from 452 (RAAF) Squadron.

Ian Milne added extra perspective:

On our return from the sweep we found that we had to land at Manston near Dover for fuel and then back to refuel again at West Malling. It was here at West Malling that we discovered that we had lost one of our number. Alex Roberts…

The other sad information we got when we got to West Malling was that we'd also damaged 'King Kong' Cox who was an ex-commercial traveller from Melbourne. Cox apparently had been detailed to follow closely behind an English boy who was flying with us that day to give us a sense of security and confidence flying with somebody, a few more people, with experience.

Cox following the English boy did not realise he had been hit by shrapnel and probably killed but certainly unconscious and so his aircraft went into a terminal dive into the sea. Cox followed him according to instructions until he realised that they were in very real danger of colliding even if they were able to pull out so he pulled out with everything in his power and just avoided the sea but saw his leader go straight into the water.

Cox arrived back, we unfortunately found out later with permanently damaged ear drums from the quick descent entailed in the dive.

Nobody had any idea what had happened to Alex Roberts in Yellow Section. Had he been killed? After Finucane's section had been attacked, nothing more was seen of him. He had not been seen to drop out of the *Circus*. It was not until months later that there was news. Years later in an interview, Ian Milne related the story in his own inimitable style:

Alex Roberts had been shot down and he actually slipped his chute to avoid landing on the perimeter of St Omer fighter aerodrome.

He walked away and made contact with some helpful people who were young ladies of doubtful repute who were not concerned with spoiling his promising attempt to get away but rather assisting it with as much loyalty as could be expected from an ally. They finished up providing him with a pushbike which enabled him to struggle his way south to Marseilles where they found him with doubtful papers and reputation so he went to gaol.

In the gaol he met a tobacco smuggler of Spanish origin who knew the way over the Pyrenees so Alex decided to go with him on his nefarious pursuits and so they went over the Pyrenees together and ultimately right through to Algeciras and Gibraltar, where Alex found himself in the hands of a lieutenant commander in command of a British destroyer en route to England. He was prepared to carry him as super cargo. There was a slight delay and the commanding officer asked Alex if there was any need he had that could be satisfied before they left and he said, certainly, the company of an attractive and co-operative young lady would be such a need that could be satisfied.

The CO of the ship said, 'Certainly son, we'll go over to Algeciras and deal with that.'

When they got back on the ship and across to England, Alex was saying goodbye and expressing his gratitude to the skipper and he said, 'What do I owe you?'

The skipper said, 'Not a thing son.'

He said, 'What about the night out in Algeciras?'

'Well', he said, 'you can put that down to an unexpected and very rare gratuity from the Crown.'

So Alex was a large participant in the largesse of His Majesty. Alex never flew with the squadron again for security reasons having been shot down and on the loose in Europe. He went on to India and considerable flying in Hurricanes...

The news they had all been waiting for came in the middle of July. The squadron was ready. It was about to be transferred into No.11 Group, the front line, and become the third squadron of the Kenley Wing.

When the Spitfires of 452 (RAAF) Squadron left the runway at Kirton-in-Lindsey in Lincolnshire on 21 July 1941, it was for the last time. They touched down at Kenley in Surrey, on one of the most famous airfields of the Royal Air Force, their new home.

Bob Bungey and his pilots were about to fly into history.

12

The Kenley Wing

The day after 452 Squadron arrived at Kenley the work started with a Channel cover patrol. Then the squadron joined No.602 Squadron RAF for a reconnaissance sweep from St Valery to Le Tréport, which passed without incident. Bob flew four times that day. In the air, 452 had been given the call sign 'Keyhole'.

On 24 July, it teamed up with 602 Squadron to act as the escort wing for bombers making a raid on Cherbourg, the second on the same target for the day. The Australian squadron was challenged briefly during the withdrawal. In an isolated attack about 15 miles (25 km) north of Cherbourg, two Me109s dived steeply on 452's starboard section, but a recent arrival in the squadron, F/O Andrew Humphrey, pounced on one of them and claimed it destroyed. He was flying Spitfire P7973, the future Australian War Memorial aircraft.

As July ended, weather conditions deteriorated. Bob's Log Book shows that he flew a convoy patrol on the 26th and a *Rhubarb* on the 30th, both entries drawing the comments 'Washout. Weather u/s'. The following day he took 452 Squadron on a *Roadstead* operation to escort four Blenheims making a low-level hunt for enemy ships in the Dieppe area. It was a long and uneventful job, lasting 1 hour 40 minutes.

The Kenley Wing was now at full strength and consisted of 485 RNZAF Squadron, 602 Squadron commanded by another New Zealand veteran, Al Deere, and finally 452 (RAAF) Squadron.

No.485 Squadron had been the first RNZAF fighter squadron established under the EATS. Like those in 452 Squadron most of its pilots were relatively inexperienced, but also like 452 it was bolstered by several veterans. It began to form on 1 March 1941 at RAF Driffield in Yorkshire, under S/Ldr M. W. B. Knight.

F/Lt Edward Wells scored 485's first success over France on 5 July. Wells soon became known as 'Hawkeye' among his fellow pilots, which was not surprising as he had been a champion at clay-pigeon shooting in New Zealand before the war. Until the end of June the New Zealanders remained at Leconfield in Yorkshire. From there they sent detachments south for particular operations. Then followed a quick move to Redhill, Surrey, where they joined 602 Squadron and became the second part of the Kenley Wing.

Now the pilots of 452 Squadron were the 'new kids on the block' and as newcomers all eyes were on them to see how they would perform. Bob realised that his training was on trial. His routines had been well rehearsed. Fred McCann, from Hobart, Tasmania, recalled that although the squadron took off in four sections of three, the RAF's standard basic formation, by the time it was over the Continent they were flying in three sections of four.

> Bob would lead off as Blue 1 with Blue 2, but he would also have White 2 as the third aircraft.
>
> Next would come Paddy Finucane as Red 1 with his Red 2 wingman, but he would also have Yellow 2 as his third aircraft.
>
> Third off would be Graham Douglas as Green 1 with his Green 2 wingman, but his third aircraft would be Black 2.
>
> Finally, the other section leaders, White 1, Yellow 1 and Black 1, would take off together last.

'This was the order so that section and flight leaders could lead in take-off,' recalled McCann, 'We changed to battle formation as we crossed the English coast, a manoeuvre worked out by Bungey that brought howls of laughter from other squadrons.'

Regardless of how humorous the other Kenley Wing pilots thought the unusual manoeuvring might be, Bob was putting into practice the ideas he had expressed to Pyker Offenberg way back in October last year: 'What we ought to avoid is flying in sections of three,' he had said, 'We ought to fly in pairs like the Germans do. The leader can then fire, knowing that his rear is protected.' Now he had the opportunity, with the support of his flight commanders, to put theory into practice.

Over the English coast the squadron rearranged itself into three sections of four: Bob (Blue 1) with Blue 2 emerged in the lead combined with White 1 and White 2 as the second pair. Behind to Bob's right was Paddy Finucane (Red 1) and Red 2 combined with Yellow 1 and Yellow 2. And on the left Graham Douglas (Green 1) and Green 2 combined with Black 1 and Black 2.

Fred McCann explained further, 'Each Spitfire in a section of two flew 250 yards (230 m) apart; Yellow 2 was 750 yards (690 m) behind Finucane. This, for AE Charlie, was a hell of a gap. Bungey insisted on it and said that if Yellow 2 was attacked he should be covered by Red 1 who would break into the attack and be in range to fire at the leading attacker providing the warning was early enough. Meantime, Red 2 and Yellow 1 were supposed to follow around after Red 1...'

McCann added: 'During August I flew twelve sweeps — all as Arse End Charlie, the last man in the formation. Twice when I was No.2 to Bungey it was like a holiday! The end man, No.4 in a flight, was the one who got shot at. The men in front did the shooting...'

What the pilots in the other units did not fully realise yet was that Bob and his squadron also had a secret weapon – Brendan Eamonn Fergus Finucane. And Paddy Finucane was about to hit his stride. He would not remain a secret for much longer.

The Kenley Wing received a new wing leader as well, W/Cdr Johnny Kent, a Canadian from Winnipeg who was posted in from the aggressive Polish Wing at Northolt. He took the opportunity to fly first with 452 Squadron as it took part in a *Circus* operation to St Omer.

In the early evening of 3 August, the wing flew over Manston at 18,000 feet (5,500 m) on its way out to cross the Channel where it encountered cloud at that level. The three squadrons reduced height, dropping to 13,000 feet (3,950 m) and proceeding below the cloud but 602 Squadron became separated. After crossing the enemy coast, course was set for St Omer, where 602 Squadron rejoined. Anti-aircraft greeted them after crossing the coast.

Near Ambleteuse, five bogeys flying in line astern were seen going in the opposite direction. They were soon identified as Messerschmitt 109s but they had rounded wingtips. New Me109Fs! Still flying in line astern, they turned and half rolled in behind the Spitfires to take up a position 1,000 feet (300 m) higher up aft to starboard and followed the wing. That was on Paddy Finucane's side, and he was waiting.

Three 109s peeled off to strike but Finucane and his wingman, Bill Eccleton, turned into them and counter-attacked as they crossed their path. Finucane's first burst missed but he followed the 109 into thin cloud, keeping track of him by his condensation trail. At the same time he saw the German leader's No.2 falling on fire – Eccleton's victim.

When Finucane broke out of the cloud he saw he was right behind his quarry at a range of 200 yards. A long burst sent the Messerschmitt down in flames. Shortly afterwards he noticed eighteen enemy aircraft above that seemed to be milling around in a loose circle evidently following a leader. Checking behind, Finucane saw he had six other Spitfires from 452 Squadron with him so he went into the attack. He picked on the last 109, gave it a burst and it broke away. Preferring not to pursue, he chose out another one and gave it a 2-second burst. Pieces flew off its tail unit and it went downwards vertically apparently out of control. He lost sight of it when it disappeared into a cloud layer at 2,000 feet (600 m).

This battle was reported later in the South Australian press:

S.A. PILOTS TAKE PART IN BIG AIR FIGHT OVER CHANNEL

The first RAAF Fighter Squadron operating in England has opened its account against the Germans and the three South Australian members Squadron Leader Robert Bungey, Sgt Pilot Ian Milne and Sgt Pilot Paul Makin, all played their part.

This week the squadron became practically 100% Australian with the arrival of the first contingent of ground personnel from Australia.

It was recently transferred from a north eastern aerodrome to an advanced striking base near London, and has taken part in 12 daylight sweeps over enemy country. Squadron Leader Bungey said that the sweeps opened the eyes of the lads who went into action with visions of last year's non-stop dog-fights.

They expected to see the air filled with combat-hungry Huns, but discovered that a more frequent sight was merely a 400 mph flash as a Messerschmitt dived from a terrific height, hoping to catch a victim unawares. Invading planes usually are at a disadvantage because the Germans are aware that they are coming, and are thus able to gain greater height, but last Sunday evening was an exception. Bungey was leading the squadron at 14,000 ft. just over an aerodrome in Northern France, near the coast when a horde of Messerschmitt stratosphere planes hurtled down on a section comprising the squadrons Irish Flight Commander, Flight-Lieutenant (Paddy) Finucane DFC, Pilot-Officer W. Eccleton and Sgt Pilot Richard Gazzard of Sydney, and Sgt Pilot Ian Milne of Adelaide.

'They became separated from the squadron but Finucane chased and shot down the leading German, while Eccleton dived after another. I got in a two second burst and saw the Messerschmitt burst into flames and then blow up,' he said.

Finucane then spotted more than 30 Messerschmitts milling around a cloud. The four RAAF fighters instantly tore into battle although they were outnumbered eight to one, and should have been annihilated. 'We chased the Huns until our ammunition ran out,' Eccleton said. 'The air was a whirling mass of planes, but I was unable to glue my sights on a single plane because the "Jerries" simply went into dives when they were in danger of being attacked. Not one of our planes even got a bullet hole in it.'

The day before Finucane and Sgt Pilot Raymond [*sic*] Chisholm, of Sydney, attacked a German transport column near Dunkirk. 'It was lovely to see lorries colliding with one another and Germans diving for the hedges as we swooped down almost to the height of the trees,' said Finucane. 'Chisholm exploded an ammunition lorry, then we beat up a few barges, and raked a small coastal steamer before making for home,' he added.

That same day, Sgt Pilot Paul Makin of Adelaide helped to put an E-boat out of action.

Sgt Pilot Alex Roberts of Lismore, New South Wales, who failed to return from a sweep made by the squadron last week is said to be interned in the south of France.[1]

There was a more determined enemy fighter response on 9 August for *Circus No.68*. The operation called for five wings of fighters to escort five Blenheims from No.2 Group while they attacked the power station at Gosnay, 4 miles south-west of Bethune. The three squadrons from Kenley shared the target support role with the Tangmere Wing, Nos.610, 616 and 41 Squadrons, led by W/Cdr Douglas 'Tin Legs' Bader, who was flying as usual with 616 Squadron. The escort wing came from North Weald and consisted of Nos.71, 222, and 111 Squadrons. Acting as the escort cover wing were 403 (RCAF), 603 and 611 Squadrons from Hornchurch; and the Northolt Wing – Nos.306, 308 and 315 Squadrons – had the role of support wing.

Over the target, the force encountered 10/10ths cloud. The bombers were unable to pinpoint Gosnay so they diverted to their secondary target at Gravelines but their escorts had to keep enemy fighters at bay all the way. On the way, the Kenley Wing, with 452 Squadron leading, ranged from 20,000 feet to 27,000 feet (6,000–8,200 m). Immediately above and behind 452 was 602 Squadron at 22,000 feet (6,700 m) and 485 Squadron on the left was the highest.

The wing was passing over St Omer at 11.32 a.m. when Finucane called up Bob and then took his flight in pursuit of eight Me109s that he had spotted. The Irishman closed to 100 yards (90 m) and fired a 4-second burst which sent his 109 target down spinning in flames. Turning after another Messerschmitt, the keen-eyed Irishman fired again. Close behind him came Ray Thorold-Smith who closed in to 50 yards (45 m) and fired off a 2-second burst allowing full deflection. The 109 half rolled and dived away vertically with its tail smashed.

In the general melee, Thorold-Smith shared another 109 with Keith Chisholm; both pilots seeing the German pilot bail out. Then Chisholm was joined by Paddy Finucane and his wingman, Pat Tainton. Finucane turned sharply after him, saw Chisholm's salvo rip into the grey fuselage of another 109 and then fired himself from 250 yards (230 m), sending it down in flames as a result of their combined assault. Bluey Truscott shattered the tail unit of yet another Messerschmitt with a 5-second burst and it plunged down, apparently out of control as it headed for the ground at phenomenal speed.

Despite these successes, 452 Squadron did not have things all its own way. The aircraft flown by Bob's wingman Jay O'Byrne, Spitfire P7682, was hit and was seen to go down streaming smoke. He did not make it back to Kenley and there were also two more who failed to return, Geoff Chapman and nineteen-year-old Barry Haydon. Three altogether! These were the first serious multiple losses for the squadron, and a shock – especially for Bob Bungey. Oh, he had experienced casualties before, particularly in France. There had been so many – Leslie Clisby, Wally Blom, Doug Cameron ... too many. But this was different. He had not been in charge back then. Now as commanding officer, the welfare of the men was his sole responsibility. Andy Costello and Alex Roberts had gone so quickly. There was kit and personal effects to be gathered up, letters to next of kin to be written. Quiet and stoic by nature, Bob felt the shock of such losses more than most, but nobody realised by just how much – not yet.

Jay O'Byrne was later reported as a prisoner of war. So too was Geoff Chapman, but he had been wounded and was not immediately transferred to a POW camp. Unfortunately, Barry Haydon succumbed to the wounds he received and he was finally buried at Louguenesse Souvenir in France.

The Tangmere Wing had been seriously hit too. One of its three missing pilots was none other than its renowned wing leader, Douglas 'Tin Legs' Bader. He had bailed out south of Le Touquet from about 24,000 feet (7,300 m) minus one of his artificial legs and with the other damaged. A Czech squadron from Northolt, No.315 Squadron, lost two pilots.

Although No.452 endured the most losses, it had also been involved in the heaviest fighting and lodged most of the claims. Fighter Command's total claims for *Circus 68* were eleven Me109s destroyed, seven probably destroyed and five damaged for the loss of five pilots. The New Zealanders of 485 Squadron missed most of the fighting and 602 could claim only one probable and one damaged.

There was a second sweep that afternoon but it was uneventful. Bob's Log Book shows that he was up again for a third time later to escort a Lysander patrolling the English Channel on the lookout for pilots who may have come down in the water.

Flying the aircraft which would ultimately reside in the Australian War Memorial's collection in Canberra, Spitfire P7973, that day was F/O Andrew Humphrey, an Englishman from Lincolnshire, who had claimed a 109 in it back on 24 July. Bob had often flown this machine during June and July and other pilots who logged time in it were Ray 'Throttle' Thorold-Smith, Jay O'Byrne and Keith 'Bluey' Truscott, who was destined to become one of the RAAF's most famous fighter aces.

Circus No.68 was probably Spitfire P7973's last operation with 452 Squadron, but its combat career was far from over. It was transferred to 313 (Czech) Squadron and flew operations until 28 September 1941 when it crashed into a telegraph pole while its pilot, Sgt Arnost Mrtvy, was avoiding anti-aircraft fire. Although badly damaged with a chunk of timber embedded in its wing, Sgt Mrtvy managed to fly it back to England where he force-landed at Predannack in Cornwall. After repairs it was relegated to OTUs and in April 1944 it was with the RAF's Central Gunnery School in Yorkshire. Acquired for preservation because of its link with Bluey Truscott, Spitfire P7973 was packed in a crate and shipped to Australia on the SS *Fort Adelaide* on 8 March 1945. It reached Melbourne after a voyage lasting three months.

Towards the middle of August, 452 Squadron began trading in its tired old Spitfire Mk IIAs for new cannon-firing Spitfire Mk VBs. The pilots found their new machines lined up outside the duty pilot's watch office. Fred McCann noted in his diary:

> Bungey demanded first pick and I followed hoping to learn from him how to choose an aircraft. He walked along the line of Spits and then said I'll have that one – the numbers add up to twenty and that's my lucky number!

Bob's random choice was Spitfire Mk VB, serial number AB857. He flew it for the first time on the 11th for a 'cannon test'. On the outside, the Spitfire Mk VB differed little from the Mk II series, the most obvious change being the addition of two cannons, one protruding from each wing. The aircraft now packed a longer-ranging, harder-hitting punch, its armament consisted of two 20-mm Hispano cannons with 120 rounds each and four 0.303-inch Browning machine guns with 350 rounds each, replacing the former eight 0.303-inch Brownings. Internal changes with Spitfire engines featured progressive increases in the Rolls-Royce Merlin's power and high altitude rating. This model was powered by a Merlin 45 Series two-stage, single-speed engine and it had the capacity to have a drop fuel tank fitted under the fuselage to increase range. Satisfied with the test flight, Bob adopted Spitfire AB857 as his own.

Paddy Finucane's method of selecting a new Spitfire was just as hit and miss. He chose Spitfire AB852 because it had the individual letter code 'W', which happened to be the letter on the first Spitfire he had flown on operations with No.65 squadron and crash-landed at Manston a year before. From now on, for good luck, he would fly aircraft marked 'W' and have his personal shamrock painted on it. They would be his individual markings.

From Friday 15th to Monday 18th, Bob took the opportunity to have some well-earned weekend leave. He again flew the squadron's Magister over to RAF Benson on Friday. From there it was on to tranquil Wallingford in the upper Thames Valley and to beautiful dark-eyed Sybil for a couple of superb rare days of affection and peace. It was actually his second time there that month. His Log Book shows that he had flown the Magister to Benson and back for a quick visit on the 4th.

The old Saxon market town was a haven, a place of safety, where for a while at least the war could be forgotten. There was time for slow walks hand-in-hand in cool, green Wallingford Park on the bank of the Thames to the open-air swimming pool where they had first met. It was summer again and a good time for a swim but the water would still be bracingly cold. Then the slow stroll back home over the long medieval stone bridge built across the river and along the narrow pathways and narrow streets. They had been engaged for more than a year now and there was much they had to talk over. Plans needed to be made for the future.

Since their engagement, Sybil had made a point of writing regularly to Bob's parents in Adelaide and she also befriended his father's cousin, Maud Hogben, who lived in London. In one of her recent letters she had enclosed 'a splendid black-and white sketch' of Bob in full flying kit. She wrote, 'Bob asked me to send the enclosed. Isn't it a good picture of him? It was done by Rothenstein, who is one of our leading Royal Academy artists. Bob had to sit for 3–5 hours and did he moan.'

Bob's mother, Ada, observed later that Sybil was 'a very level-headed, capable, and domesticated girl' and 'when he and Sybil went to London to choose the aquamarine and diamond engagement ring, Sybil wrote out and said that people turned to look at the good looking flying officer but I, am sure they turned to look at the good looking couple'.

She added, 'I sent Sybil some of Bob's favourite recipes for cakes and she used to make them and take them to him when he was in hospital recently recovering from an injury to his knee. The hospital he was in was marvellous. It is in the south of England and used to be a fashionable hotel. It has a lovely garden with tennis courts. There are squash racquet courts, a tennis court inside, and even a little theatre where artists give performances for the sick men.'

Ada Bungey also mentioned, 'I wrote to Bob a little while ago and suggested that he and Sybil should get married in the Salisbury Cathedral because that was where his father was christened.'

For Bob and Sybil the weekend passed much too quickly and, before they knew it, it was Monday morning and time for him to return to Kenley. When he left, Sybil had time to make her way to Wallingford Bridge as usual and wait for his aircraft to appear from the direction of RAF Benson as he was departing. He made his usual low swoop, skimming along just above the surface of the river, before zooming up over the bridge as she waved goodbye. Now for both came the sudden pang of loneliness as the distance between them widened and the plane disappeared from sight.

On landing back at Kenley, Bob found that much had happened during his absence. While he was away Paddy Finucane had led the squadron. Saturday, 16 August, had been a very busy day with no less than three sweeps. The first, with take off at 7.25 a.m., was to St Omer for *Circus 73*. Finucane claimed one Me109E. After an early lunch the wing was off for a second time at midday for *Circus 74* to St Omer again, but this time 452 Squadron made no claims.

Circus 75 went to St Omer yet again. Take off was in the early evening at 5.45 p.m. with Kenley as the escort wing. This time the whole circus estimated that ten Me109s were destroyed, with 452 Squadron claiming no less than seven of them without loss. Both 602 and 485 Squadrons had witnessed the action but were not involved. Both Finucane and Keith Chisholm claimed two each while Arch Stuart, Pat Tainton and Bluey Truscott all sent down one apiece. That gave Finucane three in one day!

The pace continued through August. On Tuesday 19, the day after Bob's return from leave, *Circus 81* targeted the power station at Gosnay. For this, Bob led the Kenley Wing to act as escort cover for Tangmere's squadrons, which were escorting six Blenheims from No.2 Group. The target support wings were from Northolt and Hornchurch. Biggin Hill's Spitfires were the rear support squadrons.

The dogfights started at 18,000 feet (5,500 m) off Calais at 11.10 a.m. and fighting ranged down to 4,000 feet (1,200 m). Finucane scored two more Me109s and Bluey Truscott shot part of a wing from another 109, which went down vertically with no hope of recovery. But it was costly. Two more of the squadron's promising pilots, Bill Eccleton and Dick Gazzard, failed to return and Don Willis's Spitfire V, AB794, was shot up. Although wounded, Willis managed to force-land safely and his aircraft was able to be repaired later.

Such losses greatly concerned Bob. Both of the missing young men had been among the original members of the squadron. They were *his* men and two more were gone. Both, in fact, had been killed. Bill Eccleton was buried at Dunkirk, and Dick Gazzard in Oostduinkerke Communal Cemetery (West-Vlaanderen), 4 miles (5 km) west of Nieuwpoort, Belgium, but that would not be known until after the war.

The new Zealanders had lost a pilot too, Sgt K. C. M. 'Dusty' Miller of 485 Squadron flying Spitfire IIa P7977, who was the victim of a yellow-nosed Me109 which was promptly shot down by Aucklander, F/Lt John Rae. Hawkeye Wells claimed one Messerschmitt destroyed and one damaged.

It was during the raid on Gosnay that a Blenheim carrying Douglas Bader's spare artificial leg diverted to St Omer where the crew parachuted the precious package to the legless ace's captors below. The Germans had offered to allow safe passage for an RAF Lysander to actually land at St Omer to deliver the leg, but neither Sholto-Douglas at Fighter Command nor Leigh-Mallory at Group Headquarters was willing to present the Nazis with what could be turned into a propaganda coup. One could easily imagine Heinrich Himmler's photographers waiting on the spot and ready to capture the scene on film. The offer could not be accepted.

Douglas Bader had become an RAF legend. He was known to the public through the British press and throughout Fighter Command via word of mouth on the fighter airfields. His loss had been officially reported on 12 August in accordance with the standard Air Ministry policy of delaying three days until the fate of a missing flyer was known or could be fairly safely assumed with some certainty.

Bob was not one to seek publicity but as the CO of 452 Squadron he suddenly found himself thrust into the limelight on 21 August when Sholto Douglas, Stanley Bruce (former prime minister of Australia and the current Australian High Commissioner) and AVM Frank McNamara VC from RAAF (Overseas) HQ in London visited the squadron.

Because of its successes, the squadron was attracting wider notice. The No.11 Group press officer would release two routine bulletins during the month mentioning an 'Irish DFC' in an Australian squadron (official policy was not to name names). Fighter Command's Operations Record Book for 29 August would furthermore note:

> The public relations section at this headquarters will be instructed that whenever any news is forwarded to Air Ministry for publication containing specific reference to Australian squadrons or personnel, a note is to be added requesting that the information be conveyed to the Australian Air Liaison section at the same time as it is released to the press.

Copies of combat reports were also requested to be sent to the liaison office at RAAF Overseas Headquarters at Kodak House at Kingsway, London. Sholto Douglas, who was always on the lookout for good publicity, agreed with the arrangement. Thus the die was cast to ensure that achievements of the 'Irish DFC' and those of the whole of 452 Squadron, including Bluey Truscott, would receive the widest possible coverage. It would lead to Truscott becoming a national hero at home as the Australian press followed the example of Fleet Street, and Paddy Finucane would become as well known 'down under' as he became known throughout Britain. In fact, through British eyes, Finucane would be anointed as Tin-Legs Bader's successor in the public's list of leading RAF aces.

In what was meant to be a rousing speech to the pilots of the squadron at Kenley, Sholto Douglas congratulated them on their offensive spirit and said, 'I'll keep sending my fighters over there again and again. Whenever the weather permits we'll go to the enemy and fight him until he quits.'

Fred McCann wrote in his diary that Jack Emery quietly whispered to him, 'We'll go over early to Fighter Command and breathe on the windows so he'll think the weather is duff.'

Late in the afternoon, with the VIP visit over, Bob led 452 on a Channel search ranging from Calais to Cap Gris Nez, which passed without incident.

The next day Paddy Finucane was notified that he was receiving a bar to his DFC. The citation said he had led his flight with great dash, determination and courage and stated, 'Flight Lieutenant Finucane has been largely responsible for the fine fighting spirit of the unit.' He was, in reality, shooting down almost half of the enemy aircraft that the squadron was claiming. This caused no resentment. The Australians respected his special skills and idolised him, and at the same time they were gaining valuable experience.

Fog and weather conditions limited large-scale operations for the next couple of days. Bob's Log Book shows he flew a *Rhubarb* to Le Tréport early on the 24th and later in the day he led a fighter sweep but neither drew any response from the *Luftwaffe*.

The next major engagement involving 452 Squadron, a *Circus* attack on the St Omer/Louguenesse airfields, occurred late in the day on 26 August. The Spitfires from Kenley were the high cover and after crossing the French coast, they were constantly attacked by Me109s diving out of the sun in 'threes and sixes'. Perhaps the Germans were adopting the standard British formations to momentarily confuse the escorts. Another report said they were attacking 'in fours and sixes simultaneously from all over the place'.

During the action, both on the way in and while withdrawing, Keyhole Squadron was split up. Some were able to stick with Bob while others managed, with difficulty, to reform on Paddy Finucane, who called that he was circling above and rocking his wings.

Arch Stuart was heavily engaged by several 'Huns'. He called for assistance, saying he was 'very busy' and he shot at one German fighter, which fell away in an uncontrolled dive trailing smoke. After that, the loose formations managed to reform on Finucane and withdraw safely although under constant attack.

On arriving home, they discovered that this time nobody had been lost and the thirty-four-year-old Scotsman Graham Douglas had accounted for a second Messerschmitt.

Shortly afterwards, the squadron received very unwelcome orders. The same show was set again for dawn the next morning – the same pilots, same briefing and the same target, the St Omer/Louguenesse airfields. There was one big difference though; with the sun rising in the east, they would be flying into its glare – a huge disadvantage. The enemy would have the sun at his back.

At around 4.30 a.m., they were roused from their sleep and once dressed staggered to dispersal for Bob's short briefing. There was a cup of tea, perhaps a cigarette, then it was time to get into kit and move out to their aircraft. It was 27 August and the sky was clear. *Circus 85* was waiting.

Sometimes, despite the best laid plans, things go wrong. The bombers, three Blenheims of 139 Squadron, No.2 Group, arrived 30 minutes early at the rendezvous point over Rye in Sussex. Finding no sign of a fighter escort there to greet them, they turned back for home. The hostile air over the Continent was no place for three lonely bombers.

Half-an-hour later, at 6.43 a.m., four wings of Spitfires arrived over Rye in a sky that was still clear and found nothing to escort. They went on to France anyway, flying their allotted roles: Kenley Wing (escort cover); Northolt

Wing (escort); Tangmere Wing and Biggin Hill Wing (target support). The Kenley Wing climbed from 13,000 feet (4,000 m) over Rye to 18,000 feet (5,500 m) out over the Channel. The formation crossed the French coast at Ambleteuse at 7.12 a.m., and the Messerschmitt 109s were waiting. They were in front – in the sun. It would be a memorable Wednesday morning Fred McCann recalled:

> We flew into the face of the rising sun blind spot in front, and that's where the Huns had the advantage. We got a bit of flak as we crossed the French coast with some straight dotted lines of red flak among them to show the Huns where we were. We went on for a few minutes – just long enough to get nicely in the trap...

'Keyhole squadron break right!'

The Messerschmitt 109s reacted in force as the Spitfires flew on in their prearranged positions. At the same time, Group issued a call to withdraw but it was too late and a series of running fights broke out. Afterwards, the No.11 Group's report on *Circus 85* estimated that no fewer than fifty enemy fighters had been in the air.

No.452 Squadron was split up in the first attack. The Spitfire pilots desperately rolled inwards and aileron turned into the oncoming attacks, avoiding tracer and firing brief shots at the fleeting 109s as they did so. They dived and aileron turned from 28,000 feet (8,500 m) down to the 10,000-foot (3,000-m) level. Then it was aileron turning again and again, right down to the deck, dodging more tracers with every twisting manoeuvre.

The German coastal guns opened up on the fleeing Spitfires as they recrossed the coast. The sea ahead erupted in a mass of splashes and water spouts around them and black flak bursts spotted the air in front. Once clear, the 109s dived in pursuit again trying to catch up but they had to pull up quickly to avoid splashing down into the water themselves. More often than not, the fighting deteriorated into a series of chaotic, high-speed line astern chases low over the water. The chases stretched halfway back to England across the Channel. Planes were seen to plunge into the sea. The Messerschmitts were so fast, but the Spitfires could out-turn them.

At last they were in the clear and there, in front, were the white cliffs of England and safety ahead – the cliffs never looked so welcome! Critical fuel reserves were now the major concern. It was time to throttle back and endeavour to fly/glide back to Kenley.

Singly and in pairs they returned. The pilots climbed shakily out of their cockpits, but not everyone was back. Bill Middleton, a New Zealander from 485 Squadron was missing and so too was 452's Jack Elphick, a country boy from Lismore NSW. On the credit side Paddy Finucane claimed two more Me109s shot down into the sea, and so too did 'Throttle' Thorold-Smith.

At the finish of debriefing, they wearily made their way to breakfast. Meanwhile, loath to lose another man, Bob spent time telephoning the other airfields. The news for 452 was good. Jack Elphick was OK. He had landed at Lympne short of fuel but Middleton, the Kiwi from 485, had not made it back. He had gone down somewhere near Dunkirk (and was, in fact, buried there). After breakfast, Raife Cowan and Fred McCann were walking back to dispersal, passing the site of a bombed hangar currently used by the Coldstream Guards on airfield defence, when they saw Elphick's Spitfire fly over and land. It was unanimous, though; everyone wished dawn shows to hell!

For the remainder of the month there were three more *Circus* operations for 452 Squadron and a mission providing air cover to light naval units in the English Channel but none led to air combat. The RAF flew a total of twenty-six *Circus* operations during August plus numerous *Rodeos*, sweeps involving large formations of fighters alone. As well, there were many roving missions by smaller formations against coastal shipping, port installations and airfields. After counting, it was 452 Squadron that emerged as the most successful squadron in Fighter Command for the month.

This was a remarkable achievement for a new squadron that had been so recently formed and that was composed almost entirely of new, unblooded pilots. Contemporary assessments credited it with twenty-two enemy aircraft destroyed and three probably destroyed. Although almost half of these successes were claimed by the remarkable Paddy Finucane, with every engagement the Australians were taking an increasing part in the fighting and learning more and more from their few experienced veterans. Thanks to their brilliant leadership, the full tally to the end of August, not counting probables, was assessed at: Paddy Finucane ten; Keith Chisholm three; Ray 'Throttle' Thorold-Smith two and one shared; Bluey Truscott two; Arch Stuart two; Graham Douglas RAF one; Andrew Humphrey RAF one; Bill Eccleton one; Pat Tainton one; and Don Lewis one shared.[2]

In its first full month of combat, the new RAAF squadron had toppled the Polish squadrons at Northolt from their normal highest-scoring perch. In June 1941, No.303 Squadron had headed the Fighter Command list by claiming thirty-three destroyed and the following July No.308 Squadron, Johnny Kent's former unit, topped with twenty-one destroyed. In August, the nearest any of the Northolt units could get to 452 was seventeen destroyed, claimed by No.315 Squadron.

Others in the Kenley Wing were not laughing any more. Some New Zealanders in 485 Squadron were, in fact, complaining. For August 485 claimed four destroyed, one probable and one damaged and 602 four destroyed, two probable and three damaged. The Australian squadron's success after only one month on operations was giving the other two Kenley squadrons an inferiority complex!

Hawkeye Wells told the Kenley Station Commander, Gp/Capt Tom Prickman, he thought 452 Squadron 'had spots before the eyes'. He said years later to author Doug Stokes, 'Pilots were complaining how "do the Aussies do it when we fly on the same sweeps and have seen nothing?" We were in visual contact with other squadrons when 452 reported it was all happening and this could happen occasionally but was very difficult to understand continually. Our morale was getting a bit low and I had a responsibility to correct this, but I didn't really know what to do so I phoned the station commander and asked for an interview. He said he was busy and asked what it was about so I told him there was resentment on 485 over 452's high scores, that I felt he should know about it and that this state of affairs should not be allowed to continue. He replied, "Sour grapes, Wells, sour grapes", and put the phone down.'[3]

On the other hand, some thought perhaps 452 Squadron's immediate success had actually just been beginner's luck – a fluke; they would not be able to keep it up. Whether or not these jealous rumblings of complaint reached Bob's ears at this stage remains unknown, but he was certainly made aware of them later. Good luck – being in the right place at the right time – had obviously played its part, but there had to be more to it than that.

There was no doubt that Paddy Finucane's ability as a fighter pilot was nothing less than exceptional and that he was an inspirational leader. There was no doubt that 452 Squadron's other flight commander, Graham Douglas, and its few veterans were all skilled and very capable. And there was no doubt that the Australian newcomers were eager and growing in confidence – they were good and they knew that they were good – but perhaps it was this attitude that irked others.

There were other fundamentals that contributed to the squadron's success – things that were attributable to Bob Bungey himself. These were to be found in Bob's organisation, his strong discipline and his tactics in the air. With regard to organisation, Bob had an accountant's eye for detail and he gave it proper attention. With discipline, he insisted orders should be strictly followed – they were there for a reason, especially in the air. With regard to tactics which, in Fred McCann words brought 'howls of laughter from other squadrons', far from being laughable, they actually worked. So sound was Bob's judgement in the air that Paddy Finucane and Graham Douglas, both experienced pilots, respected him and willingly followed his lead.

By flying into combat in pairs and in loose fours, 452 Squadron's twelve Spitfire pilots had six pairs of eyes scouring the sky exclusively for the enemy knowing their No.2s guarded their tails. Squadron's flying in four sections of three had only four pairs of eyes scouring the sky while their No.2s and No.3s had to concentrate both on guarding their tails and maintaining formation. It followed logically that the Australian pilots had a better chance of spotting the opposition first and acting accordingly.

However, could they keep it up? In one month Bob had lost five pilots: Jay O'Byrne, Geoff Chapman and the youngster Barry Haydon on the 9th; Bill Eccleton and Dick Gazzard ten days later. And, these losses *were* personal. He had almost lost two more: Don Willis was wounded but was OK and thank God that Jack Elphick had made it back! This was his first command, the very first RAAF Spitfire squadron in the war to see action. Sadly, such losses were a part of it all, everybody knew that, but 452 was *his* squadron and they were *his* men. It was personal, all right.

On the 29th, Bob took weekend leave again, making the 35-minute flight in the Magister to RAF Benson. It was his third visit this month. He needed to see Sybil again.

13

September Duels

They did it again in September. Topping RAF Fighter Command's list as the most successful squadron in its first full month of combat operations had been a remarkable achievement for the pilots of 452 Squadron, and one that did not go unnoticed. The front page of London's *Daily Herald* of 5 September 1941 caught their attention:

Wing Commander Douglas Bader, famous legless fighter pilot, has a successor.

He is Paddy Finucane, of 452 Squadron, otherwise Acting Flight Lieutenant Brendan Finucane, DFC and Bar, 21-year-old Irishman from Dublin and one of the youngest flight commanders in the RAF.

Bader and Finucane appear together in the RAF awards list issued yesterday. They both win a Bar to the DFC, making Bader a DSO and DFC twice over.

But Bader, the greatest fighter leader and fighter tactician that this war has produced so far, is now a prisoner of war.

I say that Finucane is Bader's successor because he has the same qualities which made Wing Commander Malan, top-scoring fighter pilot, say not long ago, 'Bader is the most brilliant of the lot.'

Bader built up his reputation as a leader and tactician when he commanded a Dominion squadron, the Canadian 242, during the battles over London last September.

Finucane leads a flight in another Dominion squadron, the Australian 452. During fighter sweeps over France his squadron has destroyed 22 Messerschmitts 109. Finucane has been responsible for nearly half of them.

Recently his score of German aircraft destroyed has risen rapidly to at least 15.

But as with all great fighter pilots he is not merely an aerial duellist. He knows the trick of manoeuvres so that the rest of his flight have a greater chance of shooting down their enemies.

Not long ago his squadron tackled 100 Messerschmitts over France.

Finucane with three other pilots held off 30 of them for 25 minutes.

The piece was by 'A. B.' Austin, a thirty-seven-year-old Scotsman known as 'Sandy' to his friends. He had been the chief press officer at RAF Fighter Command Headquarters during the Battle of Britain and directly responsible to ACM Sir Hugh Dowding for releases to the media. He and 'Stuffy' Dowding had clashed initially as Dowding did not want pressmen cluttering up his HQ but after that, a mutual trust and respect developed. Austin resigned at the end of 1940 partly in disgust because of the way Dowding was dismissed, and partly because he wanted to report more widely on the war. There was a great deal of insider knowledge and informed guesswork involved in the compiling of Austin's article but his conclusions were astute and it introduced the young Irish ace and the Australians to the British public. It marked the beginning of a cycle of publicity for them all.

Paddy Finucane became exceptionally upset over attempts to discredit the squadron's August claims. The squadron's Intelligence officer, Denys Walters, recalled years later, 'Paddy seldom lost his temper but when he did it was hot. He said, "We have enough trouble fighting the enemy without getting shot at by our own side," and ended "I'm not going to be queried." He had a lot more to say about it and we sent that officer [an officer who had arrived at Kenley to question the claims] back to 11 Group with a flea in his ear. I was never called to an official inquiry, neither was anyone else on the squadron ... As I recall it, Squadron Leader Bungey kept in the sidelines while the query was going on.'

To seek the limelight was not in Bob Bungey's nature. Ian Milne summed up perceptively the merits of Bob's leadership:

> Bob was peculiarly qualified for the particular work in hand that Fighter Command found itself in. The whole scenario had changed. The business of Fighter Command in the Battle of Britain was one of defence from the onslaught of the *Luftwaffe's* bombers, escorted by their fighter force of course, but it was distinctly a defensive action.
>
> From the time we got to Kenley forward until the squadron ceased operations in Europe, our responsibility was to take the war to the enemy. To do this we were given a token force of bombers to attack a target, whether it be a strike on shipping, a powerhouse or marshalling yard, or whatever target the bombers were concerned with.
>
> The main objective was to escort the bombers with a fleet of fighters whose principle objective was to entice German fighters to come and upset us the way the air force in England had upset the *Luftwaffe* in their attacks, and so the essential need in the commanding officer was to have the capacity to know, when he was told what time he was expected to be in position to rendezvous with the bombers to escort them over and this meant that having been given the time of rendezvous and location of rendezvous his responsibility was to calculate when he would launch his fighters into the air, to climb to that given height and position without any error in height and timing because either case of error would entail a loss of needed fuel for the operation.
>
> It was remarkable that Bob's background in his time in the Battles, where his work demanded accuracy in this field of aviation and timing, paid

handsomely in his responsibility as leader of 452. He automatically was a trained navigator; he was an experienced pilot in Battles, Hurricanes and Spitfires; and he was able to assess the ability of Paddy Finucane and give him open-ended responsibility.

Paddy had an exceptionally brilliant talent to see enemy aircraft before anybody else could see them, and he had a talent to judge their position in relation to ours. If they threatened us, he had the full authority from Bob to withdraw his four aircraft and place them in a position where they would be able to intercept any assault from the enemy. This [tactic] worked so frequently and so brilliantly that the result in enemy aircraft destroyed, damaged and probably destroyed was reflected later in a score of sixty-two enemy aircraft shot down, seven probables and seventeen damaged in the time the squadron operated in Britain. In four of those months, the squadron shared, or shared leadership of British fighter squadrons in the destruction of enemy aircraft. This established the reputation of 452 as one of the most brilliant combat units in the history of air warfare, according to published records.

In so far as the successes were concerned, they were not achieved without a price. As I recall, in the first three months there was a loss to the squadron of sixteen pilots...

The new month started slowly for RAF Fighter Command. Bob returned to Kenley in the Magister on the 1st. In the late afternoon, fighters from the adjacent No.10 Group flew a *Roadstead* to Cherbourg from which one Spitfire failed to return.

Next morning, two uneventful fighter sweeps and an abortive low-level *Roadstead* attack on ships were flown to Ostend. These were followed by a second Ostend *Roadstead* but this time two Me109s were claimed destroyed, both by pilots of 452 Squadron. The squadron had already been busy before it took part in this second, late-morning *Roadstead*. A pair of Spitfires had performed a convoy patrol, and there was a scramble to intercept a bogey, which was eventually identified as friendly.

Blenheims from 139 Squadron and some bomb-carrying Hurricanes made up the Ostend strike force, escorted by three squadrons of Spitfires: Nos.242, 452 RAAF and 485 RNZAF. As usual, Bob led 452 Squadron in his favourite machine, Spitfire Mk V AB857.

The whole force was off Zeebrugge when it found an enemy coastal convoy. Anti-aircraft fire from the ships' defences and shore batteries was extremely active, and as the bombers made their approach one Blenheim was hit. Bob probably did not realise it at the time, but he may have discovered later, what he and the others witnessed next were the last moments of a long-time friend, Kevin Walsh, with his English crew F/Sgt Alfred Hole and Sgt George Brook.

Bob and Kevin Walsh had trained at Point Cook together in 1936 and both had chosen to come to England in 1937. Both had been posted to Bomber Command. Walsh was now a squadron leader in 139 Squadron. He was the pilot of Blenheim Z7274, one of the six aircraft deployed for the operation from 139's detachment at Manston. Walsh's crippled Blenheim plunged into the sea off the coast. It fell from such a low level that there was no chance of survival. (The bodies of Kevin Walsh and Alfred Hole were later recovered and buried in Belgium, but George Brook was never found.) As a result of their attacks the bomber crews claimed the sinking of a 5,000-ton vessel and a flak ship.

While the formation was withdrawing, 452 Squadron's Don Willis reported an unescorted Blenheim returning very low at sea-level. It could be seen flying so close to the water that its slipstream was churning up the surface, leaving a long white wake trailing behind which was very likely to attract the attention of any stray German fighters in the vicinity. Bob despatched Willis and his wingman, Arch Stuart, to provide cover. They were in position just in time. Within a couple of minutes a pair of Me109s appeared obviously intending to attack the bomber. Willis and Stuart cut them off and were able to claim both shot down into the sea. By that time, the Blenheim was safe out of sight. So too was the wing so the two Spitfires returned independently to Kenley.

The day's activities were not over yet as Bob led another sweep in the afternoon, this time to St Omer, but the *Luftwaffe* did not make an appearance.

Weather conditions were not suitable for operations the next day, but they improved on the 4th. Early on there was a *Roadstead* mission to Cherbourg, and a little later *Circus No.93* saw a dozen Blenheims escorted to bomb Mazingarbe power station. The *Luftwaffe* reacted strongly this time and there were many clashes but the trip proved uneventful for the Australians as 452 Squadron was not engaged. The other squadrons claimed a total of ten enemy aircraft shot down plus ten more as probables.

A period of poor weather followed with no major operations for the Kenley Wing. Except for a few *Rhubarbs* and reconnaissance flights, most RAF fighter squadrons were virtually kept grounded until 16 September. There was some flying training but a serious mishap occurred when two of 452's new pilots collided in mid-air and were killed.

Graham Douglas and Bluey Truscott attempted to fly a *Rhubarb* mission on the 11th but conditions were so bad they had to abort. In the meantime, a number of newly trained RAAF ground personnel arrived fresh from Australia. It was a thrill to welcome such a body of lean, bronzed men in slouch hats who certainly looked the part – tanned and fit after nearly three months at sea. They were to replace a large portion of the RAF ground crews but, as things turned out, quite a few of the British troops remained because the process of handing over became a somewhat drawn-out affair.

Away from his administrative duties, Bob's Log Book shows that he carried out a 1 hour 10 minute weather test on the 7th, a 1 hour 25 minute cannon test on the 10th, and a short 15 minute night flying test the following day. On the 13th and 15th though, the weather did allow formation flying practice for the whole squadron.

When operational flying resumed on the 16th, Bob led No.452 as part of the Kenley Wing to join sweeps flown by the Northolt, North Weald and Hornchurch Wings. The Australians met no opposition. Only the Polish squadrons from Northolt found the *Luftwaffe* this time and they skirmished with Messerschmitt 109s north of St Omer.

Above left: Bob Bungey's photograph and signature on his leave pass. (Robert Bungey's memorabilia via Richard Bungey)

Above right: Front cover of Bob Bungey's leave pass. (Robert Bungey's memorabilia via Richard Bungey)

Right: Proposed 452 (RAAF) Squadron RAF badge. (Richard Bungey)

Below: Bob Bungey's service medals including the Distinguished Flying Cross and the 1939–45 Star with Battle of Britain Clasp. (Richard Bungey)

Ernest, Pauline and Ada Bungey with their dog, Bomber. (Richard Bungey)

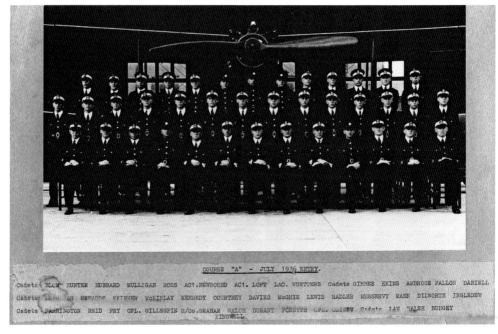

COURSE "A" - JULY 1936 ENTRY.

Cadets BLOW HUNTER HUBBARD MULLIGAN ROSS AC1.NEWBOUND AC1. LOFT LAC. WHETTERS Cadets GIBBES EKINS AMBROSE FALLON DANIELL
Cadets LEWIS OH HOWARDS SKINNER McKINLAY KENNEDY COURTNEY DAVIES McGHIE LEWIS SADLER MESSERVY MANN DILWORTH INGLEDEW
Cadets FARRINGTON REID FRY CPL. GILLESPIE U/Os.GRAHAM WALCH DURANT FORSYTH CPL. OLSEN Cadets LAW WALSH BUNGEY
RINGWELL

The cadets of 'A' Course July 1936 entry at RAAF Point Cook, Victoria. Bob Bungey is seated in the front row on the extreme right. (RAAF Museum)

R.A.A.F. POINT COOK
29TH June 1937
Group Captain MacNamara V.C.
Presenting Leslie Clisby with his wings
It was Leslie's 23rd birthday.

Above left: Bob Bungey wearing his cadet uniform at Point Cook. (Richard Bungey)

Above middle: A portrait photo of freshly graduated Bob Bungey wearing his 'wings' and his first RAAF uniform. (Richard Bungey)

Above right: Leslie Clisby receiving his wings at Point Cook. (RAAF Museum)

Below left: Pauline showing a 226 Squadron scarf which Bob had sent her to a friend. (Richard Bungey)

Below middle: Close friend, Leslie Clisby, in France in 1940. Flying Hurricanes with No.1 Squadron RAF, Les Clisby was involved in the heaviest earlier fighting and became the first Australian air ace of the Second World War before being killed in action. (RAAF Museum)

Below right: Sybil. (Richard Bungey)

Right: A formation of Fairey Battles from 226 Squadron on patrol over France during the 'Phoney War' period. Bob Bungey is at the controls of Battle 'X' in the centre. In May 1940 when the Germans invaded France and the Low Countries the Battle squadrons were decimated. They were at the mercy of the Luftwaffe's Me109s and 110s. (Richard Bungey)

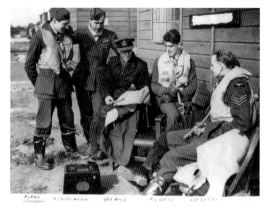

No.145 Squadron pilots at Tangmere, from left to right: the Belgian ace, Jean 'Pyker' Offenberg; Dudley Honor; S/Ldr Adrian Boyd; P/O Nigel Weir; and Sgt Duncan Sykes. (Richard Bungey)

Composite picture of a Hurricane attacking a German bomber. (RAAF Museum)

Above left: Bob Bungey with a doctor friend from the 2/3 Australian General Hospital. Approximately one-third of the Australian 6th Division, consisting of some 8,000 officers and men, arrived in Britain in June 1940 to reinforce the British defences facing possible invasion. The 2/3 Australian General Hospital was formed in England at this time. (Richard Bungey)

Above right: A publicity photo of 452 Squadron's Irish ace, Paddy Finucane. Paddy signed it as a souvenir for Bob Bungey. (Richard Bungey)

Above left: Alex Roberts was shot down on 11 July 1941 but evaded capture. He escaped over the Pyrenees and ultimately reached Algeciras and Gibraltar from where he was brought back to England on a British destroyer. Not permitted to fly operations over the Continent again, he later served in India and Burma. (Alex Roberts)

Above right: Squadron Leader Robert Bungey CO of 452 (RAAF) Squadron. (RAAF Museum)

Bluey Truscott, on the left, with Bob Bungey at Kenley. (Richard Bungey)

Before take-off, from left to right: Keith Chisholm, Ian Milne and Paddy Finucane, having a quiet moment. (RAAF Museum)

Above left: The front view of the house in Penzance, Cornwall, where Sybil was born and where the Johnsons lived before the family moved to Wallingford in Oxfordshire. (Richard Bungey)

Above right: Robert Bungey seen through the eyes of war artist Sir William Rothenstein. (Richard Bungey)

Aces of 452 Squadron, from left: Bluey Truscott, Paddy Finucane and Ray Thorold-Smith. (Richard Bungey)

Bob Bungey with Frank
McNamara VC and Sir
Charles McCann during
an official visit to Kenley.
(Richard Bungey)

Bob rushing to congratulate
Paddy Finucane for three
kills on one operation
on 20 September 1941.
(Richard Bungey)

Talking after the mission:
Bob Bungey, in sunglasses,
looks on as Paddy Finucane
congratulates Keith
Chisholm. (Richard Bungey)

Bardy Wawn and
Bluey Truscott.
(Tom Scott)

The deadly
Focke-Wulf FW
190 'Butcher Bird'
outclassed the RAF's
Spitfire Vs when it
was introduced by
the Luftwaffe towards
the end of 1941.
(RAAF Museum)

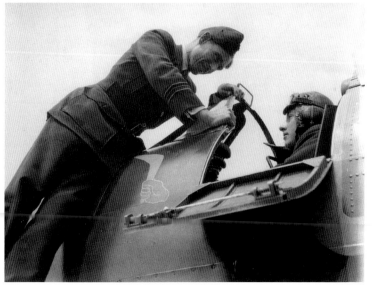

Bob Bungey in
discussion with
P/O Don Lewis before
take-off. Lewis was
lost on 22 January
1942 when his
Spitfire unexpectedly
experienced engine
trouble. He had
to bail out over
the North Sea,
where he drowned.
(Richard Bungey)

Above left: An ASR Walrus amphibian. (RAAF Museum)

Above right: Happy times that were cut so short – Richard, Sybil and Bob Bungey together. (Richard Bungey)

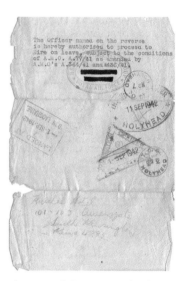

Above left: Bob made a point of writing down what was required on his special 'leave' to Ireland in August/September 1942 at a time of anticipated trouble with the IRA. Note the County Waterford address, that the pass had to be endorsed giving permission to travel in Eire, and the '200 cartridges'. (Robert Bungey's memorabilia via Richard Bungey)

Above middle: Bob's RAF leave pass for Ireland in August/September 1942. Note that the pass was endorsed giving 'privilege' permission to travel in Eire and that 'Maj Skrine' was linked to the County Waterford address. Major Walter Skrine was a high-ranking officer in Combined Operations command. Bob had dealt with him earlier during the organising of Operation *Rutter* and Operation *Jubilee*. (Robert Bungey's memorabilia via Richard Bungey)

Above right: Bob's RAF leave pass to Ireland in August/September 1942. Note that the reverse side confirms his travel from and to Holyhead. Also note that Bob pencilled in a London address in South Kensington, to which he had to report. He did not return to his command at Hawkinge. His vacant position was filled by two temporary appointments before a permanent appointment was made. Bob later returned as a supernumerary. (Robert Bungey's memorabilia via Richard Bungey)

INVALID

THE LATE Squadron-Leader R. W. Bungey, who was found shot dead yesterday, and Mrs. Bungey photographed on holiday at Somerton (S.A.). The picture was taken a few days before Mrs. Bungey's death on May 27.

Dead Airman's Worry For Motherless Child

ADELAIDE, Friday. — "Squadron-Leader Bungey told me the other night that now that he had to be a father and mother to his child he had more cause to take care of himself," said Mr. W. E. Taplin today.

Mr. Taplin was a friend of Squadron-Leader R. W. Bungey, D.F.C., famous Australian ace and Spitfire pilot.

Bungey's dead body was found on Thursday on the beach at Brighton, near his home, with a bullet wound in the head.

Alongside him was his infant son (13 months), also shot in the head.

The child is critically ill and is paralysed on one side, indicating injury to the brain.

Bungey was 28. He was to have left last night for an operational station.

Bungey's English wife, whom he married in 1941, died in a hospital in Glenelg on May 27, about three weeks after he returned from England.

Her illness resulted from complications following the birth of the child.

Shock Of Wife's Death

Mr. Taplin said: "Bungey told me he was worried about his son.

"He said that if he was away, perhaps for three or four years, the child would not know him when he returned.

"He told me it was a terrible shock when his wife died, but he had known that she could not have lived another

ALLIED FLAG DAY CELEBRATION

United Nations Flag Day will be celebrated in Australia next Monday.

The Prime Minister (Mr. Curtin) said in Canberra yesterday that arrangements for the celebration had been completed between the Government and the Commander-in-Chief of the South-west Pacific area (General MacArthur).

A ceremonial parade will be held in each of the capital cities. Representatives of all branches of the Australian and U.S. Services, including women's organisations, will take part.

Bob and Sybil's last photo together was used in this press report. (Richard Bungey)

Above: The full air force funeral of Squadron Leader Robert Bungey DFC RAAF was held at St Peter's Church, Glenelg, with the burial following at St Jude's Cemetery, Brighton. Five senior RAAF officers and Sgt David Bungey (back to camera, centre) acted as pall-bearers. (Richard Bungey)

Right: David Bungey.

Left: The Somerton Miracle – young Richard growing up into a sturdy youngster. (Richard Bungey)

Below: June 1941, an early photo of 452 Squadron. From left: Ken Cox, Arch Stuart, Brendan 'Paddy' Finucane, Ian Milne; Jim Hanigan, Fred McCann, Ray Thorold-Smith, Bob Bungey, Don Willis, Alex Roberts, Don Lewis, Graham Douglas, Andy Costello, Keith 'Bluey' Truscott and Dick Gazzard. (RAAF Museum)

The Australian War Memorial's 452 Squadron Spitfire shortly after its arrival. (AWM 148873)

Spitfire P7973 on display in the Australian War Memorial in Canberra during the 1960s. As well as being flown by Bob Bungey at times, two other pilots who flew it were the aces Bluey Truscott and Ray Thorold-Smith. (Dennis Newton)

Richard's Spitfire flight 'with his Dad'. (Nick Greenaway via Richard Bungey)

A close-up picture of Richard Bungey ready to take off and 'live the dream' in Carolyn Grace's Spitfire. (Nick Greenaway via Richard Bungey)

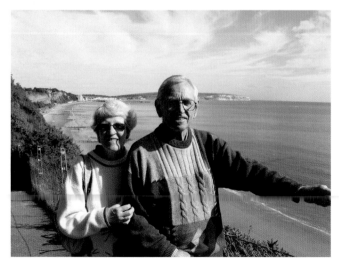

Allison and Richard Bungey on the Isle of Wight, near where his father had to ditch his Hurricane on 7 November 1940. (Nick Greenaway via Richard Bungey)

Above: The Battle of Britain memorial at Capel-le-Ferne, near Folkstone. (Dennis Newton)

Right: Bob Bungey's name on the Battle of Britain memorial in London on the bank of the Thames. (Dennis Newton)

Below right: Richard finds his father's name at Capel-le-Ferne. (Dennis Newton)

The introduction to *The Battle Within* by 60 Minutes on Channel 9, presented by Liam Bartlett. For Richard, when the documentary appeared on Australian television, the story lived up to everything the 60 Minutes team had promised. (Nick Greenaway via Richard Bungey)

Authors Dennis Newton, left, and Richard Bungey. (Dennis Newton)

The following day No.452 took part in two *Circus* operations, one of them an unusually large effort. This was the first attack, *Circus No.95* to Mazingarbe, which was becoming a regular target. This time there were twenty-three Blenheims supported by no less than twenty-five fighter squadrons. The *Luftwaffe* responded in great numbers too, but once again the Australians were not challenged.

Later in the afternoon, *Circus No.96* was of a more normal size with six Hampdens directed against the shell factory at Marquise. This too caused a strong reaction from the enemy, but not on the same scale as during the earlier mission. Again, 452 Squadron did not have a chance to tangle with any opposition.

Something ominous occurred early on the 18th. A fighter *Roadstead* was flown to Ostend, bomb-carrying Hurricanes from 615 Squadron being escorted by Spitfires from 41 Squadron. They were engaged by the usual Me109s, but among their attackers were several different-looking fighters, radial-engined types. P/O Cyril Babbage of 41 Squadron shot one of these down into the North Sea and claimed a Curtiss 'Hawk 75', an American P-36 that had been used by the French *Armée de l'Air* at the beginning of the war – but this was no Curtiss. It was a new and deadly machine that would, in fact, cost the Allies dear. Babbage's victory was the first known success scored against the new Focke-Wulf FW190.

Until now, RAF fighters had enjoyed a large measure of technical equality with, and numerical superiority over, their *Luftwaffe* opponents but that was about to change. The Spitfire V was well matched against the Me109F and superior to the earlier Me109E of the Battle of Britain, the Spitfire II and all variants of the Hurricane to a lesser extent. The new German Fw190A was a tough, radial-engined 'brute', possessing heavy armament, excellent manoeuvrability at lower altitudes, and a 15-mph speed advantage over the Spitfire V. It had started flying with *JG 26* on the Channel coast during July and August but at first had been plagued by engine problems. These teething difficulties had now been overcome and the Focke-Wulf was about to become a 'nasty shock' for Fighter Command. It would prove to be more than a match for all RAF fighters until the advent of the later Spitfire Mk IX, which would not begin to enter service for well over a year.

Mid-afternoon on 18 September, 452 Squadron was detailed with Nos.485 and 602 Squadrons to close escort *Circus No.99*, twelve Blenheims assigned to attack Rouen, but the mission became disorganised from the start. Eleven Blenheims turned up flying in two boxes, the first of six and the second of five. The Spitfires from Kenley formed up correctly but when they rendezvoused with the bombers over Beachy Head, they found a squadron of Hurricanes which had been detailed for a different operation, already closely accompanying the forward box of Blenheims.

Bob ordered 452 to take up station on the rear box but then the Hurricanes began to string out backwards over both formations. The Spitfires were, in effect, pushed away. The Australians were forced into the unwieldy necessity of dividing into flights and flying in line astern, one on either side above the bombers. Just before reaching the target, which was the port, the closely escorting Hurricanes closed in and forced 452's 'B' Flight up to the top of the escort wing as the Blenheims started their bomb run. The bombers turned to starboard after the attack and this manoeuvre left 'B' Flight isolated and dangerously exposed on the outside of the turn. Many small groups of enemy fighters were above, and the pre-arranged top cover wing for the withdrawing 'beehive' was not yet anywhere in sight.

The Messerschmitts began attacking, drawing 'B' Flight back away from the rest of the *Circus*. A series of dogfights ensued with Bob bringing 'A' Flight across to support the seriously outnumbered 'B' Flight. After this, the whole squadron was ultimately split into individuals or fighting pairs involved in a running battle. Ray Thorold-Smith, Keith Chisholm, Graham Douglas and Bluey Truscott each claimed one enemy aircraft destroyed, while Truscott claimed another as probably destroyed and Bardie Wawn two more as damaged (one of these was later assessed as destroyed). Although Bob fired several times at the attacking enemy fighters in an effort to deflect their assaults on 'B' Flight, he did not make a claim.

Unfortunately, four Australian pilots failed to return. They were P/O Don Willis, Sgt Augustus Try, Sgt Arch Stuart and Sgt Charles Manning. It was discovered later that Gus Try and Arch Stuart were POWs. Try's Spitfire was hit at low level and caught fire but he managed to bail out successfully. On the ground, he hid in a well but French civilians fearing reprisals betrayed him to the Germans. Arch Stuart went down near Rouen and according to one account he may have rammed, or been rammed by, a German fighter. Don Willis and Charles Manning were killed.

Despite the successful claims, to suffer so many losses was abhorrent to Bob, particularly after the tragic loss of the two new men in the flying accident just days earlier. All these losses were personal blows to him and although he did not show it they affected him deeply.

The 19th was quiet but the following day the RAF geared up for a major assault. Three *Circus* operations were to be launched, all against railway and shipbuilding yards in northern France in the early afternoon: *Circus No.100A*, three Blenheims escorted by three fighter wings to Hazebrouck; *Circus No.100B* to Abbeville with six Hampdens and two fighter wings; and Circus *No.100C*, twelve Blenheims escorted by another two fighter wings to attack Rouen again. Further afield, two wings of fighters from No.10 Group would escort Blenheims to Cherbourg.

The Kenley Wing's duty was to act as high cover for *Circus 100B* to Abbeville, and this time Bob Bungey would take on the role of wing leader again because Johnny Kent was absent in London. The occasion was the biggest three-pronged daylight assault on the Continent so far, and it was to be all the more important because members of the press, reporters and photographers, were on the base ready to capture everything on film.

Bob entered the smoke-filled wing briefing room accompanied by the station commander, Gp/Capt Tom Prickman. The pilots of Kenley's two squadrons, 452 and 602, were present and they rose to attention 'Sit down, chaps', they were bid.

When there was silence, Bob began his briefing, and as usual he went straight to the point:

'Here's the drill. The marshalling yard at Abbeville is the target and we'll be escorting Hampdens at 20,000 feet. 485 from Redhill [Kenley's satellite airfield] will rendezvous with us over base at 14.50; rendezvous with the bombers over Rye at 15.11 hours; crossing in at St Valery and at the target at about 15.41 hours. Biggin Hill and one squadron from Debden are the close escort. The weather? Here's the weather man (the pilots groaned in unison) and a briefing on our weather.'

'You might get some ground haze over France but perfect visibility over the target,' he said.

Special comments by the squadron commanders and flight commanders were called for, then, 'Any questions? (A pause) No? Well, good luck.'

'Happy hunting, wish I could go with you,' added Tom Prickman, which drew the usual good-natured response from the pilots.

As 14.50 approached, Bob climbed into the cockpit of his Spitfire, AB857 as usual, and was helped to strap on the Sutton harness. Time now to concentrate fully on the flight ahead; everything had been worked out to the last detail. He watched and waited as the starter battery lead was connected to the engine's ignition system. The seconds ticked away to zero. At 14.50 hours. Bob signalled. His propeller suddenly rotated and there was the harsh sound of the engine coming to life. His mechanic shouted, 'Good luck, sir' against the engine's booming growl.

All along the line the other Spitfires started up too. One by one they moved out of the blast pens and into line along the perimeter road to the left, prior to taking off from the main runway. Paddy Finucane turned right at the runway threshold and waited for Bob's section ahead of him to go –then it would be his turn into line, followed by Keith Chisholm and Ian Milne.

Bob held the aircraft with his brakes as he made the final checks, then he pushed the throttle forward. AB857 trembled with the powerful full-throated growl of its Rolls-Royce Merlin; brakes off, then he was rolling along the runway, keeping straight using plenty of rudder to counteract the powerful torque of the propeller that tried to swing the aircraft to the right before gaining flying speed.

The press photographers were waiting. They took their pre-sweep photos, including shots of the Spitfires as they lifted off in sections of three with their wheels retracting just above the runway. The New Zealanders of 485 Squadron were over from Redhill on time and formatted with 602, which had followed 452 in take-off order. Then all thirty-six Spitfires in three separate squadron formations all manoeuvred to fly in sections of four in line astern. Finally the Kenley Wing set course as one whole force and headed out over Caterham to rendezvous with the bombers above the Sussex coast.

Meanwhile, the Biggin Hill Wing met the Hampdens over Rye at 14,000 feet and stepped up its squadrons ranging from 16,000 feet to 19,000 feet. Bob brought the Kenley Wing in at 20,000 feet (6,000 m) and stepped up his squadrons in a similar manner according to the plan at briefing. With everyone in place, Circus *100B* set out across the Channel.

Trouble started immediately after they crossed the coast at St Valery. About 5 miles north-west of Abbeville twelve Me109s crossed from port to starboard 1,000 feet overhead. No.602 Squadron was well placed to deal with them. Then it was 452's turn. Paddy Finucane broke away and fired at a 109 but missed, and he quickly rejoined the squadron. More Messerschmitts were coming in from the same direction and this time the Irishman's lightning quick reflexes paid off – the 109 he fired on 'went to pieces'.

It was estimated later that about fifty enthusiastic, tenacious Messerschmitts had been involved in the various separate engagements that followed. As Bob, Finucane and Douglas had trained their pilots so often, 452 Squadron broke up into sections and counter-attacked. Within seconds there seemed to be the smoke trails from burning aircraft everywhere. At 15,000 feet cannon fire from a 109 struck the engine and radio of Ian Milne's Spitfire. That was it for him. He tried to glide back out to sea towards England but it was no good, he couldn't make it. He had to bail out fast.

In the general melee, Finucane claimed another two 109s destroyed for a total of three altogether, and Bluey Truscott shot down two, plus one Messerschmitt damaged. As well, Keith Chisholm and Sgt 'Pyfo' ('Pull Your Finger Out') Dunstan, a newcomer who had been working as a plumber's mate in Torquay but had been born in in Australia in Chelsea, Victoria, each claimed one enemy fighter destroyed while Sgt Elphick damaged two more.

The Biggin Hill Wing escorted the Hampdens to Abbeville practically unmolested, where they bombed from 14,000 feet. There was little or no flak either over the coast or the target during the whole operation, which was unusual. *Circus 100B* was an all-fighter affair with 452 bearing the brunt of the action. Incredibly, 485 Squadron saw just one Me109 which Hawkeye Wells fired on without result, and 602 Squadron reported only a few engagements, although two of their aircraft disappeared without trace, nobody seeing how or when they went down.

Back at Kenley as the early evening shadows began to lengthen, the press photographers were waiting. They had their pre-sweep shots, and now they were ready to record for posterity the excitement of the Australian squadron returning from the sweep. The pictures they captured in 452's dispersal area when the squadron landed became famous. Their great value was that they were spontaneous – the pilots were too pre-occupied with what had happened to bother noticing what the cameramen were doing. The scenes at 452's dispersal were candid, exactly as they happened.

An excited Bob Bungey was the first over to Paddy Finucane's shamrock-decorated Spitfire to help the Irish ace out of the cockpit and offer his congratulations. He then stepped back a little to let the others have the spotlight. Finucane was the star of the show. The pictures showed Bob in dark glasses off to one side, smiling; the pilots crowding around Finucane; Finucane clapping his wingman Keith Chisholm on the shoulder; Finucane with his Mae West slung over one shoulder extending his hand to accept the handshake of an informal and joyful Gp/Capt Tom Prickman; intelligence officer Denys Walters talking with a thoughtful Bluey Truscott and Keith Chisholm while making notes for the combat reports; and a tired-looking W/Cdr Johnny Kent, who had returned from London, standing nearby.

All these things and more were recorded in a remarkable series of photos which conveyed explicitly more about the men in a fighter squadron at war than any press bulletin or staged movie could possibly do. It was all there, the strain, the tension, and the excitement.

As well as going into the British tabloids, the pictures were also reproduced in Australian newspapers. Paddy Finucane and Bluey Truscott became national heroes overnight. From now on, there would be no stopping the publicity.

The official RAAF history recorded: 'On this occasion the squadron's own losses were not so severe, one Spitfire failing to return.' That was Ian Milne's machine and there was no news of him.

With his radio smashed by cannon shells, Milne had been unable to call up the squadron before he bailed out over the water. 'I finished up in my parachute landing out in the English Channel off Dieppe,' he recalled years later, 'I drifted around there in my dinghy from about Saturday midday until Tuesday afternoon sometime when I was picked up by a German flak ship and taken into Dieppe.' It was the beginning of three-and-a-half years as a POW.

All three *Circus* missions encountered opposition that day. Altogether, fifteen enemy aircraft were claimed destroyed, two probably destroyed and five damaged for the loss of seven Spitfires. Meanwhile, the No.10 Group escorted Blenheim raid to Cherbourg, known as *Gudgeon 8*, took place without incident.

Next day, Sunday the 21st, the RAF mounted two simultaneous *Circus* operations. *Circus No.101* detailed twelve Blenheims to be escorted as they bombed the power station at Gosnay again, while *Circus No.102* required the fighters to take six Hampdens to Lille. The Kenley Wing was detailed to be the high cover for the Gosnay attack, and Bob again took the role of wing leader. Though divided between the two attacks, the defending German fighters still managed to give a good account of themselves. Fighter Command was harshly treated losing fifteen fighters, including two squadron commanders.

Bob found no bombers at the rendezvous, so he led Kenley's three squadrons out over Dungeness to France, crossing the enemy coast at Le Touquet. There, he ordered the wing to orbit and keep a lookout for the missing Blenheims. Again no luck, but there were enemy fighters beginning to shadow them. As Bob and the wing finally turned towards the target, the 109s followed.

The clashes began over Desvres before reaching Lille. It was about 3.20 p.m. The melee raged for the next 10 minutes with Spitfires and Messerschmitts fighting mainly in pairs from 20,000 feet (6,000 m) down to ground level. The New Zealanders lost one aircraft and its pilot, and 602 Squadron two with one pilot evading capture and returning to the UK via Spain four months later. Miraculously, 452 Squadron emerged unscathed with Paddy Finucane claiming another two destroyed, making it five in just two days. As well,

Bluey Truscott, Bardie Wawn and Keith Chisholm each claimed a 109, plus Chisholm and Don Lewis one each damaged. On top of this, 485 Squadron's pilots claimed three Me109s destroyed, two of them by Hawkeye Wells, and one more probably destroyed, and 602 Squadron added one Messerschmitt damaged to the total.

Interestingly, Fighter Command's rules on combat claims had been tightened up after the fuss over 452's successes in August and this time two of 485's claims made on 21 September were downgraded from 'destroyed' to 'probably destroyed'. Almost as if to rub salt into the wounds of the New Zealanders, all of 452's claims were cleared as authentic.

So it was that Kenley again emerged as Fighter Command's most triumphant wing after a most difficult afternoon, and honours for the day went to 452 Squadron – again. Despite the fifteen casualties Fighter Command had suffered, or perhaps because of them, no bombers were lost in either *Circus No.101* or *Circus No.102*.

After this, air operations were restricted by fog and poor weather conditions. The lull in activity lasted until 26 September when four of 452 Squadron's aircraft flew an uneventful *Rhubarb*. Only one more *Circus* was attempted during the month, when, although the target was the marshalling yards at Amiens, the Kenley Wing encountered no enemy opposition in the air.

It was enough. They had done it again. With claims of eighteen enemy aircraft destroyed, 452 were the top of Fighter Command's tabulated scoreboard again in September. They were just ahead of the Northolt Wing's No.308 (Polish) Squadron, which claimed sixteen destroyed and was placed second. The Biggin Hill Wing, previously noted for its high scores, was not in the running. For the first time attention was centring on Kenley because of the Australian squadron's success. The official RAAF history would record:

> There was no doubt that the squadron had reached full maturity and even replacement pilots quickly became imbued with this élan, the precious corporate spirit of daring and tenacity which at the cutting edge of battle denotes the true fighter. Much of this elemental temper had been absorbed unconsciously from the experienced courage of Bungey and from Finucane's instinctive battle sense, but the fire innate in all of them burned brighter with every opportunity.
>
> The meteoric rise to prominence of No.452 owed much, as has been stated, to the complete confidence which the pilots placed in Bungey's training and administrative leadership. They were fortunate, too, in coming fresh to the battle at a time when Fighter Command was firmly seizing the initiative, and when the tactical situation was favourable. Raw as they were initially, these men were the pick of the first fruits of the EATS and, partly self-consciously but entirely whole-heartedly, they regarded themselves as the vanguard of Australian effort in the air. It was undoubtedly Finucane who turned these other assisting factors into the final success by which so brilliant a fighting team was rapidly created...

The squadron's successes created a problem for London's Daily *Herald* when news of the results of Sunday's sweep came in. Its Monday morning editions had already started to roll off the press with the headline 'FINUCANE WANTS 3 FOR HIS 21ST' –'21 FOR HIS 21ST BIRTHDAY'. For the later editions the headline was altered to read 'FINUCANE WANTS JUST ONE MORE'.

Over the next few weeks, newspapers in Australia displayed spectacular headlines like 'RAAF ON TOP AGAIN – AUSTRALIAN SQUADRON BAGS 6 NAZI PLANES'; 'FINUCANE GETS 5 IN 2 DAYS'; 'IT JUST BLEW TO BITS' in the *Melbourne Sun* (Keith Chisholm explaining his combat to Finucane; 'AUSTRALIANS TRIUMPH IN AIR' on the *Melbourne Herald*; and 'RAAF HEROES AND IRISH LEADER'. Most of these stories were illustrated with the photographs taken on the day of *Circus 100B*.

Meanwhile, although the weather had turned, there was still a lot going on. On the 23rd, word was received that Bob would be awarded the DFC and there would be decorations gazetted for others as well. 'B' Flight's commander, Graham Douglas, who was a former flying instructor (he actually owned Redhill airfield, Kenley's satellite, where he had managed a flying school before the war) was promoted and received a posting to command a squadron of his own. This turned out to be another Dominion unit, No.403 (RCAF) Squadron at Debden in Essex. Its former CO, S/Ldr Lee Knight, had been shot down by Me109s on 27 September during *Circus 103B*. Bluey Truscott, whose score now stood at six destroyed, was promoted to flight lieutenant on the 29th and Bob had him take over 'B' Flight to replace Douglas.

Bob's Log Book reveals that he only visited Wallingford once in September. On the 26th, he flew the Magister to Benson, this time via Hendon where he dropped off a passenger, Paddy Finucane, who wanted to go into London.

Bob would return to Kenley on the 29th but in-between there was much to arrange. His twenty-seventh birthday was coming up on the 4th of next month and he was organising to take ten days of well-earned leave. It would be his fifth birthday in RAF service. So much had happened since he had taken up his commission, especially recently. In 1937 on 4 October, he had been in Bomber Command in 226 Squadron at Harwell in Berkshire, with the squadron about to swap its Hawker Audax biplanes for Fairey Battles; in 1938 he was still in 226 Squadron at Harwell and still with Fairey Battles; in 1939 he and 226 Squadron had moved to France but were still flying Fairey Battles – Les Clisby had flown across France and they had celebrated his birthday together; and by October 1940 things had changed dramatically – he was in Fighter Command flying Hurricanes in 145 Squadron in Scotland at Dice about to transfer to Tangmere and into the heavy fighting over southern England; and now...

Now he was the CO of the RAAF's very first Spitfire squadron, probably its most successful fighting unit in the war so far. Paddy would be 452's acting CO while he was away, and this birthday would bring about one of the biggest changes in his life so far.

14

October Surprises

During the early afternoon of the first day of October, Bob Bungey led 452 Squadron to take part in a large-scale fighter sweep over the Boulogne area. It was one of several Fighter Command sweeps through the day. There had been a couple of minor clashes in the morning but 452's trip was uneventful.

Next day, the Kenley Wing was up again to join an early afternoon *Circus* operation but shortly after making the rendezvous with a small force of bombers over Manston, the bombers were recalled due to unfavourable weather. No.452 Squadron's twelve Spitfires were all back on the ground by 1.45 p.m.

Meanwhile, a wing of Spitfires flying a sweep over Abbeville became embroiled in heavy fighting. Without loss, No.71 Squadron claimed five destroyed and 72 Squadron one, all Me109s, but 92 Squadron was harshly treated by the new FW190s. Three Spitfires and their pilots were lost and a fourth Spitfire was shot up but managed to limp back across the English Channel to crash land near Ashford. Its pilot was safe but wounded.

There was no 'stand down' for the pilots of 452 Squadron. Their day was not over yet. Two hours after landing, Bob led his fighters up again to carry out an offensive sweep with 485 Squadron and the Tangmere Wing. They all crossed the French coast over Gravelines. Probably anticipating that bombers would be present, the *Luftwaffe* reacted strongly and a running fight developed, which spread from 8 miles east of Boulogne Harbour to 12 miles out to sea. Paddy Finucane's section was continuously engaged and the Irish ace claimed one Me109F destroyed (his twenty-first victim) and two damaged. His wingman, Sgt Raife Cowan from Brisbane, sent down another when it tried to surprise Finucane from behind. It crashed into the sea. The Kiwis claimed three probables.

Naturally, Finucane's twenty-first victory before his twenty-first birthday received wide coverage in the press. The Air Ministry even officially named him in a bulletin and this resulted in such headlines the following day as 'Finucane gets his 21st' and the like. Bluey Truscott actually missed this fight because he was on leave and not due back until the following day.

200

The 3rd was quiet with regard to operations, but it turned into a day for 452 to remember thanks to the official announcements in the *London Gazette*. Besides Paddy Finucane's success, there was a lot more to celebrate.

It was announced in the *Gazette* that Bluey Truscott was awarded the DFC for destroying six enemy aircraft. His return to Kenley also marked the beginning of his tenure in command of 'B' Flight after Graham Douglas' posting. Sgt Keith Chisholm, who also had six to his credit and was keeping pace with Bluey, received the DFM. He was the first RAAF non-commissioned pilot to win this award. Bob Bungey's DFC was announced in there too. The citation for his award read in part: 'Squadron Leader Bungey has led the squadron and occasionally the wing, on many operational sorties over Northern France. Brilliant successes have been achieved and during August ... Throughout, this officer displayed gallant and efficient leadership.'[1]

As important as this was to him, Bob was looking forward more to an exclusive celebration of his own. The 4th was his birthday and the first day of his much-anticipated, very carefully planned, ten-day leave. To begin with, he had a very special rendezvous with Sybil at the Surrey South-Eastern Register Office. It was there that they were quietly married away from the clamour and glare of publicity. Their marriage would come as a complete surprise to those at Kenley. For the next nine blissful days they would vanish into a special private world of their own, far removed from the never-ending pressure and stress of this terrible, unrelenting war.

In the meantime, the war situation away from the Channel front was far from good. Operation *Barbarossa* had been highly successful for the Germans at first but by attacking Russia and engaging in war on all fronts, the Third Reich was actually planting the seeds of its own eventual destruction. However, that was years away. This October on the Eastern Front started with the Germans about to launch their planned assault on Moscow, Operation *Typhoon*, before the onset of winter. It began on the 2nd.

This time, though, Britain and the USA pledged to send large quantities of supplies to Russia every month: 400 aircraft; 500 tanks; 200 gun carriers; 41,000 tons (41,656 tonnes) of aluminium; 22,000 tons (22,352 tonnes) of rubber; and 3,860 tons (3,922 tonnes) of machine tools plus large quantities of food, medical supplies and raw materials. For Britain it would mean a serious drain on resources that were already stretched thin elsewhere.

One wing of RAF Hurricanes (151 Wing) comprising Nos.81 and 134 Squadrons had already been deployed to northern Russia, early in September. The fighters had flown off the aircraft carrier HMS *Argus* and landed at Vaenga, near the port of Murmansk. They had been pledged by Prime Minister Churchill for the protection of this essential ice-free port, which would be a vital gateway for the delivery of supplies to the Soviets.

By 10 October, factories in Moscow involved in war production were being disassembled for evacuation out of harm's way to the east. The next day Russian-built T-34 tanks went into action for the first time and inflicted severe losses on the Germans but, despite this determined Russian resistance and increasingly poor weather, the German advance on Moscow pressed on, with Kaluga falling on the 12th.

In the Mediterranean anything could happen. Britain's 8th Army faced the Axis forces in the Western Desert where a dynamic German commander, General Erwin Rommel, was winning renown as the 'Desert Fox'. He posed a serious threat to Egypt and the Suez Canal, and if he eventually managed to be successful, India. Meanwhile the island of Malta, although besieged and battered from the air, remained a vital base from which the RAF and FAA could attack the enemy's supply lines and bases. Under siege too was Tobruk, but that situation was changing because Germany had redeployed much of its strength to its Eastern Front in the bid to speedily overcome the Soviet Union.

Despite the accomplishments of Rommel's *Afrika Korps,* British strength in the Western Desert was actually increasing. The Desert Air Force (DAF) had become a remarkably resilient weapon, thanks to its outstanding serviceability and mobility under extremely difficult conditions – its capacity to move from base to base quickly and efficiently. Not including home-based aircraft in Italy and Sicily, which were maintaining pressure on Malta, the Axis war machine could muster 180 aircraft in Greece, and in Libya Rommel could call upon 240 *Luftwaffe* aircraft plus some 300 aircraft of the Italian *Regia Aeronautica.* At this stage, with most of the *Luftwaffe* operating against the Soviets, it was mainly the *Regia Aeronautica* that was continuing the air assault on Malta.

Unknown to the Germans and Italians, Britain held a trump card – a top secret advantage. Thanks to the capture of a German 'Enigma' coding machine, the British were able to decipher the messages the German High Command was passing to its forces in North Africa and elsewhere. The stretched state of the *Afrika Korps'* supply lines was known, as were the sailing dates of almost all Axis convoys and their cargoes. Photographic Reconnaissance Unit (PRU) aircraft flying from Malta were directed where to hunt for the convoys and the RAF was able to concentrate the attacks of its relatively few anti-shipping aircraft at critical times to starve Rommel of his supplies. Resources were stretched to the limit to exploit the 'Enigma' advantage but they were being used in such a way that would not reveal that the code had been broken. With this advantage becoming more effective in October, plans were even afoot for the 8th Army to launch an offensive to relieve Tobruk.

In Britain, the onset of deteriorating weather conditions as winter approached was reducing the number of daylight air operations and the effectiveness of the pressure being applied to the Germans on the Channel front. At the same time, RAF Fighter Command was encountering increasing numbers of the *Luftwaffe*'s new formidable Focke-Wulf 190 'Butcher Bird' and realising it outclassed every fighter it had. As well, the real effectiveness of Bomber Command's night assault was under review. The times ahead would be far from easy.

If Sybil and Bob thought that their quiet, private marriage would avoid publicity, they were wrong. The Australian public was hungry for every snippet of news about its favourite Spitfire squadron. Their 'secret marriage' made headlines. One Australian newspaper report on 8 October, 'Squadron Leader Weds Secretly in London', seems to have taken most of 452 by surprise, including Finucane. The newspaper said it was not known until that day 'that he was married at the weekend. The bride's name is not known even by Flight-Lieut Finucane who is acting as squadron-leader with Flight-Lieut K. Truscott as his deputy'.[2]

Shortly after Bob returned to the squadron the press in South Australia reported:

Squadron Leader Bungey went off on his last weekend leave a bachelor and returned the husband of a lovely English girl, Sybil Johnson of Berkshire, to whom he has been engaged for about a year. 'The wedding wasn't really a surprise to us,' said the flier's parents, Mr. and Mrs. E. Bungey, who live at Glenelg South Australia.

Although they had not had a cable from their son telling them of the marriage, they have been receiving letters regularly from him and his charming English fiancée ever since their engagement. The pair appeared very much in love, and their romance can be pieced together from their letters.

'I wrote to Bob a little while ago and suggested that he and Sybil should get married in Salisbury Cathedral because that was where his father was christened.' said Mrs. Bungey.

Mr Bungey is an Englishman, but Mrs Bungey is Australian. 'But wherever they were married, I am glad to think it was a lovely English setting,' she said.

Mr. Bungey sent a cable of congratulations from the bridegroom's mother and his sister Pauline and his brother David, who is in the Air Force training in Australia. 'We are very pleased about the marriage. Sybil seems a sweet, lovable girl,' said Mrs. Bungey...

...Mrs Bungey is confident that their son and daughter-in-law will be very happy because they have many tastes in common. Bob was originally in an insurance office, and Sybil is secretary in a big business concern.

He is a very athletic type. With the idea of training for the Air Force because he has always been keen on flying, he did a course of eighteen months wrestling with former Australian amateur champion Jack Hooper. He also did six months of jujitsu with Captain McLaglan brother of the film star Victor McLaglan. The Squadron Leader is 5'11' tall, fair, and has broad shoulders like a wrestler. He is a strong swimmer and a good footballer.

'When he and Sybil went to London to choose the aquamarine and diamond engagement ring, Sybil wrote out and said that people turned to look at the good – looking flying officer but I, am sure they turned to look at the good looking couple,' said Mrs. Bungey...

...The couple met when Bob Bungey was stationed at an aerodrome near Sybil Johnson's home, Mrs. Bungey believes. The Bride wrote that Bob Bungey had to come up to our local aerodrome and sometimes stayed there for weekends. One time she said, 'I was rather expecting him yesterday but I think he must have been too busy, he loves his work in his beautiful

Hurricane... Only wishes he could get right up to the Me109s. The Huns are such dirty fighters and our boys are so grand Wizards.'

She looks forward to the time she will come out to Australia.

'I do wish I could come out to you all ... with Hubby,' she adds emphatically. We will give her a warm welcome when she does,' said Mrs Bungey...[3]

There was an unexpected shock waiting for Bob when he rejoined the squadron on the 14th. Paddy Finucane had been taken to hospital during the night, someone said with a broken leg, and Keith Chisholm was missing from a mission the day before that. Chisholm had left money in his locker with a note saying it was to be used for a suitable wake if he did not return. The night before, Finucane and Bluey Truscott and about ten others had gone in two trucks to The Greyhound pub in Croydon to do just that. At 10.30 p.m., when they were making their noisy way back through the blackout to the trucks, Finucane stopped walking to look for somewhere to relieve himself. He jumped over the stone parapet of Croydon Town Hall's balustrade and fell, heavily injuring either his foot or leg. It looked to be serious and the squadron's medical officer ordered that he be rushed to Sutton Emergency Hospital. That was hours, however, ago and they were still waiting for news.

Missing too was P/O Jackson, one of the newest pilots, and Jack Elphick who had been with the squadron much longer. There were other changes too. A huge Australian flag was flying over 452's dispersal hut. That was new; it had not been there before. On the 8th, Sir Charles McCann, Agent-General for South Australia and his opposite number for Queensland, Mr Pike, had visited Kenley informally and after an inspection of the ground personnel they had presented the new flag as a symbol of national prestige.

After Bob had left on the 3rd, Paddy Finucane being the senior flight commander was placed in temporary command of the squadron from the 4th onwards. Fog, mist and rain curtailed operational flying until *Circus No.107*, a special mission on 12 October, just the day after it was announced that the brilliant and popular Irish ace had been awarded the DSO. Twenty-three Blenheims bombed the docks at Boulogne. No.452 Squadron flew in one of the two wings provided for target support and numerous individual dogfights broke out. Finucane shot down another Me109 and Truscott damaged two others but Chisholm failed to return. He was Finucane's wingman and the Irish ace reported: 'I straightened up, and saw my No.2, Sgt Chisholm DFM, engaged by four Me 109s and spin down. I followed for about 10,000 ft but he was still spinning. By this time my Me 109 had burst into flames and I lost sight of my No. 2. I called him several times but got no reply.' Chisholm was last seen about 5 or 10 miles south-east of Le Touquet.

Next day in the early afternoon, *Circus 108A* involved six Blenheims with the task of bombing the ship lift at Arques. They were escorted by six wings of fighters. No.452 Squadron flew as close escort and as a result of the ensuing air battle, claimed its highest score for the month, all

Messerschmitt 109s: Paddy Finucane two, Bluey Truscott two, 'Throttle' Thorold-Smith one, Sgt Jack Emery one and Sgt Eric Schrader claimed a probable, which was later upgraded to destroyed.

Two Spitfires were lost. P/O E. Jackson was flying on his very first operation when he was shot down and killed by the 109s. Sgt Jack Elphick's Spitfire was crippled but he managed to bail out into the Channel close to the English coast. Thorold-Smith and Truscott circled over him so his exact position could be pinpointed by the onshore RDF stations and he was eventually picked up by the lifeboat from Dover. At least he was safe, but he had not yet returned to the squadron.

Another incident cast a shadow over the successes of that day. In the melee, Bluey Truscott had fired at the parachuting pilot of a Me109 he had shot down. After the squadron returned, the Australians were walking towards the dispersal hut when at least one man swore at him for what had done. Truscott reportedly just smiled and said, 'He might have gone up tomorrow and shot you down.' Apparently, the fiery red-headed Truscott had seen a German pilot doing that very same thing a few days earlier and swore he would return the favour.[4] It is not known if the incident was reported to Bob Bungey when he returned the following day. If it was, there is no record of Bob's reaction. Bob's day was busy enough. Many other things had happened in his absence.

Kenley had a new base commander. On the 6th, Gp/Capt Cecil Bouchier took over from Tom Prickman who transferred to No.11 Group, Fighter Command, as Group Captain Operations. After introductions Bouchier informed Bob that 452 Squadron would soon be moving to Redhill, Kenley's satellite airfield.

At the same time there was also a new wing leader flying to meet. Johnny Kent from Winnipeg, who had the reputation of being a man without nerves, had been replaced by S/Ldr Norman Ryder DFC. Before the war Kent had gained renown for his role in research at Farnborough, testing the effectiveness of barrage balloon steel-cable cutters. This was done by deliberately flying an aircraft, the prototype Fairey P4/34, into steel cables suspended below a balloon. He had been awarded an AFC for carrying out 300 deliberate test collisions. A DFC followed during the Battle of Britain. While at Kenley he was recommended for a bar to his DFC, which was gazetted on 21 October, but the time had come for him to be rested from operational flying. It was none too soon. Despite his reputation, Kent was showing signs of being affected by the constant stress of operational flying and he later admitted to feeling older than his twenty-seven years.

During a sweep back on the 22nd he'd become very ill and had to turn back. On the way, he blacked out. His aircraft fell into a spin and nearly plunged into sea but he recovered just in time. He had not flown as wing leader again since then. Sholto Douglas, who had succeeded Hugh Dowding commanding Fighter Command, decreed that his fighter pilots should be rested after 200 hours but, like many other outstanding air fighters, Kent had managed to avoid the edict until he was approaching the limits of his physical and mental endurance. The system caught up with him and his symptoms were recognised in time. He was one of the fortunate ones. Some whose warning signs were not detected in time suffered dire consequences. Officially, Kent left Kenley on 8 October to take on the role of instructor at No.53 OTU, but he actually stayed on for an extra two days to help Norman Ryder take over.

Norman Ryder (actually Edgar Norman Ryder) had received his DFC in March 1940 and he served with 41 Squadron during the Battle of Britain. He had been the commanding officer of 56 Squadron at North Weald between January and June 1941 and he had in fact come to the Kenley Wing after being an instructor at No.53 OTU. He and Johnny Kent were swapping places.

The last bit of news for Bob was that Alex Roberts had visited the squadron the day before. After being shot down, he had managed to escape from France via Spain and Gibraltar and had actually turned up, still dressed as a peasant, a week ago at a London pub frequented by the 452 Squadron boys. He was not able to rejoin the squadron because it was considered too dangerous for everybody on the Continent concerned with his escape should he happened to be shot down again and captured. He would have to serve elsewhere.[5] Bob had just missed him.

After the meetings, Bob despatched P/O Don Lewis to bring Jack Elphick back from Dover and then paid a visit to Redhill, which would soon be 452 Squadron's new home. The unrelenting pressure of command was back on his shoulders again and there was much for him to organise in his usual methodical way.

Paddy Finucane had spent a restless night in Sutton Emergency Hospital after his accident, although the painkillers kept him drowsy. An X-ray revealed a hairline fracture of his right heel bone. Next morning when the orthopaedic surgeon examined the X-rays, he had Finucane transferred to Horton Emergency Services Hospital in Epsom, which specialised in dealing with fractures and combat wounds. It was serious. He was told and he might not be able to fly for quite some time. He spent the next two days drifting in and out of sleep due to the cumulative effect of the drugs and deep-rooted exhaustion from the last three months of intense air combat.

The young Irishman was angry because it had been such a senseless accident, and devastated at not being able to return to 452 Squadron and operational flying but the diagnosis was confirmed. It was a serious fracture, and he was likely to be off any flying for several months. There was no way he would able to return to the squadron at all. It did not really help much when a written message from Leigh-Mallory arrived congratulating him on his DSO, and it helped even less when Bob had to send the October combat reports to him for signing because 11 Group were complaining about the delay. The good news was that when he did finally recover, he would be given his own squadron.

On 16 October, Bob and Sgt Jack Emery took off in misty weather to fly a *Rhubarb* mission but they were back on the ground just 5 minutes later.

Cloud was down to the tree tops, and it stayed that way. Likewise the next day, a sweep to be flown by the Kenley Wing was cancelled only 5 minutes after take off.

Good news reached 452 Squadron on 18 October that Sgt Arch Stuart was a POW. He had been reported missing a month ago. There were more good tidings the following day with the news that Sgts Gus Try and Ian Milne were also POWs. Try had been reported missing on 18 September in the same mission as Arch Stuart. Ian Milne had bailed out two days later.

Finally, to cap everything off, news arrived that Keith Chisholm was a POW as well. The resourceful dental student from Petersham NSW had bailed out into the sea near Berck-sur-Mer and been picked up by a German launch. This, in fact, actually marked the beginning of an incredible odyssey of capture, escape and evasion, which lasted almost three years. It would not finish until August 1944 when, after fighting alongside the French Resistance during the liberation of Paris, Chisholm was finally liberated and returned to England.

The squadron's move to Redhill took place on the 21st but it was still to operate as part of the Kenley Wing and joined it in a *Rodeo* mission during the day. Bob led the Spitfires trailing their coats over St Omer, going in and out of France via Le Touquet. It was again an uneventful trip for 452 except for the sighting of six Me109s in the distance but, while over St Omer, one of the New Zealand pilots of 485 Squadron, Sgt A. McNeil, was wounded in the arm by a 109 that made a speedy hit-and-run attack. McNeil managed to fly his aircraft, Spitfire W3579, back to Kenley and land safely. Although the aircraft was damaged, it was able to be repaired and return to service.

There was another uneventful sweep over St Omer on the 24th, Bob again leading. This pattern was repeated over and over again. Each time the Germans judged there were no bombers present, they decided there was no necessity to intercept unless everything was in their favour, and so they often didn't. Three Polish Spitfire squadrons from Northolt had more luck finding Me109s over the French coast. They claimed to have shot down nine plus four probables without loss.

The next active day of offensive operations occurred on 27 October but 452 Squadron was not involved. FW190s and Me109s encountered over the French and Belgian coasts must have been in a vengeful mood for they treated 401 (RCAF) Squadron very badly. Out of twelve Spitfires, half were lost, four pilots did not return and two bailed out over England, one being killed when his parachute failed. In return, the Canadians could only claim a probable and two damaged. Maintaining the pressure on the *Luftwaffe* was a very dangerous game to play.

Fighter Command flew only a couple of *Rhubarbs* on the 28th and the next day Bob led 452 to join a sweep by the Kenley Wing. There were no combats and only a small amount of inaccurate flak coming up from the Calais area. There were no operations flown at all on the 30th.

There was some activity on the last day of the month. A Spitfire pilot from 65 Squadron flying a *Rhubarb* encountered a lone Ju88 over the Channel and claimed it as probably destroyed. Later in the day a *Ramrod* was flown between Dunkirk and Gravelines, bomb-carrying Hurricanes searching for enemy shipping. Recorded in 452 Squadron's Operations Record Book, twelve Spitfires led by Bob patrolled over the Straits of Dover to act as one of the rear support units covering the withdrawal of *Circus No.110*. No enemy aircraft were engaged.

Nevertheless, the Kenley Wing did not come away unscathed. W/Cdr Norman Ryder did not return. His aircraft was shot down by flak. This machine was Spitfire W3579, which had been damaged back on 21 October. It had been repaired and put back into service. In the grim campaign on the Channel front to keep the *Luftwaffe* busy, Kenley's new wing leader had only lasted three weeks.[6]

15

Winter

The next time the Kenley Wing and 452 Squadron found trouble was on 6 November while covering the activities of three Curtiss P-40 Tomahawk army co-op aircraft.

The Tomahawk was an American fighter design, developed straight from the earlier Curtiss P-36 that had been used by the French air force in 1939–40. Powered by an Allison 1,150-hp engine, it retained the P-36's good handling qualities and was much faster at low to medium altitude. It was ordered in large quantity by the United States Army Air Corps for coastal defence and as a ground support fighter. Britain and France ordered it from 1939 to 1940 to boost their available numbers. Testing by the RAF revealed its performance was sluggish above 15,000 feet so it would have had little chance as a fighter against the latest models of the Me109 and the new FW190. RAF Tomahawks were therefore relegated to a low-level tactical reconnaissance role, or sent to theatres of war where the air opposition was less formidable.[1] On this occasion the Tomahawks had the task of spotting and directing artillery fire for the Dover coastal batteries which were sending a barrage across the English Channel.

As usual, Bob Bungey led 452 Squadron up from Redhill to join Kenley's other squadrons. They were all approximately 6 miles offshore from Calais by about 2.45 p.m. when enemy aircraft appeared. It was later calculated that there must have been about twenty German fighters involved in the encounter.

Six Me109Fs made the initial attack by diving on the RAAF fighters from above and behind but they were spotted in time. Before they could spring their surprise, Bob ordered 452 Squadron to break and the Spitfires scattered in good order.

Ray Thorold-Smith turned his section hard to port to engage the 109s and managed to score effective strikes on one of them. Then looking over his shoulder he noticed that his wingman, Sgt Eric Schrader, was not there. He had been shot down by one of the new FW190s. The Focke-Wulf was about 50 yards away on the port quarter and about to attack him too.

Thorold-Smith pulled up into a very steep climbing turn to port and throttled back. By then flipping into a vertical turn in the opposite direction, the enemy machine reappeared below and slightly ahead, crossing from left to right. He made a diving starboard beam-to-quarter attack, opening fire at 300 yards (270 m). As he closed in to 200 yards (180 m) firing short bursts, hits registered on the FW190's radial engine cowling and tail causing pieces of debris to tear away. The FW dropped into a vertical dive leaving a trail of black smoke. Thorold-Smith followed it down to 5,000 feet in case this manoeuvre was just a ploy to escape but he saw the crippled aircraft crash into the sea about 8 miles north-west of Cap Gris Nez. This would be the first of these formidable new 'Butcher Birds' to be credited to the Australian squadron. Meanwhile, Bob Bungey found he was in a good position to pursue one of the initial Me109 attackers. The German pilot realised his danger and took evasive action, gradually losing height as he did so. The chase was on!

Bob began pressing the button at about 300 yards (270 m), firing short spurts. The range varied as he closed in to less than 100 yards (90 m) using bursts of 1–3 seconds. Hits! He saw strikes from machine-gun bullets impacting on his target at least three separate times. Each occasion caused more and more smoke to flow from the Messerschmitt. They were down to about 3,000 feet, around 2 miles from Calais when he fired his last burst. Bob then broke away as he judged he had almost exhausted his ammunition. When he last saw the 109, it was gradually losing height and heading towards Calais, an unbroken trail of smoke staining the sky behind. It was heavily damaged, crippled.

Not far away, Sgt Bardie Wawn was on his way out of France when he noticed an Me109F being pursued by a Spitfire. Both planes were flying towards Calais and black smoke was trailing from the German fighter's tail. Then as he watched, it suddenly plunged down out of control into a vertical dive and disappeared into a patch of cloud at just 1,500 feet. Thick black smoke was pouring out of it. From that height it had little or no chance of pulling out of the dive. Although he did not know who was flying the Spitfire, he had seen enough to be able to confirm somebody else's success when he reached home.

During the fighting, as well as 'Throttle' Smith's Me109 and FW190, Bluey Truscott claimed another Me109 destroyed. There was apparently just one Focke-Wulf involved in the battle with 452 Squadron. Three other 109s were claimed as damaged, one each by Bob, P/O Eric Sly and P/O Don Lewis, because they had not seen conclusive results. Bob, as usual, was being conservative with his estimate. These outcomes were modified after Bardie Wawn described what he had seen outside Calais. The details he added dovetailed perfectly with Bob's claim. It was obvious his Messerschmitt did not get away. Two days later Fighter Command upgraded Bob's claim from 'damaged' to 'one Me109 destroyed'.

Adding to Kenley's tally that day, the Kiwis of 485 Squadron claimed two enemy fighters probably destroyed without losses. One was an FW190 by P/O Bill Crawford-Compton, which was allowed as 'damaged', and the other was an Me109E by Sgt Jack Rae.

Another positive outcome was that all of the Curtiss Tomahawks involved in the artillery-spotting operation returned home safely.

Unfortunately, offsetting these good results, two Australian Spitfires failed to return. One was flown by Sgt Schrader, Thorold-Smith's wingman, and the other by Sgt Geissman.

As far as Bob was concerned, two men lost was two too many. Young Geissman was a newcomer – there had hardly been time to get to know him – but Eric Schrader had been with the squadron for a couple of months. He had showed great skill and was already credited with a 109 destroyed. But now ... the Focke-Wulf had got him and it seemed certain that he had been killed. This was the part of Bob's job as commanding officer that he hated most. Every man in the squadron was his responsibility, and he took this responsibility far more seriously than anybody realised. Just how seriously would not be revealed until much later.

Trying to co-ordinate bombers and fighters in the prevailing weather conditions as winter approached was becoming progressively more difficult. *Circus No.110*, which was intended to target Lille on the 8th, was never going to be easy. In his last-minute briefing shortly before take off, Bob cautioned, 'There is an 80 mph breeze against us on our return so we will have a tough time coming out. We must keep together. No stragglers will return.'

Twelve Blenheims were in the token bombing force but things became messy almost from the outset when six of them unexpectedly turned back en route. The supporting fighter wings were thrown into confusion. When, instead of going to Lille, the remaining bombers attacked a factory near Mons, possibly the alternative target or a mistake, the situation worsened. The Kenley Spitfires tried to provide high cover to the confused beehive formation but, while withdrawing towards the French coast, 452 came under heavy attack by Me109s.

It was an unhealthy situation. The Spitfires were flying into the predicted headwind. To turn and fight meant the real danger of running out of fuel. All they could do was evade by twisting and turning to avoid each onslaught. A personal account of the operation was recorded years later by David Downs, an ex-452 pilot who was flying as Blue 2, Bob Bungey's wingman, on this particular mission. In his description, David remembered in great detail the type of aircraft that they were using at the time. In his opinion because of the intense pressure of the German attack, he owed Bob his life. He recalled:

The first RAAF Spitfire Squadron formed in England was No.452, and in November 1941 was based at Redhill, Surrey. The Spitfires in use at this time were Mark VB s (single seat, Rolls Royce Merlin engine) armed with two 20 mm cannons and four .303 inch machine guns. Max speed, straight and level was 376 mph, ceiling 37,000 feet and there were 6,479 Mark VBs built.

The CO was S/Ldr R. W. Bungey of Adelaide. He had served with distinction through the Battle of Britain with the RAF. The commander of 'B' Flight to which I had been allocated, as a sergeant pilot a month earlier was F/Lt Keith 'Bluey' Truscott of Melbourne. Prior to 8 November, I had experienced only two fighter sweeps over the French coast with no enemy aircraft seen – only some light anti-aircraft ground fire. The squadron was briefed for the sweep on the previous afternoon and they had been appointed to be top cover for escort duty to Lille in France.

There were twenty twin-engine light bombers called A-20 Havocs, very fast.[2] They were to attack the rail yards at Lille from about 15,000 feet. There were many Spitfires involved at varying heights with 452's twelve aircraft at 33,000 feet top cover, the CO was leading 'B' Flight (three pairs of Spitfires). Truscott was leading the second. The pairs flew in line astern fairly loose, comfortable formation.

'A' Flight was similarly arranged and flew out to our right. I was to fly No 2 to the CO. My job was to stay with him and protect him from rear attack. We were to rendezvous above Dover at 33,000 feet at 11.00 a.m. Climbing fairly steeply towards Dover the noses of the aircraft blotted out part of the horizon. I remember looking to the left (north-east) and noting that the weather in that direction was hazy and visibility not good whereas to the right (south-west) it was clear and the English Coast along past Dungeness towards Beachy Head very clear.

From Dover we turned a bit right towards the target. We were carrying extra thirty gallon fuel tanks under the aircraft. Soon after crossing the French Coast we had reached our height of 33,000 feet. The CO waggled his wings and we switched onto our main fuel tank and dropped the extra tank off the bottom.

As we approached Lille there was not much to see except anti-aircraft shells exploding mostly well below us. Prior to this I had not been above 23,000 feet. I remember thinking what an awful lot of space there was around us and only this little aircraft holding me up. Also noticeable was the sloppy response by the aircraft to movement of the controls in the thin air. We were to maintain radio silence for as long as possible. We turned left and we were now flying about north and right over the target.

Suddenly I found myself following the CO in a very tight turn to the left. I glanced up along my right wing and saw two aircraft coming straight at me at close range. Smoke started coming out of the nearest one and I thought, 'You poor fellow, you are going down in flames.' My next thought as tracer bullets were passing all around me was, 'You b-----d, you're shooting at me!' Each of those thoughts lasted about one hundredth of a second.

I instinctively pushed my aircraft in to a skid to avoid his line of sight. We were being attacked by Messerschmitt 109s almost continuously mostly in pairs and from above. Our Spitfire Mark VBs were more manoeuvrable than the 109s so they only stayed to mix it with us occasionally. They were higher and simply had to dive on us, squirt their guns, then with the speed gained coming down climb up for another go. While many of our other aircraft were getting away home, we at the top continued to be attacked.

Most of our evasive action as they approached was to pull into a tight turn one way or the other, sometimes for the full circle and sometimes for only 90 degrees then back the other way. On rare occasions a 109 got between the CO and me and within range and I fired my guns but I had no chance of observing results, being far too busy staying with my leader.

Under these conditions our progress to the north was slow and we were using much of our precious fuel. The first radio call I heard was the CO calling the rest of the squadron, saying that he and his No.2 were completely cut off and about trapped and could anyone help ... No reply.

In Kenley's operations room, WAAF plotters' recorded aircraft movements on their large map table, and numbers were marked on the chalkboard as messages were received through their headphones from radar observers and the aircraft. A report came in that the Australians were 'hotly engaged' and there were some tense silences on the loud speaker. Positions on the board showed them leaving the French coast. Then someone was down in the drink.

> With all that manoeuvring we had lost a lot of height and eventually crossed the coast near Dunkirk. A few miles out to sea and in that slight haze I saw before, the Germans suddenly left off their attacks and disappeared.
>
> Soon after that the unmistakable voice of 'Blue' Truscott[3] came on the radio saying he was completely cut off from the squadron, his aircraft was shot up and could anyone hear him? The CO said, 'Yes' and we did a couple of turns and saw him. His aircraft was going down in a gentle curve. There was some discussion about him bailing out. He could not roll the aircraft over and bunt himself out so he had to climb out upwards. The wind pressure against him caused his parachute pack to catch against the round head cushion near the top rear of the cockpit. There were some worrying moments as we watched him try and wriggle free which, after a while, he did and went over the side.
>
> We were about 4,000 feet by now and he opened his parachute quickly...

Truscott had been leading the starboard section of 452 when the attacks started. He pulled around fast and fired from very short range at the leading 109. His aim was good and there were cannon strikes on the engine cowling and around the cockpit. The Messerschmitt seemed to explode and drop away in an out-of-control vertical dive.

While returning towards the French coast his section came under attack again. Truscott fired at three of them without any obvious effect. By now he had dropped to the rear of the *Circus* which was just crossing the coast. Then he spotted two more Messerschmitts diving down to attack a pair of Spitfires and shouted a warning. At the same time he went after the enemy machines, which broke away to starboard. He was able to follow the second one. Firing from dead astern with a 5-second burst, he blew away the 109's tail unit. The German fighter flicked over and fell vertically.

In the same instant he felt his own Spitfire shudder and saw hits on his starboard wing. He immediately broke away to port and dived away from danger. As he made direct for the English coast, he realised that he was running out of fuel too quickly. The tank had probably been hit. He would have to parachute out. As he climbed to 3,000 feet he called for help and Bob responded, but then the fore-and-aft control of his aircraft failed. There was no other choice. He had to bail out into the sea. That was when Bob and David Downs arrived on the scene.

'We watched, circling him as he hit the water, inflated his dinghy and climbed into it,' David recalled.

Bob knew that his wingman could be was running low on fuel too. Keeping formation meant that pilots flying on the wing had to work their throttle much more than their leader using fuel up at a greater rate.

The CO said to me, 'How much fuel have you No.2?'

I said, 'less than ten gallons, sir.'

He said that he would stay a few minutes and send a radio signal to the sea rescue launch (hoping there would be one close enough) and mark the spot. He told me to set my compass on course so and so (I forget the figure), drop down to only a few feet above the water (because it was difficult to attack an aircraft at water level), throttle back to very economical cruising, following that course and I should be all right.

I had tremendous faith in my CO who was highly respected by every man in the squadron, so I was not worried as I flew slowly across that water with nothing to see but the haze. After a short time I saw ahead of me some cliffs and soon was able to pull her up over the cliffs and within a minute or two there was Manston airfield right ahead. I went straight in and landed without turning, stopped, switched off with the gauge reading zero. I got out and saw a few bullet holes in the left wing and fuselage. A tanker came straight over and refuelled my aircraft.

Meanwhile, in Kenley's operations room they realised by the call signs that it was Truscott who was down. Then Bob's voice came through the speaker, 'I am circling overhead.'

'Can you give me your position on the map?' he was asked.

Bob gave it, but his own fuel situation was already critical and he added, 'I can't last much longer.'

'Planes will relieve you,' was the response, and boats were on their way. Bob left it to the last minute before setting course for Manston.

David Downs recalled, After I had been down [at Manston] for four or five minutes, I saw the CO land and pull up about two hundred yards from me. He got out as another tanker approached to refuel his aircraft. I taxied over beside him and we took off in formation and flew back to Redhill.[4] He later told me that it was the most torrid situation and the worst mess he had been in.

'Blue' Truscott was picked up after about an hour and returned to Redhill that evening.

S/Ldr Truscott DFC and Bar ... was one of the RAAF's top fighter aces and once told me that S/Ldr Bungey was the best CO in the air force. His consideration and concern for the pilots of his squadron was outstanding, for example, his ability to give me the exact course to Manston airfield from some miles out to sea off Dunkirk with visibility down to a mile or so...

Truscott was the only pilot from 452 Squadron to claim successes, but he was not the only pilot who failed to return. 'Pyfo' Dunstan also had to use his parachute and he splashed down into the sea off North Foreland. Both men were rescued after spending about an hour in the water. Another pilot, Sgt Pat Tainton, ran out of fuel and had no choice but to force-land near Gravesend. Fortunately, he was not injured. To Bob's great relief, they were all safe.

No.452 Squadron was not the only unit to suffer. *Circus 110* deteriorated into an RAF disaster. Although four enemy fighters were claimed destroyed, plus one probably destroyed and four damaged, the cost to Fighter Command was no less than eleven fighters and nine pilots lost, including the wing leader from Kirton-in-Lindsey, W/Cdr D. R. Scott DFC, and three squadron commanders. The loss of such highly experienced airmen was especially serious. The RAF was facing the same situation that the *Luftwaffe* had faced in the Battle of Britain. Unlike the previous year when the fighting was concentrated over England, even if a downed airman survived there was next to no chance of him returning to his squadron to fly and fight again the very next day.

The RAF did not fare much better in other missions flown that day. In all, Fighter Command lost eighteen aircraft and fourteen pilots during the 8th. As a result, *Circus* missions were cancelled indefinitely and *Circus 110* was the last for the year. They would not recommence until March 1942.

To replace them, *Ramrod* and *Roadstead* operations, in which bomb-carrying Hurricanes acted as the strike force, became the norm but even these were few and far between because weather conditions severely limited operational flying. No.452 Squadron participated in just two. The first on 18 November was an attack on an alcohol distillery at Hesdin, and the other was against shipping at Boulogne on 27th. There were no engagements involving the Australian squadron in either of them but during the latter, three of the bomb-carrying Hurricanes were claimed by enemy fighters and flak.

Bob was not involved in the mission on the 27th. He was on leave. He and Sybil needed to be elsewhere. They had to travel to Liverpool for a highly emotional farewell.

Liverpool was Britain's most important strategic port on her west coast, a fact fully realised by the Germans. It was, in fact, the place where the vital Battle of the Atlantic was being planned and fought. The city had the dubious honour of suffering a blitz second only to that inflicted on London itself.

During seven consecutive nights of bombing at the beginning of last May, the environs of Liverpool/Birkenhead had suffered dreadfully. At one stage movements in and out of the docks by road and rail were brought to a standstill and seventy shipping berths out of 144 were put out of action; 66,000 homes were destroyed or damaged; ten hospitals were hit, and the area's utilities were severely affected. Casualties totalled 1,900 killed and 1,450 seriously injured. Eventually the number of homeless reached in excess of 70,000.

Since then, with the bulk of the *Luftwaffe* transferred to the east for the Nazi offensive against Russia, the widespread night bombing of the British Isles had eased considerably, although at times there were still serious sporadic attacks. Altogether, the Germans made eighty air raids on Merseyside, killing 2,500 people and causing damage to almost half the homes in the metropolitan area.

In November, more than six months after the heavy May blitz, Bob and Sybil could clearly see that Liverpool was still a mess. Bomb damage seemed to be everywhere. Nevertheless, the docks had remained in use and shipping movements continued despite the bombardment, the sinking of several and widespread carnage. It was a dangerous place, but it was where they had to be. The SS *Nestor*, a vessel belonging to the Blue Funnel Line, was here preparing to sail, and its destination was Australia.

Their plans had been made. Sybil's ultimate destination was Adelaide. She was going down under to join the Bungey family at Somerton. Bob would follow her later at the conclusion of his RAF short service commission after August next year. Under the predetermined conditions of the commission, as they were laid down when Bob was a cadet at Point Cook, when his term with the RAF concluded he was required to rejoin the RAAF so that the Australian service could benefit from his overseas experience.

The *Nestor* departed from Liverpool on 29 November to their mutual relief, and sadness. At least Sybil would be safe with his family away from the bombing and the war. They would all be out of harm's way. All that he could do now was keep busy and wait – wait for a cable with the news of her arrival safe and sound in Adelaide.

Two days later Bob was back at Redhill with 452 Squadron in his 'office', his Spitfire, training his pilots in cloud formation practice. As winter tightened its grip on Europe during December, Fighter Command flew no more large-scale operations of any kind, much to the chagrin of the Australian fliers. The war's major events were taking place elsewhere.

On Germany's Eastern Front, as the Germans were making their final plans for the offensive against Moscow, the temperatures dropped to – 12° in the first half of November and many of the *Wehrmacht's* troops began to suffer from frostbite. Outside the Russian capital by the 27th, the Panzer forces had been involved in bitter fighting around Kashira for three days, but they faced the realisation that they could not continue their drive forward because of their lack of reinforcements. Meanwhile, a Soviet counter-attack re-occupied Rostov but during the month in beleaguered Leningrad 11,000 people died of starvation.

Pressure was maintained on Moscow until 5 December when, in Germany, Adolf Hitler ordered the offensive halted because even he had come to the realisation there was no possibility of further gains. At the same time, he also instructed that *Fliegerkorps II* be transferred from the Eastern Front to the Mediterranean in preparation for a major effort against Malta. The very next day the Soviets counter-attacked along the 500 miles of the Moscow sector and met with considerable success against the overextended German troops.

In North Africa during November, the British 8th Army launched its Operation *Crusader* offensive and the Germans and Italians fell back to Agedabia. The fortress of Tobruk was relieved at last. Australian troops had already been rotated out earlier on, thanks to the Royal Navy's remarkable 'Scrap Iron Flotilla' destroyers. Unfortunately, the garrison's relief was short-lived. In December the situation suddenly changed again. Two large Axis convoys, heavily escorted by units of the Italian Fleet, succeeded in reaching

North Africa and replenishing Rommel's supplies. The *Afrika Korps* was able to go on the offensive again and the 8th Army had to retreat, losing the ground it had just gained. Tobruk would be under siege again.

Then suddenly everything changed. The focus of the war shifted abruptly to the Pacific Ocean on the other side of the world.

Early on the morning of 7 December in Hawaii, it had just seemed to be the start of another peaceful Sunday until without warning Japanese carrier-based aircraft attacked the US naval base at Pearl Harbor. There had been no declaration of war and the Americans were taken completely by surprise. Massive damage was inflicted on the USN's Pacific Fleet and shore installations, including airfields, were shattered. All eight battleships in port were hit and five of them sunk. Three cruisers and three destroyers were also lost. Casualties reached 2,403 men killed and 1,178 injured. President Roosevelt labelled it a 'Day of Infamy' as the USA found itself suddenly plunged into war.

Japan had galvanised itself into action elsewhere too. Prior to the Pearl Harbor attack, landings had already taken place simultaneously at Kota Bharu in Northern Malaya, and in Thailand at Singora and Patani near the Malayan border. They were recorded as happening on 8 December local time, because of the International Date Line lying between the two areas.

Further south, the Japanese made attacks on Guam, Wake Island and Midway. Their actions not only took the USA and the British Empire by surprise, but also the Germans. News of all these disastrous events spread like wildfire, sending shock waves around the globe. By the end of the 8th, the USA and UK in retaliation had declared war on Japan.

In Australia, Japan's assaults made the country's defence chiefs realise how totally inadequate its defences really were. Excluding overseas units, the RAAF's front-line strength consisted of seven squadrons of CAC Wirraways, seven of Lockheed Hudsons, two of PBY Catalinas, and one of Supermarine Walrus/Seagulls, totalling 177 machines. There was a reserve of Fairey Battles, Wirraways and Avro Ansons making an absolute total of 483 aircraft for home defence. Greater reconnaissance was necessary immediately, plus increased policing of the actions of Japanese pearling luggers in the north and north-west. Only eleven flying boats were available for patrolling the outer island defence line. So much depended upon the area's forward defence positions in Malaya and Singapore.

Things began happening at an accelerating pace. On the 9th in Malaya, Mitsubishi G3M 'Nells' bombed and strafed Kuantan causing heavy damage and the main airbase, Butterworth, was heavily bombed. The following day brought an absolute disaster for Britain in the South China Sea. The Royal Navy's capital ships, HMS *Prince of Wales* and HMS *Repulse*, were sunk with heavy loss of life by Japanese bombers, while only four of their number were lost. HMAS *Vampire*, one of the destroyer escorts, rescued 225 survivors. Britain's naval presence in the Pacific was all but wiped out.

In the Philippines, the Japanese invaded with landings at Aparri and Vigan, northern Luzon.

Of lingering concern to British leaders was the fact that although Britain had declared war on Japan at the same time as the USA, the United States had not yet supported her by declaring war on Germany and Italy. That situation changed on 11 December when Germany declared war on the USA in support of their Axis partner. It was another diplomatic mistake by Hitler. The Americans responded with their own declaration against Germany and Italy and the US Congress empowered its armed forces to operate anywhere in the world. The war was now truly worldwide.

On 16 December in the Pacific, the Japanese made landings in Borneo at Miri, Serh and Lutong. On the 20th, Australian National Airways (ANA), operating DC-3s, began to evacuate Australian civilians from New Guinea as the fighting spread towards Australia.

The American garrison on Wake Island surrendered on 23 December. On the same day, the Japanese launched their first air attacks on Rangoon in Burma, and in Borneo landings were made at Kuching, the capital of Sarawak. Christmas Day saw Hong Kong surrender to the Japanese.

Two days later the Philippines capital, Manila, was declared an open city, and in Australia Prime Minister John Curtin declared, 'I make it quite clear that Australia looks to America, free of any pangs as to our traditional links or kinship with the United Kingdom.' In reality, there was little else that he could do.

As the end of the year approached, ANA began evacuating civilians from Rabaul. In Malaya, the Japanese advance had been so swift that their bomber units were moved forward to bases from which they could attack Singapore Island. There, the remaining RAF and RAAF aircraft had fallen back and were gathered on four airfields. Long regarded as impregnable from the sea, Singapore's big guns were pointed the wrong way! Japan's army was coming in the back door by land. Should Singapore fall, what could happen next was unthinkable.

Awareness and anxiety levels among the Australians and New Zealanders in Britain increased as each incoming news item revealed the disastrous spread of war in the Far East and the Pacific – creeping ever closer to their homes. The Japanese seemed unstoppable.

With the arrival of the European winter, those in RAF Fighter Command had less and less to do. In December, 452 Squadron's duties consisted of covering mine-layers, escorting convoys and one uneventful fighter sweep that accounted for most of the 82 operational hours flown. It was a big drop from 137 hours in November and only a tiny proportion of the 445 hours flown during August.

There was only one air battle during the month. Shortly after midday on the 8th, Bob led the squadron's twelve other Spitfires in a 'Balbo' to cover two air-sea rescue launches operating off Boulogne. South of Dungeness they encountered bandits, the highly dangerous Focke-Wulf 190s. The Australians realised almost too late that it was a trap. While they were preoccupied with the first enemy formation, three more FW190s suddenly bounced them from above. The Spitfires scattered and in the ensuing melee only four Australian pilots managed to fire at the fleeting enemy aircraft. No obvious results could be claimed.

If it had not been realised before, the 190s now demonstrated their clear superiority. They were faster in diving and climbing than 452 Squadron's

Spitfire VBs, which had up until then maintained parity with, and even a measure of superiority over, the various models of Me109. The only edge the Spitfires seemed to have was their manoeuvrability as they tried desperately to keep out of harm's way. They had the worst of this fight. Sgt Jack Emery failed to return. He was last seen chasing an FW190 with two others on his tail.

Every loss was a blow to Bob, but Jack Emery's was particularly so. His background was similar to Bob's. To start with, he was a fellow South Australian. He had been born in Adelaide but was working as a clerk in Whyalla when he volunteered to join the RAAF. He had been credited with a Me109 destroyed back in October but there were signs that the strain of combat flying was impacting on him.

Emery had shared a room with Fred McCann in the 'Red House', which was just outside the main gates of Kenley airfield. One night a couple of the squadron's pranksters crept into where he was sleeping. They suddenly switched on the light and shouted at Emery's sleeping form, 'Break, Jack, there's a Hun on your tail.' Emery's reaction was not what they expected. He groaned and drew his knees up into his chest – the foetal position – and by doing so it became obvious he was actually experiencing immense stress. Ashamed of themselves, the two would-be comedians backed away and slipped away out of the room.[5]

As Christmas arrived and the New Year loomed, Bob was alone. He had much to think about. When spring arrived and the offensive was renewed, the air war by day would be so much harder, unless the RAF could come up with a more powerful Spitfire or a brand new fighter. If not, the Focke-Wulfs would only inflict more and more casualties – the bleak prospect loomed of a limited future. Even with the USA in the war, the situation was only going from bad to worse. But that was not all.

Sybil was out there on the ocean somewhere – but where? By now she and the SS *Nestor* could be anywhere in the South Atlantic or beyond. Not knowing was a gnawing, empty pit of frustration. Was she merely sailing from one war zone into another that was much worse – into danger rather than away from it? Was anywhere safe now?

16

452 Finale

For security reasons, it had been necessary for Bob to leave Sybil at Liverpool and start back for Surrey before the SS *Nestor* had actually departed on 29 November. Adding to the anguish of their separation, 10 hours after he had gone and before the ship actually left port, Sybil saw Bob again, this time on a theatre screen featuring in a newsreel about the Australian Spitfire squadron.

The *Nestor* was a big ship. She had a length of 589 feet, a beam of 68 feet and was a distinctive luxury liner belonged to the famous Blue Funnel line – her funnel was said at the time to have been the highest ever built. Her gross tonnage was 14,500 tons, giving her a size advantage of about 1,200 tons over the Orient liner, the SS *Orama,* and the trans-Pacific Union liner, the SS *Niagara* of that time. These were the next largest size British vessels to visit the Commonwealth in the pre-war years. Propelled by twin screws she could, if required, develop a speed of sixteen knots. This ship would have a long and busy life. During the First World War, she worked as a troopship carrying the Australian Expeditionary Force, and in the Second World War she was involved in evacuating children from Britain to Australia.

Nestor reached South Australia early in February 1942 and Sybil was warmly greeted by Bob's parents, Ernest and Ada, and sister, Pauline. She was welcomed into their home at Somerton. Bob's younger brother, David, had joined the RAAF and was in New South Wales.

She found everything was there as Bob had described it during their quiet talks together: the beautiful clear, calm water of Holdfast Bay in the Gulf of St Vincent and the long, continuous stretches of beach where he and David had swum and trained before he had joined the air force; Brighton, the next suburb just south of the Bungeys' home at Somerton Park with its landmark long pier stretching out from the beach; and to the north historic Glenelg with its own famous long jetty just a tram ride from the centre of Adelaide. She could reach the water by a short walk westward along Phillip Street, then over the road and walk straight ahead across the bright yellow sand. If she turned right she could even walk along to Glenelg or if left she could reach Brighton. Alternatively, she could cut across the sand dunes either way through low bush and coastal shrubs, just as Bob had done many times years before. Imagine walking back with him across the dunes to home, they would be relaxed and happy – at peace with the world. There would be good times ahead, happy times for them both – and their anticipated new arrival.

Sybil's arrival made a newsworthy item for Adelaide's eager press, especially because of the publicity surrounding Bob's distinguished reputation coming from his work as the commanding officer of the first Australian Spitfire squadron.

9-2-1942

NOTED S. A. AIRMAN'S WIFE HERE

Australian flying men in Britain were regarded by the people of England as airmen of outstanding skill and courage said Mrs Bungey, the young English wife of the now famous Glenelg airman, Squadron Leader R. W. Bungey DFC who arrived in Adelaide this week to join her husband's parents in Tarlton Street, Somerton. Mrs Bungey's home is in Wallingford Berkshire UK.

Mrs Bungey said that her husband had little time for anything except the hazardous work of leading his squadron. He was out on two or three sweeps over the channel almost every day and was working very hard. 'Bob says very little about his exploits,' said Mrs. Bungey, 'but he likes to talk about the work of his comrades.' Mrs. Bungey added that there were two or three South Australians in her husband's squadron...

...Ten hours after bidding good-bye to her Adelaide air-ace husband, Squadron-Leader R. W. ('Bob') Bungey his English bride unexpectedly saw him featured in newsreel at an English port.

She has now met his parents, Mr and Mrs E. Bungey of Somerton with whom she will stay.

Squadron-Leader Bungey commands the first Australian Spitfire Squadron in Britain.

'Bob is out on two and three sweeps over the Channel nearly every day, and is working very hard', said his attractive young wife. 'It is wonderful to see them set out on these sweeps. In the morning 12 or 15 planes glide through the sky and they tear back at night. My husband leads. His plane is in front so I always know where to look for him. At times he has led the wing.'

RUSH TO PHONE

We listened to the wireless news, and each time a plane was reported missing rushed to the telephone to ring the aerodrome. It was reassuring to hear his voice even if our telephone bill grew. All wives of pilots do the same.

Bob was shot down into the channel during the Battle For Britain in September 1940 [sic], but I did not know about it until he had recovered. He rarely tells me of his achievements until they slip out months afterwards.

He has been very lucky during these sweeps. Many times his plane has been punctured by bullet holes.[1]

Spitfire Leader

Sybil was even sought after for an interview on radio. The Advertiser Broadcasting Network of South Australia wrote to her on the 23rd:

Dear Mrs Bungey,
During the 'Magazine of the Air' each Friday evening, we include two 3-minute interviews under the title 'These Names Are News.' It has occurred to me that you might be interested to give some of your experiences in this broadcast. To date we have included two excellent ones by women just arrived here from the war zone.

These interviews are quite informal and are recorded quite separate from the actual broadcast. We do this to suit the convenience of the various speakers and at the same time avoiding any mike nervousness.

A fee of one guinea is paid for the interview. If you would care to give your particular experiences, and I hope you will, for there is tremendous interest in first hand news, would you communicate with me for a time appointment?

Yours Faithfully,
John Cameron

Two days later another more formal letter arrived, this time from the mayor of the adjacent Adelaide resort area of Brighton, and it acknowledged that Bob had been promoted:

Dear Madam,
May I extend, on behalf of myself and the Mayoress, the Members of my Council, the Town Clerk, and his Officers, our sincere congratulations on your husband being promoted to the high office of Acting Wing Commander in His Majesty's Royal Air Force. Will you convey to him our sincere wishes that he may have every success in his new position.

Yours faithfully,
Mr Brown
Mayor.[2]

Sybil's warm welcome to South Australia was very likely much warmer than she expected, particularly as she was accustomed to February in England. In England it was still winter but summer was at its height in Australia, a period when Adelaide's temperatures in particular could soar. It is not on record how Sybil felt at the time, but she may have been very uncomfortable indeed, especially as she was expecting Bob's child.

* * *

On the other side of the world, winter's cold, bleak weather was having its impact on the air offensive from Britain. The only real form of attacking the enemy on the Continent was through the strategic bomber offensive being staged by RAF Bomber Command at night. Complementing and gradually replacing its hard-working Wellingtons and Hampdens, new

222

heavier bombers – Avro Manchesters and four-engined Short Stirlings, Handley Page Halifaxes and Avro Lancasters – were reaching squadrons in a steady flow. Some of these would become highly successful aircraft, others temporary steps in the development of ultimate weapons.

At the same time, the supply of bomber aircraft in UK and coming from North America promised to increase at a rate well in excess of Allied losses, but the build-up would take time. The main element in Britain's favour for this was the active entry of the USA into the war, with its promise of full military support including personnel in large numbers and overwhelming quantities of supplies.

In January 1942, Bomber Command also received news of a change of leadership with the appointment of Air Marshal Arthur Harris. With the departure of Sir Richard Pierce, AVM Baldwin took over temporarily until the arrival of Harris in February. Strong-willed and aggressive, for the next three years Harris would preside over Bomber Command's transformation into an overwhelming juggernaut. He would become known to all as 'Bomber' Harris.

By comparison, the supposedly non-stop daylight air war from England was almost static and 1942 began quietly. The offensive was maintained by the method of fighter *Ramrod* operations, escorted fighter-bomber missions, and *Circuses* would not be resumed again until early in March.

As with all the squadrons in Fighter Command, 452 Squadron trained and practiced whenever the weather permitted. To start things off, Bob led the full squadron on a 'Balbo' formation exercise the day following New Year's Day.

Operations that were flown were mostly small scale compared with the 'impressive' massed raids on the Continent of the preceding autumn. Thorold-Smith and his wingman, on a *Rhubarb*, attacked an alcohol distillery at Colleville on 3 January and saw cannon hits on the top of the distillation tower as well as other installations such as storage tanks.

Next day, Bluey Truscott and P/O Ray Sly made a similar attack on a canal lock at St Valery-sur-Somme. During their approach to the target they surprised a group of German soldiers who scattered wildly. After firing on them, the two pilots damaged the lock gates with their 20-mm cannons.

That same day, Bob and his section were scrambled to escort an air-sea rescue Lysander searching for the crew of a Wellington, which had reportedly crashed into the sea off Portland Bill during the night. The overnight target for fourteen Wellingtons and four Stirlings had been Brest Harbour where the German capital ships, *Scharnhorst, Gneisenau* and *Prinz Eugen,* were still sheltering. The body of one member of the bomber's crew was in due course recovered and afterwards buried in Folkstone New Cemetery, Hawkinge. The others were never found and their names were later recorded on the Air Force memorial at Runnymede which honours airmen who have no known grave.

Six Spitfires from 452 Squadron attempted to intercept enemy aircraft reported off Beachy Head on 5 January and, during the same afternoon, another pair of Spitfires searched for German shipping off Le Havre, but neither mission produced any results.

In an attempt to bring on an air battle, Bob led 452 to take part in a *Rodeo* 'Channel sweep' the following day. Although the wing 'trailed its coat' off Mardick, no enemy planes took off to engage it. There was some reaction elsewhere. Two Spitfires and their pilots were lost, one by 134 Squadron while flying a convoy patrol in the morning and the other by 616 Squadron similarly on patrol in the afternoon.

The following days reverted mainly to air-to-air attack training but four Spitfires were 'scrambled' on 9 January to patrol after raiders between Dungeness and Beachy Head. As usual, the expected bandits failed to materialise.

Bad weather obstructed further operations until 22 January, when Bob led the squadron to Manston. From there in the afternoon they flew a protective umbrella covering mine-sweepers as they cleared an area where *Luftwaffe* bombers had been active overnight. The patrol was without incident until P/O Lewis flying Spitfire AB992 unexpectedly experienced engine trouble. He had no choice but to bail out over the sea. Don Lewis was one of 452's originals and an experienced pilot. His position was fixed before the others departed.

On returning to Manston, as soon as his section's Spitfires were refuelled Bob conducted a search to cover any rescue attempt. Lewis was spotted floating on the surface of the water still surrounded by his parachute – but he did not move. He had drowned. It was a pensive group of pilots that Bob led back to Kenley late that afternoon.

On 24 January, a late BBC bulletin opened with a sombre, poignant bugle call sounding the 'Last Post' and followed it with the Belgium national anthem. The announcer said: 'This evening we have learned with regret that the best of the Belgian fighter-pilots has been killed on active service. It is Flight Lieutenant Jean Offenberg DFC.'

To Bob, it did not seem possible; Pyker Offenberg, gone!

It had not happened in combat. Two days earlier, the weather had cleared enough for Offenberg, who was then with 609 Squadron stationed at Digby in Lincolnshire, to take up one of the new pilots for formation flying practice. For the next hour the two Spitfires manoeuvred changing close positions above the airfield. Offenberg and his companion were concentrating on each other and did not notice another Spitfire, an aircraft from 92 Squadron also up from Digby, flying nearby. The pilot of the lone Spitfire decided to make a mock attack on Pyker and his pupil, sweeping in towards them at 90°. He miscalculated. He was coming too close! He tried to avoid by pulling back on his controls and at the same time Offenberg apparently suddenly realised the danger and pulled up as well – too late. A collision! Offenberg's Spitfire lost its tail unit. It continued climbing for a fraction of a second, then turned over onto its back and plunged into a vertical dive. It was all over in seconds. The two fighters plummeted down from only 1,000 feet and crashed into the snow-covered ground. There was no chance of survival. Pyker! Don Lewis! How many more?

Out early on 25 January, Thorold-Smith and Pat Tainton came upon a small tanker escorted by four anti-aircraft trawlers moving northwards hugging the French coast. Unfortunately, before a large-scale *Ramrod* attack could be launched on the basis of their report, the ships had put into the safety of Boulogne harbour.

Later, Bob led the squadron out with 485 RNZAF Squadron and joined the Northolt Wing on a Channel sweep but just a single Me109 was seen in the distance and it was too far away to attack. It was Bob's last flight in his faithful aircraft, Spitfire Vb AB857.

However, the day did mark an important landmark in the life of 452 Squadron. RAF authorities regarded the period of guidance for the RAAF's first Spitfire unit was now completed. The time had come for Bob Bungey to move on. Although he was an Australian in charge of an RAAF squadron, he was still officially an officer of the RAF holding a short service commission and under its terms, subject to the commands of that service. Bob was promoted to acting wing commander and posted to a new command, but first he had to go to RAF Shoreham.

Almost continuously for more than two years Bob had been in the front line of the war – from the very beginning flying Fairey Battles in France, to flying Hurricanes in the fighting over Britain, and then Hurricanes followed by Spitfires in the mounting air offensive over the Continent. Possessing an organised mind capable of analysing enemy tactics and countering them in the air and of excelling with his methodical administrative skill, he applied these abilities to his leadership as a flight commander and squadron leader – always setting an example by leading from the front.

During its stay in Fighter Command's No.11 Group, 452 Squadron was credited with destroying sixty-two enemy aircraft, probably destroying seven and damaging another seventeen. It was the highest scoring unit for two consecutive months and equal highest scoring squadron the month after that. Its members were awarded one DSO, five DFCs, three bars to DFCs, one DFM and one Mentioned in Despatches. In achieving this outstanding record twenty-two pilots were lost, either killed or missing.

Bluey Truscott would later say, 'Wing Commander Bungey made the Australian Spitfire Squadron, not Finucane or anyone else. Wing Commander Bungey would not take leave so that he could continue to fly and at the head of his men. He was such a wonderful leader that we would follow him anywhere.'[3]

Bob's posting was not the only change. Bluey Truscott was promoted to acting squadron leader and took over command of the squadron. Paddy Finucane, who had temporarily rejoined 452 as a supernumerary, was also promoted to acting squadron leader and posted to command 602 Squadron at Redhill. Also arriving to take over at Kenley was another larger-than-life Irish character and RAF legend, Gp/Capt Victor Beamish.

Late that day, Bob flew the squadron's Magister to Benson with Ray Thorold-Smith in the other seat. He had some leave and needed to visit Sybil's family at Wallingford before he reported to Shoreham next month. Behind Bob's usual stoic exterior, what his real emotions were at that poignant time could only be a guess. Thorold-Smith would take the Magister back to Kenley.

Just two months later, 452 Squadron was transferred out of the line and rested. Late in May, responding to the Australian government's urgent demands, Britain agreed to release it to go to Australia. Its departure was from Liverpool on 21 June 1942. With it went its sister unit, 457 Squadron, and 54 Squadron RAF. Together the three of them would become the RAAF's 'Churchill Wing' to defend Darwin.

If Bob had been able to stay with 452 Squadron, it is possible he might have been back in Australia as early as mid-August 1942; but that was not meant to be.

17

Air-Sea Rescue

Some confusion exists as to whether Bob Bungey's initial transfer was to command RAF Hawkinge or to RAF Shoreham. Although the official RAAF history and 452 Squadron's Operations Record Book recorded it as Shoreham, Bob initially wrote 'Hawkinge' in his RAF Log Book. But then afterwards he crossed the entry out by drawing a line through it, and wrote in 'Shoreham' just above. Why? Perhaps it was simply a mistake, but given his methodical nature it seems most likely he had been initially informed, perhaps verbally, that his command would be Hawkinge. When his posting finally did arrive, he had to change his Log Book entry because his orders were to go to Shoreham first to receive further briefing and instruction.

Shoreham airfield in Sussex was originally just grazing land some 6 miles from Brighton on the western side of the River Adur, which flows between Lancing and Shoreham village. The first flying school opened there in 1913 and in the 1920s, Shoreham airfield hosted many iconic air shows and flying meets. Famous aviators such as Sir Alan Cobham attended some of these high-profile events. During 1930, the municipal authorities of Brighton, Hove and Worthing formed a joint committee to establish Shoreham as the municipal airport for all three towns. Construction of a fine art deco air terminal building began in November 1934 and on 13 June 1936 it was opened by the mayors of all three municipalities. By 1938 passenger air services were operating from Shoreham Airport to Jersey, Birmingham and Liverpool.

With the outbreak of war in 1939, major international airline companies were relocated from London Airport (Croydon) to Shoreham. These airlines included such operators as Sabena, KLM and Imperial Airways, the forerunner of British Airways; and their links extended to Copenhagen, Amsterdam, Malmo and Brussels.

In May 1940, the German invasion of France and the Low Countries changed everything again. Passenger traffic to and from the airport was suspended and, shortly afterwards, the RAF took over. With fighter airfields already being established nearby, the municipal airport was turned into something more versatile – including becoming the base for a detachment of aircraft that would eventually be formed into part of No.277 Air-Sea Rescue (ASR) Squadron. The ASR setup at the beginning of 1942 was fragmented and complicated, probably explaining the need for Bob to go to Shoreham to be properly briefed about it.

The formation of ASR squadrons had grown out of the need to rescue aircrew who had ditched their aircraft, or bailed out and come down in the sea, before they either drowned or died from exposure in their dinghies. For the first year of the war this effort was completely unco-ordinated, left as the responsibility of the missing aircraft's home station. Downed aircrew were lucky if they might be picked up in time by a navy rescue launch. During the early stages of the Battle of Britain alone, at least 225 RAF aircrew were lost at sea. It was not until the Germans began to place a chain of rescue rafts in the English Channel for their fliers and to operate specialised rescue floatplanes and launches that the RAF realised it too needed to make better arrangements and organise some sort of proper rescue service.

As the Battle of Britain progressed, the dropping of dinghies, supplies and survival equipment to downed airmen was pioneered by a few units using Supermarine Walrus amphibians which could operate from water as well as land. One of the first to initiate this was a New Zealand pilot, F/Lt R. F. 'Digger' Aitken. In June 1940 he was an instructor stationed at Gosport and he suggested employing amphibian aircraft to retrieve pilots from the sea. Given the approval of his senior officers, he 'scrounged' a Walrus from the Fleet Air Arm and began operations over the Channel off the Isle of Wight. He soon proved its worth. According to accounts, 'Sometimes a German Heinkel float plane landed nearby on a similar mission, and the two aircraft, watching each other suspiciously, would remain floating placidly on the sea until air battles started above. In the few months he was engaged on this air-sea rescue work, Aitken picked up thirty-five British and German airmen.'[1]

At the same time, various improvised equipment for dropping to airmen in distress was developed independently. RAF Station Thornaby produced the Thornaby bag, a strengthened parachute bag buoyed with floats containing food, drink, cigarettes and first-aid equipment. Then RAF Bircham Newton provided the Bircham barrel, and this was followed by the Lindholme dinghy – all proving valuable in the saving of lives.

Around the end of July 1940, the commander of Fighter Command's No.11 Group, AVM Keith Park, arranged with the Army Co-operation wings to assign twelve Westland Lysanders for offshore search duties. On 22 August, these 'borrowed' Lysanders were officially placed under Fighter Command control. They were used for searches of the sea up to 20 miles offshore, covering England's coast from the Wash to the Bristol Channel and the South Wales coastline as far as Milford Haven. Lysanders could not carry a standard Lindholme dinghy, but by early 1941 they had their own specifically designed equipment. This consisted of four small 'M' Type dinghies containing distress flares, food and water, all packed in a valise that could be fitted inside a small bomb container and carried under the Lysanders' stub wings.

Towards the end of 1940, the RAF's fleet of rescue launches was doubled and, by May 1941, another six Lysanders were added to Fighter Command's ASR network for even greater coverage.

The successes achieved by all these measures were so encouraging that early in 1941 an organisation was created to co-ordinate and control all of the fragmented, independent sections employed in rescuing ditched crews. These sections ranged from the mouth of the Humber to the Isle of Man and, to cover this vast area, two Lysanders and usually a Walrus were based at Coltishall, Exeter, Manston, Martlesham, Pembrey, Portreath, Shoreham, Tangmere and Warmwell. The rescue 'trade' increased steadily during 1941 and by the autumn, it had outgrown the capacity of just attached flights to deal with the situation. It was decided remove the attached flights from their parent army co-operation squadrons and form them into separate squadrons that had the sole task of air-sea rescue.

This required better and more direct organisation and training, and the addition of more diverse types, principally the permanent acquisition of Walrus amphibians from the navy. The first three of four of these specialised squadrons were formed in October: 275 Squadron at Valley, 276 Squadron at Harrowbeer, and 278 Squadron at Matlask. The fourth unit, 277 Squadron, came into being at the end of the year. No.277 Squadron was officially formed at Stapleford Tawney in Essex on 22 December 1941 with its fragmented detachments that were stationed at various bases around England's south coast being combined administratively for more efficiency. By February 1942, the squadron had a mixture of Lysander Mk I and Mk IIIA aircraft and Walrus amphibians but they were still spread out from Stapleford Tawney in detachments at Martlesham Heath, Shoreham and Hawkinge. Because of this wide spread, the organisation and co-ordination of the squadron presented some very challenging problems. Bob needed to be fully briefed.

Bob was familiar with Lysander co-op aircraft from his days of flying with the AASF in France in 1939–40, and he was aware of their capabilities. However, Walrus amphibians were new to him, although there had been some at RAAF Point Cook when he was a cadet. In Australian service they were called Seagulls. They were single-engined, three-seater pusher-engined biplanes, designed in the early 1930s for fleet spotter work. He was given an introduction to the type when he flew a Walrus from Shoreham to Tangmere and back on 10 February, accompanied by F/Lt Green. With both of these types operating from his future new base, he needed to be fully aware of their strengths and weaknesses.

Towards the end of February, Bob at last moved to Hawkinge, where W/Cdr W. L. Bateman was in command, and there was a Tiger Moth (T5536) at his disposal. His Log Book shows that he flew it to Redhill and back on 1 March for a final farewell visit to 452 Squadron and thereafter he used it whenever required.

Hawkinge was a grass airfield, perched on top of the cliffs high above the coastal town of Folkestone. Although he was no longer supposed to fly on operations, simply by being at his new base Bob was still very much in the front line. On a clear day the airfield could be seen by the Germans at Pas de Calais if they used strong binoculars, and there was also the ever-present danger of attracting the attention of *Luftwaffe* hit-and-run raiders.

Back in 1940 during the withdrawal of the BEF squadrons from France and the Battle of Britain, Hawkinge had become the most-used forward airfield in Fighter Command and accordingly suffered damage from bombing attacks. Thereafter, with the RAF going onto the offensive, Lysanders began to operate from Hawkinge in the Air-Sea Rescue role. These were obtained from No.4 Army Co-operation Squadron, which had arrived at nearby Manston in December 1940. Daily, a solitary machine would be despatched to Hawkinge on standby and each night it would return to Manston. This single Lysander was substituted by a complete operational rescue unit in June 1941 and, in due course, this was developed into 'A' Flight of No.277 (ASR) Squadron. In July the flight received two Walrus amphibians and these provided a new challenge for the aircrews. In the right conditions they could alight on the sea to carry out a rescue and this became a new and dangerous feature of their work.

Meanwhile, with rubber dinghies attached to its wheel spats, the slow but highly manoeuvrable Lysander was always a most welcome sight for any ditched flier. Although it carried twin Browning machine guns for defence, because of its lack of speed it was a sitting duck for any prowling enemy fighter so it was desirable for it to be escorted by a couple of RAF fighters to ward off any hostile attack. Bob had flown cover on many occasions.

'A' Flight of 277 (ASR) Squadron was not the only unit residing at Hawkinge. The other was No.91 'Jim Crow' Squadron commanded by S/Ldr Robert 'Bobbie' Oxspring who had only arrived a month earlier himself from 41 Squadron at Manston and was still in the process of settling in. However, adding to the confused nature of administering the base, 91 Squadron was split up too. Only half of this squadron was actually residing at Hawkinge – its 'A' Flight had been detached to nearby Lympne.

Hawkinge, Lympne and Manston were all forward satellite airfields in the Biggin Hill Sector but the scattered nature of the units flying from them made organisation and administration awkward at the very least and sometimes a downright nightmare. No.91 Squadron had been formed at Hawkinge on 11 January 1941, equipped with Spitfire IIAs and then Spitfire VBs. The designation 'Jim Crow' was given to the specific assignment of carrying out coastal patrols to intercept any enemy aircraft coming in over the coast. No.421 Flight at Hawkinge had been expanded to squadron strength and re-numbered No.91 Squadron for patrolling the Kent coast and finding the occasional enemy aircraft to shoot down into the sea. In February it also began *Rhubarb* operations over the Continent and anti-shipping reconnaissance flights over the North Sea. With the advent of 'A' Flight of No.277 Squadron, sorties escorting ASR Lysanders and Walruses carrying out rescue missions from Hawkinge over the Channel were added to its tasks.

In May, 91 Squadron tried flying *Rhubarbs* at night, but found that the Spitfires were not really suitable for the work and these were discontinued. During that month, besides using the Tiger Moth, and despite his now normal desk duties, Bob flew five different Spitfires for local familiarisation flights and air tests, including one for a cannon test off Beachy Head.

A few weeks before Bob's arrival at Hawkinge, there had been an emergency. Late on 11 February the German capital ships, *Scharnhorst,* *Gneisenau* and *Prinz Eugen,* had sneaked out of Brest Harbour under the cover of darkness and then, heavily escorted and hidden by poor weather, they sailed for Germany via the English Channel. It was not until 10.30 a.m. the following day when two Jim Crow pilots from Hawkinge, S/Ldr Bobbie Oxspring and his wingman Sgt Beaumont, who were flying a patrol over the Channel, spotted the German convoy. Landing at 10.50 a.m., they reported their sighting and the news was immediately sent to Fighter Command – but the authorities were not convinced that they actually were the German capital ships making a surprise 'Channel Dash'. What followed turned into a fiasco. Due to a series of blunders and the inclement weather, the enemy convoy succeeded in sailing through the Straits of Dover and escaping back to Germany in a relatively undamaged condition despite multiple RAF attacks, which were poorly co-ordinated and fragmented. Hawkinge and 91 Squadron played only a very small part after the original sighting and when the escape was over, they reverted to the normal routines.

A few weeks after Bob's arrival at his new base, exciting news reached him from Australia. The following appeared in the Adelaide press:

SON FOR NOTED AIR ACE

On Friday, March 20, at the PATAWILYA Private Hospital, a son was born to Mrs Bungey, wife of Australian air ace Wing-Commander, R. W. Bungey DFC RAF whose squadron has achieved a fine record abroad. Mrs Bungey, who arrived in Adelaide on February 11, was formerly Miss Sybil Johnson, of Wallingford, Berkshire, England,

'Son Richard Arrived'
'Your son Richard, arrived today All well
'Congratulations.'

This message has been cabled to Wing Commander Bob Bungey DFC, leader of the No.1 Australian Spitfire Squadron in England.

His reply hasn't come yet, but the proud grandparents, Mr and Mrs E. Bungey, know he will be thrilled at the news.

'Bob wanted a son', said Mr Bungey today, 'Richard is the name he chose. He used to say his son would be Richard the Lion-Hearted.'

At his early birth Richard Bungey weighed in at 5 lb 4 oz, small but strong and already with a determined spirit. Bob responded by telegram:

Telegram

Glenelg
27 Mar 42
Great Britain
Mrs. R W Bungey
Tarlton St Glenelg S A

Bless you darling knew it would be Richard feel terribly proud. Love you more than ever.

Bob Bungey.

Richard was christened in Adelaide's St Peter's Cathedral the following July. The public notice read:

July 1942, Friday.

BUNGEY JUNIOR

The four month old son of Wing Commander Bob Bungey DFC, South Australian flying ace, will be christened RICHARD WILTON in St Peter's Cathedral on Sunday afternoon.

Young Richard, who was born while his father was in England, will have two godfathers and one godmother –Wing Commander Sir Arthur Barrett, Squadron Leader Keith Truscott, and Mrs R. Clisby. Major Elliot Playford will act for Squadron Leader Truscott in his absence.

Mrs Bungey has written to her husband to tell him about the christening. She received a cable last week, sending his love and saying he was well.

***

Much had been happening to Bob in the interim. He officially took over as commanding officer of RAF Hawkinge on 30 April 1942.

Kent in south-east England's front line was probably the busiest county in the country, and Hawkinge was one of its busiest stations, particularly with the air offensive renewing as the year progressed. It was a refuelling point for squadrons carrying out *Circus* operations and other missions at greater range over the Continent, and an emergency landing ground for anyone returning with their aircraft damaged or low on fuel. On these occasions ASR was always on call and had to be ready.

The Walrus amphibians and Lysanders were extremely reliable but 277 Squadron lost Lysander V9483 on 16 April when it suffered engine failure. It crash-landed into trees and sheared off a wing at Fosholt Farm. On 1 May, the day after Bob took over, Lysander V9488 overshot the field at Hawkinge while landing and ran into a fence. Worryingly, Lysanders were becoming scarce. As well as being used for Air-Sea Rescue work, they were required for other duties such as special clandestine night flights in and out of the Continent and for army co-op work in other theatres.

In May, the squadron's four Lysanders were complemented by the addition of six Boulton Paul Defiants. Viewed from a distance, a Defiant looked like a Hurricane. It had a humped-back, a large radiator under the centre fuselage and evenly tapered, round tipped wings. It was powered by a Rolls-Royce Merlin engine like the Hurricane and Spitfire, but the hump wasn't a hump – it was a power-operated gun turret with four .303-inch Browning machine guns.

The Defiant was a throwback to the two-seater designs of the First World War, such as the Sopwith 1½ Strutter and Bristol F2B Fighter. It had been thought that the 360° traverse of its turret would give greater flexibility to the crew because the aircraft would not need to be manoeuvred behind the enemy in order to fire with fixed forward-aimed armament – in fact there wasn't any fixed forward-aimed armament at all!

Defiants were employed at first over Dunkirk, where they claimed great success when the Germans mistook them for Hurricanes and attacked them from the rear only to run into a concentrated barrage from the machine-gun turrets. But that situation did not last. Once the *Luftwaffe* pilots identified their opponents properly, they simply altered their attacking angles and hacked the slower, heavier Defiants out of the sky; two squadrons were decimated during the Battle of Britain.

Realising they were useless as day fighters, the RAF consigned Defiants to the night-fighter role where they achieved a few limited successes but with the advent of airborne radar and the formidable Bristol Beaufighters, they were now being retired from the night-fighter squadrons. They were becoming available in increasing numbers for some other new role, so they were to be tried in the ASR organisation in the hope that they would be more able to defend themselves than the Lysanders.

At this point Bob was called away for something highly top secret. Fortunately, most of the pilots and aircrew in 91 and 277 Squadrons were very experienced. In fact, one of the 91 Squadron pilots, F/Lt Roger Hall, had flown Defiants before as nightfighters with 255 Squadron. He and his gunner had actually scored that squadron's first victory by shooting down a He111 over the Humber in February 1941.

Bob had to leave the conversion onto Defiants and training in their capable hands.

18

Rutter

It was code-named Operation *Rutter* at first. Bob Bungey's involvement with it began early in June.

Bob's RAF Flying Log Book shows that on the 4th he flew the base's Magister trainer to Northolt and back to Hawkinge again that day, apparently without carrying any second person. The purpose? Given Northolt's proximity to London and the various military headquarters, he seems to have needed to go to the capital to have special papers prepared and to receive instructions in order for him to organise his future movements.

He did the Northolt trip again four days later but this time he picked up a passenger, Major Walter Skrine from Combined Operations Headquarters in Richmond Terrace. Instead of returning to Hawkinge, they flew to Cowes on the Isle of Wight.

Bob was familiar with the Isle of Wight having flown over it so many times and having been forced down into the shallow water near Shanklin in November 1940, but the atmosphere there was completely different now. It was busy – very, very busy. Troops were everywhere, lots of them – Canadians! They were called *Simmerforce* and they were going through rigorous training. There were other uniforms too: British Commandos with green berets, the dark blue of the Royal Navy and Free French, British glider troops and Paratroops with red berets, a few lighter blue RAF, and he even saw a familiar stray dark blue RAAF uniform as well.

Security was tight – exceptionally tight. No one could get onto the island without the proper identity papers, which had been especially issued for something he would learn was called *Rutter*. Once there, no one could get off the isle without the personal approval of the commanding generals or their security staffs. Civilians with homes and businesses on the island were allowed to remain but otherwise the Isle of Wight was completely isolated from the rest of England. As well as 5,000 Canadians, there were 4,000 sailors, airmen, and assorted groups of various nationalities, even including a small number of American Rangers. Most were attached to *Simmerforce* or had some other connection with it. Something dramatic was happening, or was about to happen.

Osborne Court at Cowes was the headquarters of the 2nd Canadian Division under the command of Major-General John Hamilton 'Ham' Roberts. His second-in-command was Lt/Col Churchill Mann and these men, and Combined Operations officers such as Major Skrine, were responsible for the detailed planning of Operation *Rutter* – whatever that was! Although Bob was still officially in command at RAF Hawkinge – as he would continue to record in his RAF Flying Log Book – it was here at Cowes that he would be based for at least the immediate future, attached to the Canadians or to Combined Operations.

But what was *Rutter*?

Since being invaded by the Germans in June 1941, the Soviet Union had been absorbing the impact of the main brunt of the European land war. As the fighting on the Russian Front lurched from crisis to crisis in 1942, the Soviet dictator Josef Stalin agitated for the Allies to launch a second front on Continental Europe to relieve the pressure of the German offensive on his beleaguered forces. The British, still staggering from the events of the past two years in Europe, North Africa and the Mediterranean, plus now the Far East, were not in a position to mount such a response. Although a second front was clearly not yet practical, out of several proposals that British military leaders considered, a plan was conceived to launch a surprise Combined Operations raid in force on a French coastal port or town.

In general terms, the idea was for the Royal Navy to land a large body of troops, more than three-quarters of them Canadians, at a coastal port during high tide, supported by British Commandos on the flanks to knock-out gun positions overlooking the beaches, with paratroops and glider troops landing further inland to capture and demolish heavy batteries located there. After achieving their specific objectives, at the next high tide they were to withdraw to their landing craft as quickly as they had come to be taken back to England, all under the cover of a protective air umbrella by the RAF.

No combined operation on the scale of *Rutter* had ever been attempted before and the raid was scheduled to be launched towards the end of June 1942. At this stage, the name of the French port was top secret, known only to those at the highest level. The target was Dieppe. This was Operation *Rutter.*

For the RAF to provide massive air cover for the operation, fighter squadrons in large numbers had to be deployed temporarily to the airfields in the south and south-east of England. Hawkinge had to host two of them.

Bob returned to Hawkinge on the 12th with instructions to have three corrugated blister hangars erected to accommodate the needs of the expected visitors. Hangar space was at a premium since the bombing raids of 1940 when only the No.1 hangar had survived the onslaught. Although these new structures would offer only the simplest form of protection for maintenance and servicing engines, it was considered they should be effective enough to save the ground crews from having to work in the open. After putting the necessary arrangements in place Bob returned to Cowes, this time flying his Tiger Moth T5536.

Although security placed restrictions on radio usage and normal telecommunications, there still had to be a constant back-and-forth flow of reliable information and communication between the various commands.

This made necessary much physical coming-and-going between Cowes and the War Office, Combined Operations HQ in Richmond Terrace and other special, 'secret' destinations, but it could not be conspicuous. Out-of-the-ordinary increases in the normal routines of ferry transport might attract unwanted attention, but who would pay much attention to – or be able to follow – the wanderings of an open-cockpit, two-seater biplane trainer apparently on normal training flights? Using the Tiger Moth on the 14th, Bob flew Lt/Col Churchill Mann to Northolt and return. Two days later, he took Major Skrine on the same circuit. Then on the 20th, Lt/Col J. D. McBeth,[1] the 2nd Division's Signals Commanding Officer, went with him to Netheravon in the next county, 13 miles west of Andover, and back.

On 27 June, Bob took a Hurricane first to Northolt and then delivered it to Tangmere where he picked up a special passenger to fly back to Cowes in the Tiger Moth. This was the officer in the RAAF uniform that he had noticed before, AC/mdr Adrian Cole, who was familiar. Bob realised he knew him from his days at Point Cook – a time that seemed so long ago now. All the cadets at Point Cook had been aware of the exploits of Australian fliers in the Great War and some, like Adrian 'King' Cole, were instructors. After guest night dinners, several of these legendry figures would visit the cadets' anteroom where, with a little prompting over port, they could be 'persuaded' to relate some first-hand accounts of combat over enemy lines. King Cole was one of the harder ones to get to talk but his array of medals showed that he had done more than his share, though he was fairly reserved about it.

In 1917 Adrian Cole had been posted to Egypt where he flew with No.1 Squadron, Australian Flying Corps. While flying a Martinsyde Elephant on 21 April, he was shot down by ground fire over Tel el Sheria and forced to land, but a fellow pilot landed close by and picked him up. In a similar exploit on 26 June, he and another pilot landed to pick up the pilot of a BE 2 that had a seized engine. Escorted by Cole, the other pilot took off two up but his engine seized too, and they had to land again. Cole then tried to take both pilots in his Martinsyde, but his engine stopped too and he crash-landed. It was only after a long walk through No Man's Land that they were all finally picked up by a detachment of the Light Horse. After No.1 Squadron converted to Bristol Fighters, Cole won an MC on 16 August 1917 for attacking six enemy aircraft that were about to strafe Allied cavalry. Early in the summer of 1918, Cole was posted to France where he joined 2 Squadron AFC flying SE 5As as a flight commander. During the next five months he claimed nine victories for a total of ten (six destroyed, three out of control, one driven down), receiving a DFC after the fourth. Afterwards, he joined the RAAF upon its formation in 1921 and became Director of Training, and then Commandant of Point Cook in 1926. He had been Deputy Chairman of the MacRobertson-Miller Air Race of 1934. In the Second World War, Cole was attached to the RAF and before joining *Rutter* had already served as CO of 235 Wing in North Africa. He could recall Cadet Bungey at Point Cook and was particularly aware of the achievements of 152 Squadron under Bob's leadership. Cole's role in *Rutter* was significant.[2]

Overall responsibility for *Rutter's* air umbrella was in the hands of AVM Trafford Leigh-Mallory GB DSO, Air Officer Commanding No.11 Group, RAF Fighter Command. He had previously been in charge of No.12 Group during the Battle of Britain and had taken over 11 Group from AVM Keith Park at the end of 1940. His immediate superior in 1942 was ACM William Sholto Douglas KGB MC DFC.

Leigh-Mallory would control the air operations from No.11 Group headquarters at Uxbridge, west of London. Radar reports of movements in the Channel would be relayed to him there and plotted, and he would work with the attacking force through an air liaison officer. Adrian Cole was the RAF Air Liaison Officer for *Rutter,* the direct go-between for Leigh-Mallory and General Ham Roberts, and with this came the added responsibility of being the fighter controller on a destroyer during the raid.

A formidable air fleet was being assembled. Leigh-Mallory earmarked forty-eight squadrons of Spitfires, mostly Spitfire Mark Vb and VC versions but four squadrons were equipped with the latest Mark IX Spitfires and two had the Mark VI. With a few exceptions these units would provide the vital air cover for the raid, including escorting light bombers, Bristol Blenheims IVs and Douglas Boston IIIs and covering Hurricane fighter-bombers. Supporting too were new Hawker Typhoons and Army Co-op North American Mustangs.

The aircraft would also have to provide continuous protection for the ships and boats before, during and after the raid as they withdrew to England in the afternoon and early evening. This was where Air-Sea Rescue came in. Backing up the air umbrella and the vital ASR launches would be the job of the Lysanders, Walrus amphibians and Defiants of the ASR detachments from Hawkinge, Lympne, Manston, Stapleford Tawney, Martlesham Heath, Shoreham and around the coast.

Back on 11–12 June, just after Bob had joined *Rutter,* there had been a full-scale rehearsal of the mission, which for security was called Operation *Yukon.* The West Bay (Bridport) area of Dorset, being a similar distance away from the Isle of Wight, was selected to represent Dieppe. That night Cole was with General Roberts and his team on a destroyer headquarters ship, HMS *Calype,* which was specially equipped with an impressive array of the latest electronic equipment for directing the landings and following troop movements ashore. Churchill Mann was on another destroyer equipped in a duplicate manner to monitor or be ready to take over should the systems on *Calype* fail or be disabled. Major Skrine, the appointed liaison officer between Combined Operations Headquarters and the Canadian 2nd Division was on the *Princess Beatrix,* a vessel that had been specially assigned to Combined Operations for transporting commandoes on raids. He was there to evaluate and report on the performances of the landing craft as well as the troops as they landed and then carried out their allocated objectives.

What followed was utter chaos, the RN being blamed as chiefly at fault. One group of troops was landed a mile from its allotted beach area, another group about 2 miles away from its, and the supporting tanks arrived 1½ hours late due to the crews of their landing craft losing their way in the darkness. On shore, the infantry deployed inland much too slowly and reached their objectives late, upsetting Churchill Mann's carefully worked out timetables. A couple of frontal assaults actually did function properly but only because the local troops pretending to be the enemy dutifully ducked for cover on cue when the air support Hurricanes roared overhead in a mock strafing attack.

Afterwards, with the exercise over, the Canadian 2nd Division with all its added personnel and particular attached units, returned to the Isle of Wight. On their arrival the island was again sealed off from the mainland while those in charge evaluated what had transpired.

Despite the chilling reality that if it had been the actual raid, the Germans could have transformed the confusion into a bloodbath, Operation *Yukon* planners rationalised the results. They concluded that if the landing craft crews could improve their navigation skills and punctuality, it was reasonable to anticipate the outcome might be a success. Accordingly, a second practice run, *Yukon II*, was organised for 22–23 June to be carried out at dawn across the same stretch of coast as before. Meanwhile, a tentative date for the real operation was set for when the next tides would be suitable, 4–9 July inclusive.

This time the landings were carried out at the correct locations and went according to plan, although some still noted that the assault landing craft lost direction and were late landing the troops they carried. *Yukon II* was subsequently described officially as a comparative success. General Roberts was satisfied enough with his division's performance, but not with the way the navy handled its role, even though the run from the Isle of Wight west to Bridport, with its strong tides, was far more difficult than the actual trip would be to Dieppe. The decision: Go!

Late on 27 June, the day Bob brought Adrian Cole from Tangmere to Cowes in the Tiger Moth, there was a special briefing for all officers of the 2nd Division. It was held at Divisional Headquarters Osborne Court and among the 300 key officers present as well as Adrian Cole, Bob noted the faces of General Roberts who was presiding, Colonel Mann, Colonel McBeth, and Major Skrine, but there were others there too. At the front to one side was a thin, hawk-faced figure, General Bernard Montgomery, and nearby was a taller man in naval uniform, Lord Louis Mountbatten, the head of Combined Operations himself.

Although the name 'Dieppe' was deliberately avoided, the officers were all told officially for the first time that the plan was to raid a port somewhere on the coast of France. An accurately detailed scale relief model, about 10 feet long by 6 feet wide, was unveiled of the target and its surrounding area. Apparently when someone exclaimed that he recognised the place, Roberts sprang to his feet and emphasised the absolute necessity for complete security. If somebody breached it, the penalty would be severe – at least 'penal servitude with hard labour' or worse, and the raid, which he referred to as 'the party', would have to be cancelled. Other ranks were not to be told until they were aboard their ships. He then handed the briefing over to Churchill Mann.

Mann went over the essential details using the scale model and it was revealed that meteorological experts predicted favourable weather for 4–5 July. This was in the middle of the period when the desired phase of the moon and the tides would take place. It had been decided to launch Operation *Rutter* on this night, or on one of the two following nights. And so the die was cast.

In the week that followed there was a flurry of renewed activity in order to be ready in time. For Bob it meant he had to ensure that Hawkinge was ready. On the 29th, he flew a circuit from Cowes to Northolt and Tangmere in the Tiger Moth. At Tangmere he met up with 91 Squadron's F/Lt Roger Hall and brought him to Cowes to be briefed. Bob also needed to be updated with the happenings at Hawkinge. The three blister hangars had been put up and were ready for the visiting Spitfire squadrons, which were due to arrive the following day: Nos.41 and 65 Squadrons, both equipped with Spitfire VBs like 91 Squadron so there were unlikely to be any unforeseen maintenance and servicing issues. Meanwhile, 277 Squadron's adaptation onto the Defiants was continuing, but it was more a case of the Defiants that needed to be adapted. They needed to have their wings modified to carry two of the 'M' Type dinghies but, by comparison, the Lysanders could carry four.

Bob took Roger Hall back to Tangmere on 3 July and after leaving him there to make his own way back to Hawkinge in his own aircraft, he flew on to Northolt before returning once more to Cowes. He had also transported Walter Skrine to Tangmere the previous day.

By now more than 200 vessels of all shapes and sizes had been gathered around the Isle of Wight in Cowes Roads, Newhaven, Southampton Water, and in Yarmouth Roads. Also on the 3rd, *Simmerforce* began to board the large infantry landing-ships to prepare, so the men thought, for yet another exercise, this one code-named *Klondike*. When the troops were all on board and their communication with shore had been completely severed, the news, so long top secret, was revealed. This was not another exercise; they were going to meet the enemy at long last. Shortly after midnight they would sail for France. Their target was the French port of Dieppe.

The night of 3–4 June came and went, but the fleet did not sail. The following night came and went, and still the fleet did not move. Those on board in their cramped quarters waited, and waited … and still the fleet did not move. As 5 June dawned they were still waiting.

It was the wind. The commander of the 1st Airborne Division had sent a message which said: 'Best available meteorological information indicates wind will increase in strength throughout the night from the south-west. Glider operations have been cancelled and by dawn an accurate air drop will be impossible to achieve. Accordingly, I recommend that operation be postponed.'[3]

Around the same time, Combined Operations HQ received an Intelligence report stating that a German Panzer Division had moved into Amiens, which was only 8 hours away from Dieppe. This could spell disaster. In the operation as planned, the troops had to be ashore for 15 hours between the two high tides, but this was long enough for an enemy armoured column to reach the port from Amiens.

To avoid cancelling the mission, the only thing to do was change by withdrawing before the second high tide, but that would play havoc with Churchill Mann's organisation. The whole plan could be compressed by eliminating the lengthier demolition missions and withdrawing *Simmerforce* by 1100 hours instead of late afternoon's high tide. Time was needed to make the changes and issue new instructions. Meanwhile, forecasts were that the weather was likely to deteriorate further over the next few days until 8 July when the winds would lighten. This was the last day until August when the moon and tides would be favourable. Churchill Mann worked feverishly and his extensive alterations were sent to Montgomery and Mountbatten for approval and thus for confirmation that zero hour should be dawn on the 8th.

On 5 July, the force commanders and their staffs met for a final decision on the date. Meteorological reports confirmed fair weather for 8 July with only light winds. That was three days away, but another potential problem loomed.

As the force commanders met, Bob took Colonel McBeth, the Canadian Division's Signals CO, on a 'local flight' over the Isle of Wight to inspect the area from the air. There were too many ships to be seen. Although they were all shapes and sizes and a lot of them did not have an obvious military look, the increase in numbers was not likely to go unnoticed for long by any capable *Luftwaffe* reconnaissance expert. High-altitude Junkers Ju86P reconnaissance aircraft were flying over England with impunity. The longer the fleet remained assembled in port, the greater was the danger of discovery.

After landing to refuel and so that McBeth could report back to the meeting, Walter Skrine joined Bob again and they flew to the Fleet Air Arm airfield at Lee on Solent to deliver in person an updated report to the navy.

Next day, Bob flew Churchill Mann to Northolt so he could attend an urgent meeting at Combined Operations Headquarters in Richmond Terrace. Following this, Mountbatten attended a conference of the Chiefs of Staff at the War Office where he advised that if *Rutter* did not go ahead on the 8th, the men of *Simmerforce*, who were still waiting aboard the ships, should be disbanded and dispersed. These couped up men were completely unaware of the quandary and the doubts plaguing their commanders. The mission, Mountbatten concluded, could be set in motion again on a later date.

Fears that German reconnaissance planes may have spotted the vast armada of ships seemed to be confirmed at 6.15 a.m. on 7 July when the *Luftwaffe* paid the Isle of Wight a visit. Four hit-and-run aircraft swept in low over the Yarmouth Roads and bombed the *Princess Astrid* and *Princess Josephine Charlotte*, infantry landing vessels that were carrying the troops of the Royal Regiment of Canada. Bombs hit both ships but fortunately they passed right through them before exploding in the water under their keels. The Royals suffered just four light casualties but because there was a minor probability the *Princess Josephine Charlotte* might sink, the troops were disembarked. They assembled ashore and were instructed to march to Cowes for further orders. A motorcycle dispatch rider carrying an urgent message from General Roberts stopped the column on the way with orders that the regiment was to return to its training headquarters.

The air attack was the last straw. There was no time to alter the plan yet again to cater for the loss of the damaged ships and the removal of the Royals from the attack. Reluctantly, Ham Roberts telephoned Mountbatten at Combined Operations Headquarters. This news, combined with the adverse weather forecasts, finally led Mountbatten into deciding to cancel the operation. General Roberts gave the order for all units to disembark. *Rutter* was all over before it had started.

Early on the 8th, instead of landing at Dieppe, the men of *Simmerforce* departed from the Isle of Wight to return to their previous training camps in Sussex.

The following morning, Bob took off alone in the Tiger Moth and flew east. He was on his way back to Hawkinge.

19

Jubilee

Bob Bungey had been back at Hawkinge for only a week when there was terrible news – Paddy Finucane was dead.

After fracturing his right heel at Croydon Town Hall back in October 1941, the irrepressible Irish ace was off operations until the following January by which time official regulations denied his return to 452 Squadron. Instead, he was promoted to squadron leader and given command of No.602 Squadron at Redhill. It was a change that both he and the Australians openly regretted because they had bonded so closely and successfully.

On 20 February, Paddy was slightly wounded in the leg during a clash with FW190s. He was back in action on 13 March and by the end of the month he had added four of the formidable Focke-Wulfs to his tally. As his fame spread in the press, models of his Spitfire adorned with its vivid green shamrock emblem were sold all along Piccadilly Circus and The Strand. In April, his engagement to Jean Woolford, a girl he had known for several years, was announced. Bob and the others knew they were a good match.

Paddy's score reached thirty-two in May 1942, equalling that of the famous South African ace, W/Cdr Adolf 'Sailor' Malan, who was no longer flying operations. But by now the stress of Paddy's continuous combat flying was beginning to show. The RAF was feeling the strain too. Several very experienced leaders had already failed to return, such as Douglas 'Tin Legs' Bader (9 August 1941), the flamboyant Robert Stanford-Tuck (28 January 1942), and the remarkable Victor Beamish (28 March 1942) who had taken over at Kenley.

Paddy was promoted to 'Wing Commander Flying' on 21 June – an outstanding achievement for a 21-year-old, but privately he confided to members of his family that he was feeling very tired.

15 July brought with it another routine *Ramrod* operation – fighters shooting up ground targets. For the Hornchurch Wing the target was a German Army camp at Étaples, a few miles inland from Le Touquet. The raid was timed to catch the Germans lining up for lunch. Paddy showed little concern when the intelligence officer gave details of the camp and said they could expect some light flak. Most pilots at that time did not take small arms ground fire very seriously and Paddy was one of them. He should have.

They crossed the coast of Sussex over Pevensey Bay at 12.10 and Paddy set out across the Channel at low level to make landfall at Le Touquet. It was 12.22 as they reached the beaches. A single machine-gun post near Pointe du Touquet opened fire at the oncoming thirty plus Spitfires as they suddenly loomed head-on out of the Channel mist and swept overhead.

What were the odds of a small calibre machine gun hitting a low-flying plane speeding overhead at 300 knots? Minimal! But Paddy's Spitfire was hit in the starboard wing and engine. A wisp of white vapour streamed back from the engine. Glycol! Radiator damage! Paddy made a hard vertical turn to starboard and headed for home, back across the beach and low over the water. His wingman, P/O Alan 'Butch' Aikman, a Canadian from Toronto, formed up in his normal position on the right. Paddy had throttled back, flying slowly to save his engine.

Paddy was too near the French coast. To go down or bail out would have meant capture at the very least. That was not an option. He had to try for England or get as close to it as possible for a rescue. Aikman followed. The Canadian throttled back and lowered his landing gear and flaps to maintain the slow speed and stay close by in the air.

On the R/T, Aikman heard his leader say the engine was overheating. About 10 miles from Le Touquet, Paddy's choices ran out – he had to ditch. He jettisoned the cockpit canopy.

Just before removing his helmet Paddy calmly said on the radio, 'This is it, chaps.' Or, it may have been, 'This is it, Butch,' to his loyal wingman.

Aikman could see the engine had yet not seized up. The propeller was still spinning but there was a long white cloud of escaping coolant trailing behind. Paddy gave a 'thumbs-up' signal just before he eased back on the controls. He ditched perfectly but the nose of the Spitfire dug in with a huge splash and the aircraft instantly sank like a stone. There was no escape – no chance for an air-sea rescue.

Paddy Finucane was gone. His flying mates, Bob included, were shocked by the news, and all of Britain mourned him. More than 3,000 people attended the requiem mass held in his honour at Westminster Cathedral. Later, his name was inscribed on the Runnymede Memorial.

Added to this tragedy, Bob also found out that Boudouin de Hemptinne, one of his capable Belgian friends in 145 Squadron, had failed to return from a fierce air battle somewhere near Lille. By May, Boudouin had been promoted to flight lieutenant and was a flight commander in 122 Squadron operating from Hornchurch. On the 5th during *Circus 157*, his squadron escorted Douglas Boston bombers from 226 Squadron to bomb Lille. The Germans reacted strongly and 122 Squadron had been severely mauled by FW190s. Four Spitfires and their pilots were lost. There was little hope.

In fact, the Focke-Wulfs were from the formidable *JG26* and de Hemptinne's Spitfire Vb (MT-T, BM321) was shot up apparently by *Hptm* Johannes Seifert. He was *Hptm* Seifert's thirty-third victory. According to reports, de Hemptinne was wounded in the back but managed to land his damaged machine before his life ebbed away shortly afterwards. Because he was not carrying identification papers for fear of reprisals being committed against his family, the Germans buried him as 'unknown' at Ypres. After the war, de Hemptinne's identity was established and on 27 August 1948 he was reinterred in Grave 28 of the Belgian Field of Honour in Brussels Town Cemetery.

Anguish struck Bob again deeply. It was personal. Quiet and stoic by nature, he did not show his emotions, he kept them to himself, but inside his grief was growing like a cancer – especially since Pyker Offenberg's tragic death. At least, as far as he knew, others from his former flight in 145 Squadron were still going. The Kiwi, Paul Rabone, was flying nightfighters and the Anglo-Argentine, Dudley Honor, had transferred to somewhere in the Middle East.

Death seemed to be everywhere. Pyker, Boudouin, Leslie ... so many had gone – and now Paddy. It was better not to think of such things. Work was the answer. Keep busy.

Bob did just that – he worked. There was much to catch up on.

* * *

While Bob was away at Cowes, No.65 (East India) Squadron from Great Sampford in Essex had been the first unit to arrive at Hawkinge on 30 June. It was commanded by S/Ldr A. C. Bartley, a Battle of Britain veteran who had flown with 92 Squadron in 1940. Next came 41 Squadron from Martlesham Heath, under the command of S/Ldr C. J. Fee. Both were equipped with Spitfire VBs.

As things turned out, their stay was short-lived because *Rutter* was cancelled on 7 July. Nevertheless, their time at Hawkinge was not wasted. While they were there, they became the first Spitfires using wing drop-tanks to operate from the airfield for sweeps and *Rhubarbs* over France, which allowed them to attack targets that were further afield. S/Ldr Fee's aircraft took up coastal patrols and fighter sweeps in pairs, similar to the 'Jim Crows' ranging along the French, Belgian and Dutch coasts, plus flying some night sorties for good measure. Both squadrons were moved north again shortly afterwards. No.65 Squadron transferred back to Great Sampford and 41 Squadron went to Debden.

After the two Spitfire squadrons departed, 91 Squadron had a change of command. Bobbie Oxspring was posted to Biggin Hill to take over 72 Squadron and S/Ldr Jean Demozay of the Free French Air Force arrived to take his place.

Then on the 26th, Bob had an unexpected but familiar visitor – Major Walter Skrine from Combined Operations. Skrine delivered a bombshell. *Rutter* was on again, but under a different code-name this time – Operation *Jubilee*. Political pressure by the Russians for a second front in the West had not let up and as a result just a week after the raid had been cancelled, Lord Mountbatten at Combined Operations Headquarters had actually brought it back into consideration. The target and the plan were the same as the compressed single tide assault that had been worked out so speedily and so late before. The attack force's withdrawal would begin at 1100 hours instead of late afternoon, but some other changes had been made too. There would be no glider forces or paratroops used at all, as they depended too much on perfect weather conditions. Churchill Mann had reorganised the timetable. There would be a supporting diversionary raid on the German airfield at Abbeville by Boeing B-17 Flying Fortresses of the newly established 8th USAAF, escorted by Spitfires.[1] After landing from their escort mission, the Spitfires would be redeployed to join the Dieppe air umbrella. As before, there would be no heavy naval bombardment, reliance would be placed on the element of surprise and the use of smoke screens dropped by fighter-bombers and fired from destroyers offshore.

Also as before, Hawkinge would host two Spitfire squadrons but, unlike before, they had to cope with two different types of Spitfire. One was equipped with the standard Mk VB but the other had the more powerful Spitfire VI. This was based on the Spitfire Mk VB but designed to fly and fight at high altitude making it capable of intercepting high-flying German reconnaissance aircraft such as the Junkers Ju 86P, which had been operating unmolested over Britain since early 1941. Flying as high as 40,000 feet, the Junkers had so far been virtually immune from interception. In April 1942, No.616 (South Yorkshire) Squadron had been the first unit to equip with the new Spitfire variant of which only 100 would be built.

The suitability of these Spitfires to operate from Hawkinge needed to be checked. For one thing, they had a larger wingspan because of their extended wingtips for greater lift. Would there be sufficient space for the ground crews to service them in the three corrugated blister hangars built earlier, or would there need to be some other special arrangements put in place?

A Spitfire VI was made available for evaluation two days later and in his Flying Log Book Bob recorded a climb in it up to an altitude of 38,000 feet (11,600 m), the greatest height he ever achieved. The obvious external change besides its extended wingtips was a four-bladed propeller, the first production Spitfire variant to have this feature. Internally it was powered by a Rolls-Royce Merlin 47 engine with its supercharger set to produce maximum power at greater height. Bob found that at height the controls responded much better than those of the Mk VB version.

One aspect of the Spitfire VI made the cockpit feel claustrophobic – unlike standard Spitfires, the canopy could not be slid open and shut. It had to be closed and bolted down before take off. This was to completely seal the cockpit so it could be pressurised by an engine-driven blower that forced warm air into the cabin once the pilot was strapped in and encased. The warm, sealed cockpit was good at high altitude, but lower down where the air was warmer the cockpit could become almost unbearably hot. In the event of an emergency, the whole canopy could be jettisoned to allow the pilot to escape.

The sealed cockpit was not popular with most pilots as the normal practice had been to taxi, take off and land with the canopy open. Hawkinge's ground crews had to become familiar with this different routine and proficient, particularly if a fast turnaround was needed between missions.

Meanwhile, the war went on. On 25 July, a Defiant of 277 Squadron was shot down north of Dunkirk by *Uffz* Börner, an FW190 pilot of *JG26*. Lost were Sgt John Arundel and Sgt William Bunn. Arundel had been the pilot involved in the squadron's first successful sea rescue by a Walrus on 1 June. Spitfire pilot Sgt Ron Stillwell of 65 Squadron had suffered engine trouble, bailed out and spent two hours in the water before being picked up.

Bob flew a Defiant for the first time at the end of July. His pilots were disillusioned with the type's performance, its high stalling speed and wide turning circle. He found that in terms of speed at least, it had the edge over the Lysander – but there were obvious disadvantages. Although it was powered by a Rolls-Royce Merlin engine, the added weight of the heavy, four-gun turret plus that of the air gunner made the aircraft slow climbing and less manoeuvrable. Modifications had been carried out to the wings to accommodate the Type 'M' dinghy, but it was still only capable of carrying just two of them, one under each wing.

Something more worried Bob. Compared with the Lysander's ability to manoeuvre, the Defiant's movements were sluggish. The possibility was they would be easier targets for the Focke-Wulfs and Messerschmitts than the slower but more nimble Lysanders. Time would tell, but time was at a premium. For now, by increasing 277 Squadron's numerical strength, it was beneficial to have the Defiants around until something better came along. Hopefully in the near future these would be Spitfires, which could defend themselves on equal terms if necessary. If Skrine's forewarning concerning *Jubilee* was right, every plane they had needed to be made ready quickly. Bob flew the Major back to Croydon in Defiant AA302 on 2 August.

In the meantime, with the approval of Operation *Jubilee* by the Chiefs of Staff on 27 July, troops and naval vessels gravitated back to the Isle of Wight and their previous stations. Total strength for *Jubilee* was approximately 6,100 troops – 5,000 of them Canadians.

Across the Channel, the Germans were anticipating it was likely there would be some form of hostile move against the French coast during the summer of 1942, but they could only guess at exactly how, where and when it would take place. They did know, however, the most likely times when the tides and weather might favour such a venture if it came from the sea. In August, the most favourable period would be between the 18th and 23rd. They were not far out. *Jubilee* was set for the 19th.

As before, Hawkinge became a host station. Like all the other airfields in the southeast, Bob implemented a strict security cordon around the base. Activities in and around the aerodrome were reduced to a minimum with everyone entering the station being scrutinised and their passes inspected.

Before the raid took place Bob was there to welcome in the two visiting Spitfire squadrons and they were quickly dispersed with typical efficiency. The Spitfire Vbs of No.416 RCAF Squadron (City of Oshawa) were the first to touch down. Commanded by S/Ldr Leader L. V. Chadburn, his unit had only been operational since February. The other, No.616 (South Yorkshire) Squadron from Great Sampford, arrived that same day with its high altitude Spitfire VIs. No.616 had been the last auxiliary squadron to be formed in back 1938 and now had S/Ldr H. L. I. Brown DFC commanding.

During the run-up to 19 August, Hawkinge's No.91 Squadron carried out its usual Jim Crow reconnaissance flights over the Channel between Le Havre and Ostend while the two visiting squadrons provided top cover. With three Spitfire squadrons operating from the airfield and hangar space still limited, it was decided that, except for a few to stay behind, it would be better for most of 277 Squadron to operate from Shoreham during the raid.

On the eve of the battle, movements of personnel to and from base were completely cancelled and special precautions put in place. At 5.30 p.m., all pilots were called to the briefing room where they waited in an atmosphere that was quite different from normal. A number of unfamiliar officers were there. Something was brewing. There was complete silence when Bob and the other senior officers walked in laden with maps and papers.

The briefing began with Bob's dramatic announcement that a Division of Canadian troops and commandos would land on French soil at Dieppe at dawn the next morning. When the pilots heard this there was a wave of enthusiastic excitement. At last the Continent was being invaded – but that all changed when it was added that the troops would re-embark and return to England at 1100 hours the very same morning! There was groaning and mumbling until they were brought back to order. It would be a raid in force, they were told, the largest of the war so far.

Details of the operation followed. Before dawn, squadrons of Hurricane would bomb and machine-gun the German coastal positions. At the same time, Bostons would lay smoke to cover the commandos as they landed to the east and west of the town to silence the defending gun batteries. Passing through a channel cleared by minesweepers, an entire fleet of special landing craft would bring the Canadians and their supporting tanks right onto the Dieppe beaches.

The other officers took their turns to add further details. The RAF would provide continuous protection for the troops and ships during the raid and particularly afterwards as they withdrew to England in the afternoon. It was chance at last to engage the Huns in the air on 'our terms' for a change, they said. Strong *Luftwaffe* reaction was expected but there would be nearly fifty squadrons of Spitfires in the air to take care of that. With a few exceptions these would provide the vital air cover for the raid, for escorting Blenheim and Boston bombers, and to cover the Hurricane fighter-bombers. Air cover would have to be continuous so each Spitfire squadron would have to fly up to four ops throughout the day. It was a maximum effort. There would be new Typhoons and Mustangs about too. As for ASR, Lysanders, Walruses and Defiants would have the job of backing up the vital rescue launches and they would be flying from bases all around the coast.

After take-off times for the first sorties were given, Bob closed the session by informing everyone present that the airfield was now completely sealed off and the telephones were cut off except on his own personal order.

When the pilots left the briefing, each squadron leader and his flight commanders quickly drew up the order of battle for the day's missions. Following that they went to the mess for a light dinner and spent the rest of the evening digesting what was about to take place, quietly talking to each other or privately musing over it all in their own thoughts.

The 19th finally arrived. At 06.00 hours, three Spitfires from No.91 were the first to take off, followed an hour later by 416 and 616 Squadrons. All of them were destined to tangle with the Focke-Wulfs.

Few German aircraft were seen in the initial stages of the landings as Spitfire squadrons swarmed over the whole area in a protective blanket but as the day wore on, packs of FW190s and Dornier bombers appeared. Like the other forward airfields in England's south-east, Hawkinge became a vital focal point for dozens of fighters as they returned for refuelling, rearming and making a fast turnaround – and it was a sanctuary for those seeking safety. Some of these were from the American Eagle squadrons based at Biggin Hill.

Unlike Hawkinge's two visiting Spitfire squadrons, No.91 had the task of carrying out anti-shipping patrols between Ostend and Le Havre. As they searched for E-boats or any other vessels that could interfere with the Dieppe landings, they were not involved directly in the fighting and spent most of the time searching for dinghies in the water and escorting rescue launches. During his Jim Crow to Ostend, P/O A. M. Le Maire, a Belgian, was attacked by two FW190s but managed to escape, however his aircraft was damaged while landing. Despite this, Le Maire was up again late in the afternoon with P/O I. Matthew searching for a high-speed launch. They found eight FW190s attacking another launch, which was already on fire. As the Spitfire pilots manoeuvred to attack, the Focke-Wulfs flew off. Altogether, 91 Squadron flew seventy-three sorties consisting of Jim Crows, ASR patrols and escort flights. One Spitfire was lost when Sgt C. H. Evans' machine suffered engine trouble and he had to bail out. An aircraft of 277 Squadron was scrambled from Hawkinge. It directed a rescue launch to Evans' position and he was recovered uninjured from the water.

The Canadians of 416 Squadron flew four covering missions during the day and claimed three FW190s destroyed, one Ju88 probably destroyed and six Ju88s and a Focke-Wulf damaged. One Spitfire was badly damaged but not by enemy action. As P/O P. G. Blades was taking off his aircraft struck an unseen depression in the grass, which damaged the wheels and they would not close properly. He had to abort and while touching down the undercarriage collapsed completely.

No.616 Squadron flew four missions too. It was credited with a Do217 and a FW190 destroyed and nine Focke-Wulfs damaged. Two Spitfires were lost, both shot down by FW190s: Sgt N. W. J. Coldray, a Rhodesian, was lost but F/Lt J. S. Fifield bailed out and was rescued by a minesweeper. In the late evening, Sgt N. G. Welch's Spitfire was damaged by a 190 but he managed to crash-land safely in a field just east of the airfield.

Like all the spread-out ASR units, 277 Squadron was kept busy throughout the day. One Walrus found a dinghy with two men on board and a third clinging to the side. They were the three crewmembers of a Boston that had been downed by a Focke-Wulf. The Walrus crew was able to direct a rescue launch (HSL442) to pick them all up. Not so fortunate was the pilot of a Spitfire, which was seen to crash into the sea. Although the Walrus circled the spot as long as it could, there was no sign of the airman. One Defiant was attacked by a Messerschmitt 109F but its gunner managed to get in a good burst of fire and he claimed the 109 as damaged. Another German fighter chased a Lysander inland but thanks to the Lysander's manoeuvrability, it was able to hug the terrain and evade the attacks.

Despite the quality of the air umbrella, Operation *Jubilee* turned into a disaster. The element of surprise that was so essential for success was compromised in the dark, early hours of the morning when the British fleet on its way to Dieppe unexpectedly encountered a German coastal convoy including armed trawlers. In the clash, there were casualties on both sides and a *Kriegsmarine* sub chaser, the UJ-1404, was sunk.

Regardless of the probability that the German defences would have been alerted, it was too late to turn back. The landings went ahead. The frontal assaults were subjected to murderous crossfire. Almost none of the targeted installations were reached and when the time came to withdraw only a proportion of the landing force could be evacuated. Allied casualties were heavy. Of 6,086 men who made it ashore, 3,623 (almost 60%) were either killed, wounded or captured[2] and all of the thirty tanks were lost. The Royal Navy lost thirty-three landing craft and a destroyer. On the other side, the casualties of the German defenders amounted to 311 killed and 280 wounded.

By the end of the day, the RAF and the *Luftwaffe* had fought what was regarded as the greatest air battle since the dark days of the Battle of Britain in 1940. Despite the tragic losses suffered by the Canadian troops on the ground, the RAF claimed victory in the air by shooting down ninety-six German aircraft for the loss of 106 of its own aircraft, at least thirty-two of these to flak or through accidents.[3] After the war it was discovered that *Luftwaffe* losses were actually twenty-three FW190s and twenty-five Dornier Do 217s, plus another twenty-four aircraft seriously damaged. Thirteen pilots were killed and seven wounded.

Relatively few German aircraft managed to penetrate the air shield but the headquarters ship, HMS *Calpe*, was bombed by Dornier Do217s and strafed by a FW190. Among the casualties on board was A/Cdr Adrian Cole who was wounded but his injuries were not life threatening.

A number of Australians were scattered throughout the various RAF units involved. Among these, F/Lt Tony Gaze of 616 Squadron destroyed a Do217; P/O C. Watson of 174 (Hurricane IIB) Squadron was shot down into the harbour and captured; Air gunner Sgt Henry Neville of 13 Squadron was killed when his Blenheim IV, V5380, was destroyed by flak; and Tasmanian navigator P/O D. Walch's Boston III of 226 Squadron, although damaged, returned safely. Don Walch and his crewmates set great faith in the ability of the crest painted on their Boston, Z2295/MQ-A, to bring them back, and it did. Indicating their nationalities, the crest consisted of a kangaroo, a kiwi and a Welsh dragon all on a boomerang.

In terms of personnel, RAF losses amounted to sixty-two killed, thirty wounded and seventeen captured. As Bob Bungey's attachment to *Rutter* and *Jubilee* testified, the ASR service was an important element in the planning of the raid. As well as the aircraft, thirty-four rescue launches were employed and these were among the last vessels to leave the Dieppe battle area, having waited as long as possible in case of a final late rescue call. Spitfires from 91 Squadron were still escorting launches back to England well after 6.30 p.m. About fifty distress calls were investigated by the launches and this resulted in the recovery of fifteen airmen, mostly fighter pilots. Three ASR boats were lost.

Among other lessons, the Dieppe raid proved the absolute necessity for much bigger and better preparations for air cover. It was not sufficient to simply bring in a couple of extra squadrons to each of the existing forward aerodromes for a stay of a few days. More airfields for the shorter range fighters and light bombers were needed – scores of them. They would have to be short-term airstrips because they would probably not be needed after the Continent was successfully invaded. Known as advanced landing grounds, they had to be located mostly in the south and east of England for the use of the newly arriving USAAF as well as the RAF.

In Kent, inspections were already going on to find likely sites around Hawkinge even during the lead up to Operation *Jubilee*. Out of twenty-three that were eventually built before the 1944 landings in Normandy, eleven were located in the county.

20

'Leave'

With the Dieppe raid over and the debriefings completed, the visiting Spitfire squadrons departed for their home bases leaving Hawkinge to the resident flights of 91 and 277 Squadrons. No.416 Squadron returned to Martlesham Heath and 616 went back to Great Sampford but in September it transferred to the Tangmere Wing. Meanwhile, Bob Bungey used one of the Defiants to take S/Ldr Downes, who had been at Hawkinge at the same time as Major Skrine, across to Redhill.

Although after *Jubilee* the focus of the British war effort shifted to North Africa with General Montgomery's victory at El Alamein and the Anglo/American landings (Operation *Torch*) at Algiers, Oran and three points on the Moroccan coast, there was nevertheless business as usual on the Channel Front. Meanwhile, Bob's and 277's dissatisfaction with the Defiants persisted. This disappointment was reflected in all of the ASR squadrons and nobody was surprised to see Defiants start to be phased out. The first Spitfire arrived at Hawkinge for 277 Squadron in December. It was an earlier Mk II version but even so still an infinite improvement over the Defiant.

AVM Trafford Leigh-Mallory visited Hawkinge early in November and presented 91 Squadron's official badge to S/Ldr Demozay. It carried an appropriate motto, 'We Seek Alone'. Only half of the squadron, 'B' Flight, was residing at Hawkinge, its 'A' Flight was at nearby Lympne. On the 23rd, 'B' Flight moved over to Lympne and the squadron was united at last.

Entries in Bob's Flying Log Book suggest that he may have moved to Lympne around this time too, but he could have transferred across later in December. Aside from normal work associated with administration and the routines of the two squadrons, Bob had other important decisions to make. They could no longer be put off because of temporary appointments and jobs associated with Special Operations.

Bob's RAF short service commission was ending in August and he had to choose whether he would extend this into a longer RAF commission for the duration of hostilities, or rejoin the RAAF and return to Australia as per the terms of the original short service commission contract. His head and his heart were in two different places. Prospects of promotion and advancement in the RAF were very promising, especially after his Combined Operations experience, and there were possibilities of a career after the war that could take him anywhere in the world. On the other hand, there were some very special people waiting for him in Australia.

What is known is that on 26 August at Hawkinge he received an administrative transfer to the Reserve of Air Force Officers (RAFO), but was retained for duty on the Royal Air Force Active List. He also flew the base's Magister to Biggin Hill where he apparently received some special verbal instructions before returning. These were directions to apply for 'leave' to go to Ireland, Eire in particular. He jotted them down on paper. There were two addresses with other details in-between:

Belle Ville Park,
Cappoquin,
County Waterford
* * *
Leave Pass to be endorsed
Giving permission to travel in Eire
* * *
Crossing Holy-Head [*sic*] – Kingstown
* * *
Cartridges. 200.
* * *
Eric Hall,
37 South Mall,
Cork.
Solicitor.

The following day as he awaited approval from No.11 Group via the Air Ministry, he arranged for Jean Demozay to be placed in temporary command of Hawkinge for two weeks during his absence.

His leave was approved on the 29th. Interestingly, his contact person and contract address on the pass whilst on leave were put down as:

C/o Maj. Skrine,
Belleville Park,
Cappoquin Co Waterford,
EIRE.

That Major Skrine's name was included with the address on the pass was significant. While Bob's reasons for going to Eire obviously involved Eric Hall the solicitor, with Combined Operations planner Walter Skrine involved this could not have been just ordinary 'leave'. It was undoubtedly something special required by Combined Operations command, but why would Bob have been chosen to go there?

He was certainly familiar with Ireland – or parts of it. He had been stationed near Belfast for two months with 226 Squadron after it withdrew from France in June 1940. That was before he had volunteered for Fighter Command.

Why 200 cartridges, presumably for his service revolver? This was enough ammunition for Bob to load and reload his Enfield .38-inch six-chamber firearm more than thirty times. Was it a necessary precaution? If so, what was the danger? Was it because the Irish Republican Army (IRA) had become active again?

The IRA had already campaigned against British rule in Northern Ireland during 1939–40.[1] Then, early in 1942, the prime minister of the Irish Free State, Eamon de Valera, complained about the influx of US soldiers into Northern Ireland. From his viewpoint, were they there solely as part of the build-up for combined operations against Nazi Germany? The Eire government's objections over this so-called 'occupation' by foreign troops encouraged the IRA in March to reorganise and approve a new campaign against the British military in Northern Ireland.

During the ensuing months, attacks were made against the Royal Ulster Constabulary (RUC) in Strabane, Dungannon and Belfast, which resulted in the death of two RUC constables and the wounding of two others. Six members of the IRA were arrested during the Belfast incident, which happened on Easter Sunday, and these men were sentenced to death by hanging for the murder of one of the constables. The sentences provoked hostile Irish public reaction. A petition was organised calling for mercy and a reprieve. There were some 200,000 signatures. Several days before 2 September, the date set for the executions, all the sentences were commuted save that of one man, Tom Williams.

At the same time as Bob was organising his 'leave', more trouble was brewing. IRA preparations were already underway should the hanging proceed. On the night of 30/31 August, IRA groups began to transfer arms into Northern Ireland. In one instance, two trucks were used to transport 3 tons of material over the border into Newry, County Down. They passed through RUC checkpoints without incident. The weapons were stored in a barn on a farm outside Hannahstown, County Antrim. Their distribution was set to begin but an IRA member sent to help with this was followed to the farm by members of the RUC who then raided the building. In the ensuing gun battle, one IRA man was shot dead and the arms were seized. Meanwhile, other similar shipments into Northern Ireland remained undetected.

Little is known about Bob's movements while on 'leave' in Ireland. Although 'Flying Duties' were noted on his leave pass, no flying was recorded in his Flying Log Book. His pass was stamped on the back showing that he travelled by ferry from Holyhead in Wales to Dun Laoghaire on 1 September. There is no doubt that the authorities were aware of the strong likelihood the IRA would resort to violent action if Tom Williams' execution was carried out. It was prudent for any British officer to take precautions if going anywhere in the twenty-six counties of the Irish Republic or the six counties of the Northern Ireland with their all-important deep water harbours still 'ruled' by the British. Clearly, Bob was travelling into harm's way and being properly armed was a necessary precaution.

Tom Williams was hanged at Crumlim Road Gaol, Belfast, on 2 September at 8.00 a.m. The first scheduled attack by twenty IRA members took place soon afterwards against a British Army barracks in Crossmaglen, County Armagh, in the hope of capturing a British officer and hanging him. Following this raid, the RUC and Irish Special Branch stepped up their efforts against the IRA. This led to a series of arrests and the discovery of a number of arms caches.

Violence escalated. Next day the front of a police barracks in Randaistown, County Antrim, was demolished by a mine and one RUC sergeant was injured. On the 4th, a mine failed to detonate during an attack on the RUC barracks in Belleek, County Fermanagh, and that same day in Belfast the ambushing of an IRA patrol by the police resulted in one IRA man being wounded. On 5 September, two of the RUC were killed in Clady, County Tyrone, and during a failed attack in Belfast another IRA member was wounded.

Four days later, an Irish Special Branch officer who was a former member of the IRA was shot dead outside his home in Ballyboden, County Dublin, by three IRA members. This action showed that the violence was spreading into Eire itself.

On 10 September, two members of Belfast IRA were captured when their house was surrounded.[2] The following day was the 11th, and it must have been a very relieved Bob Bungey who at last left Ireland and returned to Wales, again travelling by ferry. On reaching Holyhead, he apparently received fresh instructions to go to London. On the back of his leave pass he pencilled the address of a hotel in Queens Gate, South Kensington, where he had accommodation waiting or had to report. Exactly what Bob's 'leave' really entailed remains open to speculation, but it obviously involved being placed into an alien environment – a potentially threatening and stressful alien environment away from of his more natural element, the air.

This was also the day that Jean Demozay resumed his duties as CO of 91 Squadron, but it was not Bob who took back command of Hawkinge once more. With Bob in transit to Central London, W/Cdr R. F. Atkin temporarily stepped in at Hawkinge. Like the Frenchman, he too only held the position for a fortnight. The permanent appointment finally went to W/Cdr E. C. Jones DSO DFC who took office on 25 September.

Bob meanwhile did, in fact, return to Hawkinge sometime before the 24th as a supernumerary wing commander. His Flying Log Book shows that on the 24th he flew Defiant AA302, a machine he had flown several times before during August, to RAF Halton and back.

Thereafter, he only flew the Tiger Moth. Once each in October and November, he travelled via Benson to visit Sybil's family at Wallingford. He took the Tiger Moth to Benson again on 24 December and this time spent the Christmas period with them.

When he left Benson again on the 28th, before turning onto course for Kent he very likely followed the Thames to the Wallingford Bridge again for one last time. As he passed overhead, the familiar small, lone figure wasn't there to wave him off like before. Then, instead of returning to Hawkinge, he flew to the satellite airfield at Lympne.

* * *

Bob's attachment to Hawkinge as a supernumerary wing commander ceased officially on 9 January 1943 and he transferred to No.51 OTU at Twinwoods (Twinwood Farm) in Bedfordshire. Twinwood Farm was a satellite airfield for Cranfield located about 4 miles north of Bedford itself. No.51 OTU had been set up to train night fighter crews and its equipment there included Bristol Blenheims and Bisleys, and a few Douglas Havocs for Turbinlite interception.

Until now Bob had exclusively flown single-engined types. Probably with an eye to flying in the future, perhaps even thinking of a career in commercial aviation after the war, he began to check out on twin-engined Bisleys before returning home to Australia.

The Bisley was the last version of the Bristol Blenheim, the main Blenheim variant after the Mk I and Mk IV. Originally it was designated as the Bisley Mk I, but the new name was officially discarded for Blenheim Mk V by the Air Ministry in January 1942. Nevertheless, the Bisley name persisted among RAF crews to differentiate it from the earlier machines. It was proposed to be a specialised close tactical support version with the alternative duties of low level fighter or dual-control trainer.

In its initial form the Bisley had a 'solid' long-nose section containing four fixed, forward-firing 0.303-in Browning machine guns, each fed by a total of 1,000 rounds of ammunition; a dorsal turret with two Brownings; and an improved windscreen. The whole cockpit was externally protected by some 600-lb weight of detachable armour plate, and more armour plating was provided for the gunner's dorsal cockpit/turret.

Later, the official specification was modified, calling for a high-level bombing potential in addition to the low-level direct support role. For this additional task the solid nose was revised to permit the four-gun battery to be swapped for a navigating/bomb aiming compartment with an offset aiming window and an under-nose, rearward-firing twin Browning mounting was added for rear defence. High-level bombing versions were stripped of armour plating, but the addition of wide-ranging radio and oxygen equipment created a similar weight penalty, making it slower and less manoeuvrable than the earlier Mk IV. Production variants of the Mk V included the tropicalised Mk VD, the most produced version, and the Mk. VC, a dual-control trainer.

Bob's Log Book does not reveal on which version he gained experience but most likely it was the Mk VC trainer. Firstly, a F/Lt Innes demonstrated the controls to him on the 13th, and then Bob took over for the next hour and twenty minutes. Finally, he took the machine up solo for another hour to finish off the day. Over the next ten days as the weather permitted, he flew the Bisley on practice flights, except for two flights at the controls of a Blenheim IV, the last being a night flying test taking place on the 24th. It was his final flight as a member of the RAF.

His signature in his Flying Log Book read 'R.W. Bungey, W/C.' for the last time. The following day he transferred to the RAAF Reserve.

It was time to go home to Sybil and Richard.

21

Home

These days we have a much healthier understanding of what is known as post-traumatic stress disorder, or PTSD. In 1943 we didn't.

These days we know that PTSD can strike down anyone, especially if they have been exposed to traumatic situations that threatened life and safety, or the life and safety of those around them. It might be triggered by a car accident or some other serious incident, or incidents, such as physical assault, or torture, or disasters such as bushfires or floods – or, of course, war. The resulting intense feelings of horror, helplessness or hopelessness can surge without warning.

By the time Bob Bungey left England, he had been exposed to far in excess of what could be considered a normal quota of stress. He had done his fair share – more than his fair share. He had clocked up an impressive total of 260.20 hours of operational flying time. These had been mostly in Spitfires and Hurricanes over convoys, on defensive patrols, high-offensive patrols and low-offensive patrols – but 45.20 hours of them had been in France in those outclassed and obsolete Fairey Battles. He had destroyed and damaged enemy aircraft and nearly been destroyed and damaged himself, surviving to ditch in water that was so thankfully shallow. And then there was Hawkinge, and Cowes, and Ireland...

For more than three years anxiety and pressure had been his constant companions in a terrible, unrelenting war that seemed never-ending, almost overwhelming. Friendships forged in battle had been lost. So many, too many, had been lost. And it could happen all over again against the Japanese.

Given what did happen next, there is no doubt that at the time he departed, Bob was already struggling with PTSD's menacing, dreadful grasp.

When the Melbourne Express arrived in Adelaide on 6 May 1943, Bob Bungey disembarked to find reporters and a press photographer waiting. They approached and informed him they were there to greet an air force VIP. Bob did not acknowledge who he was and told them that the VIP was on the other end of the train. He even denied that his name was Bungey. Then, as they moved off, he tried to slip quietly away unnoticed. He hadn't managed to make good his escape before they realised they had been duped and hurried back. He was photographed but he still declined to be interviewed.

Adelaide's press was undaunted. His highly successful leadership of the first Australian Spitfire squadron was a matter of great pride – not just for Adelaide, but for the nation as well. It would not be right and proper for this local hero to be allowed to avoid the public accolades and honours due to him.

6 May 1943.

WING COMMANDER (BOB) BUNGEY DFC RETURNS HOME.

Glenelg and Somerton are proud of Wing Commander Bob Bungey DFC, who has returned home after rendering outstanding service overseas. Bob is remembered by many as a shy lad, who left here over six years ago.

Councillor Anderson reminded members of the Glenelg Council at their last meeting that Wing Commander Bungey was home once more, and agreed that he was the same unspoilt young man, with a retiring nature, as residents remembered him in his younger days. Wing Commander Bungey, said the Councillor, was outstanding in leadership as the Officer in Charge of the First Australian Spitfire Squadron, and has rendered exceptional service to the Empire, proving without question of doubt that he had outstanding ability.

The Mayor, (Mr. Frank Smith MP) said he was glad the Councillor had brought Wing Commander Bungey's name before members that evening, because he (the Mayor) and the Town Clerk (Mr. F. A. Lewis) had only that morning called to see the Wing Commander and Mrs. Bungey, but had found them in the midst of moving from Mr. and Mrs. Bungey, senior's residence to a maisonette the young couple had secured at Somerton.

'The Town Clerk and I will be calling again on Wing Commander and Mrs. Bungey on Friday next,' said the Mayor. 'We feel that Bob should not be allowed to come home unnoticed. We are making a point of letting him know how much the town appreciates his wonderful war service. We are proud of his accomplishments and proud to have both him and his wife as residents of the district.' (Applause)

PARLIAMENT HOUSE LUNCHEON

The Mayor later announced that he had arranged a luncheon at Parliament House, for tomorrow (Friday, May 28), in honour of Wing Commander Bungey, when a number of prominent Glenelg residents would be present to welcome him back to Australia. The party will meet in the Premier's Room prior to the luncheon.[1]

Sybil and Bob never made it to the luncheon.

* * *

Bob Bungey had relinquished his RAF commission on 25 January 1943, immediately after qualifying on twin-engined aircraft at Twinwoods. Just prior to leaving for Australia, his appointment to the RAAF Reserve presented a problem he did not anticipate with regard to his rank.

Gordon Olive, Bob's comrade from the old Point Cook days and when their paths crossed again later at Tangmere, faced a similar situation when he also applied to rejoin the RAAF:

When I ... visited the Australian Air Force Overseas Headquarters [in London], they seemed very keen to avail themselves of my experience. This to date was eighteen months operational experience on Spitfires almost entirely in the south-east corner of England – in addition almost a year's operations on nightfighters whilst I was a few months in the control room and nine months on training fighter pilots. This meant I'd had experience that only a few men in the RAF at this stage of the war could claim.

There was only one difficulty and that was a personal one. I had been a wing-commander for nearly eighteen months in the RAF and there was doubt that I could transfer with that rank to the RAAF as my rank was acting. However, I was assured that as I had received my acting rank on operations I would be entitled to retain it until I was re-employed in Australia. Later, I found this to be mere sales talk.

My transfer to the RAAF turned out to be a fairly simple affair and almost before I knew what was happening I found myself issued with the dark blue Australian uniform and all the trimmings. A certain amount of correspondence had gone back and forth to Australia concerning my transfer and it was said that the RAAF in Australia was very much in need of somebody with wide experience both on operations and on control of operations for staff duties...[2]

This was the state of affairs Bob ran into. Instead of a warm welcome and the retention of his rank (as had been the case for the prewar Australian short service commission volunteers when they came to England and were welcomed by the RAF), he was informed he would be reduced in rank (possibly by two levels) and lose seniority. The probability of finding himself subservient to officers with far less experience or to men who had not flown since the 1914–18 war led him to protest. His operational flying experience of bombers and fighters and his acknowledged gifts as a successful squadron leader and at times wing leader, to say nothing of his wide knowledge of administration and of combined operations, could be utilised to better advantage. His protest was in vain. He was ordered to return to Australia for service with the RAAF.

Something similar had happened to Bluey Truscott as well, although Bluey had never been a member of the RAF. In January 1942 he had been promoted to the rank of acting squadron leader in order to lead 452 Squadron. The following March he was posted back to Australia where he received a hero's welcome because of his ace status and the publicity he had received. When RAAF authorities attempted to reduce him to his substantive rank of flight lieutenant because there were no squadron commander vacancies available, there was a public outcry. The outcome was that he was allowed to retain his rank and was posted to New Guinea as a supernumerary squadron leader in 76 Squadron RAAF.

Only Bob's nearest friends were aware of his belief that he had been unjustly treated. They agreed he *had* been shabbily treated by the authorities – and it *did* rankle him to the point where he confided to one friend that he had been 'dumped and used up'.[3]

Word of what was happening to him eventually reached an anonymous 'Melbourne knight'. It is thought that this man was possibly Sir Charles McCann who controlled the South Australian Fighting Forces Comforts Fund in London. His office was a 'clearing house' for South Australian airmen when on leave. He knew Bob well and was a supporter of his work with 452 Squadron. He could also have been Sir Keith Murdoch who knew Bob and 452 Squadron equally well and was also a supporter. It was because of the influence of this benefactor that Bob was allowed to return home wearing his RAF uniform and rank. What was going to happen afterwards had to be resolved by the RAAF at home.[4]

Bob's route back to Australia was via Canada, with at least one impromptu visit over the border to the USA while in transit. By the time his ship reached Melbourne early in May the momentum of the war had changed, swinging in favour of the Allies. More than two years of destruction and hard fighting were ahead before the end, but here it seemed that Australia was already at peace. What was an amazing sight the shoreline across Port Phillip Bay presented to those returning home as it became a mass of lights after dark; how unlike a real war zone and the nightly blackouts of England!

But the war's malevolent presence was not far away. Jolting news waited. Bluey Truscott was dead.

After being posted to New Guinea in 76 Squadron, Truscott had flown P-40 Kittyhawks during the battle of Milne Bay in August/September 1942, and he became the squadron commander when the CO, S/Ldr Peter Turnbull, was killed. He led the unit back to Australia at the end of the year. Over Darwin during the night of 20/21 January 1943, he intercepted three Japanese bombers and shot one (a Mitsubishi G4M Betty) down, to bring his score up to fifteen destroyed, plus three probables and three damaged. It was his last victory. On 28 March, while making a mock attack on a Catalina flying boat that he was escorting low over the sea, he misjudged his height and flew straight into the water. His end was eerily similar to that of his best mate, Paddy Finucane.[5]

There was more. Ray 'Throttle' Thorold Smith had gone too. He was officially listed as 'missing, believed killed'. In England the tall gangling Sydneysider had taken over 452 Squadron from Bluey Truscott. He then brought it to Australia and led it to Darwin as part of the new defending 'Churchill' Spitfire Wing. His aircraft had completely disappeared on 15 March during a heavy raid on the Northern Territory's capital.[6]

Bob could only wonder just how many of the 452 Squadron originals were still alive.

All this had happened in March as Bob was coming home. On leaving the ship, he reported to the RAAF's Transit Depot at the Melbourne Cricket Ground (MCG) to present his credentials to the AOC. There he was granted leave and offered the train trip to Adelaide where he would report to

No.4 Embarkation Depot. He would be issued with new dark blue RAAF clothing, which would include two uniforms adorned with squadron leader's stripes. When his leave was over, he would be required to wear these in his new role as a squadron leader flying instructor. It must have been a very pensive Bob Bungey that boarded the train to Adelaide.

Except for his brother, David, now a sergeant in the RAAF and stationed in New South Wales, Bob found everyone at Tarlton Street, Somerton waiting, for him – his parents, Ernest and Ada, and sister, Pauline, all welcoming him home … and at long, long last Sybil!

Dear Sybil. She was as radiant as ever and looking more grown up than he remembered, more mature. Beautiful!

And for the first time here was Richard, his son, a fine and sturdy boy of thirteen months. But the boy did not know him. How could he? They had never met before. That would change. There would be plenty of time to alter that. With Richard's first smile Bob knew there would be good times ahead, happy times for them all. Now for a while they could relax and be happy – at peace again with the world. He and Richard could play and they could do all the normal things young families did. With Richard in the stroller, he and Sybil could walk down to the beach edging Holdfast Bay. Walking alongside that bright yellow sand and beautifully clear, calm water in the autumn sunshine, what could be better? The days were getting cooler. To the right they could go to Glenelg; to the left, Brighton.

When they did go walking, they took the family's fox terrier with them. As a pup he had been named 'Bomber' in honour of Bob's early days in the RAF. The dog and Bob had bonded naturally at once despite Bob's six-year absence.

Sometimes though, when they returned from their strolls, Sybil looked very tired and her legs and feet were prone to swelling. At times she did not seem at all well.

From among the gifts for his family Bob had brought home from England, he produced a fine picture of a Spitfire. Spitfires were the best planes in the world, he said, and he had flown them, and actually commanded a whole squadron of them! The picture was duly framed and given pride of place on a wall.[7]

On occasion while on their walks, Bob and Sybil took the opportunity to drop into the nearby office of an old friend of the family, W. E. Taplin, who was apparently of English extraction. They used to 'delight in talking of England,' Mr Taplin remembered later. Bob also mentioned that he hoped to play a big part in commercial aviation after the war.

David arrived home on leave from the RAAF Base at Mildura on the 14th and the two brothers had a joyful reunion. The following day they went to a football match and afterwards made their way across the sand dunes to the beach. The sand was not hot underfoot in May but the water was still warm enough for swimming, certainly, for Bob, not as cold as the water of the River Thames at Wallingford. It is not known if they swam to the Glenelg Bathing Box as they had done so many times before. Was there a tennis ball for the dog? They decided to swim again the next day.

For the first time it really did seem there were good times ahead.

With everyone home, the house at Tarlton Street was overcrowded. At the same time, Sybil and Bob were keen to set up a place they could call their own, even though she and Richard would be on their own when Bob's leave ended. Fortunately, in answer to their wishes, a maisonette was found to be available just blocks away at 20 Walkers Road in the same suburb. It was too good an opportunity to miss. They seized their chance immediately and agreed to rent.

David was still available to help them move in on the 18th, but it was only two days before he was due to depart again for Mildura. The two brothers played tennis the day before he had to go. Their friendly rivalry was still there, just as it had always been while they were growing up.

But Bob was concerned about Sybil. She seemed to be coming down with the flu or something and winter was not far off. Nor was she eating well; she wascomplaining of nausea and of feeling too full. Sometimes she felt discomfort in her mid-and lower back but the pain would go away after a while.

It was only a week later, not long after he returned to Mildura, that David received shocking news. Sybil had suddenly collapsed while at Walkers Road and been rushed to Patawilya Private Hospital in Weewanda Street, Glenelg. She was attended by the family's regular physician, Dr Kenneth Steele, but there was little that could be done. She passed away during the night, just a few hours after her admission. It had happened on Thursday, the day before they were scheduled to attend the Parliament House luncheon in Bob's honour.

The diagnosis in the medical report released afterwards recorded that the immediate cause of her death was a cerebral haemorrhage, but it also revealed that she had been unwell for a protracted period of time. For at least a couple of months she had been suffering from acute nephritis, a condition often caused by some sort of infection, or more commonly by an autoimmune disorder. This frequently had a damaging impact on major organs like the kidneys – but there was another complication as well. Most recently, over the last month, her malady had been compounded by bacterial endocarditis, an infection resulting in inflammation of the valves of the heart. Sybil was only twenty-four but she had been in 'indifferent health' for quite some time.

The whole family was shocked, as were Sybil's family and friends in Wallingford when they learned what had happened. No one was more devastated than Bob, but true to his stoic nature, he did not let it show.

Sybil Bungey's funeral was held in St Peter's Church, Glenelg, and the burial followed at St Jude's Cemetery, Brighton. At the burial service Bob stepped forward in front of the others, a solitary figure dressed in full uniform, and saluted the coffin as it was lowered to its final rest. Afterwards, he refused to accompany the others who were returning to the family home. He needed to be alone.

Bob made his way to the beach and walked back by himself, thinking of Sybil. They'd only had three precious weeks together. Three weeks! He had to think. If only they could have the time over again so they could be together come what may – but she was gone. Only three weeks! It seemed that all those he cared about were no more – Leslie… Pyker… Bedouin… Paddy… Bluey… and so many others… And now Sybil! Three weeks!

There was much that had to be done to put their affairs in order. What about Dick? What would happen to his son when his leave was over and he had to report back for duty? He'd already been granted one extension of time and had requested another. Soon he would be expected to start training new pilots, probably at Mildura, but his heart would never be in it. How could it be? And when he came home Richard would not know him all over again! What if he was posted onto operations again and this time did not return at all? Richard would be left alone in the world. Richard was all he had now. They should be together.

The only hope was for his mother and father to care for Richard until he could resign from the RAAF. They both loved their little grandson dearly, but Ada was not in a fit state of health herself. How could she properly care for an active youngster? She would not last three months. Then, when she was laid up herself there would be a bigger mess than ever! If she was younger and in better health, nothing would give him greater pride and joy than to watch Dick grow up in her care.

There was no point staying on in the new accommodation at Walkers Road. Bob and Richard moved back to Tarlton Street on 5 June. It was Saturday. Ada was well aware of her son's worry and grief. When he spoke of his concerns at home, she insisted she would be able to care for Richard while he was away – but Bob was unconvinced.

He continued with the daily walks, taking Richard in the stroller around the streets and down to the beach. Bomber would trot along beside them. The weather was colder these days, sometimes windy and the sea not so calm with white caps showing on the swell. Sometimes he went out alone.

Late on Monday he called in once more to see Mr Taplin, who recalled:

He came to my place last Monday night. We talked till late in front of the fire of his experiences overseas. He had a number of original press photographs of the men in his squadron including Paddy Finucane and Bluey Truscott.

When he was showing me one photo he said, 'That's poor Paddy. Bluey Truscott's gone since, and so have a lot of others.'

Bungey told me that he and two others in the photograph remain alive.

Before he left that evening he said he was worried about young Dick, his son. He remarked that he had to be both father and mother to the child. If he went away, perhaps for three or four years, it would mean that the boy would not know him when he returned. He said that although it was a terrible shock when his wife died, it was all for the best, because he had been told that she would not have lived for more than three months, and might have had a lot of pain.[8]

By Wednesday Bob had made his decision. In his mind he had worked out the best method of solving the problem, a solution which to him in his present state 'was as correct and clear cut as it could be'.[9] He spent much of the day in his room writing a letter to David, explaining everything in detail to make sure all was in order. 'Dear Dave,' he started, 'This is the most difficult task I have ever had to carry out...'[10]

Bob wrote four elaborate pages before finally signing the last and placing them all in an envelope prior to putting them in his suitcase.[11]

That night he went with his father to see *Eagle Squadron*, the film showing at the nearby theatre in Glenelg. They had made the arrangement earlier because Ernest believed the film held a particular interest for his son. The introductory commentary was spoken by the widely-known American war correspondent, Quentin Reynolds, with whom Bob had been friendly in England. In it there were a number of close-ups of American fighter pilots serving with the RAF, all of whom Bob had known – but many had since been killed.

Bob seemed to thoroughly enjoy the film probably because it brought back so many memories, Ernest thought. He appeared to be in good spirits. It was midnight when they finally said good night and retired.

Late Thursday morning, Bob placed Richard in the stroller again and said goodbye to his mother before they set out on their customary walk. Bomber the fox terrier went along too. It was 11.00 a.m.

To Ada, her son seemed to be his normal self, nothing was unusual. What she did not know, and nor did anybody else, Bob had with him his .38 Enfield service revolver.

22

Miracle at Somerton

On Thursday afternoon as agriculturist William Appleby was walking home along the beach from Glenelg to Brighton something unusual attracted his attention. It was about 5.15 p.m. and he had reached the Somerton area between College Road and Downing Street. A child's stroller was standing there unattended. Was it abandoned? There seemed to be a large doll or an infant sitting in it. It was a child.

Looking around, Appleby approached slowly and then suddenly stopped, frozen to the spot. Near the stroller, a man was lying on the sand. There was blood on his head and he was not moving. He appeared to be dead. Just in front of his outstretched hand was a gun.

From where Bill Appleby was standing the child appeared to be all right but he did not go any closer. Instead he hurried off, striding towards his North Brighton home, and on arriving at the beach kiosk he telephoned Brighton Police.

Constable John Moss responded to the call and accompanied by his fellow police officer, Constable Shipway, he made his way to the beach. About midway between Downing Street and College Road, they saw the man on the sand just as Appleby had described. He was lying unmoving on his right side. He did appear to be dead. The stroller was there and so was the baby which seemed to be whimpering softly – but there was something else too. A dog! There was a small dog – a fox terrier – lying between the man and the stroller and it sat up as they drew near. It was guarding the man and the baby and it tried to attack the policemen when they came too close. Moss recalled later, 'The dog definitely did not want us to touch the baby or the father.'

With Shipway restraining the dog, Moss was able to make a closer inspection. He noted there was a head wound near the man's right temple and another wound on the other side near the left temple. A hand gun was on the sand in front of the body near the right hand. It was an Enfield six chamber revolver, standard issue for the British armed forces, but the man was dressed in civilian clothes. He looked familiar but there was nothing that could be done for him.

Next, Moss directed his attention to the child's stroller. The infant was propped up in a sitting position and was a boy judging by the clothing. He was alive but there were bloodstains on his head. On examining these more closely the constable realised there were wounds on both sides of his head. Although the boy was still alive, he was obviously badly injured.

There was no time to lose. Without delay, Moss carefully lifted the child out of the stroller and carried him to Somerton Crippled Children's Home which was nearby. The matron of the home took charge at once and immediately contacted a doctor – Dr Kenneth Steele of Glenelg. Phyllis Langley would recall later:

> When the child arrived there were no signs of fright, distress or pain. He seemed normally pleased to see us and was interested in the fire. It was only when he touched his head that he whimpered at all and that very little. There wasn't a sign of tears upon his face and it lit up with interest when he came in. I really don't think that the child had been frightened nor had he suffered. What a fine little chap...

Constable Moss in the meantime telephoned Adelaide CIB requesting the attendance of a detective at the scene of the tragedy.

Dr Steele reached the home shortly afterwards and examined the wounded child. He then arranged to have him transferred to Gambier Private Hospital in Pier Street, Glenelg. There is little doubt that the doctor was aware of who the boy was, and he was apprehensive about the likely identity of the man on the beach.

With the arrangements in place, Dr Steele accompanied Constable Moss to Somerton Beach. Light was fading. At about 6.50 p.m., from a point some distance south of College Road, he saw the man on the sand. Constable Shipway was still on duty at the scene, and so was the dog – on guard even now. Looking down at the figure lying there, Steele's worst fears were realised. He knew who he was. This was the same young man he had seen grow up and had recommended so highly for the air force seven years ago.

With mixed emotions, he began his examination. There was a wound in the head just above the right ear and another jagged wound, an exit wound, on the other side near the temple. It must have happened about three to four hours earlier. Apparently the dog must have stayed there all that time. To Constable Moss the doctor made the necessary formal declaration that life was 'extinct' and then added, 'In my opinion death was consistent with a bullet wound, and from the position of the body it could have been self-inflicted.' He found no other marks of violence.

Dr Steele then made another startling declaration, 'I identify the body of the deceased as Robert Wilton Bungey, late of No.3 Tarlton Street, Somerton. The deceased was well known to me personally.'

It was about 7.30 p.m. and dark when Detective C. Hanrahan of Adelaide CIB arrived to begin his inquiry in response to Constable Moss's telephone message. He inspected the weapon and confirmed it was a .38 Enfield service revolver. It was loaded containing four live bullets and two spent cartridges.

In his report later, Detective Hanrahan noted: 'The doctor...identified the deceased, having attended him previously and treated his wife before her death a few weeks ago...' He also wrote:

> I ascertained that the deceased was Robert Wilton Bungey, 28 years of age, widower, residing with his parents at 3 Tarlton Street, Somerton. He recently returned from England, where he held the rank of Wing Commander in the Royal Air Force, and since his return he has been attached to the Royal Australian Air Force as an Instructor. He was decorated with the DFC whilst serving abroad...
>
> ... Dr Steele stated that in his opinion the wounds would probably have caused death. He considered that it was most likely that they were self-inflicted.[1]

Detective Hanrahan made an inspection of the surrounding area and was unable to find evidence of any other disturbance or violence. His next step was to visit Tarlton Street.

The body was conveyed to the city mortuary in the police ambulance with the permission of the city coroner. Bomber the fox terrier followed the stretcher to the ambulance, and was later delivered home in a police car, but exactly when that occurred is uncertain. Nor is it precisely clear when Ernest and Ada Bungey were informed of Bob's death and of their grandson's injuries. They must have been almost overwhelmed by despair.

When Bob and Richard had not returned home by 6.00 p.m., Ada had called her husband who, in turn, had reported their absence to Glenelg Police. As well as that, Pauline had gone out during the afternoon to look for them. She made her way to the beach. Once there she had to decide which way to go – right to Glenelg or left to Brighton. She turned right. It was the wrong direction, away from where they were eventually found. That decision afterwards gave rise to a nagging thought destined to trouble members of the family for years to come. Had she gone left, would she have found them before the tragedy, in time to actually have a chance of averting what happened? It was impossible wishful thinking.

Accompanied by Constable Moss, Detective Hanrahan visited the Bungey home that night and was directed to Bob's room. He found the suitcase. Inside it he discovered the envelope which contained Bob's elaborate four-page hand written letter to David, and 'other documents' including Bob's freshly written will dated Wednesday the 9th bequeathing all of his personal effects and monies to his brother in the event of his death.

When the detective showed the documents to Ernest Bungey he confirmed that they were definitely in his son's handwriting. He related that his son was 28 years of age and was a squadron leader in the Royal Australian Air Force. He had returned to Australia about five weeks ago and was on leave at the time of his death. About a fortnight ago his wife had died and since then he appeared very worried and broken hearted but at no time did he express any intention of taking his life. Ernest had last seen him alive when he retired at midnight last night. Neither he nor Ada was aware their son had a revolver.

The family contacted David at Mildura and he immediately sought leave to return to Adelaide. He noted in his diary, 'Bob died, Richard gravely ill.' He arrived home the following day.

At the same time as David was travelling home that Friday, the fingerprint expert stationed at Adelaide, Mr Dudley Aebi, was given the Enfield revolver to examine. In his report he wrote:

Plain clothes Constable Sutherland handed to me the Service Revolver, four bullets and two cartridge cases (produced) believed to be the property of Robert Wilton Bungey. In company with finger print expert Durham I examined these articles for finger prints. Several smudged finger prints were found, but no prints that would be of use for identification purposes.

Dudley Aebi submitted his report to the Acting City Coroner, Mr. M. Ziesing, who added it to the comprehensive reports he already had on the circumstances of the tragedy prepared by Detective C. Hanrahan, plain clothes Constable Sutherland and Constable Moss. These included all the statements they had gathered as a result of their investigations. As well there was Bob's Last Will and his long letter to David. Bob had given a detailed description of his assets and possessions but by its tone there could be no doubt that it was actually a farewell letter to his brother – a final letter with such passages as:

...Since Sybil died, the question of Dick's future has been constantly going through my mind, and to me it has appeared hopeless... Had Mother been younger and enjoyed better health, nothing would have given me greater pride and joy than to have watched Dick grow up. I realise that my actions will cause a lot of grief and sorrow but it would probably have been greater if we had both continued living. For myself I had no other interest in this world apart from Dick...

I cleared up all known debts of Sybil's and I have none outstanding. I hope that you are not troubled too much by all this. Tell Dad not to grieve too much over this as I am sure that we shall be much happier where we are.

Your affectionate Brother,

Bob[2]

The evidence was clear. There was no doubt about the circumstances at all. Robert Bungey was so overwhelmed by anguish that he could not think straight. He was a victim of grief and so agonised by worry that his mind was unbalanced. Mr Ziesing determined that an inquest was not necessary and wrote his conclusion at the end of the fingerprint expert's final report.

The RAAF authorities were informed immediately. Subject to his parents' approval, Bob Bungey would be given a full air force funeral at St Jude's Cemetery, Brighton, the next morning (Saturday).

***

Because of Bob's distinguished reputation coming from his work as the commanding officer of the first Australian Spitfire squadron, his funeral was widely reported in the evening press:

FIVE CHIEF AIR OFFICERS AT BUNGEY'S BURIAL

Squadron Leader R. W. Bungey DFC, a hero of the Battle of Flanders and the Battle of Britain was buried today beside his young wife in St Jude's Cemetery Brighton.

Thousands paid tribute to the airman. In addition to the crowd inside St Peter's Church, Glenelg, where the funeral service was held, hundreds congregated outside and groups watched in silence along the route to the cemetery.

The 13 month old son, who was found wounded in the head near his father's body on North Brighton beach on Thursday is still critically ill.

The five most senior officers in the Royal Australian Air Force in Adelaide acted as pall-bearers at the funeral. They were Wing Commander J. Broadbent, the Commanding Officer of the Air Training Corps (Sir Arthur Barrett), Squadron Leader E. S. Pitman, Squadron Leader Bailey, and Squadron Leader Millbrook. The other pall-bearer was Sergeant David Bungey RAAF, the airman's brother.[3]

Among those present at the funeral were two airmen in the uniform of the Royal Air Force who had fought in action with Squadron Leader Bungey, they were Flight Lieutenant Paul Makin and Pilot Officer D. W. Gray. The airman's flying cap was placed on top of the coffin which was draped with the Union Jack.[4]

At the wish of the parents it was a private funeral. Canon H. R. Cavalier, who conducted the service at St Peter's Church, Glenelg, and officiated at the burial, also conducted the service at the funeral of the airman's wife, little more than a fortnight ago.

In an address after the church service, he spoke of the profound love that existed between the airman and his wife. It was anxiety over his wife's health that had made him give up the important work he was doing in England and come to Australia, he added. Canon Cavalier said that the airman's death and the death of his wife were a great loss to the country as well as to two families – one in Australia and one in England. Boy Scouts from a troop to which Squadron Leader Bungey once belonged formed a guard of honour, through which the cortege passed.

About 100 floral tributes were borne in a special car to the cemetery.

Following the prayers delivered by Canon Cavalier at the grave, each Air Force Officer saluted in turn before leaving the burial ground.

Chief mourners were Mr E. Bungey (father), Sgt David Bungey (brother), Mr O. C. Batchelor and Mr B. Hand. Others present included the Acting Mayor of Glenelg (Alderman W. Allen), the town clerk (Mr F. A. Lewis), the Mayor of Brighton (Mr Brown), and the town clerk (Mr A. H. Saunders). Mr R. A. West headmaster of Adelaide High School, where Bungey was educated, and Mr F. A. Robertson (another teacher) were also there.

Mr Robertson coached the airman in mathematics for six months before he joined the Air Force six years ago. He also taught him at school.[5]

When he commented on the death of the Australian flier, the aviation correspondent of London's *Evening Standard* wrote:

Pilots in London today are mourning the loss of a man whose name was known throughout Australia. One who knew him well told me, 'He was a great leader. He led 452 Squadron in its heyday. All the success was due to him. He must have led them on about 70 fighter sweeps. – AAP.

The profound love between Bob and Sybil was the theme of the funeral address as he was laid to rest beside her in St Jude's Cemetery:

The joy and pride with which the people welcomed Squadron Leader R. W. Bungey DFC of Tarlton Road, Somerton, back to his young wife, his thirteen months old son, and his people was turned to genuine sorrow when a few short weeks later, Mrs. Bungey collapsed and died tragically, on Thursday, May 27, the day before she and her famous husband were to have been entertained at Parliament House, at a luncheon arranged by the Mayor of Glenelg (Mr. F. Smith MP), and to be attended by leading citizens and friends of the young airman.

There was universal sympathy for her husband, her people and his: and there was not one of the populace who could not restrain a lump from rising into their throats, and a tear into their eyes, when they thought of the bereaved young man and his sad homecoming. Everyone wanted to take him by the hand: show him in some tangible way, their sympathy, their understanding. But his great sorrow, his loneliness, their feeling that he would want to fight this thing out by himself, their respect for his loss – these, and many other genuine kind thoughts, feelings of distress, held them back, gave them too a feeling of reserve.

If we had only known: if we had only realised the maiming his soul had received; that his tortures were beyond endurance; would we have acted differently, could we have altered what fate had in store?

We are all reproaching ourselves: the sorrow, the burden is great.

Poor Bob! We who are still left here may think these things that have happened since are too terrible. We may seek, and yet not understand, that hopelessness that feeling of emptiness – everything, everything gone! What mental torture, what suffering did he go through; and that so soon following the valour and the tragedy of all those long years of war...

He told me of his friends – Paddy Finucane, Blue Truscott and the others. 'Gone, all gone,' he said.

The bestiality of one man forced a war which Bob Bungey, and others like him, carried on their shoulders.

But what do we know of what that strain did to so few? And then last Thursday, and the most tragic happening of this tragic homecoming.

The news of Bob's death cast a universal gloom: not only a gloom over the district, but over the whole Empire. We try to understand, we weep. 'Bob,' we feel, 'Why did not you tell us, old chap...?'

Bob Bungey was laid to rest at St Jude' s Cemetery, Brighton, alongside the body of his wife, at the same hour, just a fortnight after her funeral.

The same English birds – blackbirds, goldfinches, sparrows whistled and chirruped, and the sun shone forth between the clouds, just as it had done on that former occasion. Profound love existed between them. In death they are reunited.

A week after Bob's death a personal tribute was sent to his family by Sir Keith Murdoch writing from his *Herald* Office in Melbourne on the 17th.

My Dear Mr Bungey,
I was in hospital due to a riding accident when the dreadful news of your son's death came through. I am so very sorry, he seemed to me to be the last man to go that way – good, calm, clean and happy.

Alas! And alas! Some dire sickness must have overcome him. Australia has lost one of its best. I cannot hope to comfort you, but you must take comfort in the knowledge that his life was high-spirited, brave, and full of honour; of just value to his country and his cause, as a fighting man and a leader.

Yours Most Sympathetically,
Keith Murdoch.

In summing up a tribute that was printed in the *TRUTH*, Adelaide, on 19 June, the reporter concluded:

THIS, then, is the man who ended his life so pathetically, so futilely, on a lonely beach a week ago – bitter, disillusioned, broken hearted, nerves strained to breaking point by the hell he had been through – and who tried to take his infant son with him into eternity.

Say what moralists may, his was no coward's death. He died as his mates had died before him – heroically; a victim of Nazi aggression and hate, just as surely as if the bullet which blotted out his existence had been inscribed 'Manufactured by Krupp's.'

Immediately after the funeral, David Bungey paid a visit to Dr Steele. Richard, he was told, was making a remarkable fight for life. Two days after having been found with wounds from a bullet through both temples, he was still hovering between life and death. Steele and his colleagues were amazed he was still alive.

How could he not have been killed outright, shot as he was? A miracle? Was there something that caused Richard to turn his head away from the line of fire at the last instant? Did Bomber make some sort of noise or movement? Was Bob weeping? How many hours had he wandered where he and his brother had played so happily seemingly so long ago – places where he had also walked joyfully with Sybil – before he took out the revolver? In his nightmare of distress did tears blur his vision as he finally pulled the trigger?

It was not a miracle yet. Dr Steele cautioned that scant hope was held for Richard's recovery. Specialist Dr Lindon examined Richard the following day. He concurred with Dr Steele. Richard was paralysed on the left side, but was taking food and was alert, watching the doctor and nurses as they moved about the room. They were monitoring him closely owing to the dangerous possibility of infection.

In the days and weeks that followed not only the family but the whole general public also kept a close watch on the youngster's condition, thanks to the printed media. The grievously wounded boy was in their hearts and prayers. Ada Bungey cut out the various newspaper reports and pasted them into a scrapbook album. It became a precious family treasure – reminder of what happened next.

CONDITION OF AIRMAN'S BABY BETTER

The condition of the 13-month-old son of Wing Commander R. W. Bungey was today reported to be 'somewhat improved.' Dr Kenneth Steele said that the child appeared to be brighter and that the risk of infection had lessened.

The child was found with a bullet wound in the head alongside the body of his father on North Brighton beach on Thursday the 10th June.

The brother of the noted airman (Sergeant David Bungey) who is in the RAAF, said today that if the child lived he would be cared for by his grandparents, Mr and Mrs E. Bungey.

'I certainly will never see the child wanting in anything,' he added.

FLIER'S BABY SON 'MUCH IMPROVED'

The 13 month-old son of the late Wing Commander R W Bungey was 'considerably better,' Dr Kenneth Steele said today. The baby was smiling and laughing and seemed perfectly happy.

DEAD AIRMAN'S SON OUT OF DANGER.

The 13-month-old son of the late Wing Commander R.W. Bungey is now out of danger, and hopes are held that he will completely recover. The child is still in a private hospital at Glenelg. He has progressed rapidly in the last two weeks, and is now taken for walks each day. He was admitted to hospital on June 10 with a bullet wound in the head.

WING COMMANDER BUNGEY'S SON OUT OF DANGER

At last meeting of Brighton Council a letter was read from Mr E. Bungey of Tarlton Road, Somerton, thanking members for their letter of sympathy, and stating that it was a comfort to the parents to know that no single man had done more than their late son to save the Empire in its hour of need.

Bungey further stated that his grandson had made an almost miraculous recovery, and would in all probability, be quite well soon. (The child although still in a private hospital at Glenelg, has recovered sufficiently to be taken for walks each day. He was admitted to hospital on June 10.)

FLIER'S BABY NOW OUT OF HOSPITAL

23 July 1943, Friday

Richard Wilton Bungey, 15-month-old son of the late Wing Commander Bungey DFC, famous Spitfire pilot, has progressed so well, that he was able to leave hospital on Wednesday. The child is not walking yet, but is able to sit up. The left leg has been slightly affected by paralysis, but doctors hope that this will be overcome.

The baby was admitted to a private hospital on June 10.

The hearts and prayers of the public never wavered. A letter to David and the family from Phyllis Langley of the Somerton Crippled Children's Home expressed the widely shared sentiment.

Dear Mr. Bungey,

I do so regret not having been at the home the evening you and your father called. If we were able in any small way to have helped your family in their sorrow it is we who feel thankful to have been able to do it.

Any little service one could render to anyone bearing the name of Bungey is an honour and it is with profound regret that it was such a tragic time... I know you have had many offers of help and I should like to add mine to them if at any time I or this home could be of any service to the boy... and my profound sympathy for you and your family in the loss of one of Australia's greatest men.

Phyllis Langley

The Mayor of Glenelg interviewed Ada and Ernest to discuss a proposal for the State of South Australia to 'adopt' young Richard in honour of the outstanding service rendered by his father – particularly during the retreat to Dunkirk and the Battle for Britain. The Bungeys offered no objection to the proposal being discussed, but did not favour any plan that would have for its object the taking of him from the family's care. All the members of the family were greatly attached to the boy. The idea was referred to David Bungey for his consideration and approval. At this time young Richard appeared to be growing into a fine, sturdy youngster approaching the learning-to-walk, learning-to-talk stage. It was not discussed further.

On leave from the air force again in August, David took Richard to see Dr Lindon again at 10.30 a.m. on the 16th. The specialist's opinion was very encouraging. The boy would definitely walk, but might have a limp.

Two more months would pass before David could excitedly record in his diary on 14 October, 'Richard crawling!'

He was going to be alright!

23

Quest

When Ernest and Ada Bungey knew that Richard was going to live, and was 'on the mend', they had no hesitation in looking after him for as long as they could. He needed constant help with his recovery, especially at the beginning. At one point it was suggested that he should become a State ward, but both insisted that they could, and would, look after his every need. He had to have courses of physiotherapy every day for a lengthy period that stretched into the future.

On leaving the air force, David Bungey devoted his life to looking after his ageing parents and shouldering the burden of caring for his brother's injured child as well. He was quoted as saying that he would make sure his nephew would not want for anything, and he stayed true to his word for the rest of his life. After his grandparents died, Richard lived with David in the family home at Tarlton Street and when David died he ensured Richard did not need to worry about his future by bequeathing everything to him. He passed away in October 1992.

As Richard grew up he thought at first that David was his father until the family told him what had happened. Bob's sister, Pauline, later Pauline Hannaford, never forgave herself for choosing the wrong way on that fateful day the police came. She helped Richard to understand why it happened.

After his schooling, Richard worked for Myer, a major retail store in Adelaide, and at the same time he became determined to discover all he could about his father, especially by making contact with anyone who knew him. Close at hand were Mary Clisby, sister of Leslie Clisby, and her mother Faye. They had befriended Richard's mother, Sybil, when she arrived from England and they both helped to look after Richard while he was growing up and recovering. The friendship between the Clisbys and the Bungeys was close. Leslie Clisby had flown 300 miles across France to Rheims to celebrate Bob's 25th birthday back in 1939, and Faye Clisby became Richard's godmother.

In his search, Richard was helped by many former pilots who had flown in 452 Squadron. He gained a great deal of knowledge from Raife Cowan and his wife Joan. They had long talks about his father, and Raife agreed to write the Forword to this book.

Nan Wawn, the widow of ex-452 pilot Clive 'Bardy' Wawn, told Richard that her husband thought the world of Bob and considered him to have been one of the great squadron leaders of the war. He would have wanted to meet Richard and tell him that.

Ian Milne was another who thought that Bob was one of the great squadron leaders of the war. He told Richard that his father was a no-nonsense leader and a strict disciplinarian, but very fair. He also said that he was a great leader in combat. He and his wife became Richard's very good friends.

Two people who were a great help to Richard in finding out about his father were Feardar and Ray Finucane, Ray's brother being the remarkable 'Paddy' Finucane. Feardar insisted that Richard call her by her nickname, 'Dickie'. He stayed with them at Hampshire Gate during a visit to the UK in 1986, Ian Milne having a hand in arranging the get-together. They were instrumental in Richard comprehending Bob's association with Paddy and the great understanding that developed between them which made 452 Squadron so successful.

> When I went to RAF Kenley with the Finucanes, I was very fortunate to also meet Roy Dutton. This meant a great deal to me as Roy was the first CO of 452 Squadron when it was formed up at Kirton Lindsay. At Kenley, Roy presented me with an account of Bob's time in the Battle of Britain which I treasure.
>
> Roy was also instrumental in me receiving Bob's Battle of Britain Tie which only pilots that had flown in the Battle of Britain were entitled to wear. Bob never received it personally. Roy spoke highly of Bob which was very gratifying.

Although Fred McCann had attended Bob's funeral, Richard never knew him personally. He heard a lot about him through Ian Milne. When Ian passed away, his wife gave Richard a scarf that Fred had loaned Ian just before the sortie from which he did not return. Ian was shot down and became a POW. When Ian returned home to Australia after the war, he contacted Fred to return the scarf but found that he was dying of cancer. Fred told him that he wanted Bob Bungey's son to have the scarf in honour of his father.

Ex-452 pilot Bill Jefferies was known to the Bungey family as he was a bank officer in the Commonwealth Bank in Adelaide and worked with David. When Richard spoke with Bill he said that Bob was a strict CO but very good in the air when on operations. He felt safe when the combat 'got a bit hairy'. He always felt that he was going to survive when Bob was leading the squadron.

When Richard talked to Bill Thorpe about 452 Squadron, Bill was quick to point out that in his opinion Bob was a very good squadron leader, a strict CO who did not stand for anyone doing the wrong thing but was quick to praise and forgive any wrongdoing for the sake of squadron morale.

Former 452/457 Squadron ground staff expressed equally high opinions of Bob Bungey. When Richard met Bill Maudlen he told him he had a lot of material on 452 Squadron and its operations, which he wanted Richard to have. Bill had a great deal of respect for Bob and he enlightened Richard on what Bob went through as a wartime squadron leader.

In conversations with Jack Mc Kenna, Richard gained the impression that Jack had a lot of respect for his father too. He said that he was very fair but strict. If anyone got out of line, Bob would discipline them, which was the right thing to do in Jack's eyes.

Thanks to these people Richard gained great personal insight into what his father was really like.

Richard had already retired from Myer after 32 years of service before David passed away in October 1992. The following month he needed to go into the city to attend to business. He decided to catch the tram from Glenelg. He noticed a girl going the same way and he realised she had worked at Myer too. Coincidentally, he saw her again on the tram going home too. Her name was Allison Wood and she had been at Myer for 25 years. It was the beginning of a beautiful friendship, and more – Allison (Richard called her 'Ali') and Richard (Ali called him 'Rich') were married. She understood what Richard was trying to achieve in his quest to tell his father's story and she gave him great support and encouragement.

***

Early in February 2010, Richard received a telephone call that was destined to have a huge impact on him. It would start at long last to answer many of the questions he had wrestled with over the years about his father in the Royal Air Force and the Royal Australian Air Force. He would begin on a path that could give closure and peace.

On the line was an old primary school friend, Jon Waddy, who had moved to Sydney years before. He and Richard had lost contact with each other with the passage of time. Richard was delighted. Jon had an unexpected surprise. His sister, Jane, had heard an intriguing interview on ABC radio in Brisbane. It was a discussion with an author, Jack Marx, who had just had a book published titled *Australian Tragic*. The work was a collection of short stories about unusual and tragic happenings in Australia over the years, and the story of Richard's father was among them.

Jon went on to suggest that perhaps Jack Marx could be contacted through the radio station and he gave Richard the ABC's phone number. The ABC supplied the writer's phone number when Richard contacted them, 'When I rang Jack Marx,' Richard recalled, 'he told me that he was coming to Adelaide and that he would like to meet me for a more detailed "chat" about my father and his life.'

When Jack Marx arrived in Adelaide he phoned ahead to arrange a meeting at Tarlton Street.

I showed him what I had collected over the years and what my Grandmother put together about Dad. One of the items was a scrapbook with a lot of newspaper cuttings that she had put together at the time. Jack was very impressed with what I had and he asked me, what I was going to do with all this material? I explained to him that all of the material that I had would go to my wife when I went, but Allison then said that she would give it to the Aviation Museum here in South Australia for the people of future generations to see. Jack thought that it should go to the Australian War Memoria in Canberra.

Then Jack presented Richard with a special, unique surprise. It was a copy of a Second World War Movietone newsreel from 1941 which featured 452 Squadron, Bob's squadron, preparing to go to France on a raid. 'What was so special for me was that I heard my Father's voice for the very first time in my life which blew me away. I was overwhelmed!'

Jack was not finished. Before he departed, he asked for Richard's permission to approach a television station, Channel 9, to see if they would be interested in telling his father's story on their programme, *60 Minutes*.

After this several weeks went by and Richard thought little more of it but early in April he received a phone call. This one was from a producer of the programme *60 Minutes*, Kirsty Thomson. Kirsty told him that they were very interested in putting his father's story together. They discussed in more detail the life of Robert Bungey and what happened to the family. During their conversation, Richard told her about the Spitfire that was in the Australian War Memorial in Canberra and revealed that his father had flown it, but he had never seen it.

Within a week Kirsty rang back to tell him that they were definitely going ahead with the story and that they would be coming over to Adelaide to interview him at home. That was scheduled for Thursday, 26 August, and while they were there they would film various places relating to the story.

Before that, April held other surprises.

In the week before Anzac Day, Richard Bungey was 'bursting with pride' when a memorial plaque to his father was unveiled at the RAAF Association's Adelaide Headquarters at Torrens Parade Ground. This was made possible by the South Australian State President of the RSL, Bill Denny.

Interviewed by Fiona McWhirter of the *Sunday Mail* for its 'Anzac Salute' edition, Fiona described Richard as a retired salesman with nothing but love and admiration for his 'hero' dad.

Richard responded, 'How could you not see him as a hero? What he did overseas was incredible. I was so proud of him. What he did [to me] was out of love, out of consideration for me, you couldn't go past that.'

He added, 'He left a note for his brother David telling him what he was going to do. He was going to go down to Brighton. I think his comments were that its better all three of us be together in death rather than me being left alone ... If he was going to get killed, who was going to look after me? That was his concern.'

Richard was later raised by his grandparents and uncle, the only visible proof of those tragic events being a limp in his left leg. Bill Denny remarked that Bob was hailed in a 1943 RAAF publication as 'one of the greatest air organisers Australia has ever produced' and added he 'could have been suffering from an early case of post-traumatic stress disorder. When he got back he had shot down people, he had bombed people, and there had been death all around him. Death wasn't a stranger to Bob Bungey'.[1]

***

Shortly after the *Sunday Mail's* 'Anzac Salute' edition came out on 25 April, Richard received another telephone call from out of the blue. The English-sounding voice on the line introduced himself as Ray Fairminer, saying he had met Bob Bungey seventy years ago and never forgotten him.

In November 1940, Ray Fairminer had been a twelve-year-old whose family lived on the Isle of Wight near Shanklin. While at school, he heard news that a Hurricane fighter had been shot down near his home. He rushed home from school to find the RAF fighter pilot drinking tea with his parents. It was Bob Bungey. Now Ray was an eighty-two-year-old retired factory foreman living at O'Halloran Hill – only 11 kilometres away from Somerton.

Young Ray was 'thrilled to bits' to meet a Battle of Britain pilot, especially one who was an Australian – he had never met an Australian before. Bob introduced himself and told him that a Messerschmitt had got him from behind. He had been flying along and suddenly his dashboard blew up in front of him and he had to ditch. He had been rescued from a sandbank at Littlestairs near Shanklin and taken to the hospital where Ray's father, a maintenance engineer, had invited him home for a cuppa.

Bob returned to the Fairminer home the next morning and gave Ray a half-crown to share with schoolmates at the tuck shop and said before departing, 'I will be back.'

Sure enough, Ray was treated to some stunt flying by Bob the following day.

'We had a lone Hurricane come over. He put on a little bit of an aerial display, not for a long time, maybe a minute,' Ray recalled. 'Then he did a low roar over the ground, a victory roll up in the air and he was away.'

To the young schoolboy, Bob Bungey was a dashing hero and he never forgot him. In 1965 Ray Fairminer moved to Australia and settled in Adelaide. He made an effort to find Bob's relatives and discovered that several Bungey's were listed, but he hesitated and held back from making contact.

The newfound friends were interviewed by Fiona McWhirter for a follow-up article about this new twist to her 'Anzac Salute' Bob Bungey story. Ray told her that he finally discovered what had happened after reading the *Sunday Mail* on 25 April. 'My kids know the story about Bob because I've told it dozens of times, so on Anzac Day I was lying in bed and my daughter called out, she said "Dad your Australian airman has come to life". I read the story and rang Richard, much to his surprise. It was just like the last piece of a jigsaw going in and it completed the story.'

Richard was delighted to hear from and meet someone with links to his father so unexpectedly. He added, 'It's something very special to meet this fellow knowing that he knew and actually talked to my father. I was really astounded that he found me … I was very chuffed, it's fantastic really.'

Thursday, 26 August, came soon enough. The team from Channel 9's *60 Minutes* started at Tarlton Street at 9.30 a.m. While they were filming, Nick Greenaway, the producer, advised Allison and Richard that on Friday, 27 August, they would be flown to Canberra to film the Spitfire in the Australian War Memorial – a thrilling announcement. Suddenly, Richard was really going to see a plane that his father had actually flown!

Very early on the 27th, they left Adelaide, flew to Canberra and were driven straight to the Memorial. After being welcomed, they were shown into an office where were given refreshments and presented with a wonderful book to mark their visit while the Channel 9 film crew set up. The interviewer for the session was Liam Bartlett.

> Liam Bartlett walked with me to where the Spitfire was displayed and when I viewed her a strange feeling came over me. Seeing the plane and knowing Dad had flown her sent goose bumps through me. It came home to me when Liam said to me 'What do you think of that?' I was quite overcome with a proud feeling.
>
> Then Andy (sound man) wired me up. Liam and I got into a scissor lift and I was able to touch the plane just behind the squadron letters. This was where Liam asked me about Dad climbing into the cockpit and lining up the enemy ahead and opening the guns to shoot down the enemy.
>
> He said to me then, 'The next best thing would be to get into a Spitfire and fly it!'
>
> Next we moved to the front of the plane where they filmed me touching the spinner. That was so special that I was overcome and I was quite emotional.

After that, Allison and Richard returned home on the Friday evening. At that stage Richard thought that was going to be the end of his involvement in the programme.

> How wrong I was! On the following Tuesday morning Nick Greenaway rang to find out if our passports were up to date as *60 Minutes* wanted to fly both Allison and I to Britain to film some more information for the program. Then what Nick said next left me speechless! They had arranged for me to fly a WW2 Spitfire and also take us to the National Memorial for the Battle of Britain at Capel-le-Ferne near Folkstone to find Dad's name.
>
> After some running around organising some details on our travel documents, Vanessa from *60 Minutes* rang. She had organised our tickets with Qantas to fly business class. We were going via Melbourne and Hong Kong to Britain on Flight QF29 on Monday, 13 September!

The day duly arrived and the Bungeys left Adelaide and flew to Melbourne. They checked into the Qantas terminal and were given celebrity treatment while waiting for take off.

> One of the head people on the flight heard about what we were going to the UK for and arranged for Ali and I to visit the cockpit while we were in

Hong Kong. Another nice gesture from Qantas was to give us a lovely bottle of champagne after we took off. It was a very pleasant flight.

At Heathrow after clearing customs we were met by Steve, our English driver (who everybody nicknamed 'Dogsbody') and he drove us to our hotel, The Brudenell in Aldeburgh, Suffolk, where we were staying three nights. The next morning we all drove out to the airfield where the Spitfire was housed, which was an old NATO base. There we met Carolyn Grace, the pilot and owner of the Spitfire. While Carolyn briefed me on what was going to happen, Allison took some photos of the other aircraft that were housed in the hanger along with the Spitfire. Meanwhile Greg, Andy and Nick were busy putting extra cameras on the plane and I had to put on a flying suit ready for the flight.

Then it was time to climb aboard. After Carolyn received clearance from the tower, she turned over the Spitfire's Merlin engine and we taxied out to the end of the runway. Carolyn opened up the throttle and we were away.

As we lifted off, I realised that I was living a dream that I never thought would ever happen. Carolyn's voice came over the intercom and told me what was going to happen as regards the filming and what we were going to do. She then said to me to 'sit back and enjoy the flight'. After numerous manoeuvres Greg announced that he had got enough footage for the show.

With the business end over, Carolyn said that she would break away and take me for a flight. It was then that she asked to my amazement, 'Would you like to take control of the plane and fly it?'

She then explained what to do and that she would look after the rudder but I would be in control of the rest. To emphasise the point she raised her hands off the controls so then I knew that I was in complete control of this magnificent machine. It was a dream to fly, so very responsive – just a joy to fly.

After doing some other manoeuvres Carolyn asked if I would like to finish up by doing a victory roll. I said yes quickly. Doing this was the greatest thrill of all.

Finally, Carolyn took over again and we flew back to the airfield for a perfect landing. We taxied back to the hard-standing where the engine was cut. Liam came up to the cockpit and asked me what I thought.

I was on such a high. I said to him, 'I was with my Dad.'

Liam just smiled and said, 'Great.'

We all returned to the hotel late in the day feeling very satisfied with the way the filming had gone. As it was our last night at Aldeburgh we all decided to celebrate the trip. We went to a local restaurant where all the film crew let their hair down and we all got to know one another better. Nick told us what was going on the next day. We were moving on to the Battle of Britain Memorial at Capel-le-Ferne near Folkstone.

With breakfast over the following day, the crew loaded the van and after a pleasant journey we arrived at the Memorial where the boys set up for the filming. When you see this Memorial for the first time it makes you realise that these pilots gave their lives so that today we could be free. The Memorial itself is very moving and the setting is perfect with a statue of a pilot in a sitting position in full flying gear looking out over the English Channel, facing where the German threat was coming from. The statue is surrounded by an amphitheatre of grassy mounds with the names of all the pilots that took part in the Battle of Britain on a wall. At the other end there are full-size static models of a Mk.I Spitfire and a Hurricane at readiness.

Nick wanted to film me looking for Dad's name. I found it easily. Liam also talked to me about what I felt finding his name on this wonderful memorial. For me it was very special and I felt very satisfied that Dad was being honoured by *60 Minutes*.

Next day, after stopping overnight at a B&B at Gosport in Hampshire, Greg Barbara (the Cameraman), Andy Shaklis (Sound), Steve (Dogsbody), Allison and Richard went to the Isle of Wight for the day while Nick Greenaway and Liam Bartlett stayed behind to make arrangements in London. On the Isle of Wight they filmed where Richard's father had ditched in shallow water at Littlestairs Point on 7 November 1940. When filming was finished, they drove to London to their next hotel, The Athenaeum in Piccadilly, where they rested. The next day they were going to the Battle of Britain parade outside Westminster Abbey. It was an exceptional year of celebration, for September 2010 commemorated the 70th Anniversary of the Battle of Britain.

During the parade a Spitfire and Hurricane were going to fly over the parade and they were going to ask me to make a comment when the aircraft came over. When they did come, it was a grand sight and Liam interviewed me for the story when they flew over.

What had been a highly successful and smooth excursion to England was drawing to a close when misfortune struck. It was a final rest day so Allison and Richard took the opportunity to have a bus ride around London. As the bus would not be stopping outside their hotel at the end, the driver advised them when they were close by so they could get off and make their own way back. As they walked, Allison accidentally stepped on a tree guard, fell and injured her knee. When Nick Greenaway found out what happened on their return to the hotel by taxi, he took her to hospital. She had broken her kneecap. The injury strapped so she could travel back to Australia the next evening.

Nick was to fly back that day with the crew but he decided to come back to Adelaide with us to see that we got home alright. Both Ali and I appreciated what Nick did for us very much. He was wanting to shop for us before going back to Sydney, but we said to him that we were able to manage thanks. He had done enough for us and we thought that he should get back to Sydney.

When it appeared on Australian television, the story was titled *The Battle Within* and for Richard it lived up to everything the *60 Minutes* Team had promised. He relived every moment: the visit to Canberra to see his father's Spitfire; the Battle of Britain Memorial atop the White Cliffs at Capel-le-Ferne; the parade at Westminster Abbey; Littlestairs Point on the Isle of Wight; and especially he re-lived flying in the Spitfire and taking over the controls. Richard was transported to another place, another time.

'What did you think of that?' Liam had asked him when the Spitfire had landed. And Richard said: 'I was with my Dad.'

Appendix 1

'Bungey' or 'Bungay'?

Which is it? 'BUNGEY' or 'BUNGAY'? You will find Bob's surname written either way in various publications, but obviously in reference to the very same man. The official history of Australia in the War of 1939–45, *Air War Against Germany and Italy 1939–43* by John Herrington gives the following details:

> W Cdr R. W. Bungey, DFC, 40042 RAF, 257414. 226, 79 and 145 Sqns RAF, comd 452 Sqn 1941, RAF Stns Shoreham and Hawkinge 1942. Regular air force offr; of Glenelg, SA; b. Fullarton, SA, 4 Oct 1914. Died 10 Jun 1943.

BBC war correspondent, Charles Gardiner reported on the air fighting in France during May 1940. In his book, *AASF*, about the exploits of the RAF's Advanced Air Striking Force, he wrote:

> Two flights of Battles – seven in all – took off. A young Australian pilot in the first flight told me today that his flight delivered its attack at low level, and collapsed houses on both sides of the road – blocking it pretty thoroughly. (This pilot was Flying Officer Bungay)...

Noted aviation researcher/historian, Norman Franks, wrote in his book *Valiant Wings*: 'David Crooks later went onto fighters and so did another of 226's pilots, the Australian, Bob Bungay...'

Another well-known researcher/historian, John Foreman, recorded in his book, *Battle of Britain – The Forgotten Months, November and December 1940*:

> The next combat occurred off Littlehampton, at around 18.00 hours. Flight Lieutenant B. A. Bungay and Pilot Officer J. H. M. Offenberg of 145 Squadron had taken off at 15.30 hours to patrol the Shoreham area, when an He111 was sighted, a machine from II/KG27. The two Hurricane pilots attacked...

However, two previous entries in the same book referred to 'Flight Lieutenant Bungey' of 145 Squadron. Likewise, in another publication, *1941 – The Turning Point*, he wrote:

At 11.15 hours three 145 Squadron Spitfire pilots discovered a Ju88 of K.Gr.806 over the Channel. Flight Lieutenant Bungey led Flying Officer De Hemptinne and Pilot Officer Gundrey in to attack...

And so on... so which is it, 'BUNGEY' or 'BUNGAY'? Could it be both?

One of Bob Bungey's ancestors, Samuel Bungey of Wiltshire, England, immigrated to South Australia on the barque *Emily* in 1849. A young man off the land in his 20th year, he could neither read nor write. He, like many young men from the county of Wiltshire were responding to a call for agricultural labourers needed in Australia. The main form of assisted passage was provided by Britain's Colonial Office, which received funds from the South Australian Government and stipulated what type of people were needed to make the colony self-supporting. The money was expressly to finance the sending of new settlers. The various officials involved could have recorded the spelling of Samuel's surname any way they pleased. At times they may have changed 'ey' to 'ay'. At least that is one theory – but there was more to it than that.

Another suggestion for the change was that over time mail for those who could read and write was failing to reach the right people so one family decided to change to 'ay' to solve the problem. Perhaps. William Bungey, who was Samuel's youngest brother in a family of nine children, may have adopted this measure. The birth certificate of Alfred George, who was William's fifth child, was issued at Bulbridge, Wiltshire, and it shows his surname as 'Bungay', but on his marriage certificate it is 'Bungey'.

Confusing? There is more.

Kathleen Bungey, Alfred's daughter, preferred 'Bungay' because she considered it sounded better. Her nephew Peter went through his early years as a 'Bungey'. He joined the RAAF in 1959 and ran into a problem because his birth certificate showed 'Bungay'. The RAAF refused to pay him his salary unless he signed for it as 'Bungay'. Thoroughly confusing!

South Australia was not the only destination for those carrying the Bungey/ Bungay name. Another William Bungey (there were many Williams in the Bungey lineage) migrated to Moreton Bay on the *Lady Macdonald* in 1856. Newton Bungey moved to Sydney with his wife Susan on the *Stebonheath* in 1858 and there are descendants in the Sydney area to this day. The flow has continued over the years. Ralph Bungey and family arrived in Perth, Western Australia, on the SS *Otway* in 1911. Richard Bungey and family reached Brisbane by air around 1982, coming from New Zealand where more Bungey/Bungays reside.

Samuel Bungey left London on the *Emily* on 3 May 1849, and arrived at Port Adelaide on 8 August. He and another Englishman, William Merchant, settled in a hilly, wooded area that became known as Bungey Town. Its economy originally relied on the production of sawn timber, which was in demand for building in Adelaide. By the 1890s, cherries and other fruits were growing prolifically throughout the area and the village's name was officially changed to Cherryville. At the beginning of the 20th Century, Cherryville was one of the finest fruit producing areas of the state, but production declined by the 1930s chiefly owing to the steepness of the terrain. The final blow for many living there came on Black Sunday, 2 January 1955, when the area was devastated by bushfires.

Samuel's youngest brother, William Bungey and his wife Mary, née Holloway, and family, also of seven children, joined the others in the colony, arriving in Port Adelaide on 21 December 1883. Their exhausting journey aboard the *Berar* had taken just a day less than five months.

William and Mary Bungey's seventh child, Ernest, had been born in Wiltshire in 1882 and it was just a year later that the family sailed from Plymouth on the *Berar*. They had two more daughters after their arrival in South Australia increasing their family to nine: Lilian Mary in 1887, who unfortunately died as a child in 1896; and Eleanor in 1890. Ernest was the youngest of the five boys.

They lived at Norton Summit for a time then moved to Glen Osmond where William worked as a gardener in the employ of Mr Fowler, founder of D & J Fowler, a large company engaged in manufacturing and importing food products. This was where Ernest would have spent his childhood and formative years.

Like most of Adelaide's society, the family was religious. As he grew, Ernest was also keenly interested in sport, something that got him into trouble one Saturday afternoon when he sneaked out of a church prayer meeting to play cricket. For this transgression he 'got a terrible hiding' but he remarked afterwards that it 'didn't hurt too much' because his team had won!

After leaving school, Ernest began his working life as a clerk for D & J Fowler. In the meantime, his oldest brother, Walter William Bungey, founded a business, which he named Bungey Brothers, Grain and Fodder Merchants. When Ernest was in his early twenties, he worked for the company as the office manager.

There was also a theatrical side to his character. He was a reader of Shakespeare with interest in poetry and amateur dramatics. It was while he was working at a musical evening with a well-known actor of the time, Harold Parkes, that a mutual friend introduced him to an attractive young lady. Her name was Ada Rough. She was the daughter of John and Phillipa Rough of Moonta. Her father was a miner at the Moonta Copper Mines and the son of a Cornish miner who immigrated to South Australia around 1860.

Ada was very talented. She was a gifted singer, a contralto, and an accomplished pianist. She was studying at the Adelaide Conservatorium at the time. This was a common bond between them as Ernest too had a fine singing voice. Their friendship soon blossomed into romance.

Ernest and Ada were married in 1910 and their first child, a son, was born at Hutt Street Private Hospital in Adelaide on 4 October 1914.

His name?

Robert Wilton BUNGEY.

Appendix 2

Distinguished Flying Cross

RECOMMENDATION:
Station Commander, RAF Station KENLEY.
Group Captain Tom Prickman
15 September 1941

A/S/Ldr Bungey has been in command of 452 Squadron at this Station since 21st July, 1941.

He has led the Squadron in an exemplary manner on many operational flights over France. He has also led the Wing on several occasions.

Due to his personal leadership the Squadron has attained much success, in August the Squadron had the largest bag in Fighter Command, 24 enemy aircraft shot down.

Recommend that S/Ldr. Bungey should be awarded the Distinguished Flying Cross in recognition of his gallant and efficient leadership.

Further particulars of his service are attached.

COVERING REMARKS OF THE AIR OFFICER COMMANDING:
Air Vice Marshal Commanding No 11 Group, T. Leigh Mallory.
20 September 1941.
Strongly Recommended for the Award of the Distinguished Flying Cross.

APPROVAL:
Air Marshal W. S. Douglas, Air Officer Commanding–in–Chief Fighter Command
22 September 1941.

APPROVED

This Officer, who has come to England in August 1937, went to France the day before War broke out with 226 Sqdn of Battles.

They were part of the Advanced Air Striking Force and were based at Rheims. He remained in France until about June 16th, 1940 and took part in about fifteen operational sorties, mainly bombing but including reconnaissance and pamphlet dropping.

Among other operations he took part in the successful blocking of a strategic road near Zundert in which he led a flight of four Battles.

After being evacuated from France the Squadron went to Ireland and S/L. Bungey requested to be transferred to fighters or twin-engine bombers. He was posted on the 18th August to 145 Squadron which flew Hurricanes.

He was given a flight with 145 Squadron on about September 15th, and went with them to TANGMERE on October 10th.

S/Ldr Bungey took part in various combats against German fighter sweeps over this country which lasted up to the end of the year. He stayed with 145 Squadron until about April 6, 1941, when he underwent an operation on his knee.

S/Ldr Bungey was posted to 452 Squadron on June 9th 1941, the Squadron having just become day operational. Under his command the Squadron has since become night operational. The Squadron came to Kenley on July 21st, since when they have taken part in very many circus and other offensive operations and have destroyed 25 and probably destroyed 3 E/A. During August they had the highest bag for any Squadron (24). In the absence of the Wing Commander Flying, S/Ldr Bungey has led the Kenley Wing on several occasions.

SECOND SUPPLEMENT
THE LONDON GAZETTE
of Friday, 3rd OCT, 1941.
ROYAL AIR FORCE.

The KING has graciously pleased to approve the following awards in recognition of gallantry displayed in flying operations against the enemy:-

DISTINGUISHED FLYING CROSS

Acting Squadron-leader Robert Wilton Bungey (40042) No 452 RAAF, Squadron.

This officer has been almost continually engaged on operations against the enemy since the war began. During operations in France he carried out many bombing and reconnaissance missions and later fought in the Battle of Britain.

Since July 1941, Squadron Leader Bungey has led the squadron and occasionally the wing, on many operational sorties over Northern France. Brilliant successes have been achieved and during August, the unit shot down twenty-four hostile aircraft. Throughout, this officer displayed gallant and efficient leadership.

TELEGRAM: 3–10–1941
SQUADRON LEADER R. W. BUNGEY DFC RAF, RAF STATION KENLEY, SURREY
HEARTEST CONGRATULATIONS ON HONOUR BESTOWED UPON YOU BY HIS MAJESTY.

BRUCE, HIGH COMMISSIONER.

Stanley Melbourne Bruce was the twelfth prime minister of Australia (9 February 1923–12 October 1929) before being appointed Australian High Commissioner in London in 1933. He held the position until 1945. As well, he was Australia's representative to the League of Nations 1932–1939.

SUMMONS TO PALACE FOR AWARD to Squadron Leader Robert W. Bungey DFC RAF:
CENTRAL CHANCERY OF
THE ORDERS OF KNIGHTHOOD
St JAMES'S PALACE, S.W.1
19 FEBRUARY 1942.
Confidential,

Sir,
The King will hold an investiture at Buckingham Palace on Tuesday the 10th March at which your attendance is requested.

It is requested that you should be at the palace not later than 10:15 o'clock a.m.

DRESS – Service Dress, Morning Dress, or Civil Defence Uniform. This letter should be produced on entering the Palace, as no further card of admission will be issued. Two tickets for relations or friends to witness the investiture may be obtained on application to this office and you are requested to state your requirements on the form enclosed. Please complete the enclosed form and return immediately to the Secretary, Chancery of the Orders of Knighthood, St, James's Palace London, SW1.

I am, Sir,
Your obedient Servant,
W. A. Stockley
MAJOR Secretary

Also receiving awards that day were Keith 'Bluey' Truscott (a DFC) and Brendan 'Paddy' Finucane (a DSO). It was probably the last occasion they were all together. None survived the war.

Appendix 3

452 (RAAF) Squadron – The Rest of the Story

The story of 452 (RAAF) Squadron's success in the air battles over Europe during the second half of 1941 has already been related in detail in Chapters 11–16. German records examined years later after the war revealed that RAF claims during 1941–43 were highly inflated (as were those of the *Luftwaffe* in 1940, and those of the 8th USAAF 1942–45) demonstrating the difficulty of establishing accurate figures when fighting over enemy territory. No doubt this applied to 452's claims as well. However, regardless of the 'numbers game', for a new squadron to accomplish what it did in just a few short months is a remarkable tribute to the skill of its members and the tactics they employed – and to Bob Bungey's leadership. Bob was a methodical, tactical thinker and under his astute tenure 452 Squadron achieved the pinnacle of its accomplishments.

Although Bob Bungey was an Australian commanding an RAAF squadron, he was still officially an RAF short service commission officer and subject to RAF commands. When he left the squadron in January 1942, Bluey Truscott took over.

Truscott continued with Bungey's methods in the air but inclement weather that winter allowed little opportunity for combat. Scoring in 1942 did not start until 8 February when Paul Makin became separated while patrolling near Cap Gris Nez and was attacked by Me109s. Although outnumbered, he damaged one before escaping.

Three days later, the German capital ships, *Scharnhorst*, *Gneisenau* and *Prinz Eugen*, crept from Brest Harbour under the cover of darkness and poor weather and sailed for Germany via the English Channel, heavily escorted by vessels from the *Kriegsmarine*. The German convoy was not discovered until 10.30 a.m. next day. A fiasco followed. Despite repeated fragmented RAF attacks through the murk, the 'Channel Dash' convoy succeeded in escaping to Germany relatively undamaged.

The Kenley Spitfires were ordered to escort attacking torpedo-carrying Beauforts, but these failed to rendezvous. Above thick cloud the German fighter cover was nowhere to be seen so Truscott led 452 Squadron lower down. Breaking through cloud at 1,000 feet, they stumbled upon the fleet and met intense flak. Seizing his chance, Truscott led a strafing attack on a destroyer, raking it with cannon and machine gun fire. Its deck guns fell silent and smoke issued from around the bridge before 452 escaped back into the cloud cover, unscathed save for a glancing hit on Truscott's cockpit canopy!

Next day, Kenley base commander, Gp/Capt Victor Beamish, led 452 Squadron in 'annihilating' a lone He114 floatplane. All the pilots took turns shooting it down to record it as a squadron victory.

Poor weather closed in again until early March. Freshly commissioned, P/O Bardy Wawn destroyed a Me109F on 9 March, and Truscott added another Me109F and a 'damaged' to his tally. On the 13th, P/O Ray Sly claimed an FW190, and the next day another 190 was sent down by Truscott. Sgt Morrison claimed a probable Me109F. These were the squadron's final claims over Europe.

Bluey Truscott's tenure as CO was short lived. Because of the serious Japanese threat to Australia, many experienced combat pilots were ordered home. Truscott and various others were posted away from 452 and command was passed to Ray Thorold-Smith. Less than a week later, the squadron moved to Andreas on the Isle of Man where it served until it too embarked for Australia.

The personnel of 452 Squadron, 457 (RAAF) Squadron and 54 Squadron RAF, departed from Liverpool on the SS *Stirling Castle* on 21 June 1942 with all but six of their Spitfires aboard the accompanying, SS *Nigerstown*. They reached Melbourne, Australia, the following 13 August.

After leave, re-assembly began at RAAF Station Richmond NSW on 6 September where refresher training started using only six Spitfires – that was all they had. *Nigerstown's* Spitfires had been commandeered in transit for the RAF in North Africa.

Each squadron was allocated two Spitfires, two Wirraways and a Ryan ST-M trainer, but that was it. Lack of aircraft severely restricted training but the wing simply had to make do. On 9 October, Spitfire BR471 flown by 452 Squadron's Sgt Michael Clifford suffered engine failure and crashed into the sea. Clifford was the first Spitfire fatality in Australia. Another Spitfire was damaged in a landing accident.

Such were the difficult beginnings of No.1 'Churchill' Fighter Wing RAAF. Gp/Capt A. 'Wally' Walters AFC was appointed to command and his Wing Leader was W/Cdr Clive Caldwell DSO DFC, the highest scoring Allied pilot of the Desert War with twenty and a half victories.

After Australian authorities requested his return home, Caldwell was posted first to England to experience big-wing Spitfire operations over the Continent, flying briefly with the Kenley Wing from which 452 Squadron had departed only months before. With 452 and Bluey Truscott gone, the wing had reverted to the standard RAF basic flying formation of three aircraft. Bob Bungey's experiment of flying in pairs and fours had been forgotten.

Caldwell returned to Australia in September 1942 and took part in comparative tests with the new CAC Boomerang before joining No.1 Wing.

Aside from 452 Squadron, which was still commanded by Ray 'Throttle' Thorold-Smith who had trained earlier with Caldwell, there were the other two squadrons. No.457 Squadron had formed on 16 June 1941, the second RAAF Spitfire squadron formed in England under the EATS Agreement. It withdrew from operations over Europe at the end of May 1942, flying on 28 May. Its CO was S/Ldr Ken James.

No.54 Squadron had seen action covering the Dunkirk evacuation, in the Battle of Britain and participating in sweeps over France in 1941. In command was S/Ldr Eric 'Bill' Gibbs.

After sixty-four Spitfire Mk VCs finally reached Melbourne in October, the wing began receiving its aircraft during November. For security, the planes were called 'Capstans' (a popular cigarette brand) powered by 'Marvel' engines, to keep secret that Spitfires were in Australia. In early November to prevent congestion at Richmond, 452 Squadron moved to Bankstown, 457 went to Camden, and 54 Squadron stayed put. They were still close enough to practise as a wing. Throughout December training and preparation was rushed and intense. Six months after leaving England, the pilots had done little flying.

The move north began with the new year. Ground personnel were transported by ship and the aircraft commenced moving in mid-January travelling via Richmond, Mildura, Oodnadatta, Alice Springs and Daly Waters to Batchelor 90 km south of Darwin on 17 January 1943. On 31 January, 452 Squadron moved into Strauss, about 43 km south of Darwin; 457 went to Livingstone, 55 km south of Darwin, and 54 Squadron proceeded directly to RAAF Darwin. At their new bases they prepared to face renewed Japanese air activity when the wet season ended.

452 Squadron had a mixture of pilots. A few of its UK contingent remained, including F/Lt Paul Makin. Numbers were boosted by new pilots with little or no combat experience, plus a couple veteran newcomers. Two were aces from the heavy fighting over Malta, Adrian Philip 'Tim' Goldsmith and John Henry Eric Bisley.

During an intense two months of fighting starting in April 1942, Sgt Tim Goldsmith claimed at least twelve and a half enemy aircraft destroyed. He was awarded the DFM, commissioned and then received a DFC at the end of June. His last sortie on Malta was on 1 July after which he left for England. In August he was posted home.

P/O John Bisley claimed his first two victories, a Ju88 and a Ju87, off Grand Harbour on 5 April 1942 but had to crash-land wounded. He added four more victories by early July and received a DFC before leaving for England, but on 18 August he was recalled to Australia.

On 27 January 1943, less than a fortnight after arriving in the Northern Territory, 452 suffered a tragic accident 4 miles south-east of the airfield at Coomalie Creek, the home of 31 (Beaufighter) Squadron. Two Spitfires collided in mid-air while practising attacks on a B-24 of the 90th Bomb Group USAAF. Sgt Eric Hutchinson flying Spitfire A58-73 was killed. The other pilot, Sgt Henry Stockley in Spitfire A58-55 was uninjured.

Exactly a month later, in bad weather, Spitfire A58-69 (BS175) en route to Wyndham from Strauss crashed inverted at Tabletop Range, near Litchfield Park. The pilot, F/O William Ford, was killed.

With improved weather the Japanese launched a raid on 2 March. Although scrambling a pair of Spitfires early to intercept a Japanese reconnaissance aircraft (normal enemy practice was to check the weather over the target beforehand), and later having a futile chase out to sea after the retiring raiders, 452 Squadron did not manage to engage.

Japanese reconnaissance planes were slippery customers, particularly the twin-engined Mitsubishi Ki-46 Dinahs. They were fast and difficult to catch, considered as good in their role as de Havilland Mosquitoes. Japan's navy and army air arms both used them.

It was not until the next raid on 15 March that 452 Squadron could claim its first Japanese victories. Tim Goldsmith claimed a Mitsubishi G4M Betty and an escorting A6M3 Hamp, a square wingtip variant of the Zero.

Ray Thorold-Smith vanished with Zeros after him as he was attacking. He was never seen again. A Spitfire was reported to have crashed offshore from Flagstaff Hill on the northern point of the Middle Arm of Darwin Harbour. His disappearance was partially solved in 1986 when the nearly intact wreckage of his Spitfire, BS231, was found resting in mud on an even keel on the bottom at that location.

Thorold-Smith's place was temporarily filled by W/Cdr Caldwell until S/Ldr Ronald Sommerville MacDonald was appointed CO on 30 March. MacDonald, formerly CO of No.12 Vengeance dive-bomber Squadron at nearby Batchelor airfield, was an EATS graduate and former Wirraway instructor but he had limited fighter experience and had so far seen no action. Some saw his choice to command a front-line fighter squadron as unusual, but he would prove his worth.

April passed quietly and monotonously, except for several fruitless scrambles. Then, on Sunday 2 May, a Japanese raid of twenty-five bombers (seven aborted) and twenty-seven fighters had serious consequences for the defenders.

Radar plotted them over Bathurst Island at 0926 hours and at 0945 hours the Wing scrambled forty-one Spitfires including eleven from 452 Squadron. The Spitfires were still climbing while Darwin was being bombed. By the time they had assembled and climbed to make their attack the bombers were already heading for home. A running battle followed beginning 40 miles north-west of Darwin and extending 60 miles out to sea. Japanese sources claimed twenty-one Spitfires destroyed without loss, only some damaged aircraft.

In fact, fourteen Spitfires didn't return to base for a variety of reasons. Four suffered engine failure, four were shot down by escorting Zeros and one was lost ditching for unknown reasons. Five ran out of fuel, one ditching and the others force-landing elsewhere. Two out of three recovered were repaired.

As for 452 Squadron, Tim Goldsmith had to bail out after firing on a bomber. He later claimed a Nakajima Helen destroyed (actually engaged were Mitsubishi G4M Bettys of 753 AG). Three other pilots bailed out too, all landing safely. One of these was F/Sgt Ross Stagg who came down in Fog Bay. He managed to paddle ashore and spent the next sixteen days struggling through mangroves, swamp, mud and bush before being rescued, emaciated but alive. Unfortunately, it was F/O Alexander 'Sandy' McNab who perished while attempting to ditch for unknown reasons – his aircraft flipped over and plunged straight under.

Serious issues faced the Spitfire pilots and their controllers. Spitfires were short range interceptors designed to climb fast and fight over the green fields of England where they excelled. Despite their well-deserved accolades, they were much less suited to conditions in the Northern Territory. Distances were greater, landing grounds were fewer and far between, and the environment was rougher, and much dustier.

The enemy came in higher than the *Luftwaffe* did in Europe. Precious fuel was quickly consumed climbing fast and manoeuvring into the best position to attack. It took too long; many Spitfires ran out of fuel. The big wing was cumbersome and so many fighters together in the air were easier to see than the escorting Zeros that were spread out in small formations waiting to pounce using their bombers as bait. It was difficult to spot them all. Too often the Spitfires were surprised by some they had not seen in time. And the manoeuvrable Zeros were a shock. At lower speeds they were far more nimble than expected, more so than the Spitfires.

The Spitfire VC itself had shortcomings. Its de Havilland constant-speed propeller unit (CSU) suffered from oil leaks and tended to over-speed, causing engine failure. This fault would continue to plague the aircraft during the strain of engaging in combat. There were frequent cannon failures caused by the dusty conditions or severe cold at high altitude. One or both cannons of nine Spitfires failed on 2 May. If one failed, accurate gunnery became impossible. If both failed, the Australian fighters could only attack with half the firepower of the eight-machine-gun Spitfires and Hurricanes of 1940. None of Ron MacDonald's guns would fire that day. During the remainder of May and into late June, the squadron was scrambled a number of times after unidentified aircraft, but these usually proved to be stray USAAF B-24s.

The enemy did not come in force again until 20 June. In the ensuing combat a variety of Japanese types were 'identified' including Bettys, Sallys, Zeros, Haps, Oscars, Lilys and Dinahs. Recognition of Japanese aircraft would confuse the Allies for much of the war. This time Japanese Army air units were involved consisting of eighteen Nakajima Helens escorted by twenty-two Nakajima Ki-43 Oscars while nine Kawasaki Ki-48 Lilys mounted a surprise low-level attack that was unchallenged. Forty-six Spitfires were scrambled but some aborted with the usual problems.

No.1 Wing's tally was put at eight heavy bombers, five fighters and a light bomber destroyed although the Japanese admitted the loss of only two Helens and an Oscar.

For 452 Squadron, S/Ldr MacDonald and F/Lts John Bisley and David Evans each claimed a Mitsubishi Sally shot down. F/O 'Al' Mawer claimed a Zero. P/O Anthony Ruskin-Rowe was credited with two more Zeros but he was shot down and killed in Spitfire BS174. P/O William 'Bill' Nichterlein in Spitfire EE 607 was also lost.

30 June saw 452 Squadron and the wing in action against forty plus enemy aircraft, navy G4M Bettys and Zeros. S/Ldr MacDonald claimed a Betty and F/O Clive 'Bill' Lloyd a Zero before having to bail out. F/Sgt Colin Duncan after parachuting spent five days in rough country before rescue. F/O William 'Jack' Lamerton died as a result of fire during a crash landing.

The next major action, Bettys and Zeros again, took place on 6 July in which two pilots, F/O Clive 'Bill' Lloyd and Sgt Arthur 'Ross' Richardson, had to bail out. Paul Makin crash-landed with a dead engine. This turned out to be a finale for the main Japanese daylight bombing campaign on the Darwin area, though it was not realised then. Thereafter bombers were sent at night.

It was in July that 452 Squadron became involved in testing a top secret rubberised fabric flying suit made by the Dunlop Company that was meant to allow pilots to perform tight, high-speed manoeuvres without blacking out – the Cotton Aerodynamic Anti-G Suit (CAAG). The CAAG Suit was designed by Professor Frank Cotton DSc and tested in a centrifuge built in the basement of the Medical School at Sydney University. Selected pilots were sent to be 'calibrated' on the centrifuge and to carry out familiarisation flights with the intention of using the suit in operations as soon as possible. It was seen as a possible counter to the amazing manoeuvrability of the Zero.

Extensive tests eventually revealed that the pilot had a greater resistance to the effects of 'G' than the aircraft! In tight turning trials with one pilot wearing a CAAG suit and the other not, the pilot wearing the suit was on the tail of his opponent well before his opponent had recovered from blacking out during his turn. Also, he could pull out sharply from a 450-mph dive without discomfort, but both wing tips of his Spitfire would ripple under the stress. During September, two Spitfires were salvaged from 452 Squadron at Strauss with strained mainplanes.

Other drawbacks were that the pilot would have difficulty getting out of an airborne Spitfire in an emergency because of the extra restrictions of the suit, and they were extremely hot to wear, especially in the Darwin area. Air conditioning was experimented with but by that time the Japanese attacks on the north were over. CAAG suits were never used in operations over Darwin

Although August was quiet, on the 10th P/O Fred Young and Sgt Bill Coombes intercepted two Japanese floatplanes while in a detachment to defend the airstrip at Millingimbi, a low island off the coast of Arnhem Land. One was destroyed and the other declared a probable. On the 17th, F/Sgt Paul 'Paddy' Padula flying wingman to W/Cdr Caldwell shared in the destruction of a Mitsubishi Dinah, one of four Dinahs destroyed by the wing that day.

In the last major clash on 7 September, Zeros escorted the reconnaissance aircraft and bounced the wing as it climbed to intercept. Tim Goldsmith claimed a Kawasaki Ki-61 Tony [sic] destroyed, while four other enemy aircraft were claimed as probables or damaged. During the engagement S/Ldr MacDonald was wounded but bailed out safely, as also did P/O Paul Tully. In a tragic accident on the 25th, F/Os John 'Phil' Adam and Al Mawer collided in mid-air; neither survived.

The Japanese carried out their final air raid on 12 November 1943 and this marked the beginning of quiet period until early March 1944. S/Ldr Louis Spence DFC was given command of 452 Squadron on 3 February and in March, reports that a Japanese naval force may have entered the Indian Ocean led to rumours of a possible Japanese invasion, or an air raid on Perth, Western Australia. Nos.452 and 457 Squadrons were ordered to Perth to defend.

Coming down Australia's west coast, flying was made difficult by alternate dust and tropical rain accompanied by high winds. At stops along the way the pilots were greeted by mosquitoes, blinding heat and flies. One Spitfire crashed at Carnarvon and another force-landed at Gingin. Dense bushfire smoke around Perth was another hazard as they landed at Guildford airfield on 12 March. The reports were unfounded. The enemy never came.

452 Squadron relocated from Guildford back to Strauss a month later, in time to participate in the first offensive operation by Australian-based Spitfires, an attack on Japanese installations on Babar and Wetan Islands on 17 April 1944. It was the squadron's last operation with Mk V Spitfires, as conversion began to more powerful Spitfire VIIIs.

By now air combat in the theatre was rare, but it livened up on 12 June with the destruction of a Dinah. On 18 September, F/O Arthur Keith Kelly piloting Spitfire A58-435 took part in an interception exercise over Cape Van Diemen with B-24 Liberators of the 380th Bomb Group, 5th USAAF. Making a simulated head-on attack, his Spitfire collided with the B-24 and fell into the sea. His body was never recovered.

The arrival of two RAF squadrons allowed 452 Squadron to transfer to Morotai in mid-December to join the RAAF's 1st Tactical Air Force. F/O Jack Amerson Pretty shot down one of two Japanese intruders (identified as Nakajima Ki-49 Helens) over Morotai on the night of 24 December.

On 13 January 1945, Gp/Capt Caldwell led an attack on Miti airfield. During a later attack on the same target, F/Sgt Edmond McLeod 'Mac' Stevenson's Spitfire was hit by flak and crashed. He died in captivity on 14 April at Fort Oranje, Netherlands East Indies, as a result of torture by the Japanese. His body was later reinterred on Morotai.

A move to Tarakan in May 1945 saw 452 Squadron flying in support of the Balikpapan operation. S/Ldr Kevin Milne Barclay DFC took over as CO on 4 June. They flew their first operation on 30 June 1945. From July onwards, the Spitfires operated with Kittyhawks in a maximum effort ground attack role.

On the 2nd, 452 Squadron with the Kittyhawks of 75 Squadron carried out strikes on Kalabakan and Simalumong. The Spitfires made eight strafing passes on Simalumong but on his last pass, F/Lt A. Proctor crashed and was killed.

On 10 July, N. J. Cullen, another 452 Squadron pilot was last seen recovering from a dive-bombing attack. Two days later, when dive bombing the same target, S/Ldr Barclay was hit by anti-aircraft fire. He had to bail out of his damaged aircraft and was later picked up by a launch. Three days afterwards, he led an attack against Japanese pillboxes after which the Spitfires returned to their new base at Sepinang.

Raids on 19, 22 and 24 July achieved a mixed bag of motor transport, barges and fixed installations. Then on the night of the 24th, 452 Squadron scored its last air victory, F/Lt J. C. King downing a Japanese bomber in flames over Balikpapan.

The dropping of the atomic bombs in August brought about Japan's surrender. Australian casualties since 452's beginnings in Lincolnshire totalled forty-nine killed.

Limited defensive duties continued after the war until, in October, the aircraft were returned to Australia. No.452 Squadron was officially disbanded on Tarakan on 17 November 1945.

Appendix 4

Aircraft Flown on Operations by Robert Bungey

1/ FAIREY BATTLE

When it first flew in March 1936, the Fairey Battle with its modern all-metal monoplane construction, totally enclosed cockpits, retractable undercarriage, flaps and variable pitch airscrew marked a vast improvement over the existing light bombers, such as the old Hawker Hind, Hart and Gordon. The first production machine (K7558) was powered by a 1,025-hp Rolls-Royce Merlin I engine and did 243 mph at 16,200 feet, had a range of 1,050 miles, and exceeded its original P.27/32 specification figures.

The Battle went into large-scale production but some in the RAF maintained that the light bomber was already outmoded because of insufficient range and bombload to attack Britain's obvious enemy, Germany. Nevertheless, it was decided that the race for numerical parity with the *Luftwaffe* could best be maintained by producing large numbers of small machines, however unsuitable they might prove to be in the long run.

Ten squadrons of Battles went to France in September 1939 with the Advanced Air Striking Force, and early 'Phoney War' operations immediately heightened doubts about the type's survivability against modern fighter opposition. In May 1940, the Battle squadrons were decimated in daylight operations following the German invasion of France and the Low Countries. The remainder fought on, mainly at night, until mid-June, when they were finally withdrawn to England. From then on, the type was increasingly used in various advanced training roles for which its still up-to-date technical features made it suitable and useful.

FAIREY BATTLE II

Crew: 3.
Length: 52 feet 1 in.
Span: 54 feet.
Height: 15 feet 6 in over airscrew disc.
Wing area: 422 sq feet.

Engine: Rolls-Royce Merlin II, 1,030 hp at 3,000 rpm at 16,250 feet.
Maximum speed: 233 mph at 17,200 feet, 225 mph at 10,000 feet.
Landing speed: 63 mph ASI.
Best climb: 990 feet per min at 11,200 feet.
Climb: to 10,000 feet 10.8 min, to 20.000 feet 25.2 min.
Service ceiling: 25,100 feet.
Range: 1,050 miles at 200 mph at 15,000 feet.
Bomb load: 1,000 lb normal, 1,250 lb max.
Empty weight: 7,504 lb.
Loaded weight: 10,992 lb.
Armament: one .303-in Vickers Mk.V (or Browning) machine gun in starboard wing (436 rounds), one .303-in Lewis Mk IIIE (or Vickers) free-mounted machine gun. (One floor-mounted machine gun fitted later.)

2/ HAWKER HURRICANE MK I

The Hurricane evolved from the highly successful Hawker Fury biplane, a monoplane version of which was planned to be powered by a 660-hp Rolls-Royce Goshawk steam-cooled engine. When the Hawker Company's chief designer, Sydney Camm, heard of the new 1,000-hp Rolls-Royce PV12, the projected fighter was changed to take advantage of the more powerful engine. Later, the RAF's new specification for armament of eight wing-mounted guns was incorporated into the prototype. Previously there had been a long convention that the pilot must be able to reach his guns from the cockpit in order to clear stoppages, which were in those days not unusual. The new armament policy was made possible by the reliability of the Browning machine gun.

The Hurricane's structure was based on a girder-like metal framework with fabric covering but this was outdated by the all-metal monocoque structures of the Spitfire and the Me109. Technically, it did not have the built-in 'stretch' that made the Spitfire supreme. Nevertheless, its war record was outstanding, particularly as a bomber destroyer in the Battle of Britain.

Powered by the early 1,189-hp Rolls-Royce Merlin C, the prototype Hurricane K5083 flew for the first time in November 1935 and turned in a remarkably fine performance of 315 mph at 16,200 feet. Best climb rate was 2,950 feet per minute at 7,600 feet, and the ceiling was estimated at 34,500 feet. Hawker decided to put the fighter into large-scale production without waiting for full official sanction. When an Air Ministry order for 600 aircraft did come three months later, the company already had a good start towards issuing production drawings and tooling. The time saved meant that more Hurricanes were available when they were so vitally needed in the first year of the war.

First squadron deliveries of the Hurricane I with the Merlin II engine went to No.111 Squadron at Northolt late in 1937. Even so, only ninety-three of the new eight-gun fighters were available in September 1938 at the time of the Munich crisis – none were Spitfires. This handful of Hurricane fighters was also limited at the time to an operating height of 15,000 feet because of the lack of gun heating. Britain's main fighter defences still depended on 660-odd biplane fighters. By the same time the next year, more than 500 monoplane fighters, mostly Hurricanes, were in RAF squadron service.

Hurricanes first won battle honours overseas over France, the Low Countries, and in Norway. One facet of the Battle of Britain was the rush to provide British fighters with constant speed airscrews instead of the fixed-pitch and, later, two-position propellers with which they were previously equipped. The constant speed unit gave the aircraft a better rate of climb, faster diving speed and a decidedly improved ceiling, providing a vital boost to performance. Spitfires received priority for the conversion but Hurricanes were progressively modified, even in the heat of the battle. Yet another technical aspect of the conversion was the vastly increased powers made available for limited periods from the Merlin II and III by increasing the supercharger boost pressure, which uprated the maximum horsepower by as much as 40%. Nevertheless, by the end of Battle of Britain, Hurricanes were showing their limitations in fighter verses fighter combat against Messerschmitt 109Es.

HAWKER HURRICANE I
(Rotol constant-speed propeller, June 1940)

Crew: 1.
Span: 40 feet.
Length: 31 feet 4 in.
Height: 8 feet 9 in.
Wing area: 258 sq feet.
Engine: Rolls-Royce Merlin III, 1,242 hp at 3,000 rpm.
Maximum speed: 316 mph at 17,750 feet, 292 mph at 30,000 feet.
Best landing speed: 64 mph ASI.
Best climb rate: 2,645 feet per min at 11,600 feet.
Climb: to 10,000 feet 3.8 min, to 20,000 feet 8.35 min, to 30,000 feet 18.3 min.
Service ceiling: 33,750 feet.
Range: 425 miles.
Empty weight: 4,666 lb.
Loaded weight: 6,316 lb.
Armament: eight forward-firing, wing-mounted .303-in Browning machine guns.

3/ SUPERMARINE SPITFIRE Mk I and II

The designer of the Spitfire, R. J. Mitchell, at first evolved a series of high-speed monoplane seaplanes as British contenders in the Schneider Trophy Races, culminating in the superb Supermarine S.6B, which won the trophy outright for Great Britain on 13 September 1931 with an average speed of 340.8 mph. Two weeks later it raised the world's speed record to 407 mph. After these successes Mitchell continued to design of a series of monoplane fighters that led to the prototype Spitfire of 1936 powered by a Rolls-Royce twelve-cylinder in-line liquid-cooled aero engine, which later became famous as the Merlin.

Orders for Spitfires were placed in June 1936, barely three months after the prototype flew for the first time. The emergence of the first production machines was delayed considerably by the need to create new production techniques for construction of the all-metal stressed-skin airframe. Extensive sub-contracting was used to meet current and anticipated orders as war loomed closer. From June 1938 onwards finished machines began to trickle through to the RAF. The first squadron to re-equip with the new fighter was No.19 at Duxford but when the September Munich crisis flared up soon afterwards, the squadron had not worked up to operational status. Britain's fighter defences depended on 660-odd biplane fighters and a handful of Hurricanes, which were limited to an operating altitude of 15,000 feet. Spitfire and Hurricane production was pressed urgently forward and when war finally came a year later, the RAF was equipped with a small but elite fighter force centred on about 500 modern eight-gun fighters.

Some of this growing strength was drawn off to meet Continental commitments in 1939–40, but upon the insistence of Hugh Dowding in charge of Fighter Command, most of the eight-gun fighters, including all Spitfires (except for a few special high-speed reconnaissance Spitfires), were retained in Britain despite French protests. At the opening stages of the Battle of Britain, Fighter Command was largely intact and recovered from the losses over Dunkirk and France, with 620 serviceable Hurricanes and Spitfires opposed by some 800 Messerschmitt 109s and 250–300 Me110s.

Early production Spitfire Is had the 1,230-hp Merlin II driving a wooden fixed-pitch two-bladed airscrew but in time for the Battle of Britain a three-bladed constant speed unit was substituted, which significantly improved the climb rate and ceiling. Armament of the IA version was eight machine guns in the wings but some were converted to cannon armament and designated IBs. These early models were closely matched in performance with the Me109E but were more manoeuvrable and handy in the turn. The last production batches of the Mk I were re-engined with the Merlin III of 1,440 hp at 5,500 feet giving a top speed of 354–8 mph at 18–19,000 feet.

During 1940 the next model, the Mk II, began to come off the production lines and by early 1941 was the main squadron type. Practically identical to the Mk I, the new version had the 1,240-hp Merlin XII engine with a Coffman cartridge starter and was built in two versions, the IIA with the standard eight-gun armament, and the IIB with two 20-mm cannon and four .303-inch machine guns, the cannon being introduced to offset the range advantage enjoyed by cannon-armed German fighters. Like the 109, the Spitfire proved lacking in range as soon as it forsook its interceptor role.

SUPERMARINE SPITFIRE Mk IIA
(Rotol CS airscrew, September 1940)

Crew: 1.
Span: 36 feet 10 ins.
Length: 29 feet 9 in.
Height: 8 feet 10 in (12 feet 3 in over airscrew disc).
Wing area: 242 sq feet.
Engine: Rolls-Royce Merlin XII, 1,236 hp at 13,500 feet, at 3,000 rpm.
Maximum speed: 354 mph at 17,550 feet, 321 mph at 30,000 feet, 290 mph at sea level.
Landing speed: 67 mph ASI.
Best climb rate: 3,025 feet per min at 12,800 feet.
Climb: to 10,000 feet 3.4 min, to 20,000 feet 7.0 min, to 30,000 feet 13.7 min.
Service ceiling: 37,600 feet.
Combat range: 395 miles.
Empty weight: 4,783 lb.
Loaded weight: 6,172 lb.
Armament: eight forward-firing, wing-mounted .303 in Browning machine guns.

4/ SUPERMARINE SPITFIRE Mk V

The Spitfire V began to reach Fighter Command squadrons in the spring of 1941 and became the main RAF fighter in 1941–42. A variety of Merlin engines were fitted with low-, medium-, and high-altitude ratings, giving from 1,414- to 1,585-hp combat power. Late in 1941 the Mk V came up against the faster-rolling, speedier FW190. The wingtips were clipped and new all-metal ailerons fitted to improve the Spitfire's roll rate. Nevertheless the Spitfire V was outclassed on several counts by the 190 and to a lesser degree by the Me109G.

The Spitfire V was the first mark to serve overseas and many were supplied to Russia and the USAAF squadrons in Europe. Armament followed the Mk II, there being similar A and B variants, but later a 'universal' wing was introduced on the VC, which had provision for A or B type armament or for a new weapons combination of four 20-mm cannon as well as more ammunition for the heavy weapons. With the low-altitude-rated engine giving 1,585 hp at 2,750 rpm (although at the expense of a reduced engine life due to the increased boost pressures) the clipped wing VC during 1943 came to be used as a low-altitude fighter-bomber, with 250-lb or 500-lb bombs being carried on a modified fitting in place of the belly drop tank.

SUPERMARINE SPITFIRE Mk VB
(May 1942)

Crew: 1.
Span: 36 feet 10 in.
Length: 29 feet 11 in.

Height: 11 feet 5 in.

Wing area: 242 sq feet.

Engine: Rolls-Royce Merlin 45, 45M, 46, 50, 50A, 50M or 56 of 1,470 hp –1,585 hp. Maximum speed: 369 mph at 19,500 feet.

Initial climb rate: 4,750 feet per min.

Ceiling: 35,500 feet.

Range: 470 miles normal, *c.* 1,000 miles max.

Range (still air) with 170-gal. belly tank: 1,380 miles at 156 mph at 15,000 feet.

Weight empty: 5,065 lbs.

Weight loaded: 6,785 lbs.

Armament: Two 20mm Hispano cannon with 120 rounds per gun and four .303 in Browning machine guns with 350 rounds per gun, plus one 500-lb or two 250-lb bombs.

Bibliography

Bingham, Victor, *Blitzed! – The Battle of France May–June 1940* (Surrey, England, Air Research Publications, 1990).

Claasen, Adam, *Dogfight – The Battle of Britain* (Auckland, New Zealand, Anzac Battles Series, Exisle Publishing Ltd, 2012).

Collier, Richard, *1940* – The *World in Flames* (Harmondsworth, Penguin, 1980).

Cooksley, Peter G., *1940 – The Story of No. 11 Group, Fighter Command* (Robert Hale, London, 1983).

Foreman, John, *Fighter Command War Diaries – Volume 1: September 1939 to September 1940* (Walton-on-Thames, Air Research Publications, 1996).

— *Air War 1941: Vol. 1 The Turning Point* (Surrey, Air Research Publications, 1993).

— *Fighter Command War Diaries – Volume 1: September 1939 to September 1940* (Walton-on-Thames, Air Research Publications, 1996).

— *Fighter Command War Diaries – Volume 2: September 1940 to December 1941* (Walton-on-Thames, Air Research Publications, 1998).

— *RAF Fighter Command Victory Claims – Part 1: 1939–1940* (Walton-on-Thames, Red Kite, 2003).

Franks, Norman, *The Greatest Air Battle* (London, William Kimber & Co Ltd, 1979).

—*The RAF Air Sea Rescue Service in the Second World War* (South Yorkshire, Pen & Sword, 2016).

—*Valiant Wings* (Northamptonshire, William Kimber & Co, Ltd, 1988).

Gardiner, Charles, *A.A.S.F.* (Plymouth, Mayflower Press, 1940).

Halley, James J., *The Squadrons of the Royal Air Force* (Tunbridge, Air-Britain, 1980).

Herington, John, *Australia in the War of 1939–1945, (Air)* Vol. III, Air War Against Germany and Italy, 1939–1943 (Canberra, Australian War Memorial, 1962).

Houart, Victor, *Lonely Warrior, the story of Jean Offenberg* (London, Transworld Publishers, 1957).

Johnson, Frank (ed.), *R.A.A.F. Over Europe* (London, Eyre & Spottiswoode, 1946).

Long, Gavin, 'The AIF in the United Kingdom' in *Australia in The War of 1939–1945, (Army) Vol. I, To Benghazi,* (Canberra, Australian War Memorial, 1961).

Lotz, Jim, *Disaster at Dieppe* (Toronto, James Lorimer & Company Ltd, 2012).

Marx, Jack, *Australian Tragic* (Sydney, Hachette Australia, 2009).

Mason, Francis K., *Battle over Britain* (London, McWhirter, 1969).

— *The Hawker Hurricane* (Bourne End, Bucks., Aston Publications, 1987).

McCarthy, John, *Australia and the Imperial Defence 1918–1939* (St Lucia, University of Queensland Press, 1976).

Monks, Noel, *Fighter Squadrons* (Sydney, Angus and Robertson, 1940).

Morgan, E. B. & Shacklady, E., *Spitfire, the History* (Stamford, Key, 1987).

Newton, Dennis, *A Few of 'The Few' – Australians and the Battle of Britain* (Canberra, ACT, Australian War Memorial, 1990).

— *A Spitfire Pilot's Story – Pat Hughes, Battle of Britain Top Gun* (Gloucestershire, Amberley Publishing, 2016).

Olive, Gordon and Newton, Dennis, *The Devil at 6 O'Clock* (Loftus NSW, Australian Military History Publications, 2001).

Olive, Gordon DFC, (Newton, Dennis (ed.), *Spitfire Ace* (Gloucestershire, Amberley Publishing, 2015).

Parry, Simon W, *Intruders Over Britain* (Surrey, Air Research Publications, 1987).

Ramsey, Winston G. (ed.), *The Blitz Then and Now*, Vol.1 (London, After the Battle, 1987).

— (ed.), *The Blitz Then and Now*, Vol. 2 (London, After The Battle, 1988).

— (ed.), *The Battle of Britain Then and Now* (London, After The Battle, 1980), Plus versions Mk II, Mk III & Mk IV.

Rawlings, John D. R., *Fighter Squadrons of the R.A.F. and their Aircraft* (Macdonald and Jane's, London, 1976).

Richey, Paul, *Fighter Pilot* (London & Sydney, Pan Books, 1969).

Roberts, Tom, *Wingless – An Alphabetical List of Australian Airmen Detained in Wartime* (Ballarat, Australia, Thomas V. Roberts, 2011).

Robertson, Terence, *Dieppe – The Shame and the Glory* (London, Pan Books, 1965).

Shores, Christopher & Williams, Clive, *Aces High* (London, Grub Street, 1994).

Stokes, Doug, *Paddy Finucane: Fighter Ace* (London, William Kimber, 1983).

Thompson, W/Cdr H. L., *New Zealanders with the Royal Air Force*, official history of New Zealand in the Second World War 1939–45, Vol I: *European Theatre September 1939–December 1942* (Wellington, New Zealand, War History Branch, Department of Internal Affairs, 1953).

Trevor-Roper, H. R., ed.), *Hitler's War Directives 1939–1945* (London, Pan, 1973).

Wood, Derek, &L Dempster, Derek, *The Narrow Margin* (London, Hutchinson, 1961).

Wynn, Kenneth G., *A Clasp for 'The Few' – New Zealanders with the Battle of Britain Clasp*, (Auckland, New Zealand, Kenneth G. Wynn, 1981).

— *Men of the Battle of Britain* (Norwich, Norfolk, 1989).

Zuehike, Mark, *Tragedy at Dieppe: Operation Jubilee, August 19, 1942* (Vancouver BC, Douglas & McIntyre, 2012).

Notes

Foreword

1. From Brisbane, Queensland, Raife Cowan returned to Australia and in the Pacific Theatre also served in 75 Squadron RAAF. By 1945, he was in command of 78 Squadron RAAF and flying operations over Tarakan when the Second World War ended.

3. The Phoney War

1. References to various map coordinates.

4. Six Days in May

1. The Allies referred to these Messerschmitt fighters during the war years as the 'Me109s' and 'Me110s' but at the time of their design the manufacturing company was *Bayerische Flugzeugwerke* and the prefix 'Bf' was used for these types in official German handbooks and documents. Most modern writers therefore refer to them this way these days, i.e., as 'Bf109' and 'Bf110'. The design team was headed by Professor Willy Messerschmitt who joined the company in 1927 and eventually took over when it was reconstituted as the Messerschmitt A.G. Thus, later types such as the 'Me163' and 'Me262' were written so in official German handbooks and documents. To return to the mood of the times in this book, it was decided that the 'Me109' and 'Me110' references, as employed in Allied documents in the Second World War, should be used.

2. Kilmartin's identification of this rare type has to be faulty as according to records the Heinkel He112 was not used in combat by the *Luftwaffe*. It was most probably another Me109, or perhaps a stray 'gull-winged' *Stuka*.

3. Researchers suggest that the 'Arados' were actually Henschel Hs126 army co-op aircraft. They also reduce Leslie Clisby's claim to one Me109 and two Hs126s destroyed, a fine achievement anyway. Over claiming in violent air battles was not uncommon and to accurately determine the results of a combat can be well-nigh impossible. Lists of victories will remain open to question and interpretation – especially as during the haste to evacuate from France many RAF records were destroyed or lost (including those of No.1 Squadron).

4. The accounts of Leslie Clisby's death vary. Other historians, notably Brian Cull, Bruce Lander and Heinrich Weiss in *Twelve Days in May* write that he was killed on 14 May, ignoring what was recorded by Paul Ritchy and Noel Monks. Victor Bingham's *Blitzed! – The Battle of France May–June 1940* lists Leslie Clisby KIA on 14 May 1940 (p.206) but then Leslie Clisby MIA on 15 May 1940 (p.207).

5. Maydays

1. There is controversy about this. According to the Air Officer Commanding-in-Chief of Fighter Command, Hugh Dowding, he never spoke to Churchill stating the minimum number needed to be twenty-five squadrons. To defend Britain effectively against an estimated 2,000 long-range bombers operating from Germany, he had calculated that he needed forty-six squadrons at his disposal for the general defence of the country, plus four to protect convoys along the east coast, two to cover the RN naval base at Scapa Flow and one more for Northern Ireland – a total of fifty-three. Instead of the fifty-three squadrons he deemed as essential, he had no more than thirty-five when war was declared in September 1939. Given the full number of squadrons, Dowding felt confident of breaking the assaults of the *Luftwaffe*, but with anything less – and certainly with only half of them – he was not so sure. He regarded the draining away of his fighter squadrons to a war that was probably already lost in France as a recipe for ultimate disaster.
2. Records are fragmented and estimates of the number of the aircraft involved in daylight operations on 19 May range from twenty-three to thirty-three.
3. The instruction to stop had come from Adolf Hitler who was in conference with Guderian's commander, General Gerd von Rundstedt at Army Group A headquarters in Charleville. Hitler expressed fears of being caught by a French counter-offensive from the south and pressured von Rundstedt to issue orders, for the second time, that Guderian's tanks should halt their advance. At the same time, Herman Goring assured the *Führer* that his air force could administer the *coup de grâce* to the BEF trapped inside the Dunkirk perimeter. If so, this would save troops and conserve precious tanks for the forthcoming final battle for France.
4. This was probably a reference to the withdrawal of 218 Squadron's personnel to Nantes and then England after handing over their remaining Fairey Battles to 103 Squadron.

6. The End of France

1. Bob Bungey's letters have not survived. If some do still exist, their whereabouts is not known at this time. It is known, however, that at least one letter home to Australia written by Bob late in May 1940 reached Tarlton Street, Somerton Park, well before another letter which he had sent much earlier that very same month.
2. Bob's Log Book lists this mission as a night operation taking place on 31 May 1940, whereas the surviving Operations Record Book record of 226 Squadron shows that it actually occurred in the very early hours of 1 June 1940. Other 226 Squadron records for the month of June were lost.
3. This is the generally accepted figure but according to the War Office the total number of men landed in England was 336,427.
4. No.226 Squadron's records do not reveal any expanded information on the incident because those for the month of June 1940 were lost during the evacuation of France.

7. 145 Squadron RAF

1. This conversation is based on one that is recorded in the classic book *Lonely Warrior* by Jean Offenberg DFC, from notebooks translated into English by Mervyn Savill and edited by Victor Houart. There have been many releases of this work over the years but it was originally published in England by Souvenir Press Ltd in 1956. In the book, Boyd is at first mentioned as 'Robert Boyd' then later as 'Adrian Boyd'. The latter is correct. There was a F/Lt Robert Boyd who was a pilot in 602 Squadron at this time and his portrait was done by famous artist Cuthbert Orde. Perhaps this was the cause of some confusion for the biographer.

2. The Americans, who were neutral at this stage of the war, were sceptical of the figures. The reality was not revealed until research after the war – research that continues to this day. On 15 August, seventy-six German aircraft had been destroyed for the loss of thirty-five British fighters. On 31 August, thirty-nine German aircraft had been destroyed for the loss of forty-one British fighters. On the day they bombed London, forty-one German aircraft were destroyed for the loss of twenty-five British fighters. On 15 September, the day that would be called 'Battle of Britain Day', sixty-one German aircraft were destroyed for the loss of thirty-one British fighters. The figures on these random days were therefore, the Germans lost 217 aircraft and the British 132 – an approximately kill ratio of 3:2. German estimates at the time of RAF aircraft destroyed were even more wildly inaccurate, enough for the High Command to think that the British were using up their last reserves of fighters. It was a shock on 15 September when, not only did the *Luftwaffe's* bombers have to run the gauntlet of Keith Park's 11 Group on the way to London, they also suddenly ran into Leigh Mallory's 'Big Wing' over the capital!
3. Jean Offenberg's biographer actually wrote 'Group 2' or 'No.2 Group' repeatedly in the book, *Lonely Warrior*. In reality, No.2 Group was part of RAF Bomber Command with its squadrons all equipped with Bristol Blenheims at this stage of the war (see Chapter 3). It should read No.11 Group. Offenberg would not have made such a mistake. Most likely, the biographer in reading the Belgian pilot's handwritten notes made the error of interpreting '11' (eleven) as the Roman numeral 'II' (two).
4. *Lonely Warrior,* the story of Jean Offenberg, provides invaluable rare glimpses of Bob Bungey at a personal level – as a fellow combat pilot and as a friend.
5. On 27 September 1940, the *Luftwaffe* lost fifty-seven aircraft and RAF Fighter Command thirty-four.

8. Tangmere
1. The conversations over the R/T and between the members of 145 Squadron are based on those appearing in *Lonely Warrior* by Jean Offenberg.
2. There are discrepancies in the existing records at this point. Although the squadron's Operations Record Book shows that Bob next flew on the 20th, Bob's Log Book entries show that after he flew his sortie on 17 October he actually flew his next sortie on the night of the 19th. Jean Offenberg's lengthy description of the leave he and Bob had at the *Old Ship Inn* is also under the date of '19th October', which suggests that he wrote it all down immediately on his return to Tangmere. He was probably writing it at the same time as Bob was flying his night patrol in Hurricane 2696. Why the keeper of 145 Squadron's Operations Record Book did not record Bob's night patrol is unknown. Perhaps he simply overlooked it amid the constant pressure of recording operations.

9. Hurricane Winter
1. On 28 November 1940, Helmut Wick failed to return from a dogfight with RAF Spitfires over the English Channel. It was later established that he had drowned despite escaping from his crippled aircraft.
2. Victor Houart, the biographer who edited Jean Offenberg's notebooks, did not include a correction in the *Lonely Warrior*.
3. For Jean Offenberg's full comment, see Chapter 8.
4. Gordon Olive & Dennis Newton, *The Devil at 6 O'Clock* (Loftus, Australian Military History Publications, 2001, p159–160).

10. Spitfire Spring
1. From *Lonely Warrior* by Victor Houart, (London, Transworld Publishers, 1957, p.106–108.)

2. Known as 'Sam', 'Sammy' and sometimes 'Fishy' Saunders, Gerald Alfred Wellesley Saunders of 65 Squadron was awarded a DFC on 4 April 1941 and survived the war to be released from the RAF as a wing commander in 1945.
3. Robert Reid MacPherson of 65 Squadron was commissioned in November 1940 and rose to be a flight lieutenant with 129 Squadron. He failed to return after combat with Me109s on 13 October 1941.
4. New Zealander Ronald George Wigg of 65 Squadron was posted to the Middle East in mid-September 1942, where he joined No.1 (SAAF) Squadron and flew operations during the Battle of Alamein. In August 1945, he transferred to the RNZAF and was released from the RNZAF on 14 April 1946, as a squadron leader.
5. Ernest Derek 'Dave' Glaser of 65 Squadron was awarded a DFC in August 1942 when a flight lieutenant with 234 Squadron. He commanded 548 Squadron at Darwin from February 1945 until it disbanded in September 1945. Glaser retired from the RAF in June 1953 as a squadron leader.
6. William Johnson Leather was serving in the Far East at the end of the Second World War and he was released from the RAF in 1945 as a group captain.
7. Jean Henri Marie Offenberg was appointed 145 Squadron's 'B' Flight Commander on 21 May 1941. In June, he was first Belgian to receive the DFC. On 17 June he was posted to 609 Squadron at Biggin Hill and was awarded the *Croix de Guerre (Belgian)* in July. He was killed in a mid-air collision on 22 January 1942.
8. Baudouin Marie Ghislain de Hemptinne was posted to 609 Squadron at Biggin Hill on 17 June 1941 and awarded the *Croix de Guerre (Belgian)* in July. He was killed on 5 May 1942 as a flight lieutenant with 122 Squadron.
9. Michael Alan Newling, still in 145 Squadron, was shot down and killed near Lille on 6 July 1941 while flying escort to *Circus No.35*.
10. Peter William Dunning-White was awarded the DFC in June 1941 and later served in 255 Squadron in North Africa. He was afterwards posted to No.100 Group RAF Bomber Command in July 1944 and was released from the RAF on 8 October 1945 as a wing commander.
11. Charles Gordon Chaloner Olive formed and commanded 456 RAAF Squadron in June 1941, and in 1942 left the RAF to rejoin the RAAF and returned to Australia. He was at Air Defence HQ, Morotai in 1945 when the war ended and left the RAAF in 1946 as a wing commander.

11. 452 (RAAF) Squadron

1. At this time, a large formation of aircraft was commonly referred to as a Balbo. The name came from an Italian fascist leader, General Italo Balbo, who first achieved fame when he led twelve Savoia-Marchetti S.55 twin-hulled flying boats on a flight from Italy to Rio de Janeiro in 1931. On 6 January 1931, the aircraft flew from Portuguese Guinea to Natal Brazil to complete the first formation crossing of the South Atlantic. Later, in 1933, Balbo did another first in grander style. He commanded a formation of twenty-five Savoia-Marchetti S.55X flying boats on a flight of 12,430 miles (20,000 km) across the North Atlantic to Chicago via New York to take part in the Century of Progress Exhibition, and then flew back to Italy via the Azores and Lisbon. He was also instrumental in building Italy's air force, the *Regia Aeronautica,* and became the Italian Air Minister in 1929. In 1933, he was appointed Governor-General of Libya but he died when the aircraft he was flying was shot down over Tobruk by Italian gunfire.
2. Parry, Simon W, *Intruders Over Britain* (Surrey, Air Research Publications, England, 1987, p.170, 177).

12. The Kenley Wing
1. Press release via Richard Bungey, *The Story of Wing-Commander R. W. Bungey DFC RAAF.*
2. These figures are based on those in the official RAAF history, *John Herrington's Air War Against Germany and Italy 1939–1943* published by the Australian War Memorial, Canberra. Other publications sometimes quote slight variations on these figures.
3. Stokes, Doug, *Paddy Finucane: Fighter Ace* (London, William Kimber, 1983).

14. October Surprises
1. For the full citation, refer to Appendix 2.
2. Stokes, Doug, *Paddy Finucane: Fighter Ace* (London, William Kimber, 1983, p.101).
3. Press release via Richard W. Bungey, *The Story of Wing Commander R. W. Bungey DFC RAAF.*
4. According to German sources no *Luftwaffe* pilot bailed out that day so if that is true Truscott must mistakenly have fired at an RAF pilot on a parachute.
5. See Ian Milne's description of Alex Robert's adventures in Chapter 12.
6. Norman Ryder was later reported to be a POW.

15. Winter
1. The Tomahawk was a rugged aircraft suited to conditions in the Middle East. One of the first units to use the type was 3 Squadron RAAF during the Syrian campaign of June 1941 against the Vichy French. It emerged as the most successful fighter on the Allied side.
2. Although years later David Downs recalled the bombers as being twenty Douglas A-20 Havocs, records show that on this occasion they were actually twelve Bristol Blenheim IVs, as related in John Herrington's official history, *Air War Against Germany and Italy1939–1943.*
3. Those who knew him recalled that Bluey Truscott's voice was rather high pitched and it became even higher pitched when he was excited during combat.
4. Bob Bungey's Log Book shows that he and David Downs did not fly directly back to Redhill. They flew out to provide cover over Bluey Truscott's position before actually returning to base.
5. Stokes, Doug, *Paddy Finucane: Fighter Ace* (London, William Kimber, 1983, p.69).

16. 452 Finale
1. Via Richard Bungey.
2. Ibid.
3. Press interview with Bluey Truscott, 25 May 1943, via Richard Bungey.

17. Air-Sea Rescue
1. Thompson, W/Cdr H. L., *New Zealanders with the Royal Air Force*, official history of New Zealand in the Second World War 1939–45, Vol I: *European Theatre September 1939–December 1942* (Wellington, New Zealand, War History Branch, Department of Internal Affairs, 1953, p.223).

18. Rutter
1. Written as 'Col Macbeth' in Bob Bungey's RAF Flying Log Book
2. Adrian Cole would become an Air ViceMarshal CBE DSO MC DFC.
3. Robertson, Terence, *Dieppe – The Shame and the Glory* (London, Pan Books, 1965, p.160).

19. Jubilee

1. This was actually only the second heavy bomber raid carried out by the USAAF in the European theatre. The first was an attack on Rouen on 17 August 1942.
2. Regarded as the worst day in Canadian military history, Canada's casualties have been calculated as: 907 killed, 586 wounded and 1,946 captured. As well, there were 275 British commandos killed and the Royal Navy suffered 550 personnel dead and wounded.
3. A breakdown of RAF losses has been put at sixty-two Spitfires; twenty Hurricane; four Bostons; two Blenheims; two Typhoons; and ten Mustang Mk Is, but lists vary.

20. 'Leave'

1. The period 1939–40 was the second time the IRA had campaigned against British rule in Northern Ireland. The first had been during the Irish War of Independence.
2. This series of attacks by the IRA's Northern Command against the security forces in Northern Ireland lasted until December 1944 and resulted in IRA action being suppressed by the end of the Second World War. The northern command of the IRA had been reduced to a few wanted men with Northern Ireland entirely free from IRA activity. There was not another resurgence until 1956.

21. Home

1. Richard Bungey's Private Papers. This article is among numerous press clippings pasted into a scrapbook which was kept by Ada Bungey about her son. Unfortunately, the original sources and dates of these were not always included and so are often unknown. When they could be traced they have been properly acknowledged. It is thought this piece is from the Adelaide *Advertiser*.
2. Olive, Gordon DFC, (Newton, Dennis ed.), *Spitfire Ace*, (Gloucestershire, Amberley Publishing, 2015, p.227).
3. *TRUTH*, Adelaide, June 19, 1943.
4. Ibid.
5. Noted author Ivan Southall wrote Keith Truscott's biography, *Bluey Truscott*, which was published by Angus and Robertson in 1958.
6. See Appendix 3: 452 (RAAF) Squadron – The Rest of Its Story.
7. At the time of writing, the picture is still there in its rightful place on the wall.
8. Richard Bungey's Private Papers.
9. Ibid.
10. Ibid.
11. Ibid.

22. Miracle at Somerton

1. Excerpts from Detective C. Hanrahan's Report, Richard Bungey's Private Papers.
2. Richard Bungey's Private Papers, op cit.
3. Ibid.
4. Another report states that the RAAF ensign was around the coffin, and the airman's flying cap on top.
5. Richard Bungey's Private Papers.

23. Quest

1. The *Sunday Mail,* 'Anzac Salute' by Fiona McWhirter, 25 April 2010, p.7.

Index